Quality of Life Research

Quality of Life Research

A CRITICAL INTRODUCTION

Mark Rapley

SAGE Publications
London • Thousand Oaks • New Delhi

First published 2003
Reprinted 2003

SAGE Publications Ltd
6 Bonhill Street
London EC2A 4PU

SAGE Publications Inc
2455 Teller Road
Thousand Oaks, California 91320

SAGE Publications India Pvt Ltd
B-42, Panchsheel Enclave
Post Box 4109
New Delhi, 100 017

British Library Cataloguing in Publication data

A catalogue record for this book is
available from the British Library

ISBN 0 7619 5456 2
ISBN 0 7619 5457 0 (pbk)

Library of Congress Control Number: 2002107101

Typeset and designed by GCS, Leighton Buzzard, Beds.
Printed in Great Britain by Athenaeum Press, Gateshead.

CONTENTS

LIST OF FIGURES AND TABLES

Figures

Tables

APOLOGIA

Let us begin by seeing the assessment of quality of life in practice. In the extracts below, transcribed from recordings of the administration of Schalock and Keith's (1996) *Quality of Life Questionnaire*, we see how the moment-by-moment interaction of quality of life assessors and assessees produces scores on a standardized QOL measure.[1] Each question has three response options, scored 1, 2 and 3.

Extract 1

Interviewer	D'you feel out of place out an' about in social situations?
Anne	No
Interviewer	Anne? Never?
Anne	No
Interviewer	Sometimes?
Anne	No
Interviewer	Or usually?
Anne	Sometimes I do
Interviewer	Yeah? OK, we'll put a two down for that one then

Extract 2

Interviewer	Oh right, OK then, right then, so Arthur would say that your life brings out the best in you?
Arthur	Brings out the best in you
Interviewer	Or treats you like everyone else?
Arthur	Anybody else
Interviewer	Or doesn't give you a chance?
Arthur	Uh er treats yer uh uh all alright
Interviewer	The same as everyone else? You the middle one?
Arthur	Yeers.

These sorts of exchanges, typical of the administration of *any* quality of life questionnaire (Houtkoop-Steenstra, 2000), suggest that assessment of quality of life – whatever the designers of questionnaires, or the writers of survey manuals, say – is, *in practice*, far from straightforward.

If we are to get a firm grip on quality of life research, and become informed practitioners, we need to be aware of both the positive findings, persuasive theories and impressive-looking measures, and also of the practical and theoretical difficulties inherent in the ideas, concepts and assessment methods of the area. This book introduces – and offers a critical reflection upon – social scientific research on QOL, outlining those persuasive theories, impressive measures and positive findings, but also warning against uncritical acceptance. The intention is to equip students with an understanding of the main approaches to quality of life research, and the conceptual-analytic tools needed to become discerning 'consumers' of the literature. Much of this book is designed to *show*, as well as *tell*, how such a critical engagement might proceed. To support the development of a critical stance, each chapter ends with study questions.

We take as a guide Michel Foucault's (1985: 8) observation on the purpose of knowledge:

> What would be the value of the passion for knowledge if it resulted only in a certain knowingness … and not, in one way or another … in the knower's straying afield from himself … the question of knowing if one can think differently than one thinks, and perceive differently than one sees, is absolutely necessary if one is to go on thinking and reflecting at all.

We'll put a two down for that one then.

Note

1. Data are drawn from Rapley and Antaki (1996). Transcription is simplified.

PREFACE

quality *n*. 1. a characteristic, property or attribute. 2. high grade; superior.
of *prep*. A particle indicating 5, a relation of identity.
life *n*. 1. Condition which distinguishes animals and plants from inorganic
objects and dead organisms … 5, course or mode of existence.
(Macquarie Dictionary, 1992)

In 1990 the leading ethnographer of the lives of people with intellectual disabilities,[1] Robert Edgerton, suggested that the term 'Quality of Life' was the 'shibboleth of the 1990s' (1990: 149). The term 'shibboleth' implies not only the importance of the concept, but also the contentious nature of the field and the potential upshot of QOL research. In public life, and the social sciences, the notion of QOL has come – since the 1960s – to be a routinely invoked concept. The term appears in the discussion of everything from the relative 'liveability' of towns, cities and nations to the aims and effects of social policy, from the relative benefits of differing models of human service provision to the individualized outcomes of a vast number of medical and psychotherapeutic practices.

This is not to suggest that questions about what constitutes a life of quality, or what the characteristics, properties or attributes of such a life might be, only began in the 1960s. As Socrates famously noted, the unexamined life is one unworthy of living (Plato, 1903). Much of Western philosophy and literature since can be read as an extended response to his questions about life's quality and qualities. While some might dismiss such endeavours as frippery produced in 'a playground for philosophical speculation' (Veenhoven, 1997), the upshot of such questioning has always been practical and serious – both historically and in the present. The Nazi conceptualization of a life of quality entailed the idea of 'life unworthy of life' – an idea that warranted the 'euthanasia' of people with intellectual disabilities, the chronically ill, and the inmates of mental hospitals by German doctors and psychiatrists in the 1930s and 1940s (Gilbert, 1986: 239). Currently, the idea that it is possible to *quantify* the *quality* of a life – to establish numerical parameters for the relative value of lives with particular qualities – is a warrant for the selective abortion of particular foetuses (Kuhse and Singer, 1985), the provision (or not) of life-sustaining medical interventions (Nord, 1999) and, in some jurisdictions, 'physician-assisted suicide' for those whose quality of life is 'pointless and empty' (Sheldon, 2000: 1174).

It is in the contemporary social sciences that the most sustained efforts have been made to define, describe and understand quality of life. In their 1996 literature review Antaki and Rapley (1996a) identified over 2,500 journal articles specifying 'quality of life' as a keyword in the preceding three years. Hughes *et al.*'s (1995) survey identified 44 separate definitions between 1970 and 1993. Cummins (1997a: 1–2) noted 'well in excess of 100 definitions and models ... some are clearly representative of others while some are cast in such vague or inclusive terminology that their heuristic value approaches zero'. The electronic archives of the *British Medical Journal* identify 702 articles with 'quality of life' in their titles between 1994 and 2001. Muldoon *et al.* (1998: 542) state that 'over 1000 new articles a year are indexed under "quality of life"'. Entering 'quality of life' into Google returned no fewer than 'about' 3, 410, 000 webpages! QOL is, evidently, a concept of powerful – if not pervasive – resonance in contemporary life. Yet the very popularity of the concept (and use as a 'lay' rather than 'technical' term) has resulted in a fragmented literature. The literature is, furthermore, a site of considerable controversy over issues ranging from the adequacy of QOL as a scientific construct, to the meaningfulness of QOL measurement and the social policy relevance of QOL measures.

To add to the confusion the various social scientific literatures conduct their own QOL debates in isolation from each other, and sub-areas within each field show little appreciation of work in adjacent specialisms. In the developing field of health-related QOL (HRQOL) separate, and condition-specific, measures of HRQOL exist for almost every problem for which there is a medical specialty. Multiple QOL measures exist for kidney disease and end-stage renal failure specifically (Cagney *et al.*, 2000; Wu *et al.*, 2001; Martin and Thompson, 2001); for acne (Klassen *et al.*, 2000; Martin *et al.*, 2001); for head and neck cancer (Hammerlid and Taft, 2001); for respiratory disease (De Vries *et al.*, 2000) – with a number of asthma-specific measures (Ehrs *et al.*, 2001); for epilepsy (Ergene *et al.*, 2001); for vertigo (Prieto *et al.*, 1999); and for genital herpes (Spencer *et al.*, 1999). There are even QOL measures to assess the QOL of parents whose children have problems – for instance toddlers with motor disorders (Hendriks *et al.*, 2000).

Given such fragmented – often contradictory – literatures there is, says leading QOL researcher Bob Cummins, no hope of a comprehensive overview. He suggests that 'the literature is now too vast for any individual researcher to fully assimilate' (1997b: 118). Hence this book is selective. QOL is placed in its historical and cultural context; concepts underpinning QOL as a global construct are outlined; definitional controversies and commonalities across disciplines are discussed; and an introduction to key evaluative methods and tools – purpose, potential and limitations – across a range of sites is provided. My approach to the identification of exemplary studies – or, as it lacks the connotation of excellence, *illustrative* studies – is guided by Silverman's (1997) recommendation that *aesthetic criteria* be accorded a central place in the evaluation of social scientific research.

[...]volumes have been written about how theoretical or political positions (either implicit or explicit) shape the research task ... Such positions have relatively little to do with many researchers' sense of what constitutes a 'worthwhile' research problem, 'interesting data' or a 'compelling' analysis ... I believe that the most important impulse has more to do with our tacit sense of the sort of appearance or shape of a worthwhile piece of research. In that sense research is informed by an aesthetic. (Silverman, 1997: 239)

Accordingly I discuss pieces of research that offer what ethno-methodologists would describe as *perspicuous instances*. That is, work discussed has been selected by virtue of its capacity to illustrate with clarity, simplicity and economy (cf. Wittgenstein, 1961) major conceptual and methodological issues in QOL research. Each chapter concludes with suggestions for further reading, and a list of questions for further study. The Resources section (Appendix 3 page 249) lists sites providing starting points for further research, journals to consult and texts which provide more detailed guidance on various research approaches.

The book is divided into two parts: In Part 1, Chapters 1–3 offer a critical overview of key philosophical, conceptual and methodological issues. These chapters draw widely on QOL literatures across disciplines and population groups. Chapter 4 offers a review of methodological issues in quantitative and qualitative QOL research, with a discussion of the strengths and weaknesses of the principal methodological tools. The promises and pitfalls of these methods are illustrated with reference to specific QOL instruments and research approaches. Part 2 illustrates the application of the principles, concepts and methodologies discussed in Part 1. These chapters demonstrate work at a range of levels – from the analysis of social policy to service outcome research – with reference to population groups where QOL research is most developed. These chapters offer 'worked examples' of QOL research, and illustrate the diversity of approaches to the topic. The aim is, after Wittgenstein, a 'showing' rather than a 'telling'. The areas covered highlight controversial issues identified in Part 1. Thus, discussion of the adequacy of QOL as a scientific construct in Chapter 2 is picked up in Chapter 5 by an illustration of how the work of Foucauldian thinkers offers a deeper appreciation of the relationship between social scientific studies of QOL and their cultural context. Chapter 6 unpacks the ethical debate in Chapter 3 by a detailed analysis of HRQOL research. The discussion of conceptual issues in the development of generic versus population-specific QOL measures in Chapter 4 is illustrated in Chapter 7 by empirical work on these topics. Chapter 8 analyses recent developments in the psychological literature and Chapter 9 offers a recapitulation of the main themes and a response to criticisms of the philosophy, theory and practice of QOL research in the literature. Directions for research are identified.

Note

1. I use the term 'intellectual disability (-ies)' to refer to people also known as people with learning difficulties (UK) and people with mental retardation (USA).

ACKNOWLEDGMENTS

I am grateful to Charles Antaki, Steve Beyer, Bob Cummins, Hanneke Houtkoop-Steenstra, Ken Keith, John Lobley, Alec McHoul, Jim Ridgway and Bob Schalock for their analytic perspicuity, friendship, advice, discussions, disagreements and generous practical assistance. Susan Hansen has made it all possible.

I thank Bob Cummins, Mike Salvaris, Robert Schalock, the American Association on Mental Retardation and the World Health Organization for permission to reproduce copyright material.

Note

This book draws on some of my earlier work and extends analyses previously published. Chapter 3 draws on Rapley, M. (2001) Policing Happiness, in Newnes, C., Holmes, G. and Dunn, C. (eds) *This is Madness Too*. Ross-on-Wye, PCCS Books and McHoul, A. and Rapley, M. (2002) "Should we make a start then?": A strange case of a (delayed) client-initiated psychological assessment, *Research on Language and Social Interaction*, 35, 1: 73–91. Chapter 4 draws upon Antaki, C. and Rapley, M. (1996). Questions and answers to psychological assessment schedules: hidden troubles in 'Quality of Life' interviews, *Journal of Intellectual Disability Research*, 40, 5: 421–37; Rapley, M., Ridgway, J. and Beyer, S. (1998) Staff:staff and staff:client reliability of the Schalock and Keith (1993) Quality of Life Questionnaire, *Journal of Intellectual Disability Research*, 42, 1: 37–43. Chapter 5 extends Rapley, M. and Ridgway J. (1998). Quality of Life talk: the corporatisation of intellectual disability. *Disability and Society*, 13, 3: 451–71. Chapter 9 develops Antaki, C. and Rapley, M. (1996). "Quality of Life" talk: The liberal paradox of psychological testing. *Discourse and Society*, 7, 3: 293–316 (by the kind permission of Sage Publications Ltd 1996).

This book is for Ella and Tom.

PART ONE – THEORY

CHAPTER 1

Introduction – Where Has QOL Come From?

> My nominee for the key issue in the study of language and the brain dur-
> ing the first century of the third millennium is a concept that is slippery,
> burning, neglected, and crucial. That concept is definition and measur-
> ment of quality of life. (LaPointe, 2001: 135)

> The quality of life construct has a complex composition, so it is perhaps
> not surprising that there is neither an agreed definition nor a standard
> form of measurement. (Cummins, 1997a: 6)

This chapter offers a historical overview of the development of the concept
of 'quality of life' in both public life and as an object of study in the social
and human sciences. Drawing extensively on the work of Kenneth Land,
Heinz-Herbert Noll and Michael Salvaris, I outline the development of the
QOL construct, from being a social scientific index of the relative well-
being of whole populations (a measure of the state of states) to being a
measurable aspect of individual subjective experience (an index of the
state of persons). The intention is not to produce a 'Whig' history[1], but to
examine the relations between ideas of what QOL might be across what are
usually termed 'levels of analysis': that is as a property of both individual
persons *and* human collectivities.

QOL as the State of States

It is important to begin by placing the idea of quality of life (or QOL) into
historical context. To do so we must suspend both our ordinary or
commonsense understandings of what the term 'quality of life' means, and
also formal operational definitions of the idea in the social scientific
literatures (see Kendall and Wickham, 1999: chapter 1). For, as Mike
Salvaris (2000: 4) suggests in his account of the social indicators movement
in Australia:

> Political economists from Hobbes to Marx have observed that 'the most
> powerful instrument of political authority is the power to give names and to
> enforce definitions' (Chorover, 1979); and in western society since the
> Industrial Revolution, there has been no more potent idea to be defined
> (and thus harnessed) than the idea of progress. This idea, with its
> connotations of destiny and inevitability, has become almost 'the meta

narrative of history' (McLintock, 1992) – legitimating political power, elevating those who define and interpret it, and providing a unifying theme for the policies of nations.

Writing in 1996, Veenhoven suggested:

> 'In the first half of this century, quality-of-life in nations was largely measured by the material level of living. The higher that level in a country, the better the life of its citizens was presumed to be ... quality-of-life was measured by GNP related measures, currently by 'real' GDP per head ... Yet in the 1960's, the opinion climate changed ... This gave rise to a call for broader indicators of quality-of-life, which materialized into the so called 'Social Indicator' movement. (Veenhoven, 1996: 1)

While accurate in terms of its chronology, such an account – falling as it does into historicist fallacy – shows just how 'slippery' the notion of QOL can be. Clearly, if in the first half of the twentieth century it was the GNP, or 'the material level of living', that was gauged, then it was not 'quality of life' that was being measured. What Veenhoven's account suggests then is that it is possible – as indeed he himself points out later in his paper – to (re)define (or 'give a name to' as Chorover put it) almost *any* social statistic or collection of social statistics as 'QOL'.

Cummins attributes the coining of the term quality of life in its 'modern form' as a characteristic of persons *as well as* an indication of national prosperity, to a 1964 speech by President Johnson in which he is reported to have stated that *progress* on social goals 'cannot be measured by the size of our bank balance. They can only be measured by the quality of the lives our people lead' (Cummins, 1997b: 117). Similarly Noll (2000) suggests that: 'as early as in 1964 former U.S. President Lyndon Johnson stated: "the great society is concerned not with how much, but with how good – not with the quantity of goods but with the quality of their lives"'. The idea of quality of life as a measurable indicator of the 'great society's' achievements has, since its inception, been inseparable from the notion of progress. With an elegant symmetry, in the social sciences, as in political economy, 'the most powerful instrument of [political] authority is the power to give names and to enforce definitions'.

The development of a 'modern', or *individualized*, notion of QOL was neither immediate nor inevitable. Noll (2000) points to the development of two contrary conceptualizations of quality of life, one being a Scandinavian view based in the works of writers such as Drenowski (1974), Erikson and Uusitalo (1987) and Erikson (1993), centred on notions of the 'good society' and of social well-being as a welfare issue. In this work welfare is conceived of as based in access to resources by which people can control and direct their 'level of living' and, in the provision of which, public policy may have leverage. Erikson and Uusitalo (1987: 189) specify the resources citizens require in order to secure their own welfare:

'resources are defined in terms of money, property, knowledge, psychic and physical energy, social relations, security and so on'. In consequence Scandinavian thinking focuses exclusively on *objective indicators* of the level of living, or quality of life, of society as a whole.

However, as Noll notes, what he terms 'the American quality of life' approach commands more of a consensus in the 'Western' world. In this model, quality of life research – or welfare measurement – is primarily based in the assessment of *subjective indicators* at the level of individual citizens. Noll (2000) suggests of the 'American' model that

> in the tradition of the utilitarian philosophy and 'mental health research' ... this approach ultimately defines welfare as subjective well-being. The most important indicators of subjective well-being used, actually, are measures of satisfaction and happiness.

So where has the idea of 'quality of life' come from? Along with Cummins, Veenhoven and Noll, Land (2000) locates the beginnings of QOL in the 'social indicators movement' of the 1960s. The impetus, it is claimed, was the joint efforts of a NASA and the American Academy of Arts and Sciences project to predict the societal effects of the space race (Land, 1983; Noll and Zapf, 1994). Noll (2000) describes the origin of the movement thus:

> [...] social indicators research was created in the United States in the mid-1960s ... The project came to the conclusion that there was almost a complete lack not only of adequate data but also of concepts and the methodology for this purpose. Presumably it was Raymond Bauer, the director of the project, who also invented the term and concept of 'social indicators' [Bauer, 1966: 1]. In his definition, social indicators were 'statistics, statistical series, and all other forms of evidence that enable us to assess where we stand and are going with respect to our values and goals'.

Land (2000) points out that what came to be called the 'social indicators movement' by 1969 had much earlier progenitors. Carley (1981) has suggested that large scale formalization of interest in measures of the state of states was part of a broader trend towards the organization of national social, economic and demographic information that began in Western societies during the Enlightenment. This trend was consolidated through the seventeenth and eighteenth centuries and accelerated dramatically over the course of the twentieth century. Such a view resonates with Foucault's work (1973, 1977, 1978) on the rise of governmentality, surveillance and the individual subject in the emerging nation states over the same period. It is regrettable that while much current societal-level QOL work appreciates its own political relevance (for example, Veenhoven (1996) considers that his proposed measure of 'Happy Life Expectancy'

(HLE) would have 'political appeal'), most leading QOL researchers are dismissive of poststructuralist readings of the development of social indicators and their transformation into devices of individual surveillance (Cummins, 2001a).

Early in the development of such indicators Land (1975) points to the activities of the Chicago school in the 1930s and 1940s, specifically the work of Ogburn on the theory and measurement of social change and his responsibility for the production, in 1933, of *Recent Social Trends in the United States*. Noll (2000) identifies the work of Drenowski at the United Nations on systems of social indicators in the 1950s as an early contribution to the project of improving the 'measurement of the level of living by identifying components of welfare and by constructing respective indicators' (Noll, 2000). By 1969 the future direction of health economic uses of social indicators had been anticipated, as had one of the key individual-level uses of the notion of quality of life. Gudex (1990) identifies the publication by Klarman *et al.* (1968) of a cost-effectiveness analysis of chronic renal disease treatment as the beginning of the QALY (quality adjusted life year) movement in medicine (of which more in Chapter 6).

At the societal level, in 1969 the US Department of Health, Education, and Welfare document *Toward a Social Report* identified health and illness; income and poverty; the physical environment; public order and safety; social mobility; learning, science and art; and participation and alienation as key social indicators (USDHEW, 1969). The definition of a 'social indicator' in this document is attributed by Land (2000) to the economist Olson – namely a 'statistic of direct normative interest which facilitates concise, comprehensive and balanced judgements about the condition of major aspects of a society' (USDHEW, 1969: 97). In all cases, Land argues, Olson viewed such indicators as direct measures of welfare which afforded the conclusion that, if changes occurred in the right direction, all else being equal, things have improved, or that people could be understood to be 'better off'.

Both Noll and Land attribute the rapid international diffusion of social indicators work to the social and political climate of the 1960s and 1970s. Noll (2000) suggests that while this was a period of prosperity, it was also a period when questioning of economic growth as the major goal of public policy and the primary indicator of social progress began. This questioning has, more recently, again become a pressing political issue with the development of anti-globalization protest movements. Noll argues that, during this period: 'there was increasing doubt whether more should ever equal better … The concept of "quality of life" was born as an alternative to the more and more questionable concept of the affluent society and became the new, but also much more complex and multidimensional goal of societal development' (Noll, 2000). Land's (2000) description of the flurry of activity at this time – which depended on widespread acceptance of active government shaping societal structures and processes for the greater good – captures the period well. Land writes of the intellectual enthusiasm for social indicators in the United States that:

> In the early 1970s, this led to numerous developments, including the establishing in 1972, with National Science Foundation support, of the Social Science Research Council Center for Coordination of Research on Social Indicators in Washington, D.C., the publication of several major efforts to define and develop a methodology for the measurement of indicators of subjective well-being (Campbell and Converse 1972; Andrews and Withey 1976; Campbell, Converse, and Rodgers 1976); the commencement of a federal government series of comprehensive social indicators ... the initiation of several continuing data series based on periodic sample surveys of the national population ... the publication in 1974 of the first volume of the international journal *Social Indicators Research*; and the spread of social indicators/social reporting to numerous other nations and international agencies, such as the United States Nations [*sic*] and the Organization for Economic Cooperation and Development. (Land, 2000)

Land (2000) describes the social indicators movement in the USA as 'faltering' in the 1980s. These developments were much less marked in Europe, despite the rise of similar, right-wing conservative/neoliberal political ideologies and comparable economic difficulties. For example, while they vary considerably in their coverage, European countries routinely report social indicators at a national level. Of the EU member states, the Dutch biennial *Social and Cultural Report* (first published in 1974), the United Kingdom's annual *Social Trends* (first published in 1970), and France's triennial *Données Sociales* (first published in 1973) have now been in publication for over a quarter of a century (Habich and Noll, 1994).

This high level of activity, despite a hiatus in the USA in the 1980s, has continued. International agencies such as the World Bank (e.g. World Bank, 2000) and other nations (e.g. the Australian Bureau of Statistics' *Social Trends* which commenced in 1994) have joined in the publication of indicators of the social well-being of nations – in addition to the well-established measures provided by the OECD (OECD, 1982) and the United Nations' *Human Development Index* (United Nations, 1995). One can, argues Noll (2000), 'interpret the rise of social indicators research above all as an answer to the increased demands for information made by an active social policy and by the challenge to operationalize and to quantify its core formula: the concept of quality of life'. Veenhoven (1996: 1) has put it similarly: 'one of the main aims of social indicator research is to develop a comprehensive measure of quality-of-life in nations that is analogous to GNP in economic indicator research'. His HLE, as we have seen, is commended by its author not only on the grounds of its scientific merit, or its accuracy of measurement, but because it 'is likely to have political appeal'.

The role of social indicators in informing politics is also clear to writers like Zapf (1977), who suggests that they may contribute to 'enlighten[ing] us in some way about structures and processes, goals and achievements, values and opinions' (Zapf, 1977: 236). Social indicators thus offer, in Noll's (2000) words,

> standards for the level of modernization of a society and [a] register [of] progress in modernization ... [T]he primary function is not the direct guidance and efficiency control of political decisions, but broad social enlightenment and the provision of an information base which supports politics ... The primary function ... is the measurement of the level and distribution of welfare in a society, whereby welfare development can be understood as a specific dimension of the comprehensive process of modernization.

Or, as Salvaris (2000) might have it, 'progress' – with a capital P.

While Land characterizes the 1980s as a low point in social indicators research, it was during this time of 'conservative ideology' with its celebration of the market, the responsibility of individuals and the importance of 'small government', that interest in the idea of quality of life as a construct at the individual level began. Coinciding with the idea that 'there is no such thing as society, only individuals and their families' said to be at the centre of Margaret Thatcher's politics, the 1980s saw the popularity of 'total quality management', 'continuous quality improve-ment' and 'managing for quality' (Schalock, 1994: 275). In this environ-ment, the notion that quality of life was a property of individual persons became an 'idea whose time had come' (Hatton, 1995: 25). Cummins (1997b: 117–18, my emphasis) notes the intertwining of scientific and popular interest in the individualized notion of QOL:

> New interest in individual, personal values, began to emerge. Spitzer (1987) states that only four papers had QOL in their titles between 1966–1970, while this applied to 33 papers over the next five years ... This exponential rate of increase has been maintained to the present time where the term has become a *political and media catch-word*. The literature is now too vast for any individual researcher to fully assimilate.

Similarly, in their analysis of social policy for people with disabilities, Rapley and Ridgway (1998: 451) noted that:

> No less than in other areas of contemporary society, the powerful rhetoric in ... the late 1980's and early 1990's is that of 'quality'. As the concepts of competition and market economics, borrowed from commerce and

industry, have been applied to human services, so too have they been accompanied in managerial and political rhetoric by their closely associated claims of increased consumer control, enhancement of choice and quality improvement. In addition to these rhetorical claims, human services have also increasingly borrowed the rhetorical tools of corporate culture. In addition to the discourse of consumerism, human services have also begun to deploy a corporate discourse which frames their activities in terms of 'total quality management', 'performance indicators', 'business plans' and 'mission statements'.

Chapter 5 offers a detailed analysis of these developments. However, it is clear that what Cummins terms the 'modern' form of QOL has strayed a long way from the initial, and limited, conceptualization of quality of life as an index of the well-being of populations. The idea of QOL has become much more than a social policy analogue for the GDP – and is now tightly enmeshed with a set of other, and explicitly ideological, knowledges and unashamedly 'American' political and commercial projects. QOL has become not just a concept that ties together a variety of social indicators to offer an index of the success of public policy, but an integral part of the *marketing* of public policy. Land (2000) is undeniably correct when he points out that, in the 1990s, the 'widespread political, popular, and theoretical appeal of the "quality-of-life" (QOL) concept' became 'vividly apparent'. The 'QOL concept' that emerged in the 1990s, Land claims, not only offers 'a goal of social and economic policy' but also

encompasses all (or at least many) domains of life and subsumes, in addition to individual material and immaterial well-being, such collective values as freedom, justice, and the guarantee of natural conditions of life for present and future generations. The political use of the QOL notion is paralleled in the private sector by the widespread use and popularity of numerous rankings – based on weighted scales of multiple domains of well-being – of the "best" places to live, work, do business, play, etc., be they cities, states, regions, or nations. The theoretical appeal of the QOL concept as an integrating notion in the social sciences and related disciplines is, in part, due to the perceived importance of measuring individuals' subjective assessments of their satisfaction with various life domains and with life-as-a-whole .... QOL bridges the discipline of marketing research and strategic business policy with social indicators. Marketing is an importance social force – with far-reaching direct and indirect impacts on the prevailing QOL in a society – through consumer satisfaction (Samli 1987; Sirgy and Samli 1996) and its impact on satisfaction with life-as-a-whole. The intersection of marketing research with social indicators through the QOL concept led to the organization in the mid-1990s of the International Society for Quality-of-Life Studies.

QOL has become an *increasingly* slippery or complex construct over the course of its use. It is now widely used to describe everything from the state of nations' bank balances to the happiness of individuals with the contents of theirs. QOL describes outcomes of political projects, as well as how pleasant (or otherwise) it is to live in Brisbane, Berlin or Beijing. QOL describes the judgments of individuals about their happiness with their sexual relationships, club memberships and domestic arrangements, and also what will be exponentially improved (or so the marketing people claim) by the purchase of this or that washing powder, package holiday or new home. QOL simultaneously indexes the levels of crime, home ownership and participation of women in government in the nation state, and signifies the 'output' of unconscious brain states.

Varieties of Social Indicators

When the quality of life is approached as a population, or societal-level concern, two broad approaches, which, after Noll (2000), will be termed 'Scandinavian' and 'American', can be distinguished. These approaches may be separated by their position in relation to Campbell's (1972) dictum that 'quality of life must be in the eye of the beholder', that is, the relative importance of 'objective' and 'subjective' indicators of social well-being. Early American work focused on 'objective' indicators: health, poverty, unemployment rates and the like which 'represent social facts independently of personal evaluations' in contrast to 'subjective' indicators which rely upon and 'emphasize the individual perception and evaluation of social conditions' (Noll, 2000). A selection of frequently used objective and subjective social indicators is shown in Table 1.1.

It is only subsequently that the contemporary focus on 'the eye of the beholder' has become a central component of ideas about what QOL is. It is not only at the population level that debate still continues: for example, controversy continues in the mental health and intellectual disability literatures about the relative merits of either side of the objective–subjective QOL distinction, in the search for an appropriate indices of service quality at the individual level (Hatton, 1998; Cummins, 2001a).

To return to the population level, in his overview Noll offers a clear account of the two positions – and the conceptual difficulties inherent in both. He writes that:

> Using objective indicators starts from the assumption that living conditions can be judged as being favorable or unfavorable by comparing real conditions with normative criteria like values or goals. An important precondition, however, is that there is political consensus first about the dimensions that are relevant for welfare, second a consensus about good and bad conditions and third about the direction in which society should

Table 1.1 Objective and subjective social indicators

Frequently used objective social indicators (represent social data independently of individual evaluations)

Life expectancy
Crime rate
Unemployment rate
Gross Domestic Product
Poverty rate
School attendance
Working hours per week
Perinatal mortality rate
Suicide rate

Subjective social indicators (individuals' appraisal and evaluation of social conditions)

Sense of community
Material possessions
Sense of safety
Happiness
Satisfaction with 'life as a whole'
Relationships with family
Job satisfaction
Sex life
Perception of distributional justice
Class identification
Hobbies and club membership

Source: Items drawn from Cummins (1996b); Hagerty *et al.* (2001) and Noll (2000).

move. This is of course sometimes, but not always the case. Probably there is consensus that we would consider a reduction of unemployment or crime and an increase of the average income or educational level as an improvement and progress. We could perhaps be less sure, when it comes to indicators like the age of retirement; and it might indeed be debatable whether a reduction of income inequality should in general be regarded as social progress, given the fact that there is a trade-off between distributional justice and efficiency concerning economic growth ... Using subjective social indicators is, instead, based on the premise that welfare ... is perceived by individual citizens and can be judged best by them ... This position, too, is not undisputed and has caused a deep controversy about the principles of welfare measurement. Particularly Scandinavian welfare researchers criticized this subjective quality of life approach and the use of subjective indicators. One of their concerns 'with an approach based on people's own assessment of their degree of satisfaction is that it is partly determined by their level of aspiration' (Erikson 1993: 77). Looking at how satisfied people are, from this point of view is criticized as 'measuring how well they are adapted to their present conditions'. According to R. Erikson (Erikson 1993: 78) – one of the most prominent proponents of Scandinavian welfare research – people's opinions and preferences should go into the democratic political process through their activities as citizens, but not through survey questions and opinion polls. (Noll, 2000)

Land (2000) expands Noll's dichotomy of objective and subjective indicators to distinguish three types of social indicators: criterion indicators, descriptive social indicators and life satisfaction and/or happiness indicators. More recently Veenhoven (1996) has proposed 'comprehensive' social indicators or 'summary welfare indices' (Noll, 2000), which combine aspects of each of these approaches. In Veenhoven's case, the Happy Life Expectancy (HLE) index of quality of life in nations represents an arithmetic product of a happiness indicator[2] and a criterion indicator (life expectancy), of which more below.

Criterion indicators

Given the declared commitment of social indicators research to 'enlightenment' (Zapf, 1977) many indicators are intended to be directly related to social and economic policy-making considerations. This linkage may be seen in MacRae's (1985: 5) definition of criterion indicators as 'measures of those variables that are to be included in a broadly policy-relevant system of public statistics'. Such social indicators, Land (2000) suggests, may be otherwise characterized as '"target" or "output" or "outcome" or "end-value" variables, toward changes in which some public policy (program, project) is directed'. That is, they offer criteria (Ferriss, 1988) against which the success of policy initiatives may be gauged. In the summary of their *World Development Report 2000/2001* the World Bank (2000) offers a clear example of the use of such indicators on an international basis:

At the start of a new century, poverty remains a global problem of huge proportions. Of the world's 6 billion people, 2.8 billion live on less than $2 a day and 1.2 billion on less than $1 a day. Eight out of 100 infants do not live to see their 5th birthday. Nine of 100 boys and 14 of 100 girls who reach school age do not attend school. Poverty is also evident in poor people's lack of political power and voice and in their vulnerability to ill health, economic dislocation, personal violence and natural disasters.

Criterion indicators (income, life expectancy, school attendance) are also termed *normative welfare indicators* (Land, 1983: 4). As Noll (2000) has pointed out, while broad agreement may exist within and possibly even across societies about *some* of these indicators, what counts as a 'normative' indicator of welfare is likely to be culturally (even subculturally) relative, and determined by political and ideological considerations. For example, while it appears that the World Bank considers school attendance by both boys and girls of school age an unambiguous criterion indicator of (high) social welfare, there are societies – such strict Islamic states – where the presence of girls in classrooms would be considered an unambiguous social evil. Equally, the selection of criterion indicators is a matter of local choice and relative weighting. In sub-Saharan Africa, south-east Asia and Latin America, attending school is a lesser social priority than economic production: for societies where school-age children are essential contributors to the workforce, such a criterion reveals an unmistakably ethnocentric set of values.

Descriptive social indicators

Descriptive social indicators are 'indexes of the state of society and changes taking place therein' (Land, 2000). This approach 'focus[es] on social measurements and analyses designed to improve our under-standing of what the main features of society are, how they interrelate, and how these features and their relationships change'. Although these indicators appear to have much in common with criterion indicators, and indeed this category may show considerable overlap with, or even include policy or criterion indicators, unlike criterion indicators descriptive social indicators

> may be more or less directly (causally) related to the well-being goals of public policies or programs ... For instance, in the area of health, descriptive indicators might include preventive indicators such as the percent of the population that does not smoke cigarettes, as well as criterion indicators such as the number of days of activity limitations in the past month or an index of self-reported satisfaction with health. (Land, 2000)

Land (1983) has also suggested that these indicators have the flexibility of *varying degrees of abstraction*. That is, descriptive social indicators may be based on minimal data series that need little statistical manipulation (such as age-specific death rates) to more involved indices (such as years of life-expectancy at age x for men, years of disability-free life expectancy at age y for smokers). These indicators also offer the benefit of being capable of presentation as demographic- or time-budget-based systems of social accounts (Juster and Land, 1981).

Life satisfaction and/or happiness indicators

Again grounded in a decidedly Western notion – that the ultimate purpose of human experience is 'happiness' and, hence, the ultimate measure of social good must be the degree of such a state individuals have achieved – is work on so-called 'subjective' social indicators. These indicators developed from Campbell and Converse's (1972) highly influential *The Human Meaning of Social Change*.

The conceptual key to this work is acceptance of the position that measurement of individual psychological states (values, attitudes, beliefs and aspirations) in the population at large is essential to understand both social change and QOL. This position is flatly rejected by Scandinavian researchers on the grounds that the measurement of individuals' low aspiration/high adaptation is fruitless as an index of social well-being. Others, such as Rapley (2001), have pointed out the absence of a clear theoretical link between any specific policy and any particular individual avowal of happiness – and any persuasive mechanism by which such a connection might operate.

Furthermore 'social indicators' like satisfaction, happiness and life fulfilment are not truly 'social' at all in the sense that the unemployment rate, suicide rate, average life expectancy and high-school participation rate are meaningful demographic averages for a particular *society*. These indicators are only 'social' in the sense that they are collections of individuals' avowals of particular personal judgments, usually of 'contentment', 'satisfaction' or 'happiness' with *x*. As such, these indicators are of a very different kind to the criterion or descriptive social indicators discussed above. Whereas one can sensibly say that Mr Smith is out-of-work and unhappy about it, or that Jodie quit school in year 10 because she couldn't see the point of staying on, it makes no sense at all to say that Mr Smith's unemployment rate is one hundred per cent or that Jodie's high school participation rate is zero per cent.

Despite this, two major studies in the 1970s and a summary collection in the mid-1980s (Andrews and Withey 1976; Campbell *et al.*, 1976; Andrews, 1986), which examined levels of individuals' satisfaction both with the quality of life as a whole[3] and also a host of 'domains' of their lives – from the specific (house, job, family) to the global (life-as-a-whole) – have given rise to an immense literature. The idea that individual appraisals of quality of life are not just essential to understanding the quality of life of nations (the 'American' position), but may even be considered a moral imperative (Shea, 1976) commands considerable currency.

This literature itself diverges according to whether QOL is conceptualized as a *singular entity* or as a *multi-dimensional construct*, made up of a potentially limitless number of 'domains'. For example, Cummins (1996b) identified 173 domains in an analysis of 32 studies. Veenhoven (1996: 22) suggests that 'the most commonly used item is the question: 'Taking all together, how happy would you say you are? Very happy, fairly happy, not too happy, or not at all happy?' Cummins (1997b) suggests that Andrews and Withey's (1976) question 'How do you feel about your life as a whole?', is widely used as QOL index. Given the plethora of multiple-domain life satisfaction measures subsequently developed, Cummins (1996) reports comparative meta-analysis of eleven large-scale studies in which a sufficiently close relationship between scores on single-item measures and the aggregate scores of multiple-domain measures was obtained to prompt the question as to whether the latter are, as summary indicators, essentially redundant.

The current state of social indicators and population well-being research

Much work continues on the development of measures of individual well-being (the Australian Centre on Quality of Life directory includes 447 QOL measures). *Soi-disant* QOL literature also focuses on relative prosperity, GDP, unemployment rates, political democracy and so on. This is one of the major difficulties caused by the overdetermination of the notion. For example, studies addressing population health, social capital or inequalities in health (Cattell, 2001; Forbes and Wainwright, 2001; Navarro and Shi, 2001; OECD, 2001) deal in matters (such as psychological distress, well-being, poor physical health) which are also clearly within the purview of *other* literatures which claim to deal with QOL *qua* QOL (for example, Veenhoven, 1996). The comprehensive absence of rigour of thought and expression in the field (Wolfensberger, 1994) is illustrated by the OECD report *The Well-being of Nations: The Role of Human and Social Capital* (OECD, 2001).

The OECD is a clear instance of the conflation of the notion of well-being across levels of analysis: of nations and individuals respectively. The Executive Summary states that: 'human and social capital are related both to overall well-being and to economic growth ... our social objective is not simply to increase economic growth; it is also to improve well-being' (OECD, 2001: 1) and, later (2001: 4), that:

> Research links social capital, and access to such capital, with improved health – for example, one study shows that social connectedness is associated with a reduced risk of Alzheimer's disease; greater well-being according to self-reported survey measures ... [and] ... improved government – regions or states with higher levels of trust and engagement [social capital] tend to have better quality government.

Here, we see the use of 'well-being' as a construct analogous to economic growth (the notion of 'overall well-being' clearly being a measure applicable to whole populations). A couple of pages later 'well-being' is deployed as a construct that applies both to individual physical health outcomes (reduced risk of Alzheimer's disease) *and* to 'self-reported survey measures' of individual 'well-being'.

Equally, many studies describe themselves as addressing 'population health' with instruments described by their authors as 'quality of life measures'. For example Kind *et al.* (1998) report a study of the population health of the United Kingdom using the EuroQOL EQ-5D, described by its authors as offering 'a new facility for the measurement of health-related quality of life' (EuroQOL Group, 1990: 199). Kind *et al.* (1998: 736) describe their study as 'part of a wider study of practical ways of measuring health related quality of life'. However, while the EuroQOL EQ-5D claims to measure 'HRQOL', it defines QOL in terms of a three-point rating of one's 'health state today' on each of five individual-level dimensions – self-care, mobility, usual activities (study, work, housework, family or leisure), pain or discomfort and anxiety or depression. In the area of 'usual activities', for example, the choices are 'I have no problems with performing my usual activities'; 'I have some problems with performing my usual activities'; and 'I am unable to perform my usual activities'. Secondly the measure asks respondents to 'say how good or bad your own health is today' on a 0 ('worst imaginable health state') – 100 ('best imaginable health state') visual analogue scale.

In the Kind *et al.* (1998) study the average state of health recorded was 82.5, and 'a moderate problem on at least one dimension was reported by 42% of respondents' (1998: 737). Kind *et al* suggest that – as a consequence of their sampling strategy – 'the results may well underestimate the health related quality of life of the general population' (1998: 739). Thus a self-proclaimed measure of 'HRQOL' focuses on individuals' views about their health but makes no mention of the concept of quality of life *qua* quality of life. The measure does not ask respondents how they feel about being 'unable to perform my usual activities'. Yet the results are said both to have 'obvious potential' in gaining the 'patient's point of view in monitoring medical care outcomes' while also offering to account for general population level QOL outcomes (Kind *et al.*, 1998: 740).

The literature also contains numerous papers which elide individuals' health status, political movements and QOL. For example Rogers-Clark (1998: 6, my emphasis) states that 'the Women's Health movement is linked inextricably with the broader Women's movement. Feminism has two goals: to *actively improve women's quality of life*; and to remove those fundamental patriarchal ideologies within contemporary society which lead to the oppression of women.' This is very clearly to place the issue of quality of life into a socio-political frame. The current state of women's QOL, for Rogers-Clarke at least, is held to be lower than it might as a result of the dominance of 'fundamental patriarchal ideologies'. This conceptualizes QOL as a structural phenomenon – rather than construing quality of life as an aggregate of individual judgments by specific women. Farlinger (1996: 109, my emphasis) argues that the 'description of the *quality of life* today for women begins with information on indicators such as income, population, refugees, percent women in political office or boardrooms ... The key to effective policies is to measure the cause and effects of environmental degradation and find ways to provide feedback to the decision-makers and ourselves to change behavior.' Here, QOL is not an interior aspect of many individual psyches but a global attribute of a collectivity of women which may be estimated by a variety of *specific indicators* (income, refugees, women in boardrooms, etc.) rather than inferred from the continuing hegemony of 'patriarchal ideologies'.

Frey and Al-Roumi (1999: 73) ask 'why do some countries have a high quality of life?' and offer the following answer: 'One important explanation is that political democracy fosters life quality.' Proponents of this perspective argue that 'political democracy acts to center the public agenda on state actions that enhance life quality.' That Western political democracies such as the USA and the UK show reasonably high levels of happiness on most surveys (see Cummins, 2001b; Veenhoven, 1991, 1996) and at the same time low, and decreasing, levels of active participation by their citizens in the democratic process suggests that the mechanism may be less straight-forward.

Veenhoven's work attempts to link the happiness of population groups with social arrangements and political economy. Davis (1984) has shown the responsiveness of people's judgments of their 'happiness-with-life-as-a-whole' to changes in respondents' financial status as opposed to current income level. The connection of subjective well-being to income levels has been a problem since Easterlin's (1973) demonstration that, while the association of happiness with income within countries is not strong, income differences between nations predict national differences in happiness. Veenhoven (1997: 12) states that 'the richer the country, the happier its inhabitants', but qualifies Easterlin's (1973) analysis by noting that 'correlations between personal happiness and personal income are strong in poor countries and weak in rich nations' and concludes that this finding 'does not fit the theory that happiness derives from social comparison', an essential theorem of work that defines QOL as an individualized, subjective state.

While not invoking the construct of QOL, much work examines population level variables as determinants of the 'mood' of countries. Hogenraad and Grosbois (1997) describe (in the key QOL journal *Social Indicators Research*) the determinants of (what we may gloss as) a lowering of the quality of Belgian life – in their terms the level of 'threat' to the security and continued existence of the Belgian nation. Such an analysis allows us to see, in negative as it were, the factors considered conducive to an absence of threat. It is suggested that, based on 91 expert historians rating the threat severity for each year, and an analysis of objective economic, social and political indicators, a constellation of individual and population-wide factors produce 'threat'. They state that, on the basis of indicators of threat or fear, such as 'crime, unemployment, apprehension at starting a family, buying a car, or starting a new business, etc ... The present threat index ... for Belgium is found to depend on a 5-variable subset composed of: suicide, unemployment, and balance of trade, for the positive associations; and GNP and car registrations, for the negative associations' (Hogenraad and Grosbois, 1997: 221). The quality of Belgian life it would seem, then, is best enhanced by a thriving new-car market and a high GDP. The 'mood' that Belgian life is under threat, it appears, again is primarily determined by similarly macro-level phenomena (unemployment, the balance of trade). The one unequivocally individual-level indicator of threat (suicide) is, one would have thought, more likely to be an outcome of high levels of threat, rather than a predictor of it.

More Recent Developments

Veenhoven (1996: 5–6) identifies the many issues raised by the idea of measuring the quality of life of nations very clearly when he states:

> The most fundamental problem with ... QOL-indicators is that they involve criteria of a different order. They do not distinguish between means and ends, nor between societal input and societal output ... If we are not clear about what we mean with QOL, we will never have sensible measures of it ... A first thing then is to distinguish between the quality of nations and the quality-of-life in nations.

In order to facilitate such a distinction Veenhoven (1996) proposes a new index: the HLE.

Happy life expectancy

Veenhoven attempts to bridge the conceptual gap in levels of measurement between genuinely social social indicators of the quality of life (GDP, unemployment rates, etc.), with individual level indicators by suggesting that 'happiness' be considered the best indicator of individuals' satisfaction. Veenhoven identifies a range of problems with measures of quality of life in nations such as the United Nation's *Human Development Index* (1995) and Estes's (1984) *Index of Social Progress*. Extant indices show arbitrary selection and relative weighting of indicators, culture-bound indicator selection, opacity of meaning of aggregate scores and confusion of means and ends. For example, a long life is what is termed an end value – valued for itself – whereas an affluent life may offer a means to that end. Veenhoven (1996: 5) also points out the concerns raised by Salvaris (2000). That is, he questions the manner in which some of the indexes [of national quality of life] are in fact more specific and equate quality-of-life more or less with 'modernity'. They measure in fact the degree to which characteristics of the dominant Western society are present in a nation ... [I]t is misleading to call that 'quality-of-life'. Modernization should not be equated with the good life.

Veenhoven's proposal, then, is to (re)conceptualize QOL as the 'flourishing' or 'thriving' of lived existence. He draws an analogy between persons, fauna and flora to argue that:

the flourishing of plants or animals in a given ecological environment is usually measured by their functioning as apparent in growth, adequacy of behavior and absence of disease ... Can the flourishing of humans in a social environment be measured by the same criteria? To some extent yes. Human thriving also manifests physically, particularly in good health and a long life. Therefore we can induce the quality-of-life in a nation from the *health* of its citizens ... Unlike plants and animals, humans can reflect on themselves and their situation. Their suit to society is therefore also reflected in their judgments. As such we can also infer quality-of-life in a nation from the citizen's *appraisals* of life. (Veenhoven, 1996: 12, emphases in the original)

Such a conception has the merit of placing the lived experience of persons, and their appraisals of the quality of that experience, into a social context; of noting that the issue can be construed as a matter of the 'goodness of fit' between persons and their environment (cf. Zautra and Goodhart, 1979); and also of noting that (impoverished) quality of life may be evident in both 'behavioural manifestations of malaise' (Veenhoven, 1996: 17) and subjective complaints of misery.

Veenhoven (1996) suggests that while international data on un-happiness are unsuitable for computational purposes, ratings of subjective happiness across nations are sufficiently comparable to permit league tables of happy life expectancy. HLE is the product of subtracting (nation-specific) expected years in bad health from expected years of life and multiplying standard life expectancy by average happiness on a scale from 1 to 0. Or:

$$\text{HLE} = \text{Standard life expectancy} \times 0 - 1 \text{ Happiness}$$

Thus if life expectancy in country y is 50 years, with an average happiness score of 0.5, the product of $50 \times 0.5 = 25$, thus the HLE of country y is 25 years. This figure 'characterizes most of the poor nations in the present day world' whereas for 'the most livable nations' the HLE is 64 years (1996: 29). High HLE values mean that 'citizens live both long and happily' while low values suggest that 'the life of the average citizen is short and miserable.

Medium values of happy life expectancy in a country can mean three things: 1) both moderate length-of-life and moderate appreciation-of-life, 2) long but unhappy life, and 3) short but happy life' (1996: 30).

There are two conceptual and practical difficulties here. Firstly a long miserable life and a short happy one are, while numerically identical, diametrically opposite in terms of 'quality'. Secondly, the statistic describes the experience not of persons, but of a conceptual abstraction – the 'Average Citizen'. Veenhoven reports that, in a 1990 survey of 48 countries, on average, HLE in Northern Ireland (56.49) and Norway (57.16) were almost identical. That the average Norwegian citizen was unlikely to have their life expectancy, happy or otherwise, suddenly shortened by random sectarian shootings or car bombings – as were the citizens of Northern Ireland – cannot be captured by the HLE, which, it is claimed, is a 'comprehensive' indicator of the quality of life in a nation (1996: 28). Equally, while average Australian HLE in 1990 was 59.49 – putting Australia in fifth place after Switzerland, Sweden, the Netherlands and Iceland – the use of an average figure disguises the fact that, for Australia's Indigenous peoples, life expectancy (whether happy or not) has been barely 40 years since the 1950s.

Such concerns have led some workers to argue that for social indicators of well-being or quality of life to be locally meaningful, they need to be locally identified and defined. These developments are now considered.

Social indicators of the quality of life: a locally-based movement

There are now well-established sets of social indicators at the international and national levels. Chapter 2 considers the relation between *definitions* of QOL and *measures* of the construct in more detail, but for now it is important to recognize that debate about the utility of population level indices concerns issues of the meaning of measures of well-being that are deeply *practical* as well as *conceptual*. For example, Redefining Progress has suggested what they describe as a more accurate measure of progress, the *Genuine Progress Indicator* (GPI).

Cobb *et al.* (2000: 1) suggest this measure:

> starts with the same accounting framework as the GDP, but then makes some crucial distinctions: It adds in the economic contributions of household and volunteer work, but subtracts factors such as crime, pollution, and family breakdown: as such the GPI attempts to capture a more holistic picture of the *sustainable* life quality of nations, or 'genuine progress in people's quality of life'.[4]

Redefining Progress acts as an international clearing house for locally-based community indicators projects (Cobb *et al.*, 2000; Eckersley, 1998). Measures such as the GPI are a response to what Salvaris (2000: 4) has called 'a growing concern about the influence of economic output indicators, most notably the Gross Domestic Product (GDP)[5] as proxy measurements of human progress'. Salvaris and other critics of the GDP point out that it is both misleading (it is a poor measure of the actual condition of the economy and the society) and also that it is overly powerful (that is, the GDP is too influential in shaping our everyday understanding of progress and well-being). Salvaris (2000: 5) argues that:

> measuring the market value of economic production tells us very little about the broader health of the community or the environment, and nothing about the social costs of what has been produced in the economy, or about its usefulness or sustainability.

This account greatly broadens the scope of what is usually meant by the term 'social indicator'. Such concerns raise serious questions about notions like 'modernity' and 'progress' as indices of life quality complementary to those of Veenhoven (1996), but from a rather different perspective. In Box 1.1 some of the other future challenges for social indicators research, adapted from Noll, are identified.

Box 1.1 Future directions for social indicators research

1. *Reconsidering the concepts of welfare and the quality of life.* In a world of rapidly changing social contexts and problems, such as the crisis of the welfare state and global ecological problems, the usefulness of concepts – like modernization, individual welfare, subjective well-being, social capital and quality of life – needs to be reconsidered for the observation of social development at the beginning of the twenty-first century.

2. *Construction of summary welfare indices.* In the light of increasing economic and political integration in Europe, for example, and in the context of the problems of globalization and late capitalism, there is a need for internationally comparable summary indices synthesizing the various dimensions of welfare into one single measure. Examples of new summary welfare indices are the Genuine Progress Indicator (GPI).

3. *Development of local initiatives.* At the same time as developing international indices, much work will need to focus on the development of locally relevant, community-owned indices of social well-being. The National Citizenship Project and the 'Quality of life in Newcastle' projects in Australia and 'Sustainable Seattle' in the US offer models of this approach (Salvaris, 2000).

In addition to the development of indicators like the GPI, concerns about the *ethical positions* implicit in measures of life quality have spurred locally-based projects across the world in an effort to develop indicators of the quality of life of local communities, which are locally meaningful and based on explicit philosophical positions. These developments are discussed in Chapter 2. However, before we move on to these 'grassroots' indicators of the quality of life, we must consider quality of life as an individual-level construct.

QOL as a State of Persons

That there is now a 'modern form' of understanding of QOL could be taken to imply that understandings based on non-individualized notions of QOL were pre-modern, archaic or ignorant of up-to-date ideas. Yet collectivist and relational understandings of the concept continue to thrive and the appeal to modernity to warrant ideas itself has a dubious history (Chorover, 1979; Salvaris, 2000).

Brock (1993) has pointed out that theorizing the good life at the individual level has been the site of considerable historical disagreement and contestation. He distinguishes three broad approaches to QOL in terms of theories of the 'good life'. *Hedonist theory* holds that the ultimate good is to have certain kinds of conscious experiences – happiness, pleasure, satisfaction – that typically accompany pursuit of desires. *Preference satisfaction theory* (closely related to the currently influential *multiple discrepancy theory* (Michalos, 1985)) holds that the good life consists in the satisfaction of desires and preferences, with what is good being understood as people getting what they want and prefer with a minimal number of unsatisfied wants (discrepancies) equating to a better good. *Ideal theory* suggests that at least part of the good life is to do with neither conscious enjoyment nor the satisfaction of preferences, but instead consists in the satisfaction of specific normative ideals (cf. Cummins, 2000a). Megone (1990), in contrast, draws upon Aristotle to suggest that the good life consists in man's fulfilment of the *purpose of being human*, namely leading an active *rational* life. Sadly this line of reasoning seems to have been something of a cul-de-sac in the social scientific literatures, but see McHoul and Rapley (2001a) for a discussion of the philosophical implications.

As the above suggests, the observation that the link between objective conditions and subjective well-being is sometimes paradoxical at the national level is also influential at the individual level. Hence the position that subjective *and* objective states should be monitored in the 'American' social indicators literature and in endeavours derived therefrom: for example, Noll (2000) states that 'in our own German approach individual welfare or quality of life is therefore defined as "good living conditions which go together with positive subjective well-being"'. Land (2000) suggests that subjective well-being may both show 'traitlike' and 'statelike' characteristics. There is, according to Land, a consensus that subjective well-being demonstrates both reactivity to situations and events – a state alterable by circumstances – while at the same time being 'a durable psychological condition that differs among individuals and contributes to stability over time and consistency across situations' or a trait, a more or less fixed aspect of how particular individuals view their world (Stones *et al.*, 1995; Veenhoven, 1994, 1998; Ahuvia and Friedman, 1998). This synthetic view has recently been strongly contested by Cummins (1995, 1997b, 1998b, 2001b).

Subjective well-being, QOL and biological determinism

So up-to-date is Cummins' view that he has recently proposed (2001a, 2001b; 2001c; Cummins *et al.*, in press) that QOL is a 'hard-wired', homeostatically controlled, brain state. Subjective well-being is: 'a dispositional brain system that acts to keep each individual's well being within a narrow positive range' (2001a: 5) held constant at approximately 75 per cent of scale maximum (or 75%SM) on whatever quality of life, satisfaction or happiness scale it is measured.

This view is representative of the dominant form of theorizing within Western psychology and affiliated disciplines (or the psy-complex as Rose (1999) has called them), which seeks to locate the source of all of human experience within biology. Such views are a part of a broader trajectory in Western thought, which has gathered pace since the 1970s, and which has increasingly sought to replace phenomenological, social or sociological understandings of human experience and the quality of life (as much of the social indicators research discussed above may be understood) with individualized biological and/or cognitive accounts. Increasingly accounts dispense with the notion of the *person* as an explanatory 'variable': instead the focus is on putative intra-personal componentry, described in terms of computer metaphors (Button *et al.*, 1997), and often held to be the 'output' of genetically determined brain mechanisms. What may once have been viewed as transcendental human experience (joy), or existential crisis (depression), are no longer understood as states of being-in-the-world experienced by persons, but rather are respecified, as if we were discussing a faulty central heating system, as the 'consequences of homeostatic failure' (Cummins *et al.*, in press). The influential work of Cummins and colleagues on the homeostatic hypothesis is discussed in detail in Chapter 8.

In Summary

The concept of quality of life has travelled from being a shorthand term encompassing the political aims of the 'Great Society', through a period of intense social scientific formalism at both individual and population levels, back to its original status as an all-pervasive 'political and media catchword' (Cummins, 1997b). In the process the concept has developed a double life: the term 'quality of life' has come to index, simultaneously, collections of a bewildering array of 'indicators' of the quality of living conditions within the nation state, and also the 'output' of automatic brain states. Like psychology, the discipline from which the most influential formulations of QOL as an individual attribute have come, the idea has a short history, but a very long past. Again like psychology, QOL is an idea which clearly has a robust future, even if the contours of that future are both politically contentious and, presently, opaque. Quite what QOL actually *means* is the focus of Chapter 2.

Notes

1. 'Whig histories' attempt to account for how it is that past events have caused current ones. The use of history in this book owes more to Foucault, whose recommendations for the use of history entail analysis of the conditions of possibility of particular discourses, and the diagnosis of the present, as research goals.
2. Veenhoven's Happiness Index (Veenhoven, 1984) has two questions: To what extent do you regard yourself as a happy person? How satisfied are you with your present life? Both are scored on four-point scales. Psychometrics are reported by Debats (1996).
3. Andrews and Withey's (1976) measure is the single question 'How do you feel about your life as a whole?' with responses measured on a Likert scale anchored on 'delighted' ('satisfaction') and 'terrible' ('dissatisfaction'). Cummins (1996b) describes the measure as 'one of the few empirical benchmarks for life quality'. Campbell *et al.* (1976) asked respondents to rate satisfaction with health, social and family connections, material wealth/well-being and work/productive activity on a five-point scale.
4. The calculation of the GPI begins with the personal consumption component of the Gross Domestic Product (GDP), including capital investment, government spending and net exports and factors in social, environmental and economic phenomena that diminish or enhance people's quality of life, but that are not typically measured in monetary terms or included in economic analyses. For example, while the GDP simply counts money changing hands, the GPI factors in hidden environmental costs such as pollution and depletion of natural resources (Cobb *et al.*, 2000: 1).
5. The GDP is a summary measure of the total value of all goods and services traded in an economy.

Study Questions

- Should modernization be equated with the good life?
- What might be the *mechanisms* which link large-scale social indicators, social policy and individual claims of happiness?
- What are the key indicators of life quality in the community where I live?
- Should social policy be influenced by measures of the happiness of citizens?
- How do *aggregate* measures of well-being and the lived experience of *individual persons* relate to one another?

Suggestions for Further Reading

Gullone, E. and Cummins, R. A. (eds) (2002) *The Universality of Subjective Well-Being Indicators*. Dordrecht, Kluwer.

Salvaris, M. (2000) *Community and Social Indicators: How citizens can measure progress. An overview of social and community indicator projects in Australia and internationally*. Hawthorn, Victoria, Institute for Social Research, Swinburne University of Technology.

Veenhoven, R. (1996) Happy Life Expectancy: a comprehensive measure of quality-of-life in nations. *Social Indicators Research*, 39: 1–58.

CHAPTER 2

A Life of Quality – Just What Does QOL Mean?

> The term 'quality of life' is great in speeches, but when it is given the stature of a research concept, it becomes an uncertain tool unless it is controlled by a precise definition and rigorous discipline in thought and word. (Wolfensberger, 1994: 318)

Preamble

In her review of the clinical psychological and psychiatric literatures Boyle (2002) described the conceptual and practical difficulties caused by professional or technical uses of 'multi-referential lay constructs' – terms like 'depression' or 'anxiety' – which have widespread circulation in everyday language, and are also employed in the social scientific literatures with a (notionally) tightly limited 'professional' meaning. As Brown (2000: 352) notes: 'quality of life is already a well-worn term within society. Everything from clothes to condoms tends to be marketed from this perspective – a perspective where quality of life equates to pleasure.' The difficulty that the overdetermination of meaning of such terms causes in the attempt to use them scientifically is spelled out by Watson. He argues that:

> Ordinary or lay usages of technical terms, and the mundane conceptions of society that they routinely convey, both continue to operate in the technical or professional ... usage. They operate in the background through the shaping or moulding of the professional usage, despite ... attempts to redefine those ordinary meanings of such terms ... the ordinary language meanings of such terms ... can not be wished away or redefined by fiat. Thus [we] can not proceed like the Queen of Hearts in *Alice in Wonderland*, [we] can not command a word to mean whatever [we] want it to mean. (Watson, 2000: 4)

This is a critical point for social scientific research that wishes to engage with a notion such as 'quality of life' which is already imprecise in ordinary usage. Taking our cue from Watson, consider for a moment Alice's further adventures. In *Through the Looking Glass* Alice meets the Red and the White Queens – who have a remarkable set of attributes including the White Queen's ability to remember both backwards and forwards. More pertinent is the Red Queen's response to Alice's attempt to correct her answer to the Queen's inquiry about the cause of lightning: '"It's too late to correct it," said the Red Queen: "when you've once said a thing, that fixes it, and you must take the consequences"' (Carroll, 1982: 186). The QOL literature is, it would seem, unevenly distributed across these two positions. On one hand, with the Red Queen, many appear to believe that 'once you've said a thing' – having operationally defined what QOL is – that 'that fixes it'. On the other, with Alice and Rod Watson, another stream of work is less certain about what sort of a 'thing' quality of life might be, 'scientifically', and questions whether it makes any sense to regard QOL as a social scientific *thing* at all. This 'side' is, in consequence, deeply sceptical about the possibility of 'fixing it' technically. Which side of this binary one adopts does – as the Red Queen implies – make a major difference.

Defining Quality of Life

Happiness; life-satisfaction; well-being; self-actualization; freedom from want; objective functioning; 'a state of complete physical, mental and social well-being not merely the absence of disease' (WHO, 1997: 1); balance, equilibrium or 'true bliss' (Kant, 1978: 185); prosperity; fulfilment; low unemployment; psychological well-being; high GDP; the good life; enjoyment; democratic liberalism; the examined life (*pace* Socrates); a full and meaningful existence (cf. Sheldon, 2000). Not only are all of these terms used in the literature in discussions of what constitutes (a) 'quality of life' but it is difficult if not impossible to reconcile them. It is difficult to better the contention of Cummins *et al.* (in press) that:

> Among the most inconsistently used terms within the human sciences is that of 'quality of life'. Indeed, the words 'quality of life' are used with such abandon that readers must delve into the text to ascertain the intended meaning. Other terms such as 'happiness' and 'well-being' are likewise afflicted.

As we have seen in Chapter 1, when talking about QOL, the literatures invoke matters ranging from objective estimations of the life circumstances of individuals, to those individuals' 'subjective' estimations of their appreciation of those circumstances; from macroeconomic indicators, the 'amounts' of other abstract quanta such as 'human' and 'social capital' (OECD, 2001; Putnam, 1995, 2002) such economies 'possess', to individual happiness with material circumstances. QOL is linked to specific political systems, with some effectively defined *as* quality of life or as an index of it (neoliberal economic policies and democracy being the usual 'variables' related to 'high' QOL, possibly because most QOL research emanates from countries which can afford the of luxury contemplating it – see Frey and Al-Roumi, 1999; Mattes and Christie, 1997).

Some studies evaluate quality of life retrospectively – and at the remove of centuries (although the White Queen would be unimpressed by such a feat). While acknowledging that 'attempts to evaluate the quality of life in historical perspective have been hindered by the absence of data on the perceptions that people held about their well-being', Ostroot and Snyder (1996: 109) nevertheless report a study of the QOL of the people of Aix-en-Provence since 1695. Similarly, Jordan (2001) reports on the QOL of Ireland in the nineteenth century through an analysis of the writings of William Bence Jones, a resident landlord of the time. This project represents a follow-up of his earlier work on quality of life in the context of Irish emigration in the nineteenth century via Irish bootmaker John O'Neill's autobiography, *Fifty Years Experience of an Irish Shoemaker in London* (Jordan, 1999).

There are, further, legion 'indicators', 'components' or 'domains' of *both* societies' *and* individuals' quality of life. Chapter 4 considers this, primarily quantitative, approach in more detail, but for now, the state of the field may be judged by the title of another of Cummins's (1996) papers: 'The domains of life satisfaction: An attempt to order chaos'. The multiplicity of domains identified range from the commonsensical and widely applicable – the availability of decent accommodation and social relationships (Cummins, 1997b) to the highly idiosyncratic – the presence of car parking near the oncology department (Coates *et al.*, 1983). In addition to 'indicators', the literature contains a multiplicity of investigations of the 'effects' of a bewildering variety of activities and states of being-in-the-world upon QOL, variously defined. Thus we read reports on 'the effect of swimming with dolphins on human well-being and anxiety' with 'human well-being' described as 'how "positive" participants felt at that moment' (Webb and Drummond, 2001: 82). A more unusual study of 'human well-being' investigated the 'association between religion, religiosity and well-being' (Anson and Anson, 2001: 83) using *death* as the index of 'well-being' – or rather of its absence. Turning this logic on its head, there also exists a myriad of studies examining the effects of QOL *itself* (again variously defined) on other states of the world: for instance Hagerty *et al.*, (2000) study of the relationship between QOL and the outcomes of elections. Hagerty *et al.* (2000: 347) claim their work shows that QOL, as measured by 'GDP per capita, food availability, inflation, crime rates, divorce rate, and percent of females in the labor force … is the best predictor of voters' behavior' and that 'changes in QOL … significantly affect election outcomes'.

How QOL is defined (or 'fixed') is highly heterogenous across the social scientific literatures. QOL is frequently used as a synonym for the absence of post-operative complications and/or physical robustness in medical settings, as an index of the quantity and quality of staff attention in psychiatric settings and as a shorthand term for community connectedness in intellectual disability settings. In intellectual disability research the definition of QOL has been said to be 'researcher specific' (Lansdesman, 1986) or, as the Queen of Hearts would have it, the term 'means what I want it to mean'.

This chapter addresses two major ongoing theoretical debates. Firstly, what is the relative merit and status of 'objective' and 'subjective' measures of QOL? Secondly, can there be a universal definition of QOL or do definitions of QOL – and the measures derived therefrom – require calibration against the specific life circumstances of populations under study?

Definitions of QOL

In citing definitional diversity as one of the key problems of QOL research, I am recapitulating the commonest observation in reviews of the various QOL literatures. Across the social sciences literature reviews – be they focused on issues of methodology (e.g. Haase *et al.*, 1999), surveys of the QOL measures available in a particular sub-field (e.g. Cagney *et al.*, 2000; Hagerty *et al.*, 2001) or providing brief educational updates for particular professions (Higginson and Carr, 2001) – all concur in their identification of huge variability in the definition of QOL. It is routinely observed that not only do particular studies frequently lack a formal definition of QOL, but also that widely used measures of QOL fail to relate to an explicit theory of QOL and fail to show how QOL 'outputs' are related to 'inputs' in the shape of either public policy (Hagerty *et al.*, 2001), or more local circumstances (Rapley, 2001). Cagney *et al.'s* (2000: 327) account of a review of measures used in the area of end-stage renal disease is typical of the issues:

> From 436 citations, 78 articles were eligible for final review, and of those, 47 articles contained evidence of reliability or validity testing. Within this set, there were 113 uses of 53 different instruments: 82% were generic and 18% were disease specific. Only 32% defined quality of life ... Testing was completed for test-retest reliability (20%), inter-rater reliability (13%), internal consistency (22%), content validity (24%), construct validity (41%), criterion validity (55%), and responsiveness (59%). Few articles measuring quality of life in ESRD defined quality-of-life domains or adequately described instrument development and testing ... Standardized reporting and more rigorous testing could help researchers make informed choices about instruments that would best serve their own and their patients' needs.

In an era in which medicine is increasingly said to be 'evidence-based', the quality of research on QOL (at least in the area of renal disease) is at best mixed and at worst unacceptably poor. It is not only in empirical work that problems are apparent: Haase *et al.* (1999: 125) argue that 'theoretical work on health-related quality of life (HRQL) is not well developed and is often derived from a "shopping list" of concepts that lack clear identification of the theory or assumptions underlying their selection'.

The corollary of atheoretical index development and definitional heterogeneity is that the various phenomena which are taken to be contributory to QOL are equally diverse, be QOL conceptualized as either an individual-level or a population-level construct. Hence, while perhaps a majority of formal definitions in the social science literatures would agree that QOL is a multidimensional construct, neither the number nor the variety of dimensions is yet agreed despite the fact that in some areas – such as intellectual disability – a 'consensus' has been announced (Cummins, 1997a; Felce and Perry, 1996a; IASSID, 2001). This definitional diversity, and the difficulties flowing from it, is one of the problems clearly identified by writers such as Hatton (1998), Taylor (1994) and Rapley (2001) who are cautious about the use of QOL as an individual-level outcome variable: this work will be discussed in more detail in the next chapter.

Quality of Life Defined as a Population-level Construct

That what QOL might 'be' at population level is as heterogenous as it is at an individual level is shown in the diversity of indicators in the literature. Again, there is broad agreement both that quality of life is a *multi-dimensional* construct, and that QOL can be can be related to *normative expectations* about the qualities which citizens' lives may reasonably be anticipated to show (levels of access to income, for example). Precisely *which* dimensions of the lives of individuals or collectivities are selected as indicators of quality of life varies according to different authorities. Such variability occurs for theoretical and practical reasons, and often for a mixture of both. As we saw in Chapter 1, two broad camps exist with regard to the role of *objective* and *subjective* indicators in QOL assessment at both the population and the individual level.

Objective and subjective indicators of QOL

Cummins (1997a: 7) suggests that the separate measurement of objective and subjective components, or 'axes', of quality of life is essential. He states that 'the contemporary literature is quite consistent in its determination that, while both of these axes form a part of the QOL construct, they generally have a very poor relationship to one another. For example, physical health and perceived health are poorly correlated.'

Noll (2000) suggests that the possible combinations of circumstances and personal appraisals of them can be conceptualized as a 2 × 2 matrix (see Figure 2.1). He terms good living conditions and positive well-being

Categories of individual welfare

Objective Living Conditions	Subjective Well-Being	
	Good	Bad
Good	WELL-BEING	DISSONANCE
Bad	ADAPTION	DEPRIVATION

Figure 2.1 Dimensions of objective and subjective well-being (*Source*: Zapf 1984: 25).

'Well-Being' and bad living conditions with a negative evaluation of them 'Deprivation'. 'Dissonance', he suggests, refers to the 'inconsistent combination of good living conditions and dissatisfaction, and is sometimes also called the 'dissatisfaction dilemma' (clearly implying the value judgment that those who are fortunate should be happy with their lot).

'Adaptation' refers to what many researchers see as the problematic combination of bad living conditions and high levels of satisfaction, sometimes known as the 'satisfaction paradox' or 'disability paradox'. The existence of persons in this quadrant is simultaneously the driving force behind the contention that objective and subjective evaluations of QOL *must* be separately measured, the reason why 'Scandinavian' researchers ignore subjectivity altogether and instead measure only 'objective' circumstances (see Hatton, 1998), and the cause of considerable anger among disability researchers who note that only the able-bodied would *necessarily* expect people with disabilities to have an inferior quality of life (Koch, 2001).

The case is still open. Cogent and internally coherent arguments can be made for both 'Scandinavian' and 'American' positions on the objective versus the subjective in defining 'quality of life' and the indicators which are, in consequence, seen as appropriate as indices of the good life. Fundamentally, 'American' inspired researchers and government agencies accord an important role to individuals' assessments of their happiness in the assessment of population well-being, whereas 'Scandinavian' re-searchers rule out individual happiness when measuring the quality of national life. Again as we saw earlier, researchers such as Veenhoven (1990, 1996, 1997), Noll (2000) and Berger-Schmitt and Jankowitsch (1999) argue for the importance of measuring both objective and subjective quality of life, and in practice, most national governmental agencies which collect data on national well-being include both objective and subjective indicators in their systems of social statistics.

National well-being as a multidimensional concept

That the idea of quality of life is now deeply embedded in the ways that Western countries think themselves (Rose, 1992) is illustrated by the Australian Bureau of Statistics's (ABS) (2001) introduction to its new series of social indicators *Measuring Wellbeing*. The ABS states that 'a major driving force in human activity is the desire for optimal health, for better living conditions and *improved quality of life*. Individuals seek to achieve this for themselves, for their family, and for the communities of which they are a part' (ABS, 2001: 3, my emphasis). Having suggested that improving one's quality of life is a major motivator of human activity, and identified measuring well-being (apparently an interchangeable term with quality of life) as essential to governmental monitoring of the effectiveness of social policy, the ABS then enters the caveat that, when it comes to defining what it means by the term quality of life (or well-being), the 'first step in producing meaningful statistics is to map the conceptual territory that is to be measured. In the case of measuring well-being, this is a large task' (ABS, 2001: 6). However, undaunted, the ABS offers the following definition of well-being/quality of life:

> From birth to death, life enmeshes individuals within a dynamic culture consisting of the natural environment (light, heat, air, land, water, minerals, flora, fauna), the human made environment (material objects, buildings, roads, machinery, appliances, technology), social arrangements (families, social networks, associations, institutions, economies), and human consciousness (knowledge, beliefs, understanding, skills, traditions). Wellbeing depends on all the factors that interact within this culture and can be seen as a state of health or sufficiency in all aspects of life. Measuring wellbeing therefore involves mapping the whole of life, and considering each life event or social context that has the potential to affect the *quality of individual lives*, or the cohesion of society. At the individual level, this can include the physical, emotional, psychological and spiritual aspects of life. At a broader level, the social, material and natural environments surrounding each individual, through interdependency, become part of the wellbeing equation. (ABS, 2001: 6, my emphasis)

While this definition is commendably inclusive and comprehensive, it suggests that measuring well-being/quality of life, or 'mapping the whole of life' is simultaneously both a necessity and an impossibility (Morreim, 1992). Consequently, the ABS explicitly recognizes that 'measuring wellbeing involves making *value judgements* about what aspects of life are important to wellbeing and what social issues are most pressing' (ABS, 2001: 6, my emphasis).

The approach adopted by the ABS is to take the early OCED social indicators as a base set, and to recognize that the development of a system

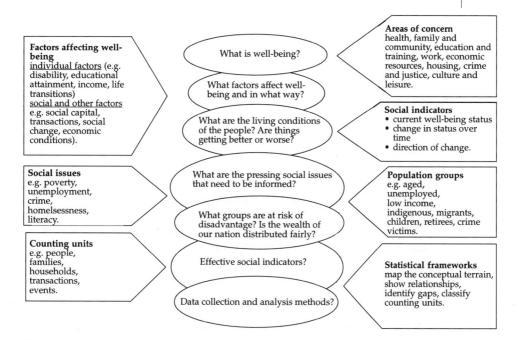

Figure 2.2 ABS system of social statistics (*Source*: Adapted from ABS, 2001: 5).

of social statistics designed to inform national policy-making *necessarily* has to involve 'making a range of pragmatic decisions about what phenomena will provide the greatest insight into these issues, how these phenomena can be measured accurately, and how the resulting measures can be combined, constructed and presented to be informative and accessible' (ABS, 2001: 6). The conceptual model adopted by the ABS is shown in Figure 2.2.

As shown, the Australian system is informed by issues of *theory and methodology* (what is well-being?), by a series of *value judgments* (which policy matters are in 'pressing need' of being informed?) – reflecting the Australian context, the inclusion of matters pertaining to Indigenous Australians in the model – and by a 'range of *pragmatic decisions*' about the available statistical base which can be used to represent, if not the whole of life, then at least Australian national well-being as accurately and completely as possible within the constraints operative (for example, government funding for census-taking).

The ABS explicitly recognizes that there probably can never be a single measure of well-being that will be approved of by all parties interested in the quality of people's lives. Rather, some indicators can, at least in affluent Western nations, be considered 'fundamental' to the measurement of the well-being of national communities (mortality rates, inequality measures and unemployment rates are cited). However, the ABS (2001: 6) also makes the crucially important point that

> at any one time the range of social indicators ... will be a subset of all possible wellbeing indicators, influenced by the preoccupations and concerns of contemporary culture. The focus of social statistics will also be constrained by what social conditions can be appropriately influenced by policy and intervention.

This point cannot be stressed too strongly. Writers such as Cummins are not persuaded of this, and an influential body of work is critical of the idea that it is both inevitable and in fact probably highly desirable that what are held to count as 'well-being indicators' should be 'influenced by the pre-occupations and concerns of contemporary culture'. Yet decisions about 'what social conditions can be appropriately influenced by policy and intervention' (and, thus, what aspects of QOL should be targets for assessment and intervention) cannot but be historically and culturally contingent. In the 1970s levels of employment in state-owned industries such as coalmining and car manufacturing were identified by countries such as the UK and Australia as appropriate for policy intervention, whereas domestic violence against women was not. By the 1980s the relative positions of these 'social conditions' had been entirely reversed.

The ABS suggests that its definition of QOL has been driven by *pragmatic* as well as by *theoretical* considerations. This is not, necessarily, a 'bad thing' but demonstrates that what the concept of 'quality of life' 'means' is dependent upon the purposes to which any given operationalization of the concept is to be put. The important point, and here the ABS is exemplary, is that such practical considerations need to be *transparent*. The ABS (2001: 7) states that:

> The ABS has given primacy to objective measures of wellbeing, largely for the pragmatic reasons that such information is most useful to government agencies concerned with the delivery of services, and is more readily interpreted. However, subjective measures can provide an important supplement to objective measures, and for this reason are provided by the ABS within specific areas of concern.

The ABS review of readily available statistics, analysis of contemporary 'preoccupations and concerns' and an appraisal of the 'social conditions [which] can be appropriately influenced by policy' has led to the identification of eight major areas of concern – shown in Table 2.1. To all intents and purposes then, the act of *identifying these areas defines quality of life* in the Australian national context.

The ABS is also exemplary in its clarity about its methods and its limitations, and in the clear links it establishes between the areas of concern, measurement units adopted and the policy relevance of the social indicators selected. In Box 2.1 the social and political questions relating to

Table 2.1 Australian system of social indicators

Aspects of life contributing to well-being	Areas of concern
Support and nurture through family and community.	Family and community
Freedom from disability and illnesss.	Health
Realization of personal potential through education.	Education and training
Satisfying and rewarding work both economic and non-economic.	Work
Command over economic resources, enabling consumption.	Economic resources
Shelter, security and privacy, through housing.	Housing
Personal safety and protection from crime.	Crime and justice
Time for and access to cultural and leisure activities.	Culture and leisure

Source: Australian Bureau of Statistics (2001: 7).

Box 2.1 Linkages between areas of concern and social policy in the Australian Bureau of Statistics Framework, *Measuring Wellbeing*

How population relates to well-being
A population can be described in terms of the well-being of its members and the resources needed to sustain and enhance their well-being. Changes in the size, composition or geographic distribution of a population are important because they present a large number of issues concerned with meeting economic and social needs. Population numbers also put pressure on the environment in ways that may not be sustainable over the longer term and potentially threaten living standards. Predicting changes in population size, composition and distribution can help in developing strategies to meet changing needs and to enhance people's well-being.

What are some key social issues relating to population?

- Ensuring that political representation and government expenditures are fairly distributed.
- Whether or not continued population growth is sustainable.
- The need to adapt to changes resulting from the ageing of the population.
- Whether the annual number and mix of migrants coming to or leaving Australia is ideal.
- Whether or not pro-birth policies should be adopted.
- Identifying communities with greatest needs for resources.
- Improving outcomes for the Indigenous population and other disadvantaged groups.

Source: Australian Bureau of Statistics (2001: 28).

the quality of life for the population as a whole that can be informed by social reporting are clearly identified.

Global quality of life

What quality of life for populations means on a global scale can be distilled from the social indicators identified by major international organizations. In *World Development Indicators*, the World Bank (1997a) identifies indicators of sustainable development as People, Environment, Economy, States and Markets and Global Linkages. In the report, *Expanding the Measure of Wealth: Indicators of Environmentally Sustainable Development* (World Bank, 1997b), it is suggested that, because poor environmental performance is, in the long-term, unsustainable and, in the short-term, deleteriously affects the health and well-being of populations, the items listed in Table 2.2 are key performance indicators of environmental life quality at a national level. The World Bank effectively defines high QOL at a population level as, at least in part, determined by patterns of land use

Table 2.2 The World Bank's 1997 World Development Indicators (WDI) – environment section

- *Land use and deforestation* Land area; rural population density; cropland, permanent pasture and other land as a percentage of total land area; total forest area; annual deforestation.
- *Protected areas and biodiversity* nationally protected area; total number and threatened species of mammals, birds and higher plants.
- *Freshwater use* Per capita freshwater resources; annual freshwater withdrawals; freshwater withdrawals by agriculture, industry and domestic use; percentage of rural and urban population with access to safe water.
- *Energy use* production and use of commercial energy; annual and per capita use of commercial energy; use of traditional fuels; growth rate and per capita production of electricity.
- *Energy efficiency, dependency and emissions* Real GDP per unit of energy use; net energy import as a percentage of commercial energy use; total carbon dioxide emissions per capita and per unit of real GDP.
- *Urbanization* Urban population; urban population as a percentage of total population; average annual growth rate of urban population; population in urban agglomerations of a million or more; population in the largest city as a percentage of total population; percentage of urban population with access to sanitation.
- *Traffic and congestion* Number of vehicles per 1,000 people; number of vehicles per kilometre of road; road traffic volumes in million vehicle-kilometres; number of people killed or injured per 1,000 vehicles.
- *Air pollution* Emissions and ambient concentrations of suspended particulate matter and sulphur dioxide.
- *Government commitment* Status of country environmental profile; national conservation strategy; biodiversity profile; compliance with Convention on International Trade in Endangered Species of Wild Flora and Fauna; participation in climate change, ozone layer, chlorofluorocarbon control and law of the sea treaties.

Source: World Bank (1997b: 107).

and extent of deforestation; the existence of protected areas and the protection of biodiversity; proportion of the population with access to usable fresh water; levels of urbanization including the percentage of the urban population who have access to sanitation; extent of air pollution; and demonstrable environmentally-friendly policies.

Likewise the European System of Social Indicators (EUSI) project (Berger-Schmitt and Noll, 2000) has been based on an inventory of the goals and objectives of the European Union and an analysis of the social indicators literature. EUSI has identified six major goal dimensions of European societal development which, with *quality of life* identified as the 'overarching objective' (Berger-Schmitt and Noll, 2000: 42) form the core of EUSI. Berger-Schmitt and Noll (2000) state that the goal dimensions were selected as directly relevant to the concepts of *quality of life*, social cohesion and sustainability. They argue that, at the European level, QOL incorporates two 'goal dimensions': the improvement of objective living conditions such as working conditions, state of health or standard of living and the enhancement of subjective well-being, as assessed by measures of happiness or satisfaction.

While the goal dimensions addressed by the concepts of *social cohesion* and *strengthening social connections and ties* are described as separate from QOL, many of the measures identified would, under other definitions, be construed as domains of life quality. Thus 'social cohesion' is described as having, as 'goal dimensions', the reduction of social disparities, social inequalities and social exclusion as may be indicated by regional disparities in the distribution of welfare within a society and equal opportunities. The third goal dimension, strengthening social connections and ties – elsewhere referred to (for example, OECD, 2001; Putnam, 1995) as 'social capital' – or the social relations within a society (informal networks, associations and organizations as well as formal societal institutions) are seen as key components.

Two other EUSI goal dimensions draw on the concept of sustainability as described in the World Bank's (1997a) 'four capital approach'. According to this approach, sustainability requires the preservation of the societal capital (physical capital, social capital, human capital, natural capital) in order to secure acceptable living conditions for future generations. The two subsidiary goal dimensions are: preservation of human capital, with indicators focusing on 'the processes and measures that affect people's skills, education and health', and the preservation of natural capital, with social indicators of the 'processes and measures that improve or deteriorate the base of natural resources' being identified as indices.

EUSI is, according to Berger-Schmitt and Noll (2000), structured by both these goal dimensions and a subset of life domains. Within each life domain up to eight goal dimensions are operationalized in terms of domain-specific measurement dimensions, subdimensions and indicators. The life domains identified as a subset of the broader scale social indicators are specified

Table 2.3 Indices of national well-being in the European System of Social Indicators: life domains, measurement dimensions, subdimensions and indicators

Life Domain: Population

Measurement Dimension: Population Size
Resident Population
Population Growth
   Crude Birth Rate
   Crude Death Rate
   Rate of Natural Population Increase
   Rate of Population Increase
Population Structure
Structure of Population by Age and Sex
   Population Aged Less than 15 Years
   Population Aged 15–24 Years
   Population Aged 25–64 Years
   Population Aged 65–79 Years
   Population Aged 80 Years and Older
Sex Ratio of Population
Dependency Structures
   Age Dependency Ratio
   Burden of Child Population
   Burden of Inactive Population
   Burden of Population in Education and Training
   Burden of Retired Population
Structure of Population by Marital Status
   Single Persons
   Married Persons
   Divorced Persons
   Widowed Persons

Measurement Dimension: Population Density and Agglomeration
Population Density
   Population Density
Agglomeration of Population
   Population of Large Cities
   Population of Small Municipalities

Measurement Dimension: Migration and Foreign Population
Internal Migration
   Inter-municipal Migration Rate
   Interregional Migration Rate
Immigration
   Immigration Rate
   Share of Non-National ImmigrantsShare of EU Immigrants
   Share of European Non-EU Immigrants
   Share of Non-European Immigrants

continued over

Table 2.3 continued

   Share of Children in Immigrants
   Share of Youth in Immigrants
   Share of Working Age Immigrants
Emigration
   Total Emigration Rate
   Share of National Emigrants
   Share of Children in Emigrants
   Share of Youth in Emigrants
   Share of Working Age Emigrants
Asylum Seekers
   Inflow of Asylum Seekers
   Share of Asylum Seekers from Europe
   Share of Asylum Seekers from Asia
   Share of Asylum Seekers from Africa
   Share of Asylum Seekers from Latin American and Caribbean Countries
   Recognition Rate of Asylum Applications
Foreign Population and Acquisition of Citizenship
   Percentage of Total Foreign Population
   Share of Foreign Population from EU Countries
   Share of Foreign Population from European Non-EU Countries
   Share of Foreign Population from Non-European Countries
   Share of Children in Foreign Population
   Share of Youth in Foreign Population
   Share of Working Age People in Foreign Population
   Acquisition of Citizenship

---

under the headings of: Population; Households and Families; Housing; Transport; Leisure, Media and Culture; Social and Political Participation and Integration; Education and Vocational Training; Labour Market and Working Conditions; Income, Standard of Living, and Consumption Patterns; Health; Environment; Social Security; Public Safety and Crime; Total Life Situation. Within each of these areas, as noted, further sub-indices are identified: for the life domain of 'Population' a further three measurement dimensions are identified (Population Size, Population Density and Agglomeration, Migration and Foreign Population), with multiple subdimensions and indicators – as shown in Table 2.3.

Assessing the quality of QOL indices

Hagerty *et al.* (2001) have reported a comprehensive survey, conducted on behalf of the International Society for Quality of Life Studies (ISQOLS), of population level QOL indices. Table 2.4 shows the major areas of life satisfaction/quality of life identified in a selection of measures designed to

Table 2.4 Domains of QOL measured by selected indices of population well-being

COMQOL (Cummins, 1997)	Index of Economic Well-Being	American Demographics Index	Johnston's QOL Index (Johnston's 1988)	UN Human Development Index (UNHDP, 1990)	Index of Social Health (Fordham Institute, 1999)	Virginia QOL Survey (Virginia Tech, 1998)	Index of Social Progress (e.g. Estes, 1997)	Swedish ULF
Relationship with family and friends (weight = 100)		Divorce rate	Family stability		Child abuse	Satisfaction with family life		Social contacts
Emotional well-being (weight = 98)					Teenage suicide	Happiness		
Material well-being (weight = 77)	GDP, housing, stock, capital investment, poverty rate	Income and employment, consumer expectations, productivity	Earnings and income, housing	PPP/capita	Average weekly earnings, access to affordable housing		Economic	Material living standards, housing, transport, leisure
Health (weight = 67)			Health	Longevity	Infant mortality, health insurance coverage, out-of-pocket health costs for >65	Satisfaction with health and health care	Health status	Health

Domain							
Work and productive activity (weight = 61)	Employment	Employment, education		Unemploy-ment, high school dropouts	Satisfaction with work and employment, satisfaction with education	Education	Employment, working environment
Feeding part of one's local community (weight = 27)	Number of endangered species	Poverty, equality	Literacy	Poverty rate >65, gap between rich and poor	Satisfaction with environment	Women status, political participation, cultural diversity, demographic	Social mobility, participation
Personal safety Crime rate (weight = 27)	Crime rate	Public safety		Homicides, alcohol-related traffic fatalities	Satisfaction with law enforcement	Defence effort, geography	Victimization
Subjective QOL					Good place to live, go to school, go to college, get job		

Source: Adapted from Hagerty et al. (2001).

inform national policy. As is apparent, the variation across measures is not only huge, but also suggests that a clear consensual theoretical specification of QOL as a population level construct, and the relation between such things as school attendance and the reports of individual citizens about their personal happiness, is yet unattained.

The difficulty of linking various phenomena to QOL as an end-state is a pervasive problem. Hagerty *et al.* (2001) note that 'most of the indexes [*sic*] reviewed failed to specify any well-established theory behind the index. By theory, we mean the "nomological net" of concepts and causal paths that specify how QOL is related to exogenous and endogenous variables.' In consequence they suggest a systems theory structural model of QOL in an attempt to define both the meaning and the mechanisms of production of quality of life (see Figure 2.3).

In the 'input' column are 'exogenous environmental variables affecting citizens' QOL'. Many of these items are familiar social indicators of QOL conceptualized as a population-level construct: socio-economic status, extent of freedom, income inequality. However, while Hagerty *et al.* (2001) note that aspects of these indicators are, at least in principle, amenable to alteration by public policy, it is of some concern that 'personality' is conceived of as an 'input variable'. Such a 'variable' may be better placed in the second column, where *throughput* variables, described as 'the *individual's response* to this environment (e.g., education achieved, marriage choice)' are itemized. It is somewhat naïve to see such matters (which are again measurable as 'objective social indicators') as being exclusively individual 'variables' which 'reflect the *individual's choice* in response to the environment and to public policy'. Such a view fails to take account of the fact that access to meaningful 'individual choice' about such things as 'consumption' or even 'marriage' is not a 'variable' normally distributed across populations, the QOL of which this model attempts to describe. QOL 'output' is disaggregated in the third column into Cummins's (1996b) domains which subsequently feed into the three higher order outputs suggested by Veenhoven (1999): happiness (or SWB), personal survival and contribution to the human heritage, described as 'the result of input and throughput'. Yet while this model may be equally comprehensible to biologists and public policy-makers, as Hagerty *et al.* (2001) contend, it is still far from explicit *how*, precisely, the model is supposed to *work*. How 'personality' determines 'marriage and children', which in turn results in happiness with 'family and friends' and, ultimately, 'SWB output' is unspecified.

Local quality of life indicators

Salvaris's (2000) review of social indicators offers a rather different perspective on the definition of QOL. Hagerty *et al.* (2001: 2–6) identify the users of reliable and valid QOL indexes as 'public policymakers'. The members of this category are identified as:

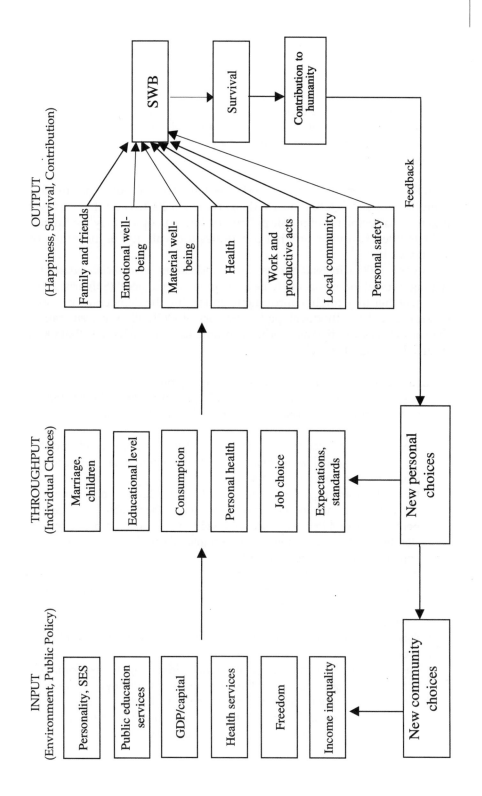

Figure 2.3 Systems theory structure of quality of life concepts and causes (*Source: Hagerty et al.* 2001).

physicians and counsellors helping individuals in need ... social workers helping families in need ... town governments developing policies and programs that can help enhance community QOL ... state bodies developing policies and programs that can assist residents of the entire state or province ... national agencies developing policies and programs that can assist citizens of that country ... international agencies developing policies and programs that can assist the world's citizens and the planet at large.

However, nowhere in their 14 criteria (see Chapter 4) for the 'validity and usefulness of such QOL indexes' (Hagerty *et al.*, 2001: 1) do they suggest that the end-recipients of public policy – ordinary people – may legitimately be entitled to a view of what constitutes the 'validity' of indicators of social well-being.

Salvaris (2000) instead views social indicators as a *social movement*. Asking if social indicators are to be a 'technocratic panacea' (Salvaris, 2000: 7) or whether they might contribute to enhancing the democratic process, he argues that locally-developed indicators of QOL allow *citizens* rather than academics, politicians or administrators to decide what it is that QOL means. He suggests that:

For three decades now, there has been a rapid growth in the development of community based planning projects using benchmarks and indicators to measure progress ... Typically, such projects have five features:

- they attempt to integrate economic, social and environmental goals around some overall vision of progress or well being, some 'path to the future' for that particular community;
- they set concrete goals or 'benchmarks' and develop appropriate 'indicators' to monitor progress in achieving them; some of these benchmarks and indicators are expressed in conventional policy and statistical categories; others (for example, those relating to social capital) are quite unconventional;
- the indicators and benchmarks are initiated, developed and monitored through some community participation process, sometimes across the whole community and sometimes through specialist panels with citizen participation;
- they are commonly long term (i.e., over 5 years) and iterative processes;
- they have, or acquire over time, some relationship to the formal processes of governance in their community; this may vary from government support or even government initiation, to de facto acceptance as legitimate policy, or at the least, they become a political obstacle that politicians and bureaucrats have to confront.

Describing the development of community social indicators across the Western world (in the USA, Canada, Norway, Australia and Ireland) as a 'social movement', Salvaris sketches the origin of the movement in the convergence of three separate phenomena; first, the general recognition that 'broad social and economic problems need community-wide solutions' (Salvaris, 2000: 2); second, 'a sense of actual or likely decline in economic and social well-being, and a desire to find integrated community wide solutions'; and third, challenging studies (such as Frey and Al-Roumi, 1999) that suggest democracy unproblematically increases QOL he argues that:

> The second factor is a democratic problem. Democracy, community and citizenship have been perceived as weakening institutions ... as a product of many factors: the size and complexity of government and society; globalisation and a perceived loss of autonomy in national policy; lack of trust in the main political parties; and the effects of a decade or more of government cuts in social and community infrastructure ... public alienation from political processes, growing social inequality, a decline in social trust and civic participation, more corporate and commercially oriented models of governments that have brought fundamental changes in the language and culture of democracy. Perhaps the most conspicuous example of the latter is the gradual transformation of citizens into 'customers' (Saul, 1997). There is no single solution to compound problems like these, but there is some agreement on the most obvious remedies. (Salvaris, 2000: 3)

Perhaps the most striking of the remedies Salvaris identifies is the proposal that genuinely *meaningful* – as opposed to 'valid' in Hagerty *et al.*'s (2001) sense – social indicators of QOL should be developed by community consultation processes, for local purposes. Also essential is: an emphasis on social inclusion; a 'community health' approach to defining life quality rather than a focus on 'improved "customer service"'; the development of social trust and stronger communities via more meaningful and cooperative governance; and the creation of 'more open and democratic processes and forums, for resolving conflicting interests, creating greater accountability and extending opportunities for citizen participation in governance' (Salvaris, 2000: 3). Assuming that the *meaning* of quality of life is a local and political matter – rather than a universal, abstract and apolitical or academic one – may enhance the quality of people's lives.

Such projects have been established at all levels from the nation-state to local communities. National-level projects, such as the Canadian Policy Research Networks (CPRN) project, has convened a citizen-based consultancy to identify national quality of life indicators. The CPRN project (*Asking Citizens What Matters for Quality of Life*) starts from the premise that:

> While there is much activity on quality of life indicators in Canada, there is no initiative underway ... that seeks input from citizens. CPRN is seeking to fill that void. It is leading and working with a Steering Committee representing a broad cross-section of organizations interested in developing a set of national indicators to track Canada's progress in quality of life, through a citizen engagement process. (CPRN, cited in Salvaris, 2000: 23)

Salvaris also describes social indicators/QOL projects in Australia. Local government-based projects in NSW, Australia also ask *citizens* rather than 'public policymakers' or academic researchers 'what matters for quality of life'. In the Sutherland Shire, in south Sydney, NSW (with a population of over 200,000 people) the Shire (the local government unit) produces a 'State of the Shire' report which monitors well-being in 12 'life spheres' drawn from a 1996 'Community Priorities' survey. Indicators of well-being in Sutherland Shire – or 'what matters for quality of life' – are measures of: community safety; community issues; decision-making; economy; education; environment; health; housing; land use; leisure; neighbourhoods; and transport.

Similarly, *Measuring the Quality of Life in Newcastle* also links community development to the articulation of locally-meaningful indices of QOL. This project has adopted 27 key social indicators developed by a community-based working group as 'local indicators' of life quality for the project. As such, what quality of life *means* in Newcastle, NSW *is the range of measures adopted by the community as indicators of the quality of life*. In Newcastle QOL means: 'clean beaches; quality of community space; air quality; appropriate educational opportunities for all; unemployment levels; appropriate transport networks; conservation of local native plants and animals; resource consumption; availability of appropriate housing for all; community participation in decision making; social support networks; perception of safety; income levels; and the diversity of employment and industry sectors' (Australia Institute and City of Newcastle, 2000, as cited in Salvaris, 2000).

Salvaris (2000: 41) describes a 'framework for national well-being indicators' as shown in Table 2.5. This collection of indicators thus represents an operational definition of what QOL actually *means* at a local population level in nation-states. Again we see that the 'health and well-being' of individuals is identified as a key indicator (in aggregate) of the well-being of collectivities.

Thus *national well-being* may be defined as populations being offered what 'enlightened societies provide for their citizens' (Edgerton, 1996: 88). That

Table 2.5 A framework for national well-being indicators

---

1. Individual health and well-being
2. Good work opportunities
3. A fair society
4. A secure and crime-free society
5. A productive and responsible economy
6. Good government and laws
7. A healthy, sustainable environment
8. Healthy communities and active citizens
9. A vigorous cultural life
10. Good international relations

Source: Salvaris (2000).

is, the quality of life of the nation-state may be judged by the extent to which individual members are healthy and active citizens; individuals have 'good work opportunities'; social relations are characterized by 'fairness', security and freedom from crime in a context of good government and legislation; where the economy is not merely productive but also 'responsible'; where the environment and human communities are healthy, sustainable and offer vigorous cultural life; and where the nation-state enjoys 'good international relations'.

Such indicators clearly share much with those described by the United Nations, the EUSI, the ABS and the World Bank. Table 2.6 shows Australia's relative standing in relation to the OECD on a range of such indicators, broken down, as for example the EUSI project does, into a series of sub-indicators. Once more, one may infer an operational definition of high life quality from such specifications. A high quality of life is indicated by: earnings growth; the absence of poverty and unemployment; decent housing; health spending and life expectancy; an educated population; high levels of cultural participation and low rates of crime; equity in social opportunities; and the absence of political corruption in the broader context of responsible environmental management.

One of the difficulties with such large-scale indices as developed by the OECD, the World Bank or the ABS is that not only may they – owing to their aggregate form – unintendedly mask very real differences between population subgroups but they may be distant from the concerns of individual citizens or local communities. Community social indicator projects are then a response to such forced abstraction. But, while Bruce and Sheila in Newcastle may feel that the cleanliness of the local beach is a key determinant of their QOL, this perception may not be universally shared.

In response to such concerns, the development of notions of QOL as an individual-level construct has occurred. Here again, we encounter a

Table 2.6 Social health in OECD countries: Australia

		Australia		
Field	**Indicator**	**Actual**	**Rank (total)**	**% best practice**
Income				
1	Real GDP per head (US$000)	19.6	14 (23)	52
2	Population below income poverty line (%)	13	15 (17)	46
3	Real earning growth by employee p.a. 1980–92	0.5	12 (19)	28
Work				
4	Total unemployment rate (%)	8.5	13 (21)	73
5	Long-term unemployment (12 months+)	2.6	10 (20)	83
6	Labour market participation %	51	7 (23)	69
Housing				
7	Home ownership rate %	70	2 (12)	93
8	Proportion of public and supported housing %	5.7	10 (12)	11
Health				
9	Life expectancy at birth (yrs)	78	5 (23)	75
10	Spending on public health (% GDP)	5.8	14 (23)	48
11	Life satisfaction/happiness (index/100)	76.7	7 (23)	96
Education				
12	Fulltime students per 100 ppl aged 5–29 yrs	55	19 (21)	19
13	Public education spending (% GDP)	5.6	11 (23)	41
14	Population with higher education (%)	24.3	7 (18)	42
Culture				
15	Ownership of TV per 1,000 ppl	641	3 (23)	71
16	Telephone lines per 1,000 ppl	510	11 (23)	46
17	Daily newspapers copies per 1,000 ppl	257	13 (22)	39
Social stress				
18	Suicides per 100,000 ppl	19	7 (18)	66
19	Prisoners per 100,000 ppl (excludes USA)	120	19 (19)	0
20	Intentional homicides by men per 1,000 ppl	2.5	18 (23)	83
Equity/democracy				
21	Income inequality (top 20% by bottom 20%)	9.6	17 (18)	1
22	Women in Parliament	24	4 (23)	47
23	Central gov. spend social security (% total CGS)	1.0	11 (17)	12
24	Comply with UN human rights conventions %	91	16 (22)	6
25	Perceived corruption (Transparency Internat.)	8.7	10 (23)	76
26	Development aid (ODA) ($ per cap. donor country)	62	13 (20)	13
Environment				
27	Energy use (000 kg oil equiv. per head)	5.3	18 (23)	42
28	Environment pollution (CO_2 emissions kg p. cap)	16.2	21 (23)	28
29	Protected areas as total land area	8.7	14 (23)	25

Indicator sources: OECD, World Bank, UN and country data.
Source: Salvaris (2000). Reproduced with permission.

tension between the proponents of universalist and individualist approaches, between those who believe that quality of life is a phenomenon that is shared universally by all persons, with definable and empirically measurable domains, and those who believe that the quality of a person's life is best understood not as a quantum of individual 'mind stuff', but rather as a 'sensitizing concept' (Taylor, 1994) which can help to alert us to the things that matter in life to particular persons. There are those who seek to 'map the world' in its entirety, and those who focus on specific, and maybe ungeneralizable, appreciations of small parts of it. It is to quality of life defined as an individual, subjective, experience that we now turn.

Quality of Life as an Individual-level Construct

To me, quality of life means to feel good and to have what is needed to cope with your life in the best way possible. (Robert Groulx, President, People First of Montreal, quoted in Groulx et al., 2000: 23)

Chapter 1 discussed the development of the idea that QOL is not merely a matter of the 'quality of the lives which ... people lead' at an aggregate population level. Recently the idea has developed that it also makes sense to conceive of QOL as an aspect of individual subjectivity, a psychological quantum expressing the satisfaction of particular people with their individual lives. A major effort has been expended on trying to arrive at a formally specified, *operational definition* of the construct. The effort, then, has been to refine unsuitably vague 'lay' notions of the good life – such as Robert Groulx's – and to replace them with formal, technical, definitions and criteria.

There are two broad approaches to this: firstly, attempts to specify generic definitions of QOL that apply to humanity as a whole and, secondly, attempts to specify locally relevant QOL constructs such as 'health-related QOL' or 'disease-specific QOL'. Such definitions vary in their specificity and levels of theoretical sophistication.

Universal QOL Definitions

Many population-level systems of social indicators can be read as specifying a definition of QOL, as it were, by default. Collections of statistics are held together not by an explicitly stated *theory* of the good life, but by a set of commonsense understandings that these various indicators make up a set of diagnostic social facts against which the goodness, or quality, of life is judged. Thus, at least in Western countries, while high levels of unemployment do not need to be explicitly defended as indicators of a (poor) quality of living in a particular society, other statistics, for example income inequality, as the work of Salvaris (2000) suggests, increasingly do.

At the individual level efforts centre on a formal operational definition of what QOL *is as such*. The question – while it sounds quite straight forward – can be asked and answered in a multiplicity of ways, and the particular ways that the social sciences go about answering such questions, by attempting to specify formal definitions of the phenomenon and operational criteria for inferring the construct, are only one, and not necessarily the best, way to go about such enquiries. To ask 'what is quality of life?' is *not* to ask the same sort of a question as asking 'what is a planet?' or 'what is electricity?' It is, in principle, not possible to say Groulx's 'definition' of QOL, 'to feel good and to have what is needed to cope with your life in the best way possible' is wrong, or that it is misguided or erroneous. This subtle but crucial point is overlooked by many writers in the social sciences who routinely claim that it is *other* researchers who have got it wrong, that what quality of life *really* is, is the way they themselves happen to define it.

There are now a small number of candidate definitions available in the literature which appear to receive wide – but not unanimous – endorsement. A range of these definitions is presented below, with brief observations about some of the difficulties each entails. All specify that QOL is an *individual psychological* perception of the *material reality* of aspects of the world. The WHOQOL Group (1993: 1) defines QOL as:

> an individual's perception of their position in life in the context of the culture and value systems in which they live and in relation to their goals, expectations values and concerns ... incorporating in a complex way the person's physical health, psychological state, level of independence, social relationships, personal beliefs and their relationship to salient features of the environment ... Quality of life refers to a subjective evaluation which is embedded in a cultural, social and environmental context ... quality of life cannot simply be equated with the terms 'health status', 'life satisfaction', 'mental state', or 'well-being'. Rather it is a multidimensional concept.

This definition of QOL benefits from comprehensiveness and efforts to relate the idea to cultural, social and environmental contexts and to local value systems. It is, however, unclear how QOL – as an 'individual's perception of their position in life' or 'a subjective evaluation' – cannot be 'simply equated with a mental state'. A similar definition appealing to cultural relativity is provided by Goode (1994a: 148):

> QOL is experienced when a person's basic needs are met and when he or she has the opportunity to pursue and achieve goals in major life settings ... The QOL of an individual is intrinsically related to the QOL of other

persons in his or her environment ... the QOL of a person reflects the cultural heritage of the person and those who surround him or her.

Efforts at universality and comprehensiveness cause problems in and of themselves. If one were to ask a Yolgnu lawman from Arnhem Land, Australia and a Los Angeles movie star for their 'subjective evaluations' of the QOL, what confidence might we have that these estimations had anything in common? Could we be confident that the 'thing' being 'subjectively evaluated' was the *same* thing in both cases? The very 'multidimensionality' built into the WHOQOL's definition and the cultural relativism central to Goode's almost certainly guarantees that whatever 'QOL' is for a Yolgnu lawman, it is not at all the same thing as it is for Harrison Ford.

A similar set of concerns arises, but for the opposite reasons, with another candidate definition. Woodill *et al.* (1994: 67) define QOL as:

The degree to which a person enjoys the important possibilities of his or her life ... This definition can be simplified to – 'How good is your life for you?'

In avoiding specificity about the component domains of QOL Woodill *et al.* (1994) dodge the difficulties caused by the WHO's specificity. The fact that the relationship between an Inuit hunter and 'salient features of the environment' is utterly different from that obtaining between a New York lawyer and her environment is accommodated, but at the price of a definition of QOL that is far from universal. As each individual has different 'important possibilities' in their life, and the extent to which they 'enjoy' them is likely to be variable, the concept becomes so individually-specific as to be of little use for comparing the QOL of different population groups. Such definitions then result in a formal operationalization of the construct that remains not only completely culturally relative but also individually specific.

Similarly problematic is the definitional preamble advanced by Schalock and Parmenter (2000: 4) in the consensus document on QOL produced for the International Association for the Scientific Study of Intellectual Disability. They write that:

It is necessary to understand the semantic meaning of the quality of life concept, and its use throughout the world to appreciate fully its importance and relevance to persons. In reference to its meaning, 'quality' makes us think of the excellence or exquisite standard associated with human characteristics and positive values such as happiness, success, wealth, health, and satisfaction; whereas, 'of life' indicates that the concept concerns the very essence or essential aspects of human existence.

This account again fails the test of universality at the same time as endeavouring to address it. Quite what the 'essence' of human existence is has bedevilled philosophy since Plato (as Schalock and Parmenter acknowledge) and there is, as yet, no sign of a 'consensus' on the question. Similarly, to claim that 'values such as happiness, success, wealth, health, and satisfaction' are universally 'positive' is simply to be blinded by ethnocentrism. Health, wealth and the pursuit of happiness may be the essence of the American dream, but to assert that this is true of humanity as a whole is intellectual and cultural imperialism. Later it is observed that:

> Quality of life encompasses the basic conditions of life such as adequate food, shelter, and safety plus life enrichers such as inclusive social, leisure, and community activities. These enrichers are based on the individual's values, beliefs, needs and interests. (Schalock and Parmenter, 2000: 7)

Again attempts at universality become immediately enmeshed in Western middle-class values. That is 'life enrichers' have every possibility of being one thing in Ulan Bator and quite another in San Diego. The taken-for-grantedness of the specification of 'life enrichers' such as 'leisure' neglects the fact that the very *idea* of 'leisure' is, in and of itself, an almost entirely modern Western concept which has little, if any, meaning – in the Western Anglophone sense of sufficient spare time and disposable income to engage in non-productive activities – if one is a rag picker living in Calcutta or an Indonesian pieceworker manufacturing 'leisure' goods like Nike trainers for Western consumers.

However, IASSID feel confident that, while a universal definition of QOL may be unavailable, in practice such a specification is possible by defining instead a set of 'conceptualization principles'. This is to attempt a definition of quality of life as an individual-level concept by the back door. It is suggested that quality of life:

1. Is composed of those same factors and relationships for people with intellectual disabilities that are important to those without disabilities.
2. Is experienced when a person's needs are met and when one has the opportunity to pursue life enrichment in major life settings.
3. Has both subjective and objective components; but it is primarily the perception of the individual that reflects the quality of life he/she experiences.
4. Is based on individual needs, choices, and control.
5. Is a multidimensional construct influenced by personal and environmental factors such as intimate relationships, family life, friendships, work, neighborhood, city or town of residence, housing, education,

health, standard of living, and the state of one's nation. (Schalock and Parmenter, 2000: 7)

The 'conceptualization principles' here are close to the earlier definition by the WHOQOL Group (1993) and have been developed from Felce and Perry (1993: 13) who define QOL, as a universal material/psychological phenomenon, as follows:

Quality of life is defined as an overall general well-being which comprises objective descriptors and subjective evaluations of physical, material, social and emotional well-being together with the extent of personal development and purposeful activity all weighted by a personal set of values.

This definition has been produced as a schematic model by Felce and Perry (1996) and is shown in diagrammatic form in Figure 2.4.

The model draws together the suggestions of the IASSID group and makes several key claims. It is suggested that 'quality of life' is the same for people whether or not they are intellectually disabled (that is QOL is the same for all of humanity); that for all people QOL is more than just the meeting of basic needs, it is derived from 'life enrichment' and the individual perception thereof. This point, it must be noted, veers into tautology: QOL is … what the individual perceives the quality of their life to be. Equally explicit is the idea that, in arriving at such a circular perception, QOL is based on 'needs, choices, and control', presumably over such things as the 'opportunity to pursue life enrichment in major life settings'. Again the culture-bound nature of such a *soi-disant* 'international' conclusion is noticeable. The final aspect of the international consensus view, 'principle 5', that quality of life 'is influenced by personal and environmental factors such as intimate relationships, family life, friendships, work, neighborhood, city or town of residence, housing, education, health, standard of living, and the state of one's nation' is in some tension with the earlier 'principle 3'. Recall that quality of life 'is primarily the perception of the individual'. If influenced by known and knowable multidimensional factors how is the perception individual? If individual, how do we know what factors influence this particular person's particular perceptions of their quality of life?

At the individual level, however, perhaps the most influential definition of quality of life is offered by Cummins (1997a: 6) who defines quality of life thus:

Quality of life is both objective and subjective, each axis being the aggregate of seven domains: material well-being, health, productivity, intimacy, safety, community and emotional well-being. Objective domains comprise culturally relevant measures of objective well-being. Subjective

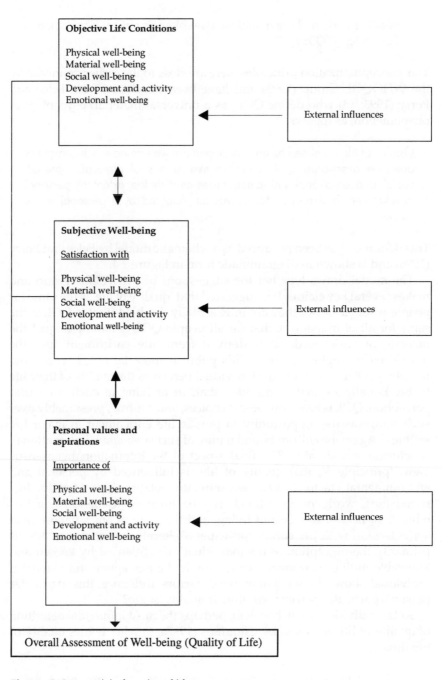

Figure 2.4 A model of quality of life.

Source: Felce and Perry (1996). Reproduced with the permission of the AAMR.

domains comprise domain satisfaction weighted by their importance to the individual.

This definition has the advantages of individual weighting of the importance of the various domains, the identification of the subjective domains via a careful review of the literature and the identification of objective domains that are 'culturally important'. Whether these domains are as likely to be important to non-Anglophone, or 'non-Western', populations is an open question. The studies of the perceptions of Aboriginal Australians in Melbourne, discussed at the end of this chapter, suggests that this is an area requiring further study.

Definitions of health-related quality of life

Many sub-areas of QOL research have developed specialty-specific definitions of QOL. Perhaps the best example is in medicine, where many definitions of 'health-related quality of life' have been advanced. Here again the ongoing debate regarding objective versus subjective descriptions of the meaning of quality of life surfaces. For example Wiklund *et al.* (1986) identify the three major components of QOL in clinical medical settings as: functional capacity, subjective perceptions, and symptoms and their consequences. Rather more broadly, Testa and Nackley (1994: 537) suggest that QOL means a range of both *objective* circumstances and *subjective perceptions* of them. They describe:

> a set of domains related to the physical, functional, psychological, and social health of the individual. When used in this context it is often referred to as 'health-related quality of life'... Health-related quality of life involves the five broad dimensions of opportunity, health perceptions, functional status, morbidity or impairment, and mortality.

Walker (1992: 265) suggests that QOL is best defined as a more centrally subjective response to a range of strictly limited, and medically-related, circumstances. For Walker, QOL means:

> a broad range of physical and psychological characteristics and limitations which describe an individual's ability to function and derive satisfaction from so doing ... health related quality of life is probably the key term and this is defined as the level of well-being and satisfaction associated with an individual's life and how this is affected by disease, accidents and treatment.

Finally Carr *et al.* (2001: 1240) suggest that quality of life is *purely* a matter of subjectively experienced health-related discrepancies. That is

> quality of life ... is those aspects of an individual's subjective experience that relate both directly and indirectly to health, disease, disability and impairment ... health related quality of life is the gap between our expectations of health and our experience of it.

Cummins (1997b: 124) provides a scathing critique of all such HRQOL definitions. The key problem in these specifications of QOL, he argues, is 'confusion as to what might constitute a reasonable set of dependent variables to measure medical outcome, and quality of life ... variables are referenced either to what is "normal" or to pathology, and ... [QOL] ... is defined through medically related measurement'. Further, Cummins (1997b) points out that the idea that people may be medically or physically compromised and yet enjoy a quality of life equal to, or higher than, that of the non-disabled general population is not countenanced in such definitions (we will return to this point briefly below). In summary, Cummins (1997b: 125) argues that:

> health-referenced QOL definitions impose an overly restricted view of the construct. They tend to produce self-fulfilling prophesies by concentrating on the negative aspects of disease and injury. In contrast, broader approaches to measurement allow for a much more positive view ... Using broader forms of measurement, people with a physical disability, an intellectual disability, or people who have survived an organ transplantation can register a level of subjective well-being as high, or higher, than the normal range for the population.

These are serious and sensible objections, but they overlook the key consideration of the *variation* that there may be in the *purpose* of QOL measurement across settings and levels of analysis. Such objections also implicitly assume that there is a singular and universally meaningful definition of the concept. As we saw earlier the ABS (2001), for example, explicitly recognizes that what counts as QOL for its particular purposes must be driven by the purposes to which such data are intended to be put. In medical settings it is reasonable that if one is interested in how patients' QOL is influenced by medical procedures, that one's definition of QOL is driven by those factors of most local importance. 'Using broader forms of measurement' may well produce different results, but there is no point using measurement tools or technologies which are not directly relevant to the questions one wishes to ask. It is, as the 'social indicators movement' has shown us, often the case that locally-derived indicators of QOL are, inherently, more meaningful. That is, the fact that many ordinary people do not appear to find academic accounts of QOL meaningful is the issue to which we now turn.

The Forced Abstraction of the Meaning of QOL

In this section the idea of HRQOL is used to illustrate a wider problem in the measurement of QOL as an individual-level construct. As we saw earlier, workers dealing with population-level social indicators such as Salvaris (2000) have argued strongly that whatever it is that QOL means, its meaning should be defined locally by those to whom it is immediately meaningful. This section looks at the issue at the level of the individual conceptualization of quality of life.

While Cummins (1997b) insists that the use of terms such as 'health-related quality of life' are conceptually incoherent in and of themselves, workers such as Mozes *et al.* (1999) have used survey techniques to evaluate the divergence between 'lay' and professional understandings of 'health-related quality of life'. Specifically they asked: 'what are the relations between the domains included in the operational definition of HRQL tools and global health ratings' (Mozes *et al.*, 1999: 269). With a representative Israeli sample multiple linear regression was used to examine the relationship between the SF-36 global rating of health-related quality of life[1], socio-economic status, presence of disease and each of the domains of the SF-36. Only 52 per cent of the variance of the global rating score was explainable by the regression model, with the SF-36 general health domain explaining 38.5 per cent of the variance. With another 7.0 per cent of the variance accounted for by the physical functioning domain, other domains of the SF-36, socio-economic variables and disease contributed minimally to the total explained variance of the global ratings of HRQL. Mozes *et al.* (1999) conclude: 'There is a considerable difference between the operational definition of the research community of HRQL and the public perception of this term.' Complicating matters further is work that suggests that there may be considerable divergence between the research community and many population groups in their understandings even of the composite *terms* of ideas such as 'health-related quality of life'.

In their analysis of problems in theoretical HRQL work Haase *et al.* (1999) identify the uncritical adoption of 'function-based' understandings of HRQL in the medical literatures. Function-based models of HRQL derive their focus 'predominantly from a biomedical perspective, emphasizing maintenance of functional abilities by management of clinical concerns, toxicity of treatments and functioning across several domains' (Haase *et al.*, 1999: 125). 'Meaning-based approaches', by contrast, develop a focus on 'the patterns and experience of illness from a subjective and holistic perspective. Meanings are derived from patients' understanding of the situation and their autonomy, beliefs, choices and relationships with others' (Haase *et al.*, 1999: 125). Advocating a 'meaning-based' approach to understanding what HRQOL means to young people with cancer, they argue that this technique can identify intervention approaches that are 'important, appropriate and acceptable to the child/adolescent and family' (Haase *et al.*, 1999: 125). Tellingly, they describe the divergence in outcomes that are likely if the a priori assumptions inherent in most function-based (HR)QOL under-standings drive the development and interpretation of measures of HRQL. Drawing on an earlier study by Haase and Rostad (1994) Haase *et al.* (1999: 125, my emphasis) point out that:

> when a child's or adolescent's social function is assessed from the function-based perspective by instrument items asking about the ability to be involved in a social activity, *involvement in the activity is assumed to be positive*. Thus, when items asking if an adolescent can attend school or visit friends are answered 'never' or 'rarely', a decreased quality of life in the social dimension is assumed. Missing from the items is the *meaning* that staying at home has for the adolescent. Remaining at home and being unable to see friends may indicate decreased HRQL for many adolescents with cancer. However … at least some adolescents and families view the time at home positively, as an opportunity to be together, strengthen family ties and focus on friendships that endure in spite of isolation.

The problems engendered by a priori assumptions about the *meaning* of broad notions like health and activity are also shown by ethnographic work by Thompson and Gifford (2000). They report a detailed 22-month ethnographic study of 'the lived experiences of diabetes and lay meanings of risk' (2000: 1457) among Aborigines living in Melbourne, Australia. Much epidemiological work in the dominant medical research/population health paradigm fails to acknowledge that 'health' is not best understood as a purely individual outcome of 'healthy lifestyles'. Thompson and Gifford (2000: 1458) point out that:

> when Melbourne Aborigines talk about trying to manage their diabetes, it is not only their sugar that is out of balance, it is their whole life. And when they talk about stabilizing their sugar, these discourses are often woven into wider narratives about individual and community struggles to maintain a sense of coherence, control and stability over present life circumstances and the future. Achieving a 'balance' in life requires the maintenance of meaningful connections to family, the land, the past and future, all of which are important for health and well being. For Aborigines, like many indigenous people throughout the world, health and identity are linked closely to land and culture.

This suggests that the very idea of 'health' as understood in 'Western' medicine (and of course presupposed and operationalized by all HRQOL-specific measures and the 'health' domains of generic QOL measures) not only is not the same 'thing' for the Aboriginal community, but can hardly be said to bear even a family resemblance. In Aboriginal terms the notions of 'health', 'balance' and community 'well-being' ('QOL'?) are not just elided but are inseparable. They are not 'variables' that can sensibly be described as quanta possessed by individuals in the here-and-now: rather the well-being of individuals *today* is part and parcel of the social trajectory of Aboriginal people as a whole in the space-time continuum that links the dreaming to the future.

Using participant observation, informal interviews, focus group discussions and in-depth interviews with senior members of the Aboriginal community, Thompson and Gifford (2000) developed an understanding of Indigenous Australians' notions of health, disease and well-being which, while focused on diabetes, have a much wider ramification. Drawing on the theoretical framework in Narrative Theory (Garro, 1992; Garro, 1994a, b; Good, 1994) they suggest that this approach was 'particularly powerful in informing the data analysis for two reasons. First, a narrative style of communication is the dominant mode of talk within the Aboriginal community, and thus an appropriate way to both collect information for this study and to interpret the results' (Thompson and Gifford, 2000: 1461). In total 52 Aborigines, both with and without diabetes took part in 38 in-depth interviews, two focus group discussions and two small group discussions, with all interviews and focus group discussions being tape-recorded, transcribed and analysed using content and thematic analysis (Bernard, 1994; Patton, 1990). By adopting such an approach it is thus possible to avoid the unsettling experience described by Mozes *et al.* (1999) of finding that the meaningfulness of the constructs with which you are working are opaque to the population you wish to study.

Furthermore, if the quality of people's lives is understood in their terms, it is possible to be much more specific about the costs and benefits of efforts to improve circumstances which deleteriously affect life quality. The understandings so afforded may be paradoxical, or as ethnomethodologists would have it 'intuitively non-apparent'. Thompson and Gifford (2000: 1458) suggest that:

> understandings and experiences ... of illness cannot be separated from people's experiences of unstable, unpredictable and disempowered realities of everyday life, as it is lived through recollections of past, experiences of present and concerns about the future ... Current epidemiological models that focus on individual level [risk] factors not only ... fail to take into consideration the wider social and political contexts of risk and well-being, but, paradoxically, some of the key factors epidemiologists have identified as 'risk' are, in many cases, factors of connection and protection when seen from the Aborigines' perspective. Indeed, some of the public health interventions that rely heavily on

individual risk factor modification, from an Aboriginal point of view, can clearly be considered to be risky, not only to their diabetes but also to their more general health and well-being.

What we see here then – but from a perspective notionally removed from QOL research *qua* QOL research – is an echo of the concerns raised by writers such as Taylor (1994) and Rapley and Ridgway (1998) – discussed in Chapter 3. That is, in construing 'health' (or QOL) as an essentialized, individualized possession or attribute, interventions designed to further the public good, the quality of services or the well-being of individuals may not only misrepresent what such notions mean in local terms, but may also serve to promote the misallocation of resources and/or to actually damage or put at risk the connectedness of persons to important social structures.

Although their discussion of the upshot of their research is placed in the context of both epidemiology in general, and health-promotion around indigenous diabetes in particular, the conclusions that Thompson and Gifford (2000: 1468–9) come to are pertinent much more broadly. They argue that:

> interventions may actually act to sever the connections that tie the individual to the wider social fabric and that is central to the promotion of health. Aborigines view diabetes as a major health issue but they are clear that it needs to be addressed within the wider political, economic and social context of their daily life; connections to kin, land and community are core to their individual identities, sense of meaning and coherence in life. They articulate that interventions must not focus only on improving health in the objective sense, but also, and perhaps more importantly, begin by cementing and strengthening the ties that bind. Our study has shown how it is vital to begin any epidemiological study by first understanding the meanings of risk and protection from the point of view of those affected.

If we take 'health' in the quote above in the Aboriginal sense then the conclusions reached are pertinent to QOL research in the social sciences *as a whole*. Arguably it is vital to begin any QOL study by first understanding the meanings of the concept from the point of view of those affected. It is this issue, the question of 'whose (quality) of life is it anyway?', that Chapter 3 considers.

In Summary

While specifications of what quality of life means at the individual level are numerous, a consensus in the social scientific literatures seems to be coalescing around an operational definition similar to that advanced by Bob Cummins (above) – at least when QOL is considered as a universal construct. This is not to suggest that these definitions are without problems: far from it. And, further, this is also not to say that QOL continues (and no doubt will continue) to be defined in very local terms, for highly specific local purposes, at many sites of social scientific research. Likewise, at the population level, what QOL means continues to be immensely varied: with indices ranging from governments' adherence to CITES to the cleanliness of local beaches. Again, this is not – in and of itself – a 'bad thing', and indeed there is reason to believe that what Salvaris has called the 'social indicators movement' may well offer a mechanism for the active enhancement of the quality of life (however it is defined) for communities at a very local level.

We have also seen that controversy continues (for both population and individual-level conceptualizations of QOL) about objective and subjective aspects of QOL definition and measurement. It is widely agreed in the literature that, however defined, 'objective' estimations of QOL and 'subjective' estimates of personal well-being not only do not covary neatly, but may be contradictory. This routinely confirmed empirical finding has long been recognized in both folk-wisdom – proverbs like 'money can't buy you happiness' – and popular culture: as the Beatles sang, 'Can't buy me love' (Lennon and McCartney, 1967). Here the issue comes down to an *aesthetic choice* by the individual researcher. The moot question is not 'which account is correct?', but rather, 'which argument do I find most compelling?'

Note

1. The SF-36 (Ware and Sherbourne, 1992) is an extremely widely used measure of HRQOL. It has 36 items tapping eight health concepts: physical functioning, bodily pain, role limitations due to physical health problems, role limitations due to personal or emotional problems, general mental health, social functioning, energy/fatigue, and general health perceptions. It also includes a single item that provides an indication of perceived change in health. The RAND 36-Item Health Survey 1.0 includes the same items but has a slightly different scoring algorithm. Psychometric reliability and validity studies are numerous: see for example Hays *et al.* (1993) and McHorney *et al.* (1993).

Study Questions

- How would I define *my* quality of life?
- What social indicators of well-being, or quality of life, are relevant in the local community where I live?
- Is the 'Scandinavian' or the 'American' approach to quality of life more compelling as far as I am concerned, and why?

- Is quality of life a universally definable concept, or should it be defined locally on an as-needs basis?

Suggestions for Further Reading

ABS (2001) *Measuring Wellbeing: Frameworks for Australian Social Statistics.* Canberra: AGPS.

Felce, D. and Perry, J. (1995) Quality of life: its definition and measurement, *Research in Developmental Disabilities*, 16, 1: 51–74.

Organization for Economic Cooperation and Development (2001) *The Wellbeing of Nations: The Role of Human and Social Capital.* Paris: OECD.

Salvaris, M. (2000) *Community and Social Indicators: How Citizens Can Measure Progress. An Overview of Social and Community Indicator Projects in Australia and Internationally.* Victoria: Institute for Social Research, Swinburne University of Technology.

Veenhoven, R. (1997) Advances in the understanding of happiness, *Revue Québécoise de Psychologie*, 18: 267–93.

CHAPTER 3

Whose Quality of Life Is It Anyway?

The development of QOL research has raised many ethical and philosophical questions. This chapter outlines the key philosophical questions in QOL research and then discusses practice issues at the interface of philosophical debate and research design/methodology. The notions of 'mainstream' and 'emancipatory' (Oliver, 1996) research paradigms will be compared and their purposes and procedures contrasted. Questions that must be addressed in any QOL research project are identified: Who is QOL research for? To what purposes may QOL research findings be put? What are the ethical obligations of researchers designing and reporting QOL studies? Is research on QOL which compromises well-being justifiable? In what way can/do the perspectives of research *participants* inform the selection of research methods and tools? What are the ethical implications of developments such as QALYs? A checklist of questions to consider in the development of a QOL research project is presented.

Conceptual and Philosophical Issues

QOL is now widely deployed as a shorthand term for the collective well-being of human groups and also as a summary description of the particulars of individual lives. Although the use of large-scale systems of social indicators necessarily presupposes a host of value judgments, and hence ethical, moral and, essentially, political positions (some of which, such as the positive valuation of widespread school participation, the presence of women in the workforce or democratic political systems have been highlighted earlier), it is QOL understood as an aspect of individual subjectivity that throws these issues into sharpest relief. This chapter discusses the major ethical and conceptual issues arising with specific reference to QOL research at the individual level.

QOL has become a driving force in service design, delivery and outcome evaluation across medicine and social care. The quality of life of 'patients'/ 'service users' is now routinely advocated as a measure of the 'quality' and 'value for money' of services. QOL is even advocated as *the* yardstick by which decisions about the (dis)continuation of not just service programmes or intervention techniques, but also individual lives, should be judged. Statements such as Blunden's (1988: 117) have begun to appear with increasing frequency:

> The quality of life of the developmentally disabled persons who live in community residences must feature prominently in any discussion of service quality ... community services should lead to a demonstrable improvement in the quality of residents' lives.

Such statements are not always framed as expectations of the outcomes of well-designed services. Rather, the assessment of QOL is increasingly presented as a *moral imperative* if human service practice is to be ethically sound. Thus:

> Several instruments are now available which allow people with cognitive impairments to record their subjective QOL. It is recommended that such measurement be regarded as an essential ethical requirement whenever issues of intervention, education or service delivery are under considera-tion. (Cummins, 1997b: 24)

There seems to be no reason why this should not be a 'good thing'. It is, surely, right that people's QOL should be an important consideration in the design of services, or that the relative contribution to the enhancement of QOL offered by different techniques should inform decisions about funding or treatment. There are, however, some very serious conceptual and ethical difficulties entailed in the use of the idea of QOL like this. The first is that of objectivity.

The problem of objectivity

The great majority of QOL studies take it for granted that the first task (at either individual or societal levels) is to *operationally define* the construct. As Chapter 2 showed, there are myriad definitions of QOL, and as many problems with them. This work is predicated upon a priori acceptance of the conjecture that QOL is an hypothetical construct (like gravity, diabetes or intelligence) which may, via strict and objective criteria, permit measurement and quantification. That is, it is presumed *in advance* that there is a single 'thing' in the world, called 'quality of life', of which it may sensibly be said that different people, communities or nations have in greater or lesser quantities (cf. Feyerabend, 1974). This approach underpins the development of *all* scales, questionnaires and indices which offer numerical values for 'QOL' states, and reaches its most extreme expression in the development of measures of quality- and disability-adjusted life years (QALYs and DALYs), which explicitly value the quality of years of life, and then express that value in terms of single number between 0 and 1. What all of these approaches share in, then, is their adherence to a theoretical (and hence methodological) position which suggests that – in principle – *all* states of being in the world are amenable to objective operational definition, and meaningful description in numerical terms.

But this approach has been subject to serious questioning. While we have become used to making sense of statements like 'Hugh is so bright, he has an IQ of 145', we tend to forget that describing aspects of persons, their experiences and their capacities in this way is a remarkably recent development (Rose, 1999). The wry humour of Douglas Adams's (1979) observation that 'the meaning of life is 42' works *precisely because* it is, in terms of our everyday sense making, nonsensical.

Similarly, while the QOL literatures may be full of statements which describe statistical aggregates of persons' happiness in such terms – for example, Cummins *et al.*'s (in press) notion that life satisfaction is best described as '75 ± 2.5%SM'– which seem, in *those contexts*, discursively unproblematic, one wonders how the researchers would take to describing their *own* satisfaction with the world in such terms. 'My QOL today is 73.75' is, of course, an outlandish formulation. That is, such numerical presentations and formally specified operational definitions may give a *spurious* impression of objectivity and of neutral scientific knowledge. The very real problems that such appearances can mask are well illustrated by thinking about an example offered by Deutscher (1973) in a discussion of the way in which *the same* 'objective' terms (and even *identical* specific numerical values) may describe very different subjective experiences. Deutscher (1973: 191) notes that:

> when an American truck driver complains to the waitress at the diner about his 'warm' beer and 'cold' soup, the 'warm' liquid may have a temperature of 50°, while the 'cold' one is 75° ... The standard for the same objects may well vary from culture to culture, from nation to nation, from region to region and, for that matter, within any given social unit – between classes, age groups, sexes, or what have you; what is 'cold' soup for an adult may be too 'hot' to give a child.

Most older British readers would probably experience the American truckie's 'warm' beer as being much too 'cold', while Australian readers would no doubt sympathize with his predicament. However, even noting this, a series of other problems are *caused by* the attempted translation of lived experiences into formally specified, operationally defined constructs. It is important to remember that, as Megone (1990), puts it: '"the quality of life" is a grandiose term. The ordinary man ... does not often talk in terms of the quality of his life, nor is the quality of life, more generally, a common topic of conversation'. And, similarly, it is important to remember that 'quality of life' is in no way the same sort of an 'object' or 'thing' as a bowl of soup or a glass of Budweiser, about which genuinely independent, objective judgments (of temperature or quantity) can be made.

The confusion of the naming of hypothetical constructs – such as 'intelligence', 'QOL' or 'schizophrenia' – with the naming of *things in the world*, reification, is an ever present problem in the social sciences (Pilgrim and Bentall, 1999). As Megone (1990) point outs, the consequence of efforts to transform 'grandiose' vernacular terms into formal, theoretical, concepts can be substantial. Megone (1990: 29, my emphasis) notes that:

> even if there is some fairly standard idea of what quality of life concerns, might it be that any attempt to produce a more refined notion for the purpose of measurement, employing theoretical devices, inevitably distorts from the original? ... The notion of quality of life is employed by theorists to address certain problems on the basis that those actually facing the problems see this as a relevant factor. But if the theorist ... solves the problem in terms of a distorted theoretical account of the factor, distorted because the theoretical refinements slant the notion in a certain way – if this is the case, then ... the theorist has *not solved the original problem*.

The existence of theoretical models of QOL which command consensus in the field may thus *appear* to offer an answer to questions such as 'what is QOL', but there is room for doubt about whether they have done so without a distorted, and distorting, account. As Hatton has observed, 'most systems for assessing quality of life also provide methods for summarizing and standardizing the experience of individuals to produce quality of life "scores" which can then be compared' (Hatton, 1998: 105), or, in other words, most systems for assessing QOL have *built into them* a set of theoretical refinements which 'distort' or 'slant the notion in a certain way' – not least transforming verbal reports into arbitrary numerical scores.

As such then, theoretical models or operational definitions of QOL – and the measurement tools which are derived from them – cannot be seen in the same terms as theoretical models or technical measures of gravity, evolution or climate. As McHoul and Rapley (2001) have noted, neutron stars, capybaras and the wind are not members of the same class as persons' accounts of the quality of their life, if for no other reason than that they are incapable of theorizing themselves. Unlike constructs such as QOL, in the case of phenomena like the wind scientists are not tempted to confuse statements about the *amount* of a property exhibited by a phenomenon and the phenomenon *itself*. This is why we hear statements on the weather forecast like 'cyclone Eliza is travelling at 200 kilometres per hour' not 'cyclone Eliza *is* 200 kilometres per hour'.

Even apparently objective scores on QOL scales are products not only of a complex set of interactions (between researchers and participants) but also of a prior set of *value judgments* about what is to *count* as QOL, which domains should be measured and the manner of the measuring. At the population level this point is perhaps more readily appreciated, as agencies such as the ABS (2001) are, as we have seen, explicit about the *pragmatic* factors influencing the selection of indicators which they use to define QOL. Quantitative individual-level research is much less explicit about the politics of operational definition, domain specification and item selection, but is no less affected by these influences than population-level QOL research. Inasmuch as quality of life is not a 'thing', so too such objective scores, however impressive they appear and however convoluted their statistical manipulation, are also not the 'thing' itself. The quality of life is, emphatically, not 42.

The problem of subjectivity

What Melbourne Aborigines define as 'health' is at considerable variance from the operational definitions of public health researchers and social epidemiologists (Chapter 2). Conversely, what constitutes 'health' from an Aboriginal perspective includes many aspects of QOL specified in many of the formal definitions of the term considered in Chapter 2. As we saw in the Apologia, achieving precise measurement of individuals' views employing standardized measures may be a hit-and-miss affair (Antaki and Rapley, 1996a, 1996b; Rapley and Antaki 1996; Antaki *et al.*, 2000). With his usual clarity, Cummins (1997b: 121–2) puts the issue well:

> but what of the subjective axis? Here the situation is not so clear. If a respondent to a QOL scale does not regard one or more of the domains as having much relevance to their personal situation, then it does not matter how satisfied or dissatisfied they are with domains that contribute little to the individual's life. If, on the other hand, a respondent regards strong links with their family and friends as integral to their life quality, then their level of satisfaction with such a domain is of paramount relevance.

This is a critical issue: the relative importance of various aspects of life may differ at any given moment for each of us, and the relative importance of specific matters may change over a lifetime. Of course if two people give different weightings to questionnaire domains, their scores are *not* directly comparable: the domains of QOL mean different things to them. If weightings change over time, the scores the person has recorded at the two time points are *not* comparable: what QOL means has changed.

These worries presuppose that any given set of domains identified by the questionnaire designer is itself genuinely representative of QOL for each and every respondent. For Melbourne Aborigines it seems that *any* standardized measure of HRQOL is unlikely to capture their subjective view of *either construct*. Interviews with adults with mild intellectual disabilities reported by Rapley *et al.* (1998) suggested that enforced sterilization; the denial of adulthood; the absence of autonomy; stigma, belittlement and rejection; and an awareness that these were the results of being identified as an 'intellectually disabled person' were inseparable from the subjective 'quality' of their lives. But items tapping these issues appear on no QOL questionnaire yet designed. Furthermore, when people

complete such questionnaires, like Anne and Arthur in the Apologia –
quite *whose* (subjective) QOL judgment is represented via a summary score
assigned by the interviewer ('we'll put a two down for that one then') is a
troubling issue (Antaki and Rapley, 1996a; Antaki *et al.*, 2000).

A second major problem in this area, and particularly troublesome in the
HRQOL and medical QOL literatures, has been identified by a number of
writers including Cummins (1997b) and Koch (2001). Koch (2001: 454–5)
points out that *all* studies seeking prospective judgments about future
health states (for example time trade-off and standard gamble studies –
discussed in detail in Chapter 6) implicitly rely on five axioms (see Box 3.1)

Box 3.1   Axioms underpinning studies of future health state preferences

Axiom 1   A person without a chronic physical deficit can accurately
compare healthy and restricted states.

Axiom 1a   Healthy persons have sufficient knowledge and experience to
make judgments about life quality and satisfaction in the
context of physical limit or disability.

Axiom 2   A healthy person can accurately predict what he or she
would want in extremes.

Axiom 3   Individuals have a core personality whose perspective and
judgments are constant whatever the physical or social
context.

Axiom 4   In public and personal health planning what is important is
solely the degree to which an individual's physical condition
deviates negatively from the norm.

Axiom 5   The discrete individual is always the sole and best judge of
appropriate treatment or non-treatment at any moment.

Source: Koch (2001)

Each of these presuppositions is conceptually problematic and Koch (2001)
offers detailed empirical work to suggest that Axioms 1 to 3 cannot be
sustained. It appears that 'healthy' people (those 'without a chronic
physical deficit') find it very difficult to make comparisons between
unimpaired and impaired states that reflect the views of people who are
already impaired, and a major reason for this is that 'healthy people' have
very little idea at all what the experience of disablement is actually like.
Such circumstances have led writers such as Oliver (1996) not only to
suggest that 'mainstream' social scientific research is oppressive of people
with disabilities, but also to demand that the research community adopt

'emancipatory' procedures or, in brief, a stance of cooperation and inclusivity – rather than one of distanced 'expertise'.

Further, all studies which ask for responses to hypothetical scenarios about future health states implicitly adopt a psychological model of the person (Axiom 3) which has come under sustained critical attack and, some would argue, is no longer tenable (see Antaki *et al.*, 1996; Edwards, 1997; McHoul and Rapley, 2001; Coulter, 1999). In consequence, accurate predictions – of future wishes when *in extremis* – can be neither expected nor relied upon. Axioms 4 and 5 are, of course, ethico-political questions through and through and not strictly speaking social scientific matters at all. The fact that a vast body of social scientific work is, however, predicated upon precisely these axioms again demonstrates that the field is not as untainted by moral, or value, judgments as is often suggested by research methods textbooks.

The problem of population-specificity

We have seen, in Chapter 2, a preview of the issue of universal vs. population- or condition-specific definitions of QOL and its measurement, an issue closely related to the controversy over objective vs. subjective indicators of QOL. The issue revolves around the purpose to which QOL measurement is to be put, and whether such measurement is understood and intended as a component of grand theory building or is intended to assist in the development of localized understandings of QOL for local purposes (for example, in human service evaluation studies). If the primary purpose is grand theory building, then there are good reasons for not supporting the development of definitions of QOL that are specific to groups like people with intellectual disabilities or the elderly, or for targeted patient populations – kidney disease, acne, vertigo and so on. Rosen (1986: 366–7) drew attention to the consequences of such group-specific definitions. While his specific concern was with people with intellectual disabilities, the point he makes applies generally. He noted that, were

> the existence of mental retardation, with its concomitant limitation in cognitive and social functioning [held to be] relevant as a factor determining quality of life requirements ... the definition of quality of life would need to be defined differently for people with mental retardation who are functioning at different developmental levels ... one might be forced into the distasteful position that individuals with more severe levels of mental retardation are entitled to less of a quality of life than those who are less severely retarded.

Rosen's worries again reflect the importance of value, or aesthetic, judgments in the field. As he noted, the logic of holding 'limitation in cognitive and social functioning relevant' *demands* that the corresponding

QOL entitlement for such persons be considered lower than for others. The problems which arise in the translation of such a priori ethical considerations into formal QOL instruments is illustrated by Cummins (1997b: 123), who notes that:

> a view that is limited to a population sub-group can restrict the view of what might constitute a high life quality for its members. Such definitions are shaped by the deficits of the groups to which they refer and, as a consequence, have been down-graded to reflect the assumption of a lower life quality than normal. Such assumptions, however, are likely to be invalid. The huge literature on positive and negative affect ... is consistent in its appreciation that each is independent of the other, such that people with serious disabilities may nevertheless describe themselves as happy, enthusiastic and excited about life.

While Cummins hints at the politics of QOL measurement in the context of his primarily methodological concern, Taylor and Bogdan (1990: 27) draw attention directly to the ethics of the QOL research programme as a whole. They note that:

> we seldom make enquiries into the QOL of people who are not disabled or disadvantaged in some way ... we usually examine QOL only when we know or suspect that people are suffering ... herein lie[s] ... the danger of studying the QOL of people with mental retardation.

Such studies also raise the ethical question of whether, and to what extent, individuals with intellectual disabilities should 'influence the selection of quality of life criteria for themselves' (Rosen, 1986: 365). To date it would seem that the research community is guilty of adopting precisely the approach that Edgerton (1990) cautioned against – namely that of 'imposing' QOL variables onto almost all respondent groups, regardless of their level of intellectual competence.

'Emancipatory' versus 'mainstream' QOL research

The issue of imposed definitions of QOL is the issue at the heart of the major criticism of writers such as Finkelstein (1993), Oliver (1996) and Duckett and Fryer (1998) of the oppressive and disempowering agenda of the 'mainstream' research 'establishment' in its relations to and with disabled people (Clements *et al.*, 1999).

The 'danger' Taylor and Bogdan (1990) draw attention to, then, is the conduct of research which does not *consult with* the people whose lives are examined, but rather treats persons as *objects of study*. Such work – 'mainstream' social scientific research – overlooks or denies Chorover's (1979) point that the power to give names (to things such as 'QOL') is exactly that: the exercise of *power*. The argument is that if QOL research is to actually be of *use* to people who *are* disabled or disadvantaged in some way, it must be explicitly 'emancipatory'. That is, to be ethically acceptable, research must be *consciously* designed, conducted and reported not only in collaboration with people who are disadvantaged, but also in a manner which respects *their* expertise on the lived experience of disablement (Goodley and Rapley, 2001). A key requirement of emancipatory research is that the results of such inquiries are not only communicated to academic peers, but also – and indeed primarily – reported back to research participants in a form that makes sense in their terms. From an emancipatory perspective research practices should always be *explicitly* politicized (as opposed to the perspective of 'mainstream' work which, in its silence on politics, itself makes a political statement) with a firm commitment to research which contributes to freeing people with disabilities from the oppression of 'normal' society.

This perspective is a major challenge to much social scientific research. While there are technical-methodological problems in operationalizing QOL differently for different groups, the pursuit of a universally applicable definition of the construct (what Cummins (1997b: 136) describes as a 'total quality of life construct') the individualized approach to its measurement is challenged here on the grounds of the politics/ethics of research into which the approach is embedded. Such a challenge reconceptualizes many of the problems already discussed in Chapter 2 as essentially *local* matters. That is, many in the disability movement (the hearing impaired for example), regard issues such as 'cultural relativity' as applying not only to gross differences between ethnic or national groups, but also as operative between the hearing and the deaf within any given society.

The 'mainstream' approach is strongly criticized not only for conceptual incoherence, but also as politically and ethically problematic, by *camouflaging* inequality (Emerson and Hatton, 1994; Hatton, 1998). If QOL is defined carefully enough it can appear that 'gross differences in objective life quality' have no bearing *at all* on people's happiness, and hence divert attention away from these matters (Hatton, 1998; Rapley, 2001). Ager and Hatton (1999: 337) put the position well:

> having argued for the value of addressing the subjective experience of individuals, it seems somewhat strange to assert the necessity of reliance upon methods underpinned by conventional psychometric theory, rather than encourage, for example, the use of more discursive analysis of individuals' accounts of their life experience ... insistence upon 'subjective' data may ... inappropriately distract attention away from the unambiguous significance of 'objective' indicators of experience. Cummins (1997) dangerously equates objective life circumstances with 'material' circumstances ... ignoring the many objective experiences which reflect differential access to power and opportunity and material resources.

The worry that concerns such as this are merely 'sensationalist' or 'postmodern' objections (Cummins, 2001a: 8) is tempered by recalling that Veenhoven (1996) specifically commended the likely 'political appeal' of the HLE. Such objections are not simply a matter for concern at the level of national social indicators (see also Reicher, 2001). The very idea of the *quality* of a life is shot through with political and ethical considerations and clear-cut personal implications.

The ethics of operational definition and scale design

If we are designing an individual-level psychometric QOL measure, *choosing* not to include an item on forced sterilization or other belittling treatment (despite the fact that many people with intellectual disabilities will have experienced this) ensures that, *even should an assessor wish to*, it is impossible for this aspect of QOL to be measured. That the circumstances of marginalized social groups entail very specific circumstances (such as having staff in authority over one) that can, sensibly, be linked to how good life might be, would seem to be an argument for the inclusion of these matters, not their exclusion, from attempts to gauge QOL.

To build a grand theory of QOL, it is of course essential to have a universally applicable unitary operational definition (if at the expense of individualized meaning). However, if one wishes to know about how this particular population group feel about their QOL, it would appear more coherent to follow, at the individual level, the 'emancipatory' paradigm, and to develop measures or indices in consultation with those directly affected. The results of adopting this approach are previewed below, and further described in Chapter 4.

Other objections to the QOL research programme

There is then reason to be cautious about using the idea of quality of life as a formal social scientific term. Taylor (1994) draws a helpful distinction between the notion of quality of life, as deployed in lay discourse, and 'quality of life' as a scientific construct, which he suggests be known as 'QOL' in order to differentiate the two ideas. Taylor (1994) suggests that the two uses are distinct in terms of both their *pragmatic use* and *phenomenological reference*, and, further, have a different *ontological* status. He proposes three key distinctions. Firstly that 'quality of life is a useful sensitizing concept whereas QOL is a reification'; secondly that 'quality of life' means something while QOL 'seems to mean everything' and, thirdly, that 'quality of life is lived and experienced while QOL is superimposed on that experience' (Taylor, 1994: 260–3). Wolfensberger has suggested that QOL is a 'Kraft cheese term', and should be abandoned in scientific discourse and replaced by a research programme in which efforts at 'total' definitions are discontinued and 'the fractioning of QOL into more clear cut components with different names' (Wolfensberger, 1994: 318) is substituted.

From a feminist perspective Eckermann has argued that existing QOL research is implicitly politicized. While the addition of QOL measures to the range of indicators traditionally used to assess health and well-being offers a richer understanding of health outcomes, most measures remain undifferentiated by *gender* and are, thus, not only insensitive to the 'subtle effects of gender socialization on health and well-being', but also disregard the particular experience of women (Eckerman, 2000: 29). Again, we see a call for the further *fractioning* – rather than 'totalizing' – of the concept. All of these objections may, in summary, be held to pivot on the central question: 'Whose quality of life is it anyway?' That is, who should define what QOL actually is?

The Views of 'Patients'

Whether notions like QOL are viable as 'technical' constructs has been questioned by a number of writers. There may, also, be serious differences between 'lay' and 'technical' views of matters such as what HRQOL 'is'. Much of the literature (at both individual and population levels) may then be characterized by its inadequate attention to the views of everyday people – be they described as 'patients' or otherwise – about the lay usage of the notion.

In their study of people with chronic obstructive pulmonary disease Leidy and Haase (1999: 70) conducted in-depth interviews with a small group of twelve people about the 'quality' of their lives. They summarize informants' views by noting that:

> participants ... were engaged in the challenge of preserving their personal integrity as they faced increasing limitations in their ability to perform day-to-day activities ... Personal integrity represents a sense of satisfying wholeness that encompasses the integration, totality, and collective of intra-personal and inter-personal characteristics, including one's physical appearance and functioning, skills, roles, knowledge, memories, environment, family, and friends. It is a sense of one's individuality and wholeness as a human being. Two characteristics are central to a sense of personal integrity: effectiveness, or 'being able,' and connectedness, or 'being with,' each of which are expressed through daily activity and challenged through limitations in physical capacity.

What Leidy and Haase (1999) suggest is that 'personal integrity', or the quality of a life, is not a one-off judgment but a *process* of engagement with lived experience. Similarly, in their analysis of the quality of life of people coping with kidney dialysis, Martin and Thompson (2001: 57, my emphasis) suggest that: 'the crucial issue in obtaining an optimal quality of life is the *process of adaptation* and acceptance of chronic illness'. The difficulty of formal, psychometric QOL measurement, is that quality of life is assessed in cross-sectional, or one-off, snapshots via the completion of questionnaires and, hence, cannot capture an adaptation *process* (Wenzel, 2001). Perhaps the most troubling aspect of such a divorcing of measurement from the process of a lived life is seen in efforts to fix, numerically, the value of particular forms of life or health states. It is to the ethics of such attempts – in the shape of quality- and disability-adjusted life years – that we now turn.

Quality of Life and the Value of Life

It is a widely accepted view that the state of one's health may (dramatically) affect an assessment of the quality of one's life, of whether life is worth living or not, despite empirical evidence to challenge this view (further discussed in Chapter 6). If we concede that some people have lives so appalling they are not worth living, 'it becomes hard to deny the existence of a grey area where a life may be worth living but is less worth living than normal. Then we may say that the condition that makes that life less worth living than normal is its low "quality of life"' (Aksoy, 2000: 19; Glover, 1977). Such judgments are problematic even as subjective, personal and private ones made by terminally ill people and their physicians – as the case of Jack Kervorkian ('Doctor Death') shows. Such subjective judgments – that death is preferable to a 'low quality of life' – are, however, routinely made (as we shall see in more detail in Chapter 6) by doctors in the Netherlands on behalf of, and without necessarily consulting, their intellectually disabled 'patients'.

Cubbon (1991) argues that, given limited health care resources, even in affluent Western societies, there is no principled way of allocating resources that produces a win: win outcome. Because resource allocation – or 'rationing' – has to occur, decision-makers need a mechanism whereby they can choose between patients, and it is unfortunate but inevitable therefore that some groups of people will be *knowingly deprived*. Statistics like Quality Adjusted Life Years (QALYs) are no worse and no better than any other alternative: they have a transparent calculation protocol and there is no option that leaves *everyone* better off. Ends justify means.

There are serious ethical dilemmas here, and the development of QALYs has always been predicated upon the notion that transparent, explicit, public statements about the quality of particular lives, expressed in a common, numerical form offers one way out of the difficulties of variation in subjective, personal opinion. However, as Aksoy (2000: 21) points out:

to consider (extreme) suffering as something worse than death is a consideration based upon supposition since no one knows what kind of experience dying is, nor how it feels to have one's life terminated (not merely threatened) by another ... The idea that the quality of someone's life could be judged 'worse than being dead' has always met with criticism. It could be argued that the opportunity for choice from among a reasonable array of life plans is an important and independent component of quality of life, but, whether being dead can be counted one such life plan is rather open to dispute. It is possible to compare the quality of two lives, or of a single person's life under two conditions, but it is not possible to make the QOL comparison needed here, because one of the alternatives to be compared is non-existence. If a person no longer exists, there is no life that could possibly have any quality so as to enter into a comparison with the quality of life sustained by treatment.

It also seems to be the case that, although people may rate the *hypothetical* outcomes (of road accidents for example), as being as bad, or even as worse than death, when people experience these events they tend not regard their lives as valueless or as having a negative value (Koch, 2000; Jones-Lee *et al.*, 1985; Loomes and McKenzie, 1990). These studies also show that doctors regularly and reliably rate hypothetical health states more negatively, and often as little better than death, than do their patients. Given that such evaluations are widely accepted in the medical literatures as guiding doctors' decision-making about treatment, and also given that techniques such as QALYs are *designedly* independent of patients' views, again we see the problems in asking the question, whose quality of life is it anyway?

Against 'realist' justifications for QALYs (Cubbon, 1991) Harris (1991: 186) has argued that 'each person has an equal claim upon the health resources of the world and in particular those of his/her own society: that no individual or group or type of individual has a more valuable life or a greater claim to life-saving resources than any other. This is part of the claim that all people are entitled to treatment as equals.' Bridging the gap between earlier discussions of social indicators of the quality of life in nation-states (Chapter 1) and the apparently esoteric and medically specific nature of QALYs (Chapter 6), Harris locates the argument against QALYs firmly in terms of the broader questions of the political economy of health. In a neat twist on one of the prevailing tropes of the 'enterprise culture' (Rose, 1992 – see Chapter 5), the idea of 'mutual obligation' between citizen and state, Harris (1991: 187) writes that:

any nation state's claim to the allegiance of its citizens is contingent upon it being willing and able to protect the lives and liberties of its citizens. In the absence of plausible threats of foreign domination, the greatest threat to the life and liberty of citizens of most democracies comes from threats to health. A society that says that particular citizens, whether individually identifiable in advance or not, will not be so protected has effectively declared such individuals to be outlaws – outside the protection of the State – and forfeited its claim to their allegiance.

Singer *et al.* (1995) argue, in contrast, that spending taxpayers' money on publicly provided health care entails a fiscal responsibility to get value for money. If resources are limited we cannot save every life that might be saved: is it then unfair to give a lower priority to saving the lives of those with incurable conditions that significantly reduce their quality of life? Harris (1995) argues that this does indeed place people in double jeopardy and is inherently unfair. Respecting persons *as such* means adhering to the *equality principle* that each individual is valued as an individual, as one, and as no more – or less – than one, whatever their life expectancy or present or predicted quality of life.

Thus, while all QOL judgments may be held to violate the equality principle, that is to violate the principled viewing of all persons as sharing in *equality of life*, QALYs can also be held to shift the question from asking 'is this treatment beneficial for this patient?' to 'is the patients' life of benefit to them?' (Ramsey, 1978; Harris, 1987). One of the most basic problems with the QALY approach, then, is the focus on quality of life in terms of abstract *life years*, rather than in terms of the *daily lives of persons*. QALYs shift our focus onto QOL as an abstract, technological concept – life years – rather than the experience of actual living, breathing people. The consequences of such technologies are, of course, shouldered by living, breathing people. It is the unintended consequences of QOL measurement that occupy the final part of this chapter.

Can QOL Assessment Negatively Affect Quality of Life?

The presumption in most of the literature is that QOL assessment is a 'good thing'. Although many caveats are entered about the present limitations of particular measures or approaches, in general terms, and from whichever tradition the work is drawn, QOL assessment tends to be framed as making a positive contribution. Thus QOL assessment assists service providers to evaluate how well services are performing (Schalock, 1997; Anderson and Lewis, 2000); it offers patients a chance to have their say (Rapley and Beyer, 1996; Costantini *et al.*, 2000); QOL assessment permits the 'rational' allocation of scarce resources (Sprangers *et al.*, 2000); it adds information not routinely available from the usual medical focus on symptomatic change (Carr and Higginson, 2001); and it offers a means to direct research funding (Fayers and Bjordal, 2001) among many other benefits. But what if assessing QOL were actually detrimental to the well-being and quality of life of those who participate in the exercise?

The medical literature recognizes that QOL measurement may raise ethical issues related to negative outcomes. Ravenscroft and Bell (2000) found that, whereas in over half of the intensive care units they surveyed 'perceived quality of life' was one of the most common reasons for terminating patients' life support, in over half staff agreed that end-of-life decisions were made on the basis of 'arbitrary quality of life (QOL) judgements' (Ravenscroft and Bell, 2000: 437). The conclusions drawn about medical termination of life included the observation that 'an obvious area for attention is the absence of accurate assessment of premorbid health and QOL, and more comprehensive audit of outcome' (Ravenscroft and Bell, 2000: 439). While on the face of it this may seem an eminently reasonable suggestion, in response to their article, Woodrow (2001) suggests – to the contrary – that 'the comment that belated or absent measurement of Quality of Life is "clearly inadequate" ignores the contentious nature of measuring Quality of Life. Another recent review [Aksoy, 2000] concludes that: "quality of life cannot be measured either accurately or reliably, and so should not be used as a criterion for health care services"'(Woodrow, 2001: 205).

Higginson and Carr (2001: 1297–8) put the theoretical issues clearly:

> the breadth of quality of life as a concept means that problems might be identified that are outside the usual remit of medical care. This raises a number of ethical concerns. Firstly the act of measuring quality of life in a clinical setting may generate the expectation that the clinician will be able to influence it … In situations where this is not possible, patients may be seen to be harmed by the process of measurement. Secondly, some … have opposed the clinical measurement of quality of life on the grounds that it represents the 'overmedicalisation' of life and clinical interference in aspects of patients' lives that should not be the concern of the clinician.

Another close ethnomethodological look at the administration of the *Quality of Life Questionnaire* (Schalock and Keith, 1996) illustrates the issues.[1] Whereas the bulk of the literature presents QOL as *scores* (of individuals, patient groups, service systems or nation-states) ethnomethodological approaches, and other qualitative methods, try to gain access to what happens in the *process* of score generation which quantitative methods present as a problematic (but basically uninteresting) procedural issue. In other words, the focus now is on trying to understand *how* it is that scores are arrived at when QOL is actually assessed in practice.

A number of papers in the medical literature have noted that the forms of QOL assessment derived by academics and researchers are often perceived by patients as puzzling or irrelevant to the issues *they* feel are pertinent to QOL (Carr and Higginson, 2001; Bowling, 1995; Coates *et al.*, 1983). Similarly, Lauritzen and Sachs (2001) have noted how the practices of routine health surveillance, monitoring and reporting *in and of themselves* introduce unpleasant and possibly aversive threats into patients' lives.

In the two examples[2] below the people whose QOL is being assessed show *their* appreciation of the exercise in similar terms. That is, what is assumed by the bulk of the literature to be a positive, or at least benign, activity (the assessment of their QOL) may be received by the recipients of such monitoring not as a useful and empowering exercise, but rather as a very real and immediate threat to their well-being.

In the first extract we enter at a point five minutes into the session where Mike (the interviewer) and Bob (the 'intellectually disabled' interviewee) are engaged in the preliminaries to the assessment proper over a cup of tea, discussing Bob's holiday plans. This extract is, necessarily, quite long and illustrates, I hope, at least one of the benefits of qualitative approaches – namely that really interesting data about the quality of people's lives are available in the fine-grained detail of interaction, not only in quantitative summaries of those interactions.

Extract 1: From McHoul and Rapley (2000b)

```
93 M:     how long will you go for (..)
94 B:     just a wee:k=
95 M:     =°huh° (1.0) and who you gonna go with
96        (2.0)
97 B:     °Henry° (..) Ste:ven: ('t) (1.0) the other
98        Steven (.) Rod >(no– no)< Steven Pallister (..)
99        you wouldn't know 'im ⌈°would  you°=
100 M:                          ⌊no::
101 M:    =°no° is he staff? (..)
102 B:    eh?
103 M:    is he staff?=
104 B:    =no: (.) °err° res:ident
...
129       (7.0) ((2 knocks and    ⌈pouring  sound))
130 B:                            ⌊(sings)) °Sa:nta  Claus
131       is comin' to town (.) Sa:nta Claus is co:ming
132       to town .h San:ta Claus is co:::ming: to:::
133       tow::n:°
134       ((stirring sound)) (16.0)
135 B:    there y'are
136 M:    thank you
...
144 B:    hhh (do you know more) than the residents
145       there?
146 M:    erm?
147 B:    (at the County Castle)
```

```
148 M:    I think so              ⌐yeah (..) I know quite a lot of them
149 B:                            L((slurping  noise))  eh?
150 M:    I know quite a lot of them (.) there's not many
151       people left there now though
152 B:    no: (.) °er° .h >most of< um:: died didn't
153       they?
154 M:    hmm died or moved out (..) °hm?° did you used
155       to (..) °hhh° be at the Castle
156 B:    yeh=
157 M:    =°yeh°
158 B:    I didn't like it much
159 M:    no:?
160 B:    .hhh I'd sooner be 'ere
161 M:    yeah (.) how long have you been here Bob
162 B:    since from nineteen eighty nine
163 M:    (right) that's about >(so)< for five years now
164       (..)
165 B:    yeah
166 M:    yeah (1.0) and you wouldn't wanna go back
167 B:    <no> ((throaty syllable)) °y' can: sti–° (..)
168       you know what you can do: with it?
169 M:    what's that then
170 B:    .hh stick it up °where° the monkeys keep their
171       nuts
```

McHoul and Rapley (2002b) offer an extended analysis of this conversation. However, for present purposes it is important to note not so much the mundane nature of this chat, but rather the very careful design of Bob's contributions to it. The *topics* of these preliminaries to the actual QOL assessment, which may be thought to be off the point or irrelevant, repay close attention. While, with the possible exception of his singing (though as the interview was conducted two days before Christmas this is moot), these matters are ubiquitous topics for chat (places of origin, one's holidays, one's job, persons possibly known in common). However, it is also the case (and this time including the singing) that they *display* a deep and insightful knowledge (on Bob's part) of the kind of encounter this is. Namely, Mike is a psychologist, there to perform an assessment of his happiness and well-being. More precisely, Bob shows Mike (and us, the overhearing analysts) that he is conscious, should he be found wanting in the QOL department, that his place of residence could be altered – and, on his own estimation (see lines 170–1), for the worse.

Accordingly, and even before the official questioning starts, it is incumbent on Bob to *display* that he is extremely happy. Thus we discover that he takes overseas holidays, he sings and so forth. Thus Bob is not only *telling* Mike, in answers to the official questions to come, that he is happy or that his QOL is acceptable to him. In addition to this, he *shows* this appreciation of his life circumstances by *doing* having a great quality of life, or at least being content with his lot.

That Bob is not anomalous in this is also shown in the second extract, again taken from the opening moments of the administration of the *QOL.Q.* Arthur makes *his* understanding of the questioning to come explicit. In line 3 (arrowed) Arthur's question about the 'hardness' of the questions he is to be asked suggests that, for him too, this is not just a cosy chat about his happiness or 'quality of his life', but instead may include ''ard' questions: to wit this is another *test*.

Extract 2: Code: CA/KK/CD (From Rapley and Antaki, 1996)

```
1    I      erm (…) and I'd ↑like you to ↑answer some questio::ns to tell
2           me how you feel about the ⌈(unintell)
3 →  AR                                ⌊they're not 'ard ones are they (.)
4    I      not very ⌈hard
5    AR             ⌊no:o
6    I      no (.) and ↑if you don't understand ↓them Arthur you can just
            tell me (.)
7    AR     yeus
8    I      and I'll I'll say them differently (.)
9    AR     ym
…
17   I      so there's no ↓hurry     ⌈(..) °do you have any° ↓ques↑tions?
            (.)
18                                   ⌊(paper shuffling)
19   I      to ↓ask ↑me?
20   AR     ye: ↑e:r↓:::s
21   I      what would you like to ↓ask me
22 → AR     I ↑like being I like being er (..) in 'ere (.)
23   I      you ↑like   ⌈being =
24 → AR                 ⌊(living) in 'ere like I like living in 'ere
```

That the reassurances offered by the interviewer are not heard by Arthur as such, and that he understands that his 'results' may be used by other people to inform decisions affecting the quality of his life, is made clear in lines 22 and 24. Rather than 'asking a question' as invited by his interviewer (in lines 17–21), Arthur uses the opportunity to make it clear, at the start of the interview, that he is happy living where he is. Adopting a more direct approach to matters than Bob, Arthur leaves no room for uncertainty on the interviewer's part. He repeats 'I like living in 'ere' three times. Why might this be? It is, I think, hard to avoid reading this exchange as other than a worried Arthur taking pains to state his understanding of the encounter. He knows, that is, that the answers he provides to a set of test questions are highly consequential. He is aware that his continued residence in his house is on the line. He fears that the likely upshot of a 'poor' performance is being relocated. 'I like living in 'ere', then, may be heard as conveying that his 'quality of life' interview *scares* him. Unfortunately, however, 'do you like living here' does not feature as a specified item on the questionnaire schedule, so this particular datum – despite its apparent importance to the quality of Arthur's life – must be disregarded in calculating his QOL score.

Table 3.1 Some ethical questions to consider when developing and designing a QOL study

- Whose quality of life is it anyway?
- Who is/are the expert(s) on QOL in the population I wish to study: academics or the people themselves?
- What is the relationship between the theoretical/operational definition of QOL used by the measures that I am going to employ and the everyday understandings of QOL of the people to whom I am going to administer them?
- What *are* the everyday understandings of QOL of the people I am working with?
- What procedures or methods might I adopt that would assist me to find out?
- Whose quality of life is it anyway?
- If everyday understandings are different from those proposed by the measure I intend to use, what are the ethical issues here?
- What *direct* and *specific* benefits to my research participants will flow from this quality of life project?
- If I cannot specify such direct benefits, in advance, what are the ethical implications of this failure?
- Is my proposed research 'mainstream' or 'emancipatory'? If 'mainstream' how could it be redesigned to give a genuine voice to my participants?
- what harm (physical, emotional, psychological) might my study of the quality of their lives cause to my participants?
- What indirect benefits may accrue to participants/the wider research community from my quality of life study?
- Whose quality of life is it anyway?

In Summary

There are serious ethical, conceptual and philosophical difficulties inherent in the study and assessment of QOL (see Table 3.1). At an individual level not only may QOL judgments be employed to make literally life-threatening decisions, they may also, in the gathering of data to inform them, be seen to do immediate harm (albeit of a less physically serious nature) to the people whose 'life quality' is supposedly 'objectively' being measured. That such harm may be caused to research participants is, in many jurisdictions (including the university where I work), sufficient for Human Research Ethics Committees to refuse a research permit.

From a wider perspective, attention has been drawn to the capacity for QOL research to offer an appearance of 'scientific' legitimacy to fundamentally ethically problematic practices in medicine (for example selective abortion, the allocation of resources to particular groups at the expense of others and (in)voluntary euthanasia) and in the operation of national economies on the basis of what some see as deeply flawed indices. Such concerns have included the recognition that, historically, not only have 'mainstream' research practices silenced disadvantaged people, but also that notions of 'lives worth living' have slipped into ideas such as 'lives unworthy of life'.

In this respect, writers cautioning against the use of QOL research have pointed to the active collaboration of medical, psychological and psychiatric professionals with both Nazi and Fascist regimes in the 'solution' of the problems such 'useless mouths' posed to the well-being, or quality of life, of the nation-state. Such concerns resonate with contemporary alarm about the creeping 'medicalization' and 'surveillance' of ever-wider areas of people's lives in the guise of concern for their well-being raised by writers such as Hatton (1998), Higginson and Carr (2001) and Taylor (1994). Such concerns also raise difficult questions about the ethics of employing as research tools measures which are based not on the views of the people to whom they are applied, but rather upon *researchers'* ideas about what quality of life is.

In the light of the ethical concerns raised in this chapter, Chapter 4 turns to examine research approaches that draw upon both 'mainstream' and 'emancipatory' thinking. Work which has focused upon the identification and the demarcation – or 'fractioning' – of domains of QOL is discussed. Workers in this stream of the quantitative tradition, such as Cummins, believe that it is possible to develop a formal operational definition of QOL which contributes both to theory building and that also offers individual persons, policy-makers, service providers and the research community a widely applicable and socially relevant measurement tool. Workers in the qualitative area have, traditionally, been more interested in the approach described by Ager and Hatton (1999): that of using a 'more discursive analysis of individuals' accounts of their life experience' to understand – in a manner which is attentive to the criticisms of writers such as Koch (2001) and Oliver (1996) – the quality of peoples' lives as they themselves experience it and, in so doing, contributing to the development of 'emancipatory' research practices.

Notes

1. The *QOL.Q* is a 40-item questionnaire which measures both objective circumstances and subjective perceptions of satisfaction with life in terms of four factors: Satisfaction; Competence/Productivity; Social Belonging and Empowerment/Independence. The other leading intellectual disability QOL

measure is the *ComQOL-ID-5* (Cummins, 1997a), a psychometrically more complex instrument which also measures objective circumstances and subjective perceptions of satisfaction in seven areas (Material Well-being, Health, Productivity, Intimacy, Safety, Place in Community and Emotional Well-being) but provides for the subjective weighting of objective factors by their level of importance to the individual. Broadly speaking the *QOL.Q* can be said to measure how happy people are in normalization-congruent service settings, whereas the *ComQOL-ID* provides for a direct comparison of (aspects of) life satisfaction between people with an intellectual disability and the normal population. Psychometrics for the QOL.Q are provided by Rapley and Lobley (1995); Rapley *et al.* (1998) and Schalock and Keith (1993). Psychometric studies of the *ComQOL-ID* can be found in Cummins (1997).

2. Extracts are transcriptions of audiotaped interviews. Transcription conventions for extract 1 are those developed by Gail Jefferson and are designed to capture the most important prosodic aspects of speech. Other extracts employ a simplified transcription. Appendix 1 shows Jeffersonian transcription conventions.

Study Questions

- Whose quality of life is it anyway?
- Is it ethically acceptable to employ predictions of future quality of life as a guide to end-of-life, or beginning-of-life, decision-making?
- What would the quality of my life be if I had Down syndrome/Alzheimer's disease/dialysis-dependent kidney disease?
- Is there such a thing as a life not worth living?

Suggestions for Further Reading

Clements, J., Rapley, M. and Cummins, R.A. (1999) On, to, for or with? Vulnerable people and the practices of the research community, *Behavioural and Cognitive Psychotherapy*, 27, 2: 103–16.

Hatton, C. (1998) Whose quality of life is it anyway? Some problems with the emerging quality of life consensus, *Mental Retardation*, 36: 104–15.

Kuhse, H. and Singer, P. (1985) *Should the Baby Live?* Oxford: Oxford University Press.

Ramsey, P. (1978) *Ethics at the Edges of Life*. New Haven, CT: Yale University Press.

CHAPTER 4

Quantitative and Qualitative Approaches

> Some, then, believe that [QOL] can only be assessed by asking the person directly (where possible); others doubt that such subjectivity is to be trusted, and prefer observable measures. Crudely: one school will want to ask how happy you are; the other will want to ask you or your guardians whether you have a job, a key to your house, and fresh linen every week, and will calculate your happiness from that. (Antaki and Rapley, 1996a)

Introduction – What is QOL Research for?

This chapter offers an overview of the major quantitative and qualitative approaches to QOL research. As is suggested by the quote from Antaki and Rapley (1996a) at the head of this chapter, and as we have seen elsewhere in Part 1, much, if not a majority, of QOL research is *not* primarily driven by a disinterested academic curiosity, but rather is functional or pragmatic. That is, across the social sciences, QOL research is conducted for a range of purposes, as Table 4.1 shows.

It is a basic principle in all social scientific work that the purposes of the research, and the specific research questions, should determine the methodology employed to seek answers. Another way to approach this is to remember that, as Edwards *et al.* (1995) put it, 'method is theory in disguise'. The adequacy of any research study is thus, to a greater or lesser extent, (pre)determined by the ability of the methodology adopted to provide sensible answers to the questions asked – and as we have already seen in Chapter 3, there are many QOL researchers (Hatton, 1998; Taylor, 1996; Wolfensberger, 1994; Rapley, 2001) who have raised serious questions about the ability of many of the research practices in the field to provide intellectually coherent answers to questions like 'what is quality of life?' Indeed, the final chapter of this book pursues this particular question – and its implications – in greater detail.

If we look at Table 4.1 it is apparent that there is a multiplicity of research questions, from disciplines as diverse as economics and health economics, nursing, epidemiology, medicine, disability studies, sociology and psychology, that can be brought together under the banner of 'QOL research'. In many cases, the methods by which answers are sought to the questions posed will often be determined by the dominant, or traditional, approach to research within the disciplinary field of study concerned. In most cases,

Table 4.1 Purposes of QOL research advanced in the literature

---

- Large-scale evaluation of effects of social policy (Baldwin *et al.*, 1990).
- To set a 'national agenda' for human services (Goode, 1994a).
- To assist in the 'process which defines some individuals in society as deserving and others as undeserving ... who should live, and who will therefore die' (Baldwin *et al.*, 1990a: 3).
- Political activism (Rogers-Clarke, 1996; Farlinger, 1996; Brown, 2000).
- Developing a more sophisticated understanding of the historical development of particular societies (Jordan, 1998, 2001).
- Developing a more sophisticated understanding of contemporary societies and social problems (Navarro and Shi, 2001).
- Promotion of human rights and equitable distribution of resources (OECD, 2001).
- Comparative evaluation of different models of human service provision or therapeutic methods (Emerson and Hatton, 1994; Bonicatto *et al.*, 2001).
- To direct research, training and service development funding to specific 'needy' areas (Sprangers *et al.*, 2000).
- To guide macro-level decisions about resource allocation (Fayers and Bjordal, 2001).
- Clinical governance (Carr *et al.*, 2001).
- Clinical audit and systematic review of quality of medical care (Higginson, 1993) and residential services (Keith and Schalock, 2000).
- To provide 'the ultimate criterion of the effectiveness of social care delivery' (Perry and Felce, 1995: 1).
- Staff training in medical and nursing settings (Maguire *et al.*, 1996).
- To direct professional focus onto 'patient-related' rather than technical aspects of health care (Higginson and Carr, 2001).
- To intervene in staff value systems to promote choice, independence and lifestyle of service recipients (Brown, 1997).
- To provide a common language for service providers (Schalock and Keith, 2000).
- To assist staff in human services to provide a more individually-centred service (Butterworth *et al.*, 1997).
- To screen for patients' 'hidden problems' in medical settings (Higginson and Carr, 2001).
- Provision of an opportunity for 'consumers' to provide feedback on matters of concern to them (Bryant *et al.*, 2001).
- To enable ideologically progressive coalitions between professionals and service users (Schalock *et al.*, 2000; Schalock, 1997).
- Refinement of theoretical models of quality of life and development of more sensitive measurement approaches (Cummins, 1995; 1997b).
- Development of clearer understandings of the meaning of the term 'quality of life' and its relation to cultural theories of 'being human' (Rose, 1992; Rapley and Ridgway, 1998; McHoul and Rapley, 2001).

---

the approach will be primarily *quantitative*: that is 'amounts' of QOL will in some manner be measured. Increasingly, however, *qualitative* approaches to a number of these questions are being put forward.

Research questions can also be distinguished in terms of their *level of analysis* (Schalock, 1996): thus QOL research concerned with the large-scale evaluation of social policy (Baldwin *et al.*, 1990), to set a 'national agenda' for human services (Goode, 1994a), to contribute to developing a more sophisticated understanding of contemporary societies and social problems (Navarro and Shi, 2001) or which aims to inform the promotion of human rights and equitable distribution of resources (OECD, 2001) is clearly operating at a societal, or *macro*, level of analysis. Studies that look at matters such as clinical governance, audit and the systematic review of the quality of medical care (Carr *et al.*, 2001; Higginson, 1993) or the effectiveness of social care residential services (Perry and Felce, 1995) may be described as operating at an intermediate, or *meso*, level of analysis. At the *micro*, or individual, level of analysis, QOL research can be concerned with assisting staff in human services to provide a more individual-centred service (Butterworth *et al.*, 1997), screening for patients' 'hidden problems' (Higginson and Carr, 2001) and offering 'consumers' of various medical or social care services the opportunity to provide feedback on matters of concern to them (Bryant *et al.*, 2001). Some studies – for example those refining theoretical models of QOL and developing measurement approaches (Cummins *et al.*, 1997, 1997a) – may span levels of analysis.

As is also evident from Table 4.1, there are other questions that do not fall neatly into these 'levels of analysis'. For example, work which seeks to develop a more sophisticated understanding of the historical development of life quality in particular societies (Jordan, 1998, 2001) and work that tries to understand how the very idea of 'QOL research' has come to be possible in the first place (Rose, 1992; Rapley and Ridgway, 1998, McHoul and Rapley, 2001) cannot be fitted into such a conceptualization. Such work may rather be described as 'metatheoretical' or philosophical and draws more naturally on techniques from disciplines such philosophy, history or cultural studies.

While there are good reasons for regarding the qualitative–quantitative dichotomy as in many ways misleading, it serves present purposes. In particular this difference serves to keep in focus two of the issues raised in Chapter 3 – 'whose quality of life is it anyway?' and the closely related question – 'to whom do QOL research results belong?' It is primarily in qualitative work that the ethics of method have been explicitly debated, and particularly the question of whether research in general, and QOL research in particular, is in the best interests of the people who researchers often refer to as 'subjects', and without whose cooperation research could not be conducted. In response to such questions, a considerable body of qualitative QOL research is, more or less explicitly, allied to the 'emancipatory' research paradigm (Oliver, 1996) which adopts as one of its goals advocacy on behalf of particular groups. Such a stance shows up very clearly a major difference between qualitative and quantitative approaches – broadly speaking – in that whereas quantitative research methods operate on the assumption that research should be characterized by objectivity, neutrality and an apolitical position, many, but not all, qualitative approaches hold that such notions cannot stand up to scrutiny (see, for example, Edwards *et al.*, 1995).

As such many qualitative researchers hold that 'subjective' factors influence everything from the choice of research questions to the preference for one 'objective' operational definition over another – not to mention which studies eventually get published (see for example Schrecker *et al's.*, 2001, discussion of 'mental illness prevention' research). 'Neutrality' is simply not an accurate description of how the 'hard' sciences, let alone the social s ciences, work, particularly given the tendency for 'awkward' statistics to be unreported or explained away – even in studies of the QOL of patients taking part in randomized controlled trials of cardiovascular and oncology treatments listed in the prestigious Cochrane Register (Sanders *et al.*, 1998) – or for favourable statistical results to be selectively reported (McNamee and Horton, 1996) (see Potter 1996, especially Chapter 1, for a discussion of social studies of science) and that claims of an apolitical stance are simply to take a political stand with the status quo by refusing to question it (Barnes *et al.*, 1999; Finkelstein, 1993; Goodley, 1996).

On account of these *political* differences about epistemology proponents of qualitative and quantitative approaches to QOL research are frequently dismissive of each other's contribution. Many quantitative researchers mistakenly conflate *quantification* with *empirical analysis*. In this Chapter I outline major qualitative and quantitative approaches to QOL and demonstrate empirically rigorous work using a range of qualitative approaches drawn from ethnomethodology, conversation analysis and discourse analysis.[1] As space precludes more than an overview of the key issues, a range of texts which detail the nuts and bolts of specific approaches (for instance guides to particular quantitative statistical methods such as factor analysis and introductory level texts in qualitative areas such as conversation analysis) is included in the *Resources* section at the end of the book.

The aim of the chapter then is to offer an overview of the costs and benefits of various approaches, and to illustrate the methodological and conceptual issues with discussions of empirical work in the literature. Conversation analytic work on the administration of structured QOL interviews (Antaki and Rapley, 1996a, 1996b; Rapley and Antaki, 1996) illustrates the use of interview methods. Work on the QOL perceptions of adults with intellectual disabilities (Alderson, 2001) expands on this issue and also demonstrates the design and conduct of studies using discourse analytic methodology in QOL research.

Quantitative approaches are discussed via a description of two widely used psychometric measures of QOL and with reference to issues of rater and inter-rater reliability, particularly reliability in situations of proxy response. Again, these conceptual and methodological issues are illustrated with a discussion of empirical data bearing on the questions in the literature, and by the description and analysis of model studies approaching these questions.

Quantitative Approaches to QOL Research

Cummins (1996: 303) suggests that 'there are two basic approaches to the definition and measurement of subjective quality of life ... One regards the construct as a single, unitary entity, while the other considers it to be composed of discrete domains.' As we have seen in Chapters 1 and 2, this has prompted a considerable body of work attempting to specify the QOL of nation-states as an *aggregate*, or sum, of quanta of various material circumstances and/or reports of citizens' levels of satisfaction with their circumstances or their happiness as a whole. Similarly, at the individual level, there is an immense number of quantitative measures of QOL which vary in both their degree of generality/specificity, and in terms of the explicitness of the link between the items they measure and their theoretical base.

What quantitative approaches share is an insistence that the theoretical model of QOL adopted and the research design which follows from it must be congruent; that item selection in questionnaire design should be guided by empirical studies; that any QOL measure should demonstrate psychometric reliability and validity; and that studies of QOL should *triangulate* the construct with other theoretically congruent measures or relevant supplementary variables. As is evident from Table 4.2, however, much quantitative research – at least as reported in the medical literature – fails to meet even these basic criteria of statistical and study design adequacy.

The relation of theoretical models of QOL to research design is illustrated in this chapter by an overview of instruments designed to measure the QOL of nations, and a discussion of two key quantitative instruments for the measurement of individual quality of life. Cummins's ComQol and the World Health Organization's WHOQOL (Appendix 2) are examined here. ComQol was selected as it is an exemplary individual-level measure that theorizes QOL as a *universal* construct, and the WHOQOL was selected as it represents an exemplary health-related QOL instrument developed and promulgated by a major international agency. Field studies using both of these measures are discussed in Chapter 7, which also considers the triangulation of QOL with other measures.

In the first half of this chapter, issues of the reliability of QOL measures are addressed in *quantitative terms*, via a discussion of studies examining the inter-rater reliability of persons and their proxies on psychometric measures. The questionable reliability and validity of individual measures is also illustrated in the second part of this chapter by the use of *qualitative* research methods.

Measures to assess the QOL of nations

The approach adopted by the ABS is an exemplary illustration of the

Table 4.2 Most common flaws in QOL research studies in the medical literature

- Trials involving QOL measurement are not comparative.
- Sample size is not justified and is either too small to have statistical power, or too large, leading to statistical significance in the absence of clinical relevance.
- The QOL measure used is idiosyncratic, not validated and/or has not had its responsiveness assessed.
- No follow-up data on patients is provided.
- No description is provided of sample attrition and/or of the handling of missing data.
- Presentation of QOL results is flawed – for example, graphs are presented with no values given or standard deviations of scores in different domains of quality of life are omitted.
- Confidence intervals and/or effect sizes for differences between conditions are not presented.
- Levels of significance adopted do not take account of the number of comparisons performed, leading to false positive results.
- The clinical relevance of statistical changes in measured QOL are not discussed.

Source: Chassany et al. (1999).

explicit specification of the relationship between the theory of QOL adopted and the design of (a set of) measures to quantify it. The ABS (2001: 6) states that:

> individual wellbeing can be measured using people's subjective evalua- tion of themselves, based on their feelings, or by collating any number of observable attributes that reflect on their wellbeing. In some ways, wellbeing might best be assessed subjectively, as it is strongly associated with notions of happiness and life satisfaction. Thus personal wellbeing might be measured in terms of how happy or satisfied people are with their life or with aspects of their life (their job, health, etc.). While such measures can be difficult to interpret, subjective measures, as with other statistics, can be aggregated and monitored over time, and, in theory, provide a picture of the nation's view as to whether living conditions are getting better or worse.

This clear theoretical statement (based as it is in a recognizably 'American' conceptualization of QOL) thus underpins the selection by the ABS of the 'areas of concern' (Family and Community, Health, Education and Training, Work, Economic Resources, Housing, Crime and Justice, Culture and Leisure) that they specify as measures of the QOL in Australia. Unfortunately, as we saw in Chapter 2, not all such measures derive their indices so directly (if at all) from an explicit theory of quality of life.

However, in their review of 22 indexes proposed as measures of well-being for national policy formulation and evaluation, Hagerty *et al.* suggest that 'only recently have we had the resources and the science to begin measuring the "good life" and how it arises' (2001: 1) and suggest 14 criteria (Table 4.3) for evaluating such indices.

As reinventing the wheel serves little purpose, it is sufficient to note here that, for quantitative studies at population levels, meeting these standards should be considered the necessary and sufficient criteria for the use of *any* quantitative measure in QOL research. It is also clear that, with slight modifications, these criteria can also be held to apply to measures of the QOL of individuals – as is shown in Table 4.4.

However, it is important to recognize that while many of these criteria for the 'validity and usefulness of such QOL indexes to public policy' are eminently reasonable, others are problematic. Firstly, it must be noticed that these criteria mix those that can sensibly apply at the population level (for example, Criterion 3: 'The index should be based on time series to allow periodic monitoring and control') with those that are equally clearly only applicable to persons (Veenhoven, 1996) (for example, Criterion 14: 'The subjective dimension of each domain has both a cognitive and an affective component. They are measured by questions concerning "satisfaction"'. It is difficult to imagine that the economy of Bolivia has either a cognitive or an affective component, even though individual Bolivians may well get emotional about the GDP. Secondly, the existence of a real, universally meaningful, QOL construct 'out there' to be measured, is presumed, regardless of social and cultural differences around the globe (as is clearly implied by notions such as a construct needing to encompass

Table 4.3 Necessary and sufficient criteria for measures of the quality of life of nations

1. The index must have a clear practical purpose.
2. The index should help public policy-makers develop and assess programmes at all levels of aggregation.
3. The index should be based on time series to allow periodic monitoring and control.
4. The index should be grounded in well-established theory.
5. The components of the index should be reliable, valid and sensitive.
6. The index should be reported as a single number, but can be broken down into components.
7. The domains in aggregate must encompass the totality of life experience.
8. Each domain must encompass a substantial but discrete portion of the QOL construct.
9. Each domain must have the potential to be measured in both objective and subjective dimensions.
10. Each domain within a generic QOL instrument must have relevance for most people.
11. If a specific domain is proposed for a non-generic instrument, it must be demonstrated to contribute unique variance to the QOL construct beyond the generic domains for the target group.
12. Domains must be potentially neutral, positive or negative in their contribution to the QOL construct.
13. Domains must differ from the dimensions of personality, cognitive processes and affect in that they cannot be measured objectively.
14. The subjective dimension of each domain has both a cognitive and an affective component. They are measured by questions concerning 'satisfaction'.

Source: Hagerty et al. (2001: 1–11).

Table 4.4 Necessary qualities of individual-level QOL measures

Issue	Sub-type	Questions
Validity	Face	Does the measure cover issues that are clearly relevant to its users, for example, 'patients', professionals and carers?
	Construct	Does the measure show theoretically congruent relationships with other measures of the construct? For example, if a QOL measure is based on a theory of QOL that suggests work is an important domain, do scores on the measure correlate with respondents' employment status?
	Discrimination	Does the measure discriminate between groups in a manner consistent with the theory underlying it?
	Content	Does the measure contain domains/items that are pertinent to the study population?
Reliability	Test-retest	Do repeat administrations of the measure produce comparable results, all else being equal?
	Inter-rater	Do separate raters arrive at the same QOL judgments?
	Internal consistency	High levels of internal consistency imply reliability but also a degree of item redundancy.
Appropriateness		Is the measure well-validated?
		Is the format and content of the measure appropriate to the intended study group? Are the items well-phrased and conceptually clear? For example, if a measure is to be used with persons with an intellectual disability, is the level of complexity of the items appropriate?
		Is the measure both sufficiently brief, and sufficiently comprehensive, to avoid respondent fatigue and to capture all necessary information?
		Has the measure been used in the current setting before and with what results?
		If the measure is a translation or from another culture, what steps have been taken to ensure local comparability?
Sensitivity		Is the measure sufficiently sensitive to detect changes that are meaningful in relation to the study?
		For example, do changes in service/treatment practice which would be expected to produce changes in QOL scores actually do so?
Interpretabilty		Does the manual for the measure provide comprehensive data on reliability, validity and other trials of its use?
		Are comparative and/or normative data available?
		Can the results of the measure be readily translated into implications for individual treatment, service practice or policy development?

Source: Adapted from Higginson and Carr (2001).

'the totality of life experience', Criterion 7). Studies critical of this idea are discussed in the second part of this chapter.

Two measures: the WHOQOL-BREF and the comprehensive quality of life scales (ComQOL)

As we saw in Chapter 2 (p. 50), the WHOQOL Group (1993) defines QOL as a multidimensional concept and has developed the WHOQOL such that the structure of the instrument reflects both their theoretical definition of QOL and also 'the issues that a group of scientific experts as well as lay people in each of the field centers felt were important to quality of life' (WHO, 1997: 3). The WHOQOL-100 measures six domains of quality of life, with 24 facets (see Table 4.5). Each facet is measured by the use of four items scored on a five-point scale. A study examining the validity of the WHOQOL-100 with people diagnosed with 'depression' (Skevington and Wright, 2001) is discussed in Chapter 7.

The WHOQOL-BREF consists of 26 questions, comprising one item from each of the 24 facets (or dimensions) of QOL as operationalized in the 100-item scale, with the addition of two single items to measure 'overall quality of life' and 'general health'. Items chosen were selected on the basis of their correlation with facet total scores (WHOQOL Group, 1998).

The six domains of QOL identified in the WHOQOL-100 are cut down to four in the short form, as the WHOQOL Group state that 'recent analysis of available data, using structural equation modelling, has shown a four domain solution to be more appropriate' (WHOQOL Group, 1996: 7). The four-factor solution reported by the WHOQOL Group (1998), and which represents the theoretical structure of the BREF instrument, explains 58 per cent of the total variance of scores on the measure, but Hagerty *et al.* (2001) note that even in this reduced factor structure there are a high number of complex loadings (that is, items load onto more than one factor). They suggest that 'using the authors' criterion for facet inclusion as a loading >.3, Factor 1 ('health') contains eight facets and one that cross-loaded (7/8 non-complex facets), Factor 2 comprises (5/9), Factor 3 comprises (3/8), and Factor 4 comprises (2/6). It seems clear that only the first factor can be asserted with confidence' (Hagerty *et al.*, 2001: 18). These authors also raise questions about the comparability of the WHOQOL Group's reported confirmatory four-factor model and their prior principal components analysis. For example, they note that two of the 'psychological' items, 'positive feelings' and 'negative feelings', load onto single factors, but that these factors are *different*. Similarly, they point out that the 'bodily image and appearance' item loads, statistically, onto the 'social relationships' domain in the preliminary analyses, but is included in the 'psychological' domain in the confirmatory model.

In their summary of the adequacy of the WHOQOL instruments against the 14 criteria they propose, Hagerty *et al.*, (2001) are highly critical. While

Table 4.5 WHOQOL-BREF domains

Domain	Facets incorporated within domains
1. Physical health	Activities of daily living Dependence on medicinal substances and medical aids Energy and fatigue Mobility Pain and discomfort Sleep and rest Work capacity
2. Psychological/bodily image and appearance	Negative feelings Positive feelings Self-esteem Spirituality/religion/personal beliefs Thinking, learning, memory and concentration
3. Social relationships	Personal relationships Social support Sexual activity
4. Environment	Financial resources Freedom, physical safety and security Health and social care: accessibility and quality Home environment Opportunities for acquiring new information and skills Participation in and opportunities for recreation/leisure activities Physical environment (pollution/noise/traffic/climate) Transport

Source: World Health Organization (1996).

the WHO instruments are exemplary in their specification of an operational definition of QOL, it appears that this, in and of itself, is far from adequate as a guide to subsequent instrument development. It appears that item selection has been guided by other factors in addition to the existing empirical literature and, indeed, the statistical analyses the WHO conducted as part of instrument field trials. The theoretical model of QOL derived from the (common-sense) views of 'experts and lay people' appears at least as powerful a determinant of item facet placement as the powerful statistical techniques applied to the data. It is instructive that a scientific instrument developed by an international organization as well resourced and respected as the WHO should be described as follows. Hagerty *et al.,* (2001) state of the entire WHOQOL project that:

this exercise has been flawed in that: (a) the authors did not use their vast array of data to deduce domains, but rather adopted the six domains they proposed at the outset; (b) the processes of data reduction to arrive at the 24 facets are opaque as far as published material is concerned, and evidence is now available to cast doubt on the adequacy of assumed facet content; and (c) three of the four domains forming the WHOQOL-100 and BREF contain considerable cross-loading facets ... the weakest of the four domains is social relationships, and yet there is a high level of agreement within the QOL literature that this domain is preeminent in its contribution to the life quality of most people ... In summary, at this stage of its development, the WHOQOL cannot be recommended as a scale to measure overall QOL. (Hagerty et al., 2001: 19–20)

Cummins's comprehensive quality of life scales (ComQOL)

These parallel scales were developed by Cummins and his colleagues at Deakin University. Work on their development is described in Cummins (1995, 1996, 1997a). As we have seen in Chapter 2, Cummins defines QOL as both objective and subjective, with QOL the aggregate of seven domains: Material well-being, Health, Productivity, Intimacy, Safety, Community and Emotional well-being. Accordingly, the ComQOL scales (parallel forms exist, for example, for people with and without intellectual disabilities) include measures of the seven domains specified in Cummins's definition. Cummins (1996) reports a detailed semantic and psychometric analysis of over 170 proposed QOL domains in the literature which, he suggests, can be reduced to the seven domains he operationalizes as his definition and measure of QOL. Cummins (1996: 307–8) notes that the seven domains of ComQOL capture 83 per cent of the reported domain descriptions cited in the 32 studies analysed.

Each domain of the ComQOL scales has three objective and two subjective measures. The three objective measures for each domain are summed, and the domain sums, when aggregated, provide a unitary measure of objective well-being. One of the subjective measures of each domain is a satisfaction measure (a seven-point item measured on a 'delightful/terrible' scale), and an importance measure (presented as a five-point item). The product of the satisfaction multiplied by the importance score for each domain provides a measure of the subjective QOL represented by the domain, and the seven products sum to obtain a single measure of subjective well-being. The conceptual structure of ComQOL is presented in Table 4.6.

Cummins admits that the ComQOL is not based on a single theory of QOL (Hagerty et al., 2001). Instead he offers a range of theoretical arguments and selected empirical observations in support of his position. For example, his justification of the use of satisfaction × importance scores as indices of QOL is explicitly based on the work of Andrews and Withey (1976). However, extensive and solid psychometric studies of the ComQOL scales have been reported. In terms of internal consistency, for example, Cummins (1997a:

Table 4.6 Conceptual framework for the ComQOL

The instrument is based on the following propositions:

- Quality of life (QOL) can be described in both objective (O) and subjective (S) terms.
- Each objective (OQOL) and subjective (SQOL) axis is composed of seven domains:
    1. Material well-being
    2. Health
    3. Productivity
    4. Intimacy
    5. Safety
    6. Place in community
    7. Emotional well-being
- The measurement of each OQOL domain is achieved by obtaining an aggregate score based on the measurement of three objective indices relevant to that domain. For example, 'material well-being' is measured by an aggregate score of income, type of accommodation and personal possessions.
- The measurement of each SQOL domain is achieved by obtaining a satisfaction score of that domain which is weighted by the perceived importance of the domain for the individual. Thus SQOL = Σ (Domain satisfaction $\times$ Domain importance).

Source: Cummins (1997: 8–9).

45–8) reports Cronbach alphas for the ComQOL of $\alpha = 0.54$ for the sum of the objective measures, $\alpha = 0.65$ to 0.69 for the sum of importance measures, and $\alpha = 0.73$ to 0.81 for the sum of satisfaction measures. Test/retest reliability correlations are reported at 0.60 for the sum of importance and 0.36 for the sum of satisfaction measures. In terms of convergent validity, the ComQOL also performs well. For example, the ComQOL subjective health sub-scale correlates with the MOS Short Form 36 (SF-36) Physical Functioning scale at $r = 0.45$ and with the SF-36 Mental Health scale at $r = 0.60$ (Cummins, 1997a: 50).

It is also a helpful feature that a range of parallel forms exist to measure the QOL of, for example, people with intellectual disabilities using items directly comparable to those in the general adult form of the ComQOL. As Cummins (1998) notes, measures such as Schalock and Keith's (1993) *QOL.Q*, and the immensity of disease-specific QOL measures, have been designed for specific population sub-groups such as people with intellectual disabilities, people with acne or children and, strictly, cannot be used to make comparisons with the general adult population. Cummins (1997a: 6) notes that 'this is an important limitation since it means that the QOL experienced by such groups cannot be norm-referenced back to the general population'. As yet, the ComQOL has not been as widely used as its psychometric properties deserve. It is possible that this is due to both the length of the scale and to the complex pre-testing procedure involved in the intellectual disability parallel form.

Inter-rater reliability and proxy responses in QOL measurement

In the assessment of the adequacy of any quantitative measure, it is a canonical requirement that the instrument should produce the same results when applied to the same item by separate raters. If two people use the same ruler to measure the same piece of wood and one returns a measurement of six centimetres and the other nine centimetres, all else being equal, one would have grounds for concern about the precision of the measuring device. Such a measure would not have a high level of inter-rater reliability. The same requirement holds for all psychometric measures, including those of QOL.

In the area of much individual-level QOL research, however, matters are complicated by the fact that researchers often want to collect information about the QOL of people who find it difficult to provide accounts of their views: for example people with severe intellectual disabilities, people with dementing conditions, children or other 'patient' groups who are believed to be unreliable reporters on how they 'really' feel – for example, people in receipt of psychiatric services. In these cases the question becomes one of assessing the level of agreement between 'patients' and proxies answering on their behalf – carers, doctors, nursing staff and the like.

In general the literature suggests that when QOL is defined in objective terms, that is in terms of matters that can be readily observed by others (for example memberships of clubs and societies in the *QOL.Q* (Schalock and Keith, 1996) and the *ComQOL-ID* (Cummins, 1997a)) or the presence/absence of physical problems (for example the *Children's Quality of Life Questionnaire – TACQOL* (Vogels *et al.*, 1998)), agreement both between independent raters and also between professionals or carers as proxies and people themselves tends to be reasonably high. The literature is also clear that when QOL is defined either in subjective terms, or when subjective aspects of lived experience are included as domains of a composite measure, the picture is much less rosy. It seems to be the case that a task that Lovett (1993: 3) termed 'guessing at another's comfort' is indeed a problematic exercise.

For example, Sawyer *et al.* (1999) report a study comparing child/patient and parent ratings of HRQOL for adolescents undergoing treatment for cancer. Seventy adolescents (aged 10 to 18 years) and their parents completed what are described as 'standard' HRQOL question-naires. Participants completed the Child Health Questionnaire (Landgraf *et al.*, 1996),[2] the Functional Status II(R) Questionnaire (Stein and Jessop, 1990, 1991),[3] and the Impact-on-Family Scale (Stein and Riessman, 1980).[4] In general, the study found that there was good agreement between parent and adolescent HRQOL reports. However, parents of adolescents receiving active treatment for cancer reported that their child's illness was having a greater impact on their child's physical functioning, social and school activities than was reported by the adolescents themselves. Adolescents reported significantly higher scores for themselves than their parents did on the Child Health Questionnaire Role/Social-Physical and Self-Esteem scales. Sawyer *et al.* (1999: 43) concluded that:

despite generally good agreement between parent and adolescent reports … it cannot be assumed that reports from parents are always an accurate reflection of the views of the adolescents. Studies examining the influence of independent factors on adolescents' HRQL must take into account differences in reports from these 2 informants and the possibility that key independent variables have differing relationships with the various domains which comprise adolescents' HRQL.

Similarly, Shaw *et al.* (2000) examined the agreement between proxies and older people with 'objective' issues of continence management. Their study examined the concordance of proxy responses and index respondents (women aged 65 years and older with neck of femur fractures) on issues around continence five days following surgery. Index respondents nominated a proxy respondent who was interviewed using the same schedule. Responses were compared using percentage agreement and Cohen's Kappa statistic. For questions relating to functional ability, Shaw *et al.* (2000) found that proxy responses were more reliable for personal care activities than for activities of daily living. They suggest that this result may be a consequence of instrumental activities questions being more ambiguous and open to individual interpretation. Interestingly, the study found that the more distant the relationship, and the lower the level of contact between staff and index respondents, the better the agreement found. However, proxy responses were found to be systematically biased, with their responses suggesting an *overestimation* of functional incapacity. Good concordance was found for questions directly addressing urinary and faecal incontinence, but fell for more detailed questions concerning the timing and frequency of incontinence. Shaw *et al.* (2000) attribute this higher level of disagreement to the use for these questions of graded response options rather than simple yes/no responses.

As with elderly people, in services for people with intellectual disabilities, proxy responses have often been employed to gauge QOL. The manuals for both of the most extensively psychometrically validated intellectual disability QOL measures, the QOL.Q (Schalock *et al.*, 1990; Schalock and Keith, 1996) and the ComQOL-ID (Cummins, 1997a), acknowledge that it may be necessary for staff members, or other significant persons, to act as proxy respondents, to complete the questionnaire 'as if they were the person'. Equally, both questionnaires recognize that this procedure is fraught with difficulty. However, if the vicarious – or proxy – feedback of more severely impaired service users is to be employed in service evaluation studies, then it is important that some measure of the success of staff members as proxy respondents be demonstrated. 'Success' in this context has usually been conceived of as the level of agreement between two independent members of staff; in other words staff–staff reliability.

Success in this respect is, however, an index of only limited utility. It is quite conceivable that staff responses may be highly reliable, yet also at considerable variance from the 'true' opinion of the service user. Clearly with non-verbal individuals there is no possibility of estimating the existence or extent of such possible discrepancies. However, the extent to which a measure supports consensual understandings of items across staff and participant groups can be estimated. In this sense success can also be construed as the extent to which staff and verbal participants agree on responses to items. The assumption underlying this procedure is that if staff members can assess, reasonably accurately, the QOL judgments of *verbal* individuals, then this ability will also hold true for *non-verbal* participants. The inferential step here is a large one. However, it seems reasonable to suggest that if a measure can be shown to elicit at least minimally acceptable levels of staff–participant concordance, then the confidence which can be placed in staff–staff reliability coefficients for non-verbal individuals would be correspondingly raised. Low correlations between the ratings of staff and verbal participants would suggest that evaluative judgments based on proxy respondents must be considered as deeply suspect.

Cummins (1997a) noted that proxy response data for the ComQOL-ID are very unreliable. A study reported by Reiter and Bendov (1996) likewise reported low correlations between staff and participant ratings on the QOL.Q (coefficients of between 0.26 and 0.31 for the Satisfaction, Competence/Productivity and Social Belonging/Community Integration factors) and a very low correlation coefficient ($r = 0.07$) between staff and service users on the Empowerment/Independence factor, with staff members consistently rating the quality of residents' lives more favourably than the residents themselves.

Rapley et al. (1998) report a similar study to those of Reiter and Bendov (1996) and Shaw et al. (2000) designed to assess the ability of the QOL.Q to support proxy responding. In the Rapley et al. (1998) reliability studies 13 pairs took part in the staff–client study and for the staff–staff study two members of staff completed the QOL.Q for 33 supported housing participants and a further 33 service users living in an institution, giving a total sample size of 66. For the staff–participant reliability study the QOL.Q was completed as a structured interview in the person's home.

Analysis of the data was conducted in three stages. Because of the small sample size for the staff–participant reliability study non-parametric statistics were used. Firstly Pearson Product Moment correlation coefficients between staff members' scores were computed and, secondly, relationships between individual proxy respondents and 'their' participants' scores were calculated. Thirdly, with the larger sample, the relation-

Table 4.7 Staff–staff reliability for the QOL.Q ($n = 63$)

Factor		Respondent	
Satisfaction	Staff 2	p value	r^2
Staff 1	0.877	0.001	0.76
Competence			
Staff 1	0.825	0.001	0.68
Empowerment			
Staff 1	0.881	0.001	0.77
Social Belonging			
Staff 1	0.829	0.001	0.68
QOL.Q total			
Staff 1	0.886	0.001	0.78

Source: Rapley et al. (1998).

ship between the proxy responses and participants' scores was analysed using t-tests for related samples.

The results showed that staff–staff reliability coefficients were comparable to those obtained by Schalock et al. (1990). Percentage predictive variance (r^2) values are high. Table 4.7 shows the correlation coefficients found, and their associated p values. As is apparent all correlation values are high, with significance being achieved at $p < 0.01$.

For the staff–participant reliability study staff–staff reliability coefficients for the proxy respondents, coefficients obtaining between participants' scores and the mean proxy response (the value Schalock et al. (1990) recommend be reported) and staff–participant reliability coefficients are shown in Table 4.8.

As can be seen in Table 4.8, with the exception of the Empowerment factor, the QOL.Q achieves a respectable level of staff–participant agreement. For the Empowerment factor the results suggest that staff and participants show a statistically non-significant, but serious, level of disagreement with each other. Staff proxies' scores, while being positively correlated, are also not closely related. Inspection of raw data revealed that the disagreement was accounted for by a pattern of disagreement in the context of a general staff overestimation of scores. In 9 of the 13 cases both staff members' scores on Empowerment were higher than those of participants. In general, staff–staff agreement appeared to be moderately stronger than staff–participant agreement.

Rapley et al. (1998) point out that, if proxy's scores are to be used to estimate participant's scores, two criteria must be satisfied. The first criterion is that *score reliability* is high; the second criterion is that the *mean scores* obtained from the two measures are *roughly equal*. Clearly, one could have perfect reliability, yet at the same time find that staff estimates of participant QOL are far higher than the participant's own estimates. Table

Table 4.8 Staff–participant and staff–staff reliability for the QOL.Q (n = 13)

Factor	Participant (r)	p	Staff 2 (r)	p
Respondent				
Satisfaction	Participant (r)	p	Staff 2 (r)	p
Staff 1	0.733	0.004	0.905	0.001
Staff 2	0.820	0.001		
Mean staff	0.765	0.002		
Competence				
Staff 1	0.651	0.016	0.962	0.001
Staff 2	0.648	0.016		
Mean staff	0.653	0.015		
Empowerment				
Staff 1	−0.268	0.343	0.159	0.603
Staff 2	−0.361	0.224		
Mean staff	−0.428	0.144		
Social Belonging				
Staff 1	0.694	0.008	0.746	0.003
Staff 2	0.628	0.022		
Mean staff	0.710	0.007		
QOL.Q total				
Staff 1	0.820	0.001	0.901	0.001
Staff 2	0.785	0.001		
Mean staff	0.823	0.001		

Source: Rapley et al. (1998).

Table 4.9 Comparison of staff and participant mean scores by factor and total QOL.Q score (n = 13, df = 12)

Factor	Staff mean	Participant mean	t-value	1-tailed p
Satisfaction	22.6	23.7	−1.75	0.05
Competence/ Productivity	13.2	14.1	−0.78	0.22
Empowerment/ Independence	25.0	23.5	1.38	0.09
Social Belonging/ Comm. Integ.	22.1	19.4	3.53	0.01
QOL.Q total	82.1	80.8	0.83	0.21

Source: Rapley et al. (1998).

4.9 shows mean scores from staff and participants on each factor of the QOL.Q and the results of paired-sample t-tests, comparing staff mean vs. participant mean scores.

The inter-rater reliability data reported above suggested a worrying level of disagreement between staff and participants on the Empowerment factor. Data on mean scores suggest further causes for concern. As Table 4.9 shows, marginally significant differences in staff and participants' mean scores on the Empowerment factor were obtained. These results suggest that staff and participants' scores are also likely to show statistically significant differences on other factors. Inspection of the raw data for Social Belonging scores again showed a pattern of staff overestimations of participant scores in 11 out of 13 cases. Satisfaction results showed the opposite pattern, however. Here staff overestimated participant's scores in only four instances.

Staff–staff correlation coefficients seem to be consistently positive and statistically significant across the studies. Similarly, a cursory examination of the staff–participant reliability coefficients, with the exception of the extremely poor result for the Empowerment factor, would seem to suggest that staff proxies can make reasonably accurate judgments on behalf of participants. Reliability for the other factors is acceptable. The correlations suggest that for these factors, the measure elicits relatively accurate perceptions of participants' own QOL judgments by staff that know them well. Further analysis indicates, however, that this appearance of agreement is deceptive. In and of themselves, the marginal correlation result for the Competence factor and the poor agreement between staff and participants' scores on the Empowerment factor, replicating the Reiter and Bendov (1996) result, are cause for concern, particularly given staff overestimation of participant's judgments. Such a view is strengthened by the differences obtained in the analysis of mean scores on the Satisfaction and, particularly, on the Social Belonging factors. Here, although apparently in agreement and with highly correlated scores, staff and participants show statistically significant differences in mean scores, and very different patterns of response to items.

These results add weight to the view expressed in the literature that the use of proxy responses to QOL measures is highly problematic (Cummins, 1996). Proxy administration must always raise the possibility of respondent bias (in human services, often in favour of positive outcomes). In this study, values for items pertaining to staff performance, or to circumstances over which staff may exercise some control, are likely to be inflated by staff proxy respondents. Items addressing more general satisfaction with life circumstances appear less at risk of such a bias, but here are at risk of staff underestimation. Indeed, Rapley et al. (1998) were moved to speculate whether staff might not be prone to 'gild the lily', to inflate some QOL scores and not others. Box 4.1 summarizes the key issues in the use of proxy response in QOL research.

Box 4.1 Summary of key points relating to proxy respondents and quality of life assessments

General factors	Factors related to the person	Factors related to the proxy
Agreement depends on the concreteness, visibility and importance of the aspects of quality of life under consideration.	People may not complete quality of life measures in ways that accurately reflect their feelings. For example, people may seek to answer questions in ways that present themselves favourably. This may be related to findings of lesser agreement between respondents and proxies.	The lay caregivers' experience of caring, the amount of time they spend with the person and their own distress may influence their assessment of the person's quality of life.
Agreement is better for concrete, observable aspects and less good for more subjective domains, such as emotional health.	Proxies have a better chance of accurately reflecting quality of life if people are open with them about their problems and feelings.	Lower quality of life scores have been associated with increases in the burden on the caregiver, time spent together, the carer's distress and with the carer having a lower quality of life.
Agreement may improve over time, but evidence is contradictory.	Agreement between respondents and proxies seems to be greater when quality of life is either very good or very poor.	Extent of agreement may be influenced by the relationship between the patient and proxy, although the evidence for this is limited.
	Although people with severe and profound intellectual disabilities may not be able to complete self-report measures, people with mild and moderate intellectual impairment can and do respond validly.	The psychometric properties of the measure are important: if the measure is unreliable, then high agreement cannot be expected.
		Health professionals may project their own feelings of hopelessness and distress onto the people when assessing their quality of life.

Source: Adapted from Addington-Hall and Kalra (2001).

In summary

Quantitative approaches have produced an extraordinary number of definitions and measures of QOL. Studies of the QOL of an immense diversity of population groups have been conducted, and published accounts run into the tens of thousands. At the level of the nation-state a number of statistical series have been established which appear to be theoretically grounded and methodologically sound. However, the quality of much of the individual-level research published, and the psychometric adequacy of many of the measures employed, are deeply questionable. Of current individual QOL measures, Cummins's ComQOL is probably the most robust generic measure and clearly has much potential. However, many questions still remain open: the issue of proxy response still awaits resolution, and inventive approaches to matters such as this will occupy the field for a considerable time to come. It is also the case, however, that many researchers view what Edgerton (1990) called the 'American passion' for quantification with considerable scepticism. It is to qualitative studies of QOL that we now turn.

Qualitative Approaches

> Exact sciences give correct answers to certain aspects of life problems, but very incomplete answers. It is important of course to count and measure what is countable and measurable, but the most precious values in human life are aspirations which laboratory experiments cannot yet reproduce. (Dubos, 1959: 279)

Interest in qualitative research methods has increased greatly in the last few years. Even disciplines which have modelled themselves upon the 'hard' sciences, such as psychology, have recognized that even the 'hard' sciences can be understood as 'socially constructed' (Potter, 1996); that there are issues about ownership of 'expertise' in what QOL 'is'; and that traditional measurement technologies may not only have hidden troubles, but also may misrepresent informants. However, qualitative research is not homogenous, and writers such as Silverman (1998) have identified the dangerous contribution much qualitative work also makes to romanticizing the idea of persons as beings with 'deep interiors' (Gergen, 1992: 208). As Silverman points out, much of this variety of qualitative work, which claims to document the 'authentic personal experience' of individuals, is not only neglectful of the locally produced nature of social order and subjectivity, but also relies on romanticized notions which allow researchers to retain their version of what is 'really' going on. Of course, what this variety of qualitative work thus manages to do is not only to rely on the sort of a priori assumptions about 'reality' which it criticizes quantitative work for, but also slips in the privileged position of the analyst through the back door (see proponents of 'critical realist' qualitative methods such as Parker, 1998).

Having said this, much qualitative work has started from a recognition expressed by Westerhof *et al.*'s (2001: 179) study of the QOL of older persons. They note that 'existing studies on subjective well-being and successful aging ... appear to focus too narrowly on life satisfaction at the expense of other personally meaningful dimensions of life judgments'. That is, much qualitative work adopts an 'emic' approach – attempting to understand QOL from the perspective of research informants. These approaches ask questions flowing from such a recognition: rather than asking 'etic' (or analyst's) questions such as 'is the QOL of Italians higher than the QOL of Australians' (Verri *et al.*, 1999), these studies will ask questions like 'how do Italians understand "quality of life"?' This type of study is taking an 'emic' approach, offering the perspective of participants an equal footing with the theoretical, epistemological and methodological 'expertise' of the researcher. Wallcraft and Michaelson (2001) put this position well (at the risk of incurring Silverman's disapproval) when they describe research participants as 'experts by experience'. Put simply, most qualitative work in the traditions discussed here would seek to pass what Potter calls the 'dead psychologist test', that is examine social interaction – for example discussions of the quality of life – that would have occurred *anyway*, even if the psychologist who wished to study it was no longer with us.

Epistemology, conversation and discourse analysis

Ethnomethodologically-inspired qualitative work starts from Sacks' (1992) insight that, in coming to understand a culture, one may assume that cultures show *order at all points*. Secondly, *that descriptions of activities, persons and their qualities* may be 'correct' in infinite ways. Schegloff (in Sacks, 1992: xlvi) describes the Sacksian position clearly:

> Sacks points out that [sampling] depends on the sort of order one takes it that the social world exhibits. An alternative to the possibility that order manifests itself at an aggregate level and is statistical in character is what he terms the 'order at all points' view. This view understands order not to be present only at aggregate levels and therefore subject to an overall differential distribution, but to be present in detail on a case by case, environment by environment basis. A culture is not then to be found only by aggregating all of its venues; it is substantially present in each of its venues.

Much qualitative work in conversation analysis, discourse analysis and discursive psychology follows Sacks' lead more or less closely (and without necessarily citing Sacks) in assuming that, in the examination of *fragments* of a culture (for example, how people talk about the quality of their lives), that which operates *across a culture as a whole* will come clearly into view. As such, quantitative concerns about sample sizes, representative sampling and so on do not assume importance in this work. Secondly, Sacks shows us that when we talk about matters of human experience there are, in principle, multiple 'correct' descriptors. Hence while it may be 'important ...to count and measure what is countable and measurable' much – though by no means all – qualitative work takes a *relativist* position towards the sort of 'exact' truth statements sought by quantitative methodologies (Edwards *et al.*, 1995; Edwards and Potter, 2001).

The third distinguishing feature of most qualitative work (with the notable exceptions of Content Analysis and much Grounded Theory (Glaser and Strauss, 1967) – see Willig, 2001; Richardson, 1996) is the insistence on the presentation of data for *the reader* to inspect (rather than just the end results in the form of p values and so on) to allow the reader to interrogate the adequacy of the analysis. The fourth and final core difference between quantitative and qualitative work is the criteria that are employed to gauge the quality of studies and the analyses they report. Unlike the lists of 14 criteria by which to assess psychometric measures we encountered earlier (Hagerty *et al.*, 2001), or publicly agreed standards for alpha values, inter-rater reliability coefficients and the like, the quality of qualitative work is judged against criteria of analytic rigour, fidelity to previous empirically-documented instances and aesthetic power (see Peräkylä, 1997). That is, unlike quantitative studies, the merit of qualitative work is judged in terms of the *persuasiveness of the argument* presented, rather than simply taking a suitably low probability value as making, and simultaneously closing, the case.

Interviews

Interviews (structured or semi-structured) with individual respondents, or in the form of group interviews (often known as 'focus groups' – see Puchta and Potter, 1999 and Puchta and Potter, forthcoming), are increasingly popular across the social sciences. This section considers the use that can be made of such methods and some of the difficulties with their use.

Alderson (2001) describes an exploratory study based on interviews with 40 adults who have congenital conditions for which prenatal tests are routinely conducted. In the published study, she reports detailed interview data from conversations with five adults with Down syndrome. Her study has been selected for inclusion here as an example of interview-based discourse analytic work for four reasons.

- Firstly, the study *directly addresses serious and important questions about the use of the QOL concept* – in this case the use of medical technologies to inform, literally, life and death decisions.

- Secondly, the study *questions everyday commonsense* – rather than respecifying it in academic terms. In this case, the study problematizes the view that prenatal testing is a 'good thing', and that the lives of people with Down syndrome are, inevitably, lives of lesser quality.
- Thirdly, the study problem is expressed with clarity, the implications of the research are placed in academic and applied contexts, and the *study design and methods of analysis are closely, explicitly and directly tied to the research questions* asked.
- Fourthly, the study explicitly recognizes the *limitations and difficulties* (both ethical and methodological) of the research approach adopted.

Alderson (2001) starts with the identification of the key research issue. That is, the taken-for-granted upshot of a positive amniocentesis result (for Down syndrome in this case) is the recommendation of selective abortion, on the assumption that affected foetuses will have a low quality of life. Alderson's study follows from the recognition that this *assumption* is exactly that, an *assumption*. The research question thus becomes, simply, 'how good is the evidence that Down syndrome inevitably leads to a low quality of life?' Alderson (2001: 627) states:

> Routine prenatal screening is based on the assumption that it is reasonable for prospective parents to choose to prevent a life with Down's Syndrome. This paper questions whether Down's Syndrome necessarily involves the costs, limitations and suffering which are assumed in the prenatal literature, and examines the lack of evidence about the value and quality of life with Down's Syndrome. Tensions between the aims of prenatal screening policies to support women's personal choices, prevent distress, and reduce the suffering and costs of disability, versus the inadvertent effects of screening which can undermine these aims, are considered.

The study is also exemplary in its clear specification of the procedural and ethical problems in conducting research in this area. Alderson (2001) notes that asking people questions about whether their parents had wanted them, or perhaps had been tempted to abort them, may be very distressing. She says (2001: 630), openly, that:

> I felt anxious about asking people, in effect: 'What are your views about the value and quality of your life? Do you feel your life is worth living? Did/do your parents want you and what might they have decided if prenatal tests had been available to them before you were born?' These sensitive questions were not asked directly, although several interviewees, including one with Down's syndrome, raised the later ones. Most of the 40 interviewees talked openly about screening, but those with Down's syndrome and spina bifida were most likely to express or imply distress about this topic, so that direct questions were more limited with them.

It is important, then, to recognize that despite the fact that 'official' questions on a structured interview schedule (or probes in a semi-structured protocol) do not *explicitly* ask 'did your parents want you?' interviewees are very likely to understand what they are, 'in effect', being asked. As we saw in Chapter 3, while some think that people with an intellectual disability are incapable of validly responding to interviews or questionnaires (Heal and Sigelman, 1990), Alderson's respondents, like Bob and Arthur, demonstrate to the contrary that they are well aware of the underlying agenda.

Alderson goes on to show how, by the use of semi-structured interviews – rather than, say, a fixed response questionnaire – the methodology of the study was directly driven by the aim of the research:

> [T]hrough enquiring about their everyday and past lives, and their hopes and concerns, we aimed to create a picture with each person of their positive and negative experiences, of the value and quality of their life to them, and of potential lives with their condition. (Alderson, 2001: 630–1)

This sort of study produces very different data to that derived from quantitative work. Rather than 'thin', quantified scores that represent, for example, a person's level of happiness with their sexual relationships with a single number, qualitative studies produce large quantities of transcribed interview material, at varying levels of orthographic sophistication. Thus while conversation analytic studies routinely use the Jeffersonian notation (Appendix 1) with details of pitch changes, pauses timed in tenths of seconds and phonetic orthography, many variants of discourse analysis (such as Alderson's study) employ a simple verbatim transcription. Alderson (2001: 631) describes her discourse analytic/thematic analysis approach to her data:

> I analysed transcripts by hand, and reread them for the overt themes, reported here in the order they were discussed during interviews, and for underlying themes: quality and value of life, costs, dependence, contributions to family and society, discrimination, replies which fitted mainly the medical or social model of disability.

As is evident, the discourse analytic approach here blends emic and etic concerns. Alderson attends to the views reported by her respondents in their terms, but at the same time is attentive to the way in which the things people say can *also* be understood in analysts' terms, here in terms of the extent to which they 'fit' academic theories, or models, of disability. Alderson's study offers material such as the extract reproduced below as her *primary data*. In this sort of work, then, the regular encountering of descriptions is considered sufficient (under the rubric of 'order at all points') to make limited, and non-statistical, claims about the generality of people's experience. The data fragment below, from a section of an interview dealing with recreational activities (here drama), with two informants with Down syndrome is preceded by a brief analytic observation. The extract illustrates clearly how what participants say at interview directly informs the analysis offered.

> In their current play, *Mongol Boy*, a Victorian industrialist rejected his son who had Down's Syndrome and who joined a circus of freaks. Peter and Philip distinguished between the denigratory language in the play and their own views, raising a main theme of all 40 interviews: discrimination against disabled people.

Int:	So do you like that kind of drama, that you're really involved in?
Peter:	Oh yes, it's amazing.
Philip:	It is very important, and when you learn to say the part you can. But it's not very nice to say this, and I'm not a very rude person, but I think that a learning disability part – I don't want to be rude –.
Int:	You seem to me to be a very polite person.
Philip:	I don't like to take the mickey of people because I know they've got rights, they're a human being like us you see, but they are 'freaks' very small people and it's wrong to take the mickey out of them … and make them upset because they've got rights as well.
Int:	Yes, very important.
Philip:	It is important.
Int:	Yes, and do you think – with people with learning difficulties – that other people think enough about your rights?
Philip:	Some people don't understand. They want us to keep quiet. Because they think, you've got a learning disability – like when I came out [of the house], somebody pushed me, just out here, pushed me and didn't apologise and I didn't like that at all.
Int:	Did they push you by accident or on purpose?
Philip:	I think they did it on purpose. They're very strange people.
Peter:	And that happened at [names another place] –.
Philip:	Yes, I know Peter, and it happened here too, a man and a woman tried to push me.
Int:	And what did you do?
Philip:	Well, the point is this, we are not allowed to talk to strange people.

(Alderson, 2001: 632)

On the basis of five such interviews, during which her informants discussed topics as diverse as discrimination, relationships, education, employment, leisure interests, hopes and their views on prenatal screening, Alderson draws telling conclusions, both about people with Down syndrome and also about the quality of the lives which these people reported. She states (Alderson, 2001: 627) that:

> they [the data] show how some people with Down's Syndrome live creative, rewarding and fairly independent lives, and are not inevitably non-contributing dependents. Like the other 35 interviewees, they illustrate the importance of social supports, and their problems with excluding attitudes and barriers. Much more social research with people who have congenital conditions is required, if prenatal screening policies and counselling are to be evidence based.

Alderson's study thus illustrates how qualitative work can shed important light upon the use of practices that rely on 'taken-for-granted' beliefs about the QOL of people with congenital disorders. Qualitative methods of study can also be brought to bear on quantitative approaches to measuring quality of life. As we have seen, increasing use is made of questionnaire-driven interview schedules in an effort to find out what people feel about the quality of their lives 'in their own words'. However, there are reasons for being cautious about interpreting the results of quantitative assessment instruments – even if they meet public criteria for *psychometric* validity and reliability. In the quantitative tradition it is crucial (so crucial, indeed, that it is usually simply assumed to be the case) that scores on such instruments represent records of *authentic answers* to *clear questions*. However, both the traditional forms of publication of quantitative work (which usually offer – at best – aggregate statistical data) and inattention to the interactional dynamics at work in interviews may disguise inauthenticity and unclarity. Work that illustrates these problems, using the methods of conversation analysis, is discussed below.

Conversation analysis

Assessing somebody's QOL using a standardized questionnaire requires that both interviewer and interviewee manage an interaction in order to record the respondent's views. This will necessarily be done in a series of turns at talk, where the precise placement of an utterance crucially affects its meaning. Information on the sequential positioning of utterances – and the subtleties of interaction – is, however, lost when talk is analysed in terms of numerical scores, by quasi-qualitative methods such as content analysis (see, for example, Atkinson, 1988), or when it is subjected to a pre-given categorization scheme (as was, influentially, done to the talk of people with intellectual disabilities by Sigelman *et al.*, 1981). The principled avoidance of the pre-categorization of talk is a foundational principle of conversation analysis (CA). Conversation analysis is a theoretically-driven approach to social interaction, with a firm base in sociology and pragmatics (Atkinson and Heritage, 1984; Boden and Zimmerman 1991; Sacks, 1992; Silverman, 1998) and a growing influence in psychology (Edwards, 1995; Edwards and Potter, 2001). The use of CA illuminates the fine-grained interplay between speakers in interaction that is lost in grounded theory, content analysis and 'critical realist' discourse analysis. CA, then, offers the most sensitive possible tool to gain access to what is going on in QOL assessment interviews.

In other words, CA offers a method of analysis which pays attention not only to the content of what is said in QOL interviews, but also to the exact delivery of what is said, which has crucial effects on meaning. The techniques of CA have accumulated into a comprehensive vocabulary applicable to a wide range of social phenomena, including interaction in institutional settings (see, for example, Drew and Heritage, 1992; Hester and Francis, 2001; ten Have, 2001).

The 'reliability' and 'validity' of QOL assessment

Antaki and Rapley (1996a) used conversation analysis to examine the validity and reliability of standardized QOL measurement. They argued that, even though they may demonstrate acceptable validity and reliability in *psychometric* terms, QOL questionnaires may actually *distort* interviewees' 'own words' by severely underestimating the degree to which questions and answers are determined by the dynamics of QOL interviews. As such, their study examines the working out in practice of the theoretical concerns expressed by Megone (1990), Hatton (1998) and Mulkay *et al.* (1987) discussed in Chapter 3. That is, by using CA, the study actually *showed* in practice the theoretical concerns raised by these writers about the 'slanting' or 'distortion' that the 'theoretical refinement' of the notion of QOL into a psychometric schedule may cause.

Typical administration of the Schalock and Keith (1996) QOL Questionnaire involved two sorts of distortions. Firstly, there were distortions of the *questions* brought about by the need to paraphrase complex items, and the inevitable use of pre-questions and response listing. Secondly, and, perhaps more disturbingly, Antaki and Rapley (1996a) documented systematic distortions of *answers* brought about by interviewers' pursuit of answers and non-take-up of interviewees' matters. As space is limited, only a brief overview of their study is possible here; discussion focuses on the distortions caused by the question/answer format of the questionnaire and the transformations of respondents' answers brought about by interviewers' pursuing what appears to be their own QOL agenda rather than that of their interviewees.

Transformations of questions

The administration of face-to-face questionnaires very often requires, in practice, that items be paraphrased in order for respondents to grasp their meaning. Houtkoop-Steenstra's extensive work (2000) shows that this feature of interview interaction applies broadly, regardless of the cognitive skills of interviewees and *regardless* of the instructions to interviewers printed on formal measures that they use the *exact* wording of standardized questions. The *QOL.Q* manual is, then, unusual in that it specifically states that it is 'okay to paraphrase an item to improve understanding' (Schalock and Keith, 1996: 13). This causes severe problems – and not only in the case of items with obviously difficult words or expressions (for example Q. 19 asks about 'the benefits you receive at the workplace' and Q. 28 asks 'Do you have a guardian or conservator'). Serious difficulties regularly arise with apparently simple questions such as Question 9 – 'How successful do you think you are, compared to others?' Extract 1 shows a typical administration of this item.

Extract 1: Code: CA/MR/WM

```
 1   Int.    ↑how successful (.) d'you think you are (.) compared to
 2           other ↓people (.) ↑yeh? (..)
 3   Will    ↑m
 4   Int.    ↑more successful than average (.) a↑bout as successful
 5           as average (.) or ↓less successful (..)
 6   Will    °(syll)° (..)
 7   Int.    gi' me one of them
 8   Will    ↑yeh
 9   Int.    ↑which ↓one (...) >↑d'you think you do< ↑better at things
10           than the    ⌈(public) (syll syll)
11   Will                ⌊↑better (..) better ↓now
12   Int.    ↑yeh? (.)
13   Will    yes
```

In Extract 1 and the extracts that follow, 'Int.' is the psychologist conducting the QOL assessment. In Extract 1, Will is the respondent whose quality of life is being assessed. Will's first utterances where an answer might be expected are noncommittal (at line 3) and inaudible (line 6). When the interviewer asks explicitly for a choice among the alternatives (at line 7) Will offers an illegitimate reply – 'yeh': he does not specify which of the three alternatives he wishes to endorse. The interviewer paraphrases the original question 'how successful do you think you are, compared to others?' which now becomes 'd'you think you do better at things than the public?' Whether or not the candidate answer offered at line 11 – 'I do better (than the public) now' – is a legitimate response is arguable. In any case, the interviewer accepts it, and an official score (3) is recorded.

Extract 2 again shows the manner in which official QOL scores are generated by *changing the official question*. Thus the item 'do you feel that your job or other daily activities is worthwhile and relevant to you or other people?' becomes, by line 9, 'd'you think what you do is good?'

Extract 2: Code MT/I/JW

```
 1    Int.    d'you feel your job or other (.) daily activities-
 2    Anne    yes=
 3    Int.    =worth whi↑ well ↑wait till I finish (.) yeah? d'you think it's
 4            ↑worth↓while an'↑ and ↓relevant to you or (.)  ┌ other
 5            people
 6    Anne                                                  └yeah (.)
 7            other people
 8            (3.00)
 9    Int.    d'you think what you do is (..) good Anne? (.) d'you think
10            it's worth ↑do↓ing
11            (...)
12    Anne    .hh yes
13    Int.    (..) definitely?
14    Anne    yes
15    Int.    yeah? (..) ok (..)
```

The problem for us here, of course, is that the indexical 'what you do' and 'it' of the official QOL item are now undefined. There is no secure basis for supposing it is the 'job or other daily activities' of the official item that Anne's response refers to, and the twin official criteria of relevance to 'yourself or others' have disappeared. However, again, in line 15, we hear the interviewer accepting Anne's answer – that 'what she does' is 'good' and recording an official QOL score of 3. QOL.Q items always have three alternative answers. Item 1, for example, asks:

Overall, would you say that life: Brings out the best in you? (Score = 3) Treats you like everybody else? (Score = 2) Doesn't give you a chance? (Score = 1).

The serial listing of the alternatives provides for interviewees to offer candidate answers *before* the full set of alternatives has been presented, and this causes more trouble. The list structure of the interviewer's turn requires that the interviewee delays their answer, but the fact that each alternative is *in itself* a well-formed question prompts an immediate answer. Extract 3 shows how the *questionnaire format* produces three quite different 'answers' to a question:

Extract 3: Code: CA/KK/TH

```
 1   Int.    °right° (..) .hh d'you ever feel ↑lonely John?
 2   John    yeah (.) ↑very ↓lonely
 3   Int.    do you?
 4   John    hmm
 5   Int.    d'you feel lonely every ↓day?
 6   John    yeah
 7   Int.    (..) or (..) once a week?
 8   John    once a week
 9   Int.    (...)°right° (..) 'kay? (..) or ↑once a ↓month
10   John    ↑once a ↓month
11   Int.    (..)°↑once a ↓month°
12   (3 secs)
```

John, it appears, feels lonely every day (QOL score = 1), once a week (QOL score = 2) and once a month (QOL score = 3). It appears, by virtue of the interviewer's recycle of 'once a month' and the long silence following in lines 11–12, that he accepts this last utterance as John's official answer and gives him the highest possible QOL score.

What counts as the interviewee's answer?

We can see that the 'official' QOL questions are prone to serious distortion. Interactional dynamics also caused distortions in what counts as an 'official' answer to the questions asked. Antaki and Rapley (1996a) identified two sources of significant trouble in this respect: (1) the interviewer's pursuit of an *alternative* to apparently acceptable candidate answers; and (2) the ignoring of respondents' material, even though it often appeared designed to be informative about the respondent's quality of life.

Pursuing the 'right' answer

Antaki and Rapley (1996a) identified three reasons for interviewers to pursue a 'right' answer: the three-part listing structure of the scale seen above; the use by respondents of 'non-official' vocabulary; and the interviewer's own perceptions of what the respondent 'really' felt or believed. Extract 4 shows again how the three-part list structure of QOL questions *prompts changes* in what interviewees say about their quality of life. A legitimate candidate answer, at what the interviewer treats as the wrong place, has significant results:

Extract 4: Code MT/I/JW

```
 1   Int.    D'you ↑feel out of ↓place (..) >out an' about in<
 2           ↓social situ↓ations?
```

3	Anne	⌈No
4	Int.	⌊Anne? (.) Never?
5	Anne	No
6	Int.	Sometimes?
7	Anne	↓°No°
8	Int.	Or usually?
9	Anne	↑Some↓times I ↑do
10	Int.	Yeah? (..) OK, we'll ↑put a two down for that one then
11		(sniff)

Anne's reply 'No' at line 3 seems unambiguous. The need for the interviewer to offer all three official alternatives (which occur at lines 4, 6 and 8) evidently implies to Anne that her original answer (repeated in lines 5 and 7) requires change or correction. By line 9, Anne has got the point: she says 'sometimes I do'. While this is a *clear change* from her emphatic 'no' in lines 3, 5 and 7 it is *this* response that is recorded as her official QOL score.

Interviewer's expectations

Interviewer's expectations were also identified by Antaki and Rapley (1996a) as contributing to distortions of answers. It seems that interviewer's expectations of what was actually the right answer – what the respondent *really* thought – could interfere with QOL assessment. A good example of this is seen in Extract 5.

Extract 5: Code HB/I/TT

1	Int.	okay (.) overall would you say ↑that (.) ↓life brings ↑out (.)
2		the ↓best in you
3	Bob	↑yes
4	Int.	treats you like everybody ↓else=
5	Bob	↑yes:
6	Int.	or doesn't give you a chance
7	Bob	eh:?
8		(1 sec)
9	Int.	what >do you think ↓that< (.) life (.) brings out the best in
10		↓you (..) ⌈or (syll syll)
11	Bob	⌊yeah the ↑best yeah yeah
12	Int.	right (..) so that's ↓your (.) your answer ↑yeah ⌈life>br< life
13	Bob	⌊↓yes yes
14	Int.	brings out the best in you does it?
15	Bob	(what's to do) with yer ↑lip:
16	Int.	↓yeah I: I ↑cut it (.) shaving
17	Bob	(syll syll syll syll syll)
18	Int.	okay (.) so of those ↑three (.) you think ↓life brings out the
19		best it doesn't (.) treat ↓you like everyone ↓else an ↑it (.) it

```
20              ↓doesn't (.) not give you a chance
21    Bob       (hhh)=
22    Int.      yeah?
23              (2 sec)
24    Bob       °°(doesn't) give me a ↑chance°° .h        ⌈hh ((sniff))
25    Int.                                                 ⌊okay (1sec)
26              al↑right (..)
```

Bob gives a well designed answer in line 11: the answer shows an agreement token ('yeah'), a legitimate, 'official', response alternative delivered with an appropriate intonation contour ('the best') and two further agreement tokens in confirmation. Bob has previously (in lines 3 and 5) indicated that he has understood the options on offer, and in line 7 successfully sought a recycle of the third option from the interviewer. Despite this, the interviewer does not accept his selection of the official answer 'life brings out the best in me' as his QOL judgment. At lines 25–6 Bob's official QOL score is not recorded as the '3' he initially selected, but rather as a '1'.

Antaki and Rapley (1996a) concluded that the very serious interactional difficulties observed in their study (difficulties which were confirmed in a series of subsequent analyses) prevented easy reduction of these QOL assessment interviews to a quantitative score. Such a conclusion, they argued, means that these observations on the administration of a typical QOL questionnaire raise tricky questions about the whole enterprise of trying to find out people how feel about the quality of their lives. They suggested that:

> it is important to be clear that although there is one particular instrument of contemporary interest under examination … the argument generalises to *any* attempt to evaluate *any* psychological state of mind that requires the respondent to fit deeply-held beliefs or feelings (life satisfaction judgements, interpersonal evaluations or personal motivations) into pre-organised question and answer categories. Such avowals of belief and feeling are, we have seen, not independent of the particular question, the sequential run of questions and previous answers, and interpersonal and institutional context in which those questions are asked. (Antaki and Rapley, 1996a; my emphasis)

A Synthesis?

A major concern of this chapter has been to stress the necessity of explicit links between the way QOL is theorized and the methods chosen to study the concept. In the quantitative tradition this means that QOL measures must be based on an adequately theorized, a priori specification (or operational definition), of the model of QOL adopted, demonstrate psychometric reliability and validity, and show that they are sensitive to the circumstances in which people find themselves. In the qualitative tradition, the issues are more centrally concerned with clarity about the theoretical underpinnings of the analytic methods used and the purpose of proposed studies (not that this isn't also true for quantitative work). In either tradition the adoption of research designs and methods should be critically informed by a deep understanding of the research tradition within which the work is conducted. Where the traditions diverge perhaps most clearly is in their stance towards emic and etic perspectives in research – although, as we have seen in the second half of this chapter, it is entirely feasible to conduct studies which attend to both perspectives. It is of course also the case that it is possible – again as we have seen above – to employ qualitative methodologies to ask searching questions about the adequacy of quantitative work.

Notes

1. A discourse can be understood as an 'organized' way of speaking of (some aspect of) experience. Potter and Wetherell (1987) describe discourses as 'interpretative repertoires': constellations of grammatically and semantically coherent terms which collectively provide particular interpretations or descriptions of the 'way the world is'. A clear and problematic example is the use of medical discourse (with its talk of 'signs', 'symptoms' and 'illness') to describe psychological distress. From a Foucauldian perspective, a 'discourse' also includes those *practices* which, together with texts, establish, for example, subject positions. From a Foucauldian perspective, the example of medical discourse would also include analysis of the manner in which such practices as the establishment of 'mental health clinics' and 'psychiatric hospitals' staffed by people described as 'doctors' and 'psychiatric nurses', the prescription and consumption of 'antidepressants' and the appearance of 'problem pages' in magazines work to constitute persons as 'patients'.
2. The CHQ-PF-50 consists of 50 items assessing 14 aspects of functioning, including physical functioning, mental health, school and social limitations arising from their illness, family functioning and the impact of their physical and psycho-social health on their parents. Two summary scales, the Physical Summary Scale and the Psychosocial Summary Scale, are also scored. Psychometric data on the validity and reliability of this measure is available in Landgraf *et al.* (1996).
3. The Functional Status II(R) Questionnaire (FSQ) (Stein and Jessop, 1990, 1991) uses 14 items which rate the interference a child's illness causes in daily functioning, covering areas such as sleeping, eating, communication, energy and mood. Higher scores indicate better functional health status.
4. The Impact-on-Family Scale (Stein and Riessman, 1980) is a 24-item scale rating the impact of child illness on family functioning in four areas (changes in economic status of a family; quality of interaction with persons outside the immediate household; interactions between family members; subjective

distress for the child's caretaker). Validity and reliability is discussed by Stein and Riessman (1980).

Study Questions

- What are the losses and gains involved in representing the quality of a person's life as a numerical score?
- Who knows best about a person's quality of life?
- My QOL today is ... ?
- How can qualitative studies of QOL assist in the development of quantitative approaches?

Suggestions for Further Reading

Berger-Schmitt, R. and Noll, H.-H. (2000). *Conceptual Framework and Structure of a European System of Social Indicators*, EuReporting Working Paper No. 9. Mannheim: Centre for Survey Research and Methodology. Available from: <http://www.gesis.org/en/social_monitoring/social_indicators/EU_Reporting/concept.htm>.

Edwards, D., Ashmore, M. and Potter, J. (1995) Death and furniture: the rhetoric, politics and theology of bottom-line arguments against relativism, *History of the Human Sciences*, 8, 2: 25–49.

McHoul, A. and Rapley, M. (eds) (2002) *How to Analyse Talk in Institutional Settings: A Casebook of Methods*. London and New York: Continuum International.

Puchta, C. and Potter, J. (forthcoming) *Focus Group Practice: Moderating Interaction in Market Research Focus Groups*. London: Sage.

Richardson, J. T. E. (1996) *Handbook of Qualitative Research Methods for Psychology and the Social Sciences*. Leicester: BPS Books.

Silverman, D. (1998) *Harvey Sacks: Social Science and Conversation Analysis*. Cambridge: Polity Press.

Willig, C. (2001) *Introducing Qualitative Research in Psychology: Adventures in Theory and Method*. Buckingham: Open University Press.

Yates, S., Taylor, S. and Wetherell, M. (2001) *Discourse as Data: A Guide for Analysis*. London: Sage.

PART TWO – PRACTICE

In Part 1, I identified some of the key conceptual, procedural and ethical concerns in contemporary QOL research. These chapters sought to place QOL research into its historical and cultural context, and to offer an account of both the prevailing consensus views and of the critical voices in the field. While we saw some brief examples of current research in these chapters, in Part 2 the focus is on the direct practical application of the ideas we have encountered so far. It is, of course, difficult to separate out theory and practice, or method, and this differentiation is – as has been seen – hard to sustain in practice. However, what the following chapters do is to *show* at greater length what QOL research actually looks like. The breadth of the field, and the space available, means that these chapters will not discuss the details of specific research procedures (statistical techniques like factor analysis, multidimensional scaling or logistic regression) or offer a detailed analysis and description of the variety of possible approaches to research (for example, questionnaire surveys, ethnographic work or action research). Where these matters arise methods texts that offer detailed guidance on the specific issues are identified. Rather the intention here is to offer an introductory overview, a flavour of some of the variety of research approaches in the field, and to identify important concerns that need to be addressed in the design and conduct of a range of QOL research projects.

Chapter 5 offers a worked example of an archaeological approach, based on the work of Michel Foucault, to develop an understanding of quality of life as a cultural object. Chapter 6 offers an overview of the use of the notion of quality of life to develop numerical indicators of life quality (QALYs and DALYs) in medicine, health economics and epidemiology. Chapter 7 considers the use of quality of life as an organizing construct in service evaluation research looking at the quality of services for people with mental health problems and intellectual disabilities. In Chapter 8, a worked example of the critical analysis of the literature in contemporary psychology is presented. Chapter 9, the final chapter, attempts to draw together the major themes of the book, and offers some tentative conclusions about where we go from here.

Throughout Part 2, it is *essential* to remember that while one particular population group ('schizophrenics', for example) may be the stated focus of the study under discussion, *all* of the work discussed here has been selected in order to illustrate *generally applicable* issues and problems. Throughout Part 2, key points about the conduct of quality of life research apply regardless of people's measured IQ or their possession (or otherwise) of a medical or psychiatric diagnosis.

CHAPTER 5

Researching QOL as Cultural Object

Chapters 1–4 outlined some of the key philosophical questions in QOL research, and some of the theoretical and methodological tensions between quantitative and qualitative research approaches. This chapter takes up these issues and offers a 'worked example' of the use of a qualitative approach to the study of QOL as a social phenomenon, at the level of the cultural production of 'quality of life' as both a meaningful device in lay discourse, and also as a legitimate object of social scientific study.

The concepts of 'quality', 'quality of life' and their variants are closely related in public discourse. They are discursive objects which have become, since the early 1980s, routinely deployed in all forms of public talk – from the promises of the advertisers of consumer products (*Build with Dale Alcock for quality lifestyles!!* being an entirely unremarkable property developer's advertisement in my local paper recently) to being the stated policy objectives of governments across the world (for example, enhancing 'quality of life' being a key objective of the British government's *Health of the Nation* White Paper and also that of the Health Department of Victoria, Australia).

The chapter introduces the key epistemological and methodological positions of Foucauldian thinkers (Rose, 1999; Kendall and Wickham, 1999), the work of discursive psychologists (Edwards and Potter, 1992; Potter, 1996) and a range of other critical theorists in what may be broadly be described as the postmodern, or social constructionist, tradition (Fairclough, 2001). The analytic tools these approaches provide are outlined. It is beyond the scope of this book to address these issues in detail, so here a qualitative analysis of the social production of 'QOL' as the necessary outcome of government policy is described to illustrate the methods and the relevance of the case study methodology to the conceptual issues raised in Part 1 (for example, the historical contingency of social scientific interest in QOL) is detailed. Kendall and Wickham (1999) provide a detailed introduction to the use of Foucault's methods of *archaeological* and *genealogical* inquiry. McHoul and Rapley (2002) offer an introductory level text describing, and showing through worked examples, the use of applied conversation analysis, discursive psychology and critical discourse analysis.

Quality of Life in Popular Culture – the Contribution of Foucauldian Thought

Rose (1992) offers what, on the surface, appears to be an insubstantial account of a small ad he began to notice appearing in the *The Guardian*, a British 'quality' daily newspaper, in 1989. Rose (1992: 141, *my emphasis*) writes that:

> it was for a private organization called 'Self-Helpline' and offered a range of telephone numbers for people to ring for answers to some apparently troubling questions. There were 'Emotional problems', from 'Dealing with infidelity' to 'Overcoming shyness'. There were 'Parenthood problems', from 'My child won't sleep' to 'I feel like hitting my baby'. There were 'Work problems', such as 'Am I in the right job' or 'Becoming a supervisor'. And there were 'Sexual problems' from 'Impotence' to 'Better orgasms'. For the cost of a telephone call, callers could obtain 'self-help step by step answers to dealing with your problems and improving the *quality of your life*'.

Rose notes that it may be thought that the ad is trivial, and its preoccupations far removed from something as 'weighty' as 'enterprise culture' (Rose, 1992: 141), in much the same way that the claims of Australian house builders to be able to 'improve the quality of your lifestyle' are apparently far removed from the concerns about quality of life discussed in earlier chapters. However, what Rose demonstrates is that such advertisements resonate with much broader and deeper presuppositions concerning what it means to be human *at all* in contemporary Western societies. That is to say the 'enterprise culture' – a phenomenon precisely coterminous with what Schalock (1994: 266) describes as the 'quality revolution' – and the 'forms of political reason' that promote it 'accord a vital *political* value to a certain image of the self.' Such a value, as Rose notes, is far from being any longer, if it ever truly was, a pet project of the political right, but rather has become the dominant political mentality of the 'West' and is increasingly so in what were once 'Eastern bloc' countries. It is, in the terms of an earlier chapter, a peculiarly 'American' – as opposed to 'Scandinavian' – view of self and the relation between self and society.

Rose argues that the extraordinarily potent view of the individual as the 'enterprising self', which now dominates 'Western' political mentality, furnishes the conditions of possibility for Self-Helpline, Dale Alcock and a raft of other 'experts of subjectivity' to proffer their services in the improvement of the citizen's quality of life. Such a view of the self, suggests Rose (1992: 141–2):

> resonates with basic presuppositions concerning the contemporary self

that are widely distributed in our present, presuppositions that are embodied in the very language that we use to make persons thinkable, and in our ideal conceptions of what people should be ... The self is to be a subjective being, it is to aspire to autonomy, it is to strive for personal fulfilment in its earthly life, it is to interpret its reality and destiny as matters of individual responsibility, it is to find meaning in existence by shaping its life through acts of choice ... The guidance of selves is no longer dependent upon the authority of religion or traditional morality; it has been allocated to 'experts of subjectivity' who transfigure existential questions about the purpose of life and the meaning of suffering into technical questions about the most effective ways of managing malfunction and improving 'quality of life'.

The critical point that Foucauldian scholarship then makes is that these are *ways* of *thinking* about selves, they are ways of *judging* those selves and, importantly, they prescribe ways of *acting* upon those selves – but that they could always have been (indeed historically have been) – otherwise. As such, while Cummins *et al.*'s (in press) 'homeostatic model of subjective well-being' discussed in Chapters 2 and 8 may appear on the surface to be nothing but the dispassionate description of empirical particulars forced upon us by the ineluctable progress of science, a Foucauldian position notes that this is *but one way* of thinking selves, and, moreover, one which is dependent not upon 'objective science' in its own presuppositions, but rather upon the *prior* acceptance of a particular cultural, political under-standing of the nature of personhood and the correct ways of investigating such a condition (see also Feyerabend, 1974).

That is to say the model, as but one example, *takes for granted* that the proper object of its enquiry and explanation is the *individual* self, which is a subjective being, aspiring to autonomy, striving for personal fulfilment (a promotion at work, or a satisfying meal perhaps proffering such an outcome), interpreting reality in terms of individual responsibility and finding meaning in existence (and, it must be said, satisfaction with the quality of its earthly life) by shaping its life through acts of choice.

Further, such scholarship recognizes that these *new* ways of thinking selves are not only historically, but also culturally, contingent. That is, whereas in the West since the Enlightenment the development of advanced liberal democracies has seen the transformation of the populace from 'subjects with duties and obligations' to 'individuals with rights and freedoms' (Rose, 1992: 142) it is also the case that contemporary thinkings of the self, or notions of personhood, vary enormously across cultures. As we will see in the 'worked example' below, it is only very recently indeed that such a way of thinking selves has been extended to some marginal groups – such as people with an intellectual disability – even in modern Western societies. It is also the case that such a way of thinking furnishes the criteria by which selves are currently judged to be competent members of a shared social and moral order: the 'mad' for example, are at root identifiable as such by their failure to enact self-hood in these terms (see Coulter, 1979).

The use of Foucauldian methods (though see Kendall and Wickham's caution about such a term) is, then, an exercise in the careful description of the 'order of things' (Foucault, 1970) which is aware that causal explanations must be partial (in both senses of the term) and that, rather than engaging in contestable *causal* accounts, it is necessary to recognize that the production of the present – quite as much as any historical event – is dependent upon a host of *contingencies*. That is, the present is as historically adventitious (Sacks, 1992) as the past. The course of events, or of any particular event (the emergence of quality of life as an organizing notion in the social sciences), is then seen not as the necessary outcome of a chain of causes (a Marxist view), but rather as one possible result of a complex set of relations between a range of other events. In other words, as Gavin Kendall and Gary Wickham (1999: 4) say, the

> use of history is not a turn to teleology, that is it does not involve assumptions of progress (or regress). This is why we say it involves histories that never stop: they cannot be said to stop because they cannot be said to be going anywhere ... Foucauldian histories are histories of the present not because understanding an ideal or complete present is the spur to investigation ... Foucauldians are not seeking to find out how the present has emerged from the past. Rather the point is to use history as a way of diagnosing the present.

Kendell and Wickham would, therefore, probably throw up (their hands in horror) at the shades of Whig historicism in the account of the emergence and development of the idea of 'quality of life' presented in Chapter 1.

Drawing upon the work of Foucault and Rose, the remainder of this chapter offers a worked example, to show how QOL – as a cultural object – may be researched, and to demonstrate how such an analysis offers us a view of the conditions of possibility of the present. The example considers, in detail, the case of the public pronouncements of government and professionals about social policy for people with intellectual disabilities in the United Kingdom between the late 1960s and the early 1990s. However, the specificity of the case materials is of little consequence: what matters here is the method of analysis. As such, even if one knows little of the detail of the subject matter, what is important is to *see* how (any) official texts can be used to develop an understanding of the practical uses of ideas like quality of life in forming both persons and social practices towards them.

As elsewhere in the social sciences the notion of 'quality of life' has recently become a key device in the intellectual disability research community. Historical study of the rhetoric of government and academia in the United Kingdom suggests that the idea of QOL has come to be intimately bound up with broader discourses of managerialism and corporatism in contemporary Western societies. That is, rather than being the ideologically pure and scientifically untroubled notion the research community, implicitly, claims it to be, QOL discourse can be understood as *mutually constructed* by government and 'psy-complex' practices.

As we saw earlier, notions of 'quality' and 'customer satisfaction' have come, since the mid-1980s, to occupy a central position in the discourse of commercial, professional and public life. A couple of clear examples of the changes in language occurring during this period are the transformation, by what was then British Rail, of people who were once 'passengers' into 'customers' and the similar transformation, in universities, of both those who give and those who attend lectures. Universities now tend to speak of themselves as having 'consumers' of 'educational services' rather than 'students' and, with appropriate symmetry, lecturers are now often construed not as scholars, but as 'content providers'.

'Ideas' such as quality of life are, then, much more than useful professional shorthand (Antaki, 1994; Potter, 1996). Such ideas do not act, neutrally, to describe established realities, but rather actively shape the social world (Potter and Wetherell, 1987; Potter, 1996), and in consequence, the place of people (with or without intellectual disabilities) within it. Antaki suggests that the function of such discursive objects, in talk, be it ministerial rhetoric, service providers' 'mission statements' or planners' 'strategic visions' is to 'do some work on the setting up or knocking down of social realities' (Antaki, 1994: 120). This suggests that an understanding of the rhetorical use of such notions as QOL by government and service providers is of considerable importance. The inspection of the 'talk' of government, in the shape of ministerial speeches or policy documents, the pronouncements of the academic or of the applied research community – the 'psy-complex' in Rose's (1986) analysis – may show the nature of the social realities to which their authors are committed, and which they wish to be accepted as 'true' in society as a whole.

The Psy-complex and the Social Regulation of (Dis)order

Greig (1993: 5) noted the widespread acceptance of what he termed the 'language' of normalization[1] by UK health authorities and direct service providers over the course of the 1980s. This acceptance may be construed as a function of the ready subsumability of its consumerist themes within another – corporatist – discourse, specifically that of a government committed to 'consumer choice'. For example, the Personal Social Services Research Unit (1987: 4) noted that :

various labels for describing aspects of consumerism in Care in the Community can be used. Involvement, participation, self-determination, choice, opportunities, power and control are all components of user involvement.

The 'labels' for 'consumerism' identified here closely approximate to versions of normalization (Wolfensberger, 1972) which describe a set of desirable service 'accomplishments'. However, by simply replacing the term 'consumerism' with 'normalization', the PSSRU's analysis of factors influencing government social policy may be translated into a typical statement of the aims and objectives – or in currently popular managerialist rhetoric the 'mission statement' or 'vision' – of all community-based (and probably many institutional) service providers across the human services. It thus seems clear that other discursive forces, in addition to normalization, may be implicated in the development of both community care and of the notion of 'quality of life' as a 'master construct'. The widespread deployment of the corporatist discursive themes of 'quality' and 'consumerism' has been precisely contemporaneous with the wholesale adoption of the 'language of normalization' (Greig, 1993) in human services.

Sociological and archaeological (Foucault, 1978) work on the social management of 'mental disorder' and the development of what Rose (1999) termed the psy-complex – psychiatry, clinical psychology, social work, mental health nursing – has relevance here. Rose's (1986, 1999) analyses of the psy-complex, or 'all those disciplines concerned with troubles and disorders of conduct, emotion and thought and the conditions for mental health' (1986: 284), with their echoes of the 'military-industrial complex', make explicit the reciprocal, indeed symbiotic, relationship between government and the regulators and researchers of mental order and disorder. Following Foucault, Rose's analyses point to the increasing 'psychologization' of society at large, and the contingent development of a broad societal focus upon individual subjectivity as the locus of well-being, (mental) health and quality of life.

Miller (1986) argues that the development of the psy-complex has greatly broadened the range of available mechanisms and locations, or sites, for the social regulation of disorder. Part of this process has been achieved by the placing of responsibility for order upon the self: as we saw in the introduction to this chapter, even 'quality' daily newspapers are now sites for the advertisements of 'experts of subjectivity' touting for business. A consequence of this, in terms of the regulatory machinery of 'liberal' societies, is that 'as far as possible individuals remain a part of society [and] become responsible for maximising their potential contribution to society' (Miller, 1986: 32) by, if possible, 'helping them selves' (see Miller and McHoul (1998) for an extended analysis of these developments). In the present context, this responsibility has also come to be construed, very recently, as also applying to persons with intellectual disabilities, but with an additional gloss that allows for assistance with the regulation of order by the self, by the provision in Western societies of intellectual disability services in the community. Such services, provided by the psy-complex on behalf of government, have – and this is, arguably, no coincidence – in the last thirty years increasingly come to stress the importance of the development of social and behavioural competence on the part of 'clients' as a key service goal (Evans *et al.*, 1987; Emerson and Hatton, 1994). Miller's (1986) conceptualization of both the development and the current nature of Western liberal societies, the relation of the individual to the state in such societies, and the role of members of the psy-complex within them, illuminates clearly the progression in the declared, rhetorical, objectives of government vis-à-vis people with intellectual disabilities. This analysis sheds light upon the development of the indices selected as appropriate outcome measures of service practice, by academic psychologists or other members of the psy-complex, warranted by government to evaluate the efficacy of these systems.

As a topic for the attention of the psy-complex the 'lifestyle', or quality of the life, of people with intellectual disabilities is very recent. While Schalock (1996) has suggested that QOL has always been a concern of the psy-complex, it is only since the 1980s that the style of life that intellectually disabled people may be thought as having, has become explicitly constructed in rhetoric as an object of interest (Antaki and Rapley, 1996a). This rhetoric reflects dramatic changes in prevailing social constructions of persons with intellectual disabilities. The development of political rhetoric and the publicly avowed construction of intellectual disability which has advanced with it have legitimated a new social construction of intellectual disability and, consequently, of the role of human services. It can be argued that it is this new social construction of intellectual disability, mutually constructed by government and the psy-complex, which has facilitated and legitimated not only a new set of public policies concerning people with intellectual disabilities – 'community care' – but which, in keeping with the 'sponsoring' corporatist/managerialist discourse, has also put in place the conditions of possibility for the emergence of talk about the quality of life of people with intellectual disabilities to develop into an organizing construct in human service/psy-complex practice.

Thus, in the light of discursive psychology's observations on the 'work' of discourse, in particular of rhetoric (see Antaki, 1994; Billig, 1991; Edwards and Potter, 2001; Potter and Wetherell, 1987), and the analyses offered by Miller and Rose of the role of the psy-complex/government partnership in the regulation of order, an analysis of the rhetoric constructing intellectual disability and QOL is warranted. The rhetoric of government defines the nature of the 'social realities' that academia and the psy-complex are empowered to regulate, and acts as legitimation of action on the part of those authorized to dispose of resources on its part. Thus inspection of the rhetoric of government and its agents, and the discourses they deploy, may then demonstrate the social construction of, among other things, social identities such as 'persons with an intellectual disability' and the rights, obligations and expectations of the 'lifestyle' or 'quality of life' to be associated with such identities.

Lifestyles and Intellectual Disability in 'Community Care' Policy: The Uses of QOL

The 'standard history' of the development of community care policy (which, in brief, appeals to developments in conscience and science as warrants for 'progress') can be contrasted with an analysis of the rhetoric of the executive and of the psy-complex. The aim of the analysis is to examine the nature of the 'social realities' (Antaki, 1994) – and the policy positions they buttress or necessitate – constructed by the rhetoric of official texts, and to argue that not only is community care comprehensible in terms of the coherence of the rhetorical and political commitments of the dominant political mentality of the 'enterprising self', but also that QOL (as a discursive object) has a parentage considerably less ideologically and scientifically 'pure' than the social scientific literatures would imply.

Collins (1992: 7) identifies the first usage of the term 'community care' in an official government publication in the *Report of the Royal Commission on the Law Relating to Mental Illness and Mental Deficiency* (1957). However, the formal adoption of community care as explicit social policy did not occur until after the executive's response to the Ely scandal (DHSS, 1969)[2] and the subsequent policy guidance in the command paper *Better Services for the Mentally Handicapped* (DHSS, 1971). The *Report of the Committee of Enquiry into Mental Handicap Nursing and Care* (DHSS, 1979) offered an explicit model of 'care' clearly influenced by what has subsequently become known as the 'ordinary life' perspective. The report suggested a range of service developments flowing from a 'belief in the primacy of a 'normal' lifestyle' (DHSS, 1979: 22) which aimed towards: 'a decent and dignified life for mentally handicapped people' (DHSS, 1979: 139). In Wales, official thinking was further advanced. The *All-Wales Strategy for the Development of Services for Mentally Handicapped People* (AWS) (Welsh Office, 1983) was explicitly based upon statements of respect for the individuality of people with intellectual disabilities; for example the Strategy review document published in 1991 reiterated the 1983 principle that people with intellectual disabilities have a right to 'ordinary patterns of life within the community' and the clear recognition that people with intellectual disabilities 'can expect … additional help from the communities in which they live … to develop their maximum potential' (Welsh Office, 1991: para. 38).

Statements in the AWS about the 'rights' of people with intellectual disabilities, and the description of people with intellectual disabilities as capable of development, is a very different discourse to that of the 1980

DHSS policy review *Mental Handicap: Progress, Problems and Priorities* (DHSS, 1980). The rhetoric of the AWS made two debts clear. The use of the term 'ordinary' to describe life styles acknowledged the King's Fund Centre's (1980) position paper *An Ordinary Life* which had laid out a detailed framework for community-based services to complement the strategic vision of the Jay Report. The employment of the term 'ordinary' in the King's Fund document itself represented a masterstroke of rhetorical understatement in response to those – for example government – who claimed the continuing necessity for 'extra-ordinary', or special, facilities such as mental handicap institutions at the time (DHSS, 1980).

In order for this 'ordinary' model of care to be more widely acceptable, however, a number of rhetorical accommodations, and a new public social construction of the nature of intellectual disability, were required. Such a construction began to emerge in the Second Report of the House of Commons Select Committee on Social Services, *Community Care: With Special Reference to Adult Mentally Ill and Mentally Handicapped People* (HMSO, 1985), which concluded that, with sufficient financial and human resources, local authorities – rather than hospitals or other health service providers – could and would provide an adequate lifestyle for people with intellectual disabilities. Further, in a subtle but significant shift in terminology, what may now – in managerialist discourse – be termed the 'client group' was referred to as 'mentally handicapped people' rather than '*the* mentally handicapped'. The Committee recommended that 'new residential services for all but a small minority of mentally handicapped adults be in the form of ordinary housing within the wider community' (HMSO, 1985, Vol. 1: cxvii). Shortly afterwards, in a major review of policy in the field the Griffiths Report (1988) laid out, explicitly, the central corporatist/managerialist, market economic tropes of 'cost-effectiveness' and 'value for money' that were to become central to government policy. In keeping with the government's consumerist rhetoric Griffiths (1998: para. 3.4) suggested that:

> There is value in a multiplicity of provision, not least from the consumers' point of view, because of the widening of choice, flexibility, innovation and competition it should stimulate. The proposals are therefore aimed at stimulating the further development of the 'mixed economy' of care.

It should be noted here that Griffiths, the expert appointed by government to advise on future policy directions, explicitly refers to people with intellectual disabilities as 'consumers'. Community-based care is constructed as offering 'consumers' the advantages of the (multiplicity of the market) in the provision of a 'mixed economy' care. In the subsequent NHS and Community Care Act 1990 corporatist notions of value for money, cost-effectiveness and quality monitoring were cemented into a nascent 'contracting culture' with the establishment – in another borrowing from the discourse of commercial banking – of organizational units called National Health Service 'Trusts' (see Collins, 1992, 1993 for a detailed discussion). Contemporaneous with the Act a range of other key changes in the social construction of intellectual disability invoked by the rhetoric of the executive and members of the psy-complex are evident.

'Quality of Life' – Core Theme in the Corporate Discourse

The sharpness of the shifts in social policy and the public social construction of people with intellectual disabilities offered by government can be gauged by comparing the rhetoric of the so-called *MENCAP Speech* by Stephen Dorrell, the then Minister of Health, in June 1991 (DOH, 1991) and the *Local Authority Circular (92)15* (LAC (92) 15) (DOH, 1992) with the social constructions of persons with an intellectual disability invoked in the earlier policy guidance and Acts of Parliament briefly discussed above.

Although no longer sustaining the eugenic theory that intellectual disability was caused by inherited degeneracy or wilful moral degradation legislated by the Mental Deficiency Act 1913, the rhetoric of government in the period prior to the NHS and Community Care Act 1990 routinely invoked a social construction of people with intellectual disabilities as a homogenous group – 'the mentally handicapped', a group which required 'nursing and care'. Before *Caring for People* (the White Paper which preceded that Act), people with intellectual disabilities were constructed in official texts not as individuals with rights, not even as 'people', but rather what would now be termed – again in the discourse of commerce – as a 'client' group, a client group, furthermore, which was not composed of individual 'service users', but rather could be constructed as a group noun describing a 'condition' which, as we will see below, could pose 'problems', upon which there could be 'progress' and for which government could set 'priorities'. While *Caring for People* represented a major change in the direction of social policy, perhaps more striking was the appropriation of the theme of 'care' into the lexicon of the corporate/managerial discourse: government now, like the manufacturers of washing powder, the international airlines and the providers of telephones, claimed to be 'caring'.

In the earlier White Paper *Mental Handicap: Progress, Problems and Priorities* (DHSS, 1980) implementation of the 1971 policy guidance had been reviewed. Consistent with its title was the policy that there was a strong case for 'special units … for certain groups … [some] … may need to live permanently in such units' (DHSS, 1980: 34). The White Paper made it clear that 'current Department policy is that some require long-term health care whilst others require long-term placement' (DHSS, 1980: 18). The assumption underpinning government policy was made explicit: it is 'taken for granted that there are some mentally handicapped people who need hospital care and a distinct group of others who need local authority or other similar residential care' (DHSS, 1980: 22). The construction here is not the now familiar, indeed formulaic, 'people with an intellectual disability' but consists in references to 'certain groups' or a similarly vague 'some mentally handicapped people' and 'others'.

In contrast, Stephen Dorrell's so-called MENCAP speech[3] of 25 June 1991 (DOH, 1991) not only displayed a reflexive awareness of its own rhetoric in the explicit use of the new term 'learning disability' rather than the previously officially preferred 'mental handicap', but also explicitly deploys the corporatist/managerialist discourse referred to above as offering a candidate organizing principle in service provision – with a particular emphasis laid on 'quality'. The speech explicitly allows for the notion of 'quality of life' as an outcome of service practice, in effect a formal governmental endorsement of the idea. Furthermore Dorrell legitimates, by virtue of the stress laid on the theme of consumerism, a view of service users as customers, as 'citizens', and in so doing offers formal validation of the explicit deployment of the themes of the corporatist discourse in the rhetoric of the psy-complex.

As we have seen, Rose (1992) suggests that the thinking of persons in terms of the 'enterprising self', which now dominates 'Western' political mentality, furnishes a version of self as subjective being, aspiring to independence and seeking fulfilment though individual responsibility and acts of choice. Seeking approval for governments' new policy goals, in the MENCAP speech government-as-corporation deploys a rhetorical emphasis on the newness and modernity of its products. Thus Dorrell urges that 'individuals', rather than 'the mentally handicapped' or 'mentally handicapped people', should 'not be offered predetermined sets of services because of ill-considered or outdated notions' (DOH, 1991: para. 6). However, in the context of social care, the managerialist, corporate discourse does not make sense without 'customers': it is necessary therefore to transform 'the mentally handicapped' from a homogenous population who require 'care' *en masse*, into one affording recognition to 'individuals' – people who are capable of being consumers; people who can, or can be assisted to, choose between 'packages of care' or 'accept it as their mission' (DOH, 1991: para. 47) to work together with providers to plan and implement services. On this reading the Minister's assertion that changes in terminology 'reflect … the values which inform our thinking' is absolutely consistent: it is the values of the enterprise culture that demand that 'the mentally handicapped' become here, rhetorically at least, '*citizens* … full members of our society …* ' (DOH, 1991: 1–2, my emphasis).

The MENCAP speech exemplifies the deployment of the theme of 'quality', indeed of 'quality of life', as the central component in the broader corporate discourse. Often invoked alongside the consumerist rhetoric, appeals to subjectivity and the individualized pursuit of 'the good life' are frequent, both as goals for individuals and as 'service principles' (DOH,

1991, para. 5). Services are to offer, with a (knowing) nod to the 'language of normalization' (Greig, 1993), 'appropriate support and opportunities founded on the *right values* and service principles' (DOH, 1991: para. 5, emphasis added). This support is to be offered to 'individuals' with 'respect and dignity'. Addressing 'individual' 'social care needs', with an explicit recognition of the 'ordinary life model' (DOH, 1991: para. 17), is to be the statutory responsibility of local authorities who are to 'contract' with a range of 'care providers' that are 'outward looking and closely associated with the general community' (DOH, 1991: para. 19).

Like the MENCAP speech, the subsequent policy paper *Social Care for Adults with Learning Disabilities (Mental Handicap)* (LAC (92) 15) (DOH, 1992), is explicit in the construction of intellectual disability it offers. The new 'citizens' of the MENCAP speech, 'people with learning disabilities', are no longer permanently deficient invalids who require nursing and other specialist care in hospital settings or special units. Unlike the 1980 position, which held that some would always need the special facilities of hospitals, the Circular constructs a radically different social reality. Here, rather than identifying a population group that requires extraordinary attention to a permanent, unchanging condition, the Circular suggests that, 'with appropriate support and opportunities … [they] … are capable of considerable personal development and of making a positive contribution to society. Few, if any, need to live in hospitals' (DOH, 1992: 1). These 'individuals' then are no longer people incapable of subjective being, of aspiring to independence, of making acts of choice.

Social Care for Adults with Learning Disabilities (Mental Handicap) (DOH, 1992) exemplifies the deployment of the managerial discourse, and specifically the 'quality' theme, in government rhetoric. *Social Care for Adults with Learning Disabilities (Mental Handicap)* gives specific guidance to local authorities on the provision of services to adults with learning disabilities: throughout the client group is referred to as 'people with learning disabilities', with the use of the parenthetical term 'mental handicap' of its title discouraged. The policy advice spells out the requirement for 'social' rather than 'hospital' or 'health' care, and instructs local authority social services departments in matters to be addressed when 'designing and developing care management and quality assurance arrangements' (DOH, 1992: 1). Having introduced the notion of the 'care package', it is of note that 'care' is no longer something offered as part of an ongoing and intimate personal relationship between people: rather it is now a something that, like any other 'product' or commodity, may be 'packaged' and which needs also to be 'contracted' and 'managed'. Furthermore the 'quality' of the product is apparently sufficiently unpredictable that (formalized) 'quality assurance' mechanisms need to be 'designed'.

The discourse invoked here is that of the corporation. We see the key device of 'quality' and the failure to refer to the objects of attention as a homogenized population group, 'the learning disabled', are not discussed. Rather, people formerly referred to as '*the* mentally handicapped' are now consumers, consumers who may have a grievance: the rhetoric of consumer choice and empowerment is invoked. 'The personal preferences of the individual' are to guide service planning and 'people should be helped to express their views and preferences ... sometimes people with learning disabilities ... will be dissatisfied with the services offered' (DOH, 1992:2). *Social Care for Adults with Learning Disabilities (Mental Handicap)* is explicit in its references to 'meeting the social needs of people ... within a mixed economy of care' (DOH, 1992: 2). Our newly disgruntled consumers, it appears, are no longer are in need of nursing.

In the light of Rose's and Miller's analyses of the endeavour to maintain people as contributory members of the society of which they are a part, the annex to *Social Care for Adults with Learning Disabilities (Mental Handicap)* is telling. In a subsection considering employment, the document appeals not only to subjectivity and intersubjectivity as sites for the regulation of conduct but also to the national interest in self-regulated conduct. The Circular (DOH, 1992: 9–10) suggests that:

> Participation in a paid job will help them to achieve a greater social independence and self-assurance. If they go out to work and pay their own way in the world, they are likely to see themselves as more valued members of the community making a contribution to that community ... it is important that the country makes the best use of the skills and potential contribution from all its citizens.

The implications of this are far reaching. Here full 'citizenship', with its rights and obligations, is held out to people who only just over a decade earlier had been described in governmental policy advice as a homogenous, and problematic, client group in need of better nursing care. These newly minted 'enterprising selves', it is suggested, will too come to find their subjectivity enhanced by producing and consuming; they will gain autonomy – 'independence and self-assurance' – and they will come, via the intersubjective ratification of their fellow citizens, to self-fulfilment, to see themselves as 'valued members of the community'.

The Welsh Office's review of the All-Wales Strategy (AWS) (Welsh Office, 1991) replicates the construction of intellectual-disability-as-enterprising-self seen in the MENCAP speech. The AWS review deploys the themes of quality and consumerism as way stations for the explicit invocation of the notion of 'quality of life' as an organizing construct within the corporatist/managerialist framework of service provision which the text constructs. Again invoking intersubjectivity as the site of concern, the document (Welsh Office, 1991: para. 2) claims that the All-Wales Strategy:

enable[s] people ... to live fulfilled lives, as independently as possible, in their own homes in the wider community, with care and support tailored to their needs as individuals ... the Strategy has demonstrated that ... local services can provide improved quality, more choice for individuals, and greater responsiveness to their needs ... people ... are experiencing greater independence and have more control over their lives.

In the same way that university students have been transformed into 'customers', here people with intellectual disabilities are transformed from a homogenized population to become 'individuals' who happen to be users of services. As 'users' or 'consumers'/'customers' of services, they have preferences ('choices') and can be expected to express them in their search for 'fulfilled lives'. The adoption, by service providers, of such a consumerist approach is what allows 'individual' enterprising selves to acquire Rose's (1992) 'autonomy' – here, 'independence' and 'control'. One of the roles of services thus becomes not just the provision of social care but also to 'assist service users to find their voice in individual and local planning ... to ensure that their needs and wishes are properly identified' (Welsh Office, 1991: 17). Most radically, perhaps, while newly enfranchised as citizens in England, in Wales people with intellectual disabilities are called upon to become the 'partners' of government. The Welsh Office (1991: 33) argues that:

the contribution which users, carers, the voluntary and private sectors can and should make to planning ... needs careful management to ensure that each partner ... can make a valuable contribution.

The term 'partner', with its echoes of the world of commerce, and the identification of people with intellectual disabilities as 'valuable' contributors to a 'managed' planning process, positions them as not just the recipients of the care of the state, but as the *colleagues* of both state and the voluntary and private sectors.

The theme of 'quality' is routinely invoked, and equally routinely linked to the notions of 'care', 'responsiveness' to 'individuals' and fiscal rectitude. Thus 'the new framework set out in the *Caring for People* White paper provides the right basis for social services authorities to work ... to develop quality care' (Welsh Office, 1991: para. 20). Further, in paragraph 31, the document states that:

The Secretary of State places great importance on improving monitoring and evaluation to ensure that services are of high quality and provide consistent value for money ... he proposes to establish mechanisms better to assure quality and assess value for money ... to implement ... practices that are responsive to the wishes and needs of individuals.

At a first reading it is entirely plausible that the Minister might be referring here to library services, the fire brigade or even to the state of the sewers. That is to say, this construction of the role of government in the provision of 'services' is not immediately identifiable as referring to the particular and specific needs of a particularly vulnerable group of people. What we have here is the state-as-corporation describing its governing political mentality. With an appeal to modernity as warrant, the implication is that neither 'value for money' nor 'quality care' was available under the 'old' framework: a framework incapable of 'quality' not just because it had inadequate measures in place to 'assure quality' but on account of the fact that it was unresponsive to the 'wishes and needs of individuals'.

It was not just government that adopted this new rhetoric in the 1980s and 1990s: the psy-complex too adopted the now linked 'languages' (Greig, 1993) – or discourses – of normalization and corporatism. Thus *Services for People with Learning Disabilities and Challenging Behaviour or Mental Health Needs* (DOH, 1993) – the report of an expert panel of academics and service providers convened by government – not only promotes 'the supported ordinary housing model' of care (DOH, 1993: 12) but also stresses the fact that 'successful services' are 'individualised' (DOH, 1993: 9). In 'successful' services the report claims, 'packages of care are constructed' on the basis of 'thoroughly knowing and understanding the individual' (DOH, 1993: 9).

Furthermore, in direct advice to 'commissioners' of services (another term making explicit the link between markets and the development of so-called 'social care'), the report stresses that 'value for money cannot be judged solely on the basis of costs … commissioners … should attend to the general *quality of life* as measured by, for example, the widely used "five service accomplishments" as well as by user satisfaction' (DOH, 1993: 19, my emphasis). In assessing value for money, 'service purchasers' are advised to 'attend to the general *quality of life* in addition to the specific treatment of challenging behaviour.' (DOH, 1993: 28, my emphasis). The regular measurement of the quality of life of service users is promoted as an example of 'good practice' (DOH, 1993: 22). It is noted that many services deploy the rhetoric of normalization while showing widely different standards of performance. Therefore commissioners are said to need to be able to: 'distinguish good outcomes from window-dressing' (DOH, 1993: 20). Again we note that the term 'window-dressing' is another a borrowing from the discourse of commerce, in this case retailing.

The rhetoric of these texts invokes a discourse recognizable as that dissected by academic theoreticians of 'quality of life'. The person with an intellectual disability is constructed as an 'enterprising self', as an individual with subjective wishes and preferences. The response of the state is no longer the direct control of deviance – a dispenser of institutional nursing care to the 'mentally handicapped' – but rather is to function as the 'caring' chair in the boardroom deliberations of a range of 'partners'. There is a range of individualized demands – 'wishes and needs' – which it is the function of services to negotiate meeting. Human services are positioned as the 'providers' (retailers?) of a range of aids (and accessories) that may be 'purchased' with a view to achieving a 'fulfilled' life. The individual 'service user' is an impaired consumer – almost a confused shopper – with the rights of citizenship, but also the concomitant personal responsibility to consume and to contribute.

In adopting these positions it should be noted that the rhetoric of government not only makes regular reference to the notion of 'quality', but also that the construct of 'quality of life' is explicitly used. Not only is 'quality of life' deployed as an *aspect of individual subjectivity*, it is also construed as an *outcome of service practice*. In the MENCAP speech it is what 'mental handicap nurses' in 'large mental handicap hospitals' have historically provided (DOH, 1991: para. 15). A high quality of life is what well-considered and up-to-date policy, by treating people with 'respect and dignity' (DOH, 1991: para. 6) – as individualized 'consumers' – offers as its latest product. In the All-Wales Strategy review (Welsh Office, 1991) 'quality of life' is invoked by the claims that the AWS has provided people with 'a fulfilled life', an outcome of services responsive to individual wishes and needs. In *Services for People with Learning Disabilities and Challenging Behaviour or Mental Health Needs* 'quality of life' is one of the 'good' outcomes which 'successful services' will deliver.

In these documents what has become an individualized outcome of service activity – a high 'quality of life' – is, in keeping with the idea that 'the customer is always right', to be assessed by assisting people to 'find their voice' (Welsh Office, 1991), to report on their own satisfaction with life. Such an idea is also expressed in the House of Commons Select Committee on the Social Services Seventh Report. The report, on 'quality', explicitly suggests that 'inspection units be *required* to take account of the views of service users' in assessing the quality of service provision (Social Services Committee, 1990: para. 106, my emphasis). Clearly, then, if this is the discursive position of government, the most appropriate index for the psy-complex to select in the process of 'monitoring and evaluation to ensure that services are of high quality and provide consistent value for money' (Welsh Office, 1991) is the quality of life achieved by people with intellectual disabilities and reported on by themselves.

In Summary

Rather than being ideologically pure developments of normalization, notions of 'consumerism', 'quality' and 'quality of life' are, rather, intimately bound up in the powerful discourse of corporatism and managerialism which, although pervading most strongly the rhetoric of the right, is, as Rose (1992) notes, the dominant political mentality of the present. As such, we have seen here how, over the course of the twenty years after 1980, a group of people previously 'thought' as a degenerate moral threat have been transformed into candidate enterprising selves.

That is, in the texts analysed in this chapter, people with an intellectual disability have moved from being represented as a homogenous population group in need of the care of others, into *individual* selves or subjective beings who can be understood as aspiring to autonomy and striving for personal fulfilment. The anonymous undifferentiated mass of 1980 – 'the mentally handicapped' – have become, by the 1990s, identifiable persons with individual responsibilities and duties, who may be expected to seek meaning in existence, be motivated by the search for satisfaction with earthly life and, most importantly, exercise such subjectivity by acts of choice. People with intellectual disabilities are, thus, recruited as 'enterprising selves'.

From this perspective it seems plausible that the notion of quality (of life) derives its legitimation as a site of social scientific study not so much from advances in science (as Hagerty *et al.* (2001) for example claim), but rather from its subsumability into projects of governmentality and the discourse of enterprise culture. The fact that the quality of life/QOL of service users has an 'intuitive' appeal as a template against which to test the 'success' of community services merely reflects this new way of thinking (intellectually disabled) selves. The resonance of this new thinking of people with intellectual disabilities as candidate enterprising selves with our everyday thinking of our selves in this way has doubtless assisted in the concept's ready assimilation into academic discourse. As has been noted, considerable rhetorical energy has been expended by government and the psy-complex in promoting the concept as a 'service quality' measure. Indeed the frequency and enthusiasm with which the social scientific literature endorses QOL as furnishing services with a means of comparing the 'number of satisfied customers' under different regimes, and rewarding these regimes appropriately, might be taken to suggest a widespread approval of this approach.

However, the analysis here would suggest that the contingencies for the adoption of the notion by the executive and its psy-complex partners may differ. The executive deploys a range of common tropes ('quality', 'consumerism', 'individual choice') as key elements of a superordinate discourse of commerce, managerialism and market economics – of 'enterprise culture'. Conversely, in the intellectual disability research community at least, the notion of QOL is understood as following from the normalization movement and as inheriting its social justice ideological commitments. Examination of a prototypical psy-complex QOL measure (Schalock and Keith's, 1996, *Quality of Life Questionnaire*) indeed reveals a strong welfarist commitment to the position of the individual inconsistent with, indeed on occasion subversive of, the hegemony of corporatized service provision and the managerialist rationale for its employment (Antaki and Rapley, 1996a; Antaki and Rapley, 1996b; Rapley and Antaki, 1996).

Notes

1. Normalization was a controversial theory of human service practice that captured the imagination of many service providers and planners from the mid-1970s onwards. In brief, normalization suggested that services should attempt to offer their 'clients' a life as close to the 'normal' as was possible. See Wolfensberger (1972) for an overview.
2. The 'Ely scandal' flowed from revelations in the newspaper *The News of the World* of appalling living conditions and abusive treatment of residents at a hospital for people with intellectual disabilities (then a so-called 'subnormality' hospital) in Ely, a suburb of Cardiff, Wales.
3. MENCAP is the major British charity, or NGO (non-governmental organization) which provides services for people with intellectual disabilities and their families, runs public education campaigns and lobbies government over the direction of social policy.

Study Questions

- How are other 'marginalized' groups – such as elderly people, homeless people or people described as 'mentally ill' – currently thought with respect to the 'enterprise culture' in the West?
- How are people with intellectual disabilities, the 'mentally ill' and elderly people thought of in non-Western cultures?
- In what other sites has 'quality', or enterprise culture talk, risen to prominence over the past twenty years?
- If possible at all, how can 'quality of life' be thought in non-Western cultures?

Suggestions for Further Reading

Foucault, M. (1977) *Discipline and Punish: The Birth of the Prison*. London: Allen Lane.

Kendall, G. and Wickham, G. (1999) *Using Foucault's Methods*. London: Sage.

Miller, T. and McHoul, A. (1998) *Popular Culture and Everyday Life*. London: Sage.

Rose, N. (1999) *Governing the Soul: The Shaping of the Private Self, 2nd edn*. London: Free Association Books.

CHAPTER 6

QOL in Health and Social Care Research

QOL research in medical settings focuses most clearly on issues of the objective operationalization and quantification of the construct. A second (though not necessarily secondary) key concern has been the ethically difficult development of QALYs and DALYs, and more recently, a focus on the related concept of 'customer satisfaction' with health/social care provision as an adjunct variable to concern with QOL. This chapter draws on the work of key critical thinkers such as Nord to review methodological approaches used in the development of QOL indices, such as QALYs and HRQOL measures, routinely used in health and social care settings.

Health-related QOL

Some authorities (most notably Cummins) are deeply sceptical of notions such as 'HRQOL' and the use of condition- or disease-specific measures. Much of this debate is a consequence of two different endeavours talking past each other. Cummins's work attempts to specify QOL as a global construct, whereas QOL research in the vast majority of medical settings revolves around pragmatic concerns. Usually, these are efforts to evaluate whether *this* procedure, for *these* patients, with *this* condition, produces an identifiable increase in QOL (in whatever way, locally, for this particular condition, it is defined).

QOL work in this area has contributed to the development of what, in the UK, may be a new approach to medicine. In view of Rose's (1992) conception of the rights and duties of 'entrepreneurial selves' in postmodernity, this 'new' approach is understandable as another instance of the increasing responsibility of persons to collaborate with the professions in the use of technologies of the self. However, in the policy document *The Expert Patient*, the British Department of Health (2001: 5) suggests that:

> an observation often made by doctors, nurses and other health profes-
> sionals … is 'my patient understands their disease better than I do.' This
> knowledge and experience held by the patient has for too long been an
> untapped resource. It is something that could greatly benefit the quality of
> patients' care and ultimately their quality of life … today's patients with
> chronic diseases need not be mere recipients of care. They can become
> key decision-makers in the treatment process … Self-management

programmes can be specifically designed to reduce the severity of symptoms and improve confidence, resourcefulness and self-efficacy.

Such an approach may, by reducing the severity of symptoms and improving 'confidence, resourcefulness and self-efficacy', be understood as contributing directly to improving patients' health-related quality of life (HRQOL).

What is HRQOL?

The US Centers for Disease Control and Prevention offer a definition of HRQOL that would probably command a consensus. HRQOL encompasses those aspects of overall QOL that can be clearly shown to affect health – be it physical or mental health (CDC, 2000). As with the concept of QOL itself, HRQOL is conceptualized as being both an individual- and a population-level construct. The CDC (2000: 6) contends that for individuals, HRQOL 'includes physical and mental health perceptions and their correlates, including health risks and conditions, functional status, social support, and socioeconomic status … On the community level, HRQOL includes resources, conditions, policies, and practices that influence a population's health perceptions and functional status.'

Why measure HRQOL?

Many Western governments claim the intent to 'increase quality of life' (DOH, 2001). Their agencies state that their 'mission' is 'to promote health and *quality of life* by preventing, and controlling disease, injury and disability' (CDC, 2000, my emphasis). Accordingly, it is necessary to adopt procedures to gauge success in these endeavours (see Petersen and Lupton, (1996). The CDC (2000: 6) suggest that:

> measuring HRQOL can help determine the burden of preventable disease, injuries, and disabilities, and it can provide valuable new insights into the relationships between HRQOL and risk factors. Measuring HRQOL will help monitor progress in achieving the nation's health objectives. Analysis of HRQOL surveillance data can identify subgroups with relatively poor perceived health and help to guide interventions to improve their situations and avert more serious consequences.

Idler and Benyamini (1997) have suggested that self-assessed health status better predicts mortality and morbidity than many objective measures of health: thus there is considerable potential in assessing the HRQOL individuals. Essentially what QOL research seeks to do in the medical/health area, then, is to answer questions, at both individual and community levels, like 'what are the effects on patients' QOL of using procedure *x*?' 'What QOL benefits flow from adopting policy *y*?' 'What endpoints should be used for clinical trials or to evaluate the efficacy of therapeutic interventions?' and 'How should effectiveness be quantified for cost-effectiveness analysis (CEA)?'

At the community level HRQOL is assessed using a wide range of specific measures – such as the EuroQOL–5D (described below) – and by summary indices in the form of QALYs and DALYs. At the individual level a huge number of HRQOL measures supplement traditional outcome indicators such as mortality rates, tumour size or blood sugar control. More recently, medical literatures have adopted three broad approaches to the use of QOL as an 'endpoint'. Studies report physician or patient judgments of the patient's QOL (in terms of symptoms or functional status) and patient evaluations of health states (in terms of preferences, 'utilities' or values). Morreim (1992) distinguishes 'Consensus Quality of Life research' (CQL) – asking healthy people to answer hypothetical health questions known as 'time trade-offs' or to assign relative values to differential impairments in terms of their 'utility' impact on QOL – and Personal Quality of Life research (PQL), which evaluates individuals' own judgements about the QOL in terms of the effects of disease and therapeutic intervention.

Morreim (1992) notes that PQL is generally more helpful in the *individual practice of* medicine. As the task of medicine is to assist *individual* patients, it makes more sense to ask patients about their QOL than to seek the judgments of healthy citizens about hypothetical situations. Examples of both approaches are considered below. However, a moment of reflection and an overview of the current state of the art is in order.

The quality of QOL research in medical settings

In considering QOL in medical settings – where judgments of life quality have life-threatening consequences – we must remember that quality of life is not an object or thing but a *judgment of the value* of life circumstances. As such, it is crucial that treatment decisions involving relative valuations of the quality of a patient's life, and the decision-making tools which inform them, are based in ethically sound research conducted and reported to rigorous standards.

Van der Maas *et al.* (1996) estimate that, in the Netherlands, 43 per cent of all deaths involve 'end-of-life' decisions by doctors (the decision to withdraw or withhold treatment, the prescription of lethal doses of analgesics or the active killing of the patient) with higher rates for people with intellectual disabilities or psychiatric problems. Van Thiel *et al.*'s (1997) study of end-of-life decisions involving people with intellectual disabilities found that, while only two patients had actively asked to die, doctors felt that *their* estimation of the patient's suffering was sufficient to 'assist' the patient to die, in three cases by lethal injection. Van Thiel *et al.*

(1997: 90) note that 'all of them were incompetent and did not express their wishes about the decision ... deaths were reported as natural in all cases'. Groenewoud *et al.* (1996) surveyed nearly half of all Dutch psychiatrists: 37 per cent had received at least one request for assisted suicide, and twelve had complied. Groenewoud *et al.* (1996) estimate each psychiatrist conducts between two and five assisted suicides a year. They suggest:

> excluding those who had ever assisted ... 64 percent thought physician-assisted suicide because of a mental disorder could be acceptable, including 241 who said they could conceive of instances in which they themselves would be willing to assist.

Such findings put evaluations of the quality of a life firmly onto centre stage, even in specialisms like psychiatry which are distant from those where QOL judgments are a routine aspect of practice (oncology, intensive care or transplant surgery). That Dutch psychiatrists kill people they describe as 'mentally disordered' or 'incompetent' raises serious ethical questions about informed consent, about the criteria against which the quality of these lives were judged and found wanting, and the evidence base upon which these judgments were made.

Much HRQOL research – even that published in prestigious journals – fails on the counts above. Much is based in dubious ethical practices and research design (e.g. not consulting patients about their QOL) and/or is methodologically so flawed as to be worthless. In their study of the quality of QOL reporting in medicine, Gill and Feinstein (1994) found that only 15 per cent of investigators defined QOL, just over a third justified selection of the measure used, and a mere 13 per cent asked patients to assess their QOL. Sanders *et al.* (1998) found QOL reporting rose from 0.63 per cent of studies in 1980 to 4.2 per cent in 1997. While, by 1987, 8.2 per cent of cancer trials reported QOL data, Sanders *et al.* (1998: 1193) noted that the field was confounded by a bewildering array of measures and that:

> of the 67 studies sampled ... 48 used 62 different pre-existing instruments and a further 15 studies reported new measures, with few following the methods proposed [by the *Lancet*] for the development and testing of instruments ... it is implausible that some 40 different measures of generic or psychological well-being could be justified in 48 trials.

Even in RCTs (randomized controlled trials), then, the 'gold standard' of outcome studies, reporting of QOL research is, say Sanders *et al.* (1998: 1194), 'poor'. Not only were patients generally not consulted about their QOL (despite QOL being defined as the most important outcome variable in 23 of the 67 studies), but also 'in about 30 per cent of studies it remained unclear whether patients had contributed any information at all'. Citing

Slevin *et al.*'s, (1988) study, it is concluded: 'Clearly some investigators continue to believe that health professionals can make a valid assessment of their patients' QOL in spite of evidence to the contrary' (Sanders *et al.*, 1998: 1194). These assessments are most technically developed in the form of QALYs and DALYs.

What are QALYs and DALYs?

Nord (1992a, 1992b) notes that the QALY concept is central to the health status approach to QOL research. Quality adjusted life years (QALYs) are derived from the notion that the relative effectiveness of medical interventions, or the value of health care programmes, is a function of the significance of the health improvements delivered to patients: the longer patients survive to enjoy the benefits of medical/healthcare intervention and the greater the number of patients who are helped by a given system. Phillips and Thompson (1998: 1) suggest that:

> QALYs provide a common currency to assess the extent of the benefits gained from a variety of interventions in terms of health-related quality of life and survival for the patient. When combined with the costs of providing the interventions, cost-utility ratios result; these indicate the additional costs required to generate a year of perfect health (one QALY). Comparisons can be made between interventions, and priorities can be established based on those interventions that are relatively inexpensive (low cost per QALY) and those that are relatively expensive (high cost per QALY).

The QALY is a straightforward statistic. The QALY represents life expectancy adjusted for QOL. In health economic terms QALYs allow comparisons across medical interventions that differ in their effects on longevity and on different aspects of QOL. Years of life in different states of physical or mental dysfunction or various symptomatic states are assigned values on a scale of 1.0 (healthy) to 0.0 (dead). These values reflect the relative quality of the states and allow morbidity and mortality improvements to be combined into a single weighted measure – QALYs gained. Thus, for example, 10 years of life in perfect health = 10 QALYs; 15 years of life with a mildly compromised QOL (e.g. persistent back pain) may be rated at 0.8 relative to perfect health, with QALY value calculated as the product of the QOL rating of 0.8 multiplied by the years of life = (15×0.8) = 12 QALYs.

Alternatively, if one lives five years on medication with perfect health followed by seven years with lowered QOL from side effects, scoring 0.5, this intervention would return 8.5 QALYs $((5 \times 1) + (7 \times 0.5) = 8.5)$. The argument for QALYs is that it is possible by, assigning a numerical value to the lowered 'utility' of a life with medical problems, to arrive at an objective 'bottom line' judgment about whether intervention is 'worth it'. If the projected value of life after intervention is less than that which might be expected with untreated disease, treatment should be withheld.

Such calculations can compare different treatments. If John has kidney failure and renal transplant improves his health from 0.3 to 0.9 for one year, and renal dialysis extends Jane's life for five years in a 0.6 state, then by simple arithmetic renal dialysis has returned 3.6 QALYs gained ((0.9 – 0.3) + (5.0 × 0.6) = 3.6). The cost per QALY gained (the 'cost : utility ratio' or the 'cost-effectiveness ratio') may then be calculated. For example, an analysis of QALYs gained by kidney transplants may return a higher absolute number of QALYs, say 5.2 QALYs. However, if the cost of dialysis is $100 per QALY gained and the cost of kidney transplantation is $500 per QALY gained, dialysis has a much better cost : utility ratio than transplantation. More QOL is purchased for less outlay: dialysis produces 'more bang for your buck' allowing resource allocation choices producing maximal health for money spent (Hyder *et al.*, 1998).

Such calculations may be expressed as cost-utility ratios using the formula.

$$\text{Cost-utility ratio} = \frac{\text{Cost of Intervention A} - \text{Cost of Intervention B}}{\text{No. of QALYs produced by Intervention A} - \text{No. of QALYs produced by Intervention B}}$$

Nord (1992a: 875) points out that 'when prioritising between them the standard health economist recommendation is to rank the programmes from the lowest cost per QALY value to the highest and to select from the top until available resources are exhausted'. However such statistics cannot tell us anything about the benefits – or 'utility' – to Jane's two toddlers of having a mum around for another five years in a health state of 0.6, as opposed to no mum in health state 0.0.

Calculating QALYs

Measuring QOL to compute QALYs primarily uses two methods, psychometric scales measuring HRQOL (e.g. WHOQOL (WHO, 1997), the CDC's HRQOL 14 or EuroQOL EQ5D (see Table 6.1)). Many studies employ psychometric measures as stand-alone instruments and report scale scores rather than QALYs. Joseph and Rao (1999) report a comparative study of the effects of leprosy on the QOL of people with and without the disease in Andhra Pradesh using the WHOQOL.[1] Alternatively, studies may opt for the direct assessment of the 'utility' of various health/ill-health states, a concept sometimes phrased in terms of 'health preferences'.

Use of psychometric QOL scales varies across studies. In some cases patients report on activities or symptoms in the recent past, providing an evaluation of their current health state, whereas in others they may make relative judgments about changes in their health status or future hypothetical health states. For the purposes of calculation present state is used. Such patient-reported facts do not necessarily indicate the relative importance to the patient of different aspects of health, nor place values on the effects of poor health on life activities. Such an approach also often relies on the expert judgment of researchers or health professionals to give the patient an overall QOL score ranging from 0.0 to 1.0, where 0.0 = death and 1.0 = perfect health, drawing on utility weights of values generated by general population surveys.

Tables 6.1 and 6.2 show health states from the EuroQOL-5D and a selection of average utility weights for various health states based on the ratings of over 3,000 people in the UK. A variety of health states are rated as progressively less desirable than perfect health, with the final state being ranked (with a minus value) as being worse than death. It should be noted that while such studies may be statistically representative of nations, they may also misrepresent the utilities assigned by patients themselves. For example, in a comparison of the utilities of members of the general public and patients with aneurysmal subarachnoid haemorrhage Polsky *et al.* (2001) found that pairwise comparisons of 243 of the EuroQol's 245 health states diverged, with 95 per cent of these differences being statistically significant. Polsky *et al.* (2001: 33) note that 'the general public rated states with the highest levels of function higher but states with worse levels of function lower, than did … patients'. In such hypothetical tasks, the general public tend to overestimate the decrease in QOL associated with impaired health states.

The same approach was employed by Salkeld *et al.* (2000) who report a combined methodology using the EuroQOL-5D and a utility measure, a time trade-off task (TTO), to investigate the relationship between fear of falling, hip fracture and QOL in older women.

EQ-5D scores were calculated using the utility weights of values from the UK general population survey, and combined with the results of a preference task (rank-ordering four hypothetical hip-fracture scenarios) and the TTO to conclude that the preference weight for a 'bad' hip fracture was valued at 0.05, with a 'good' hip fracture valued at 0.31. Salkeld *et al.* (2000: 341) note that 'of the women surveyed, 80 per cent would rather be dead (utility = 0) than experience the loss of independence and QOL that results from a bad hip fracture and admission to a nursing home'. Phillips and Thompson (1998) report a comparative evaluation of two drugs for breast cancer, with health states describing patients' experience of the disease from pre-treatment to terminal illness scored by oncology nurses. Phillips and Thompson's (1998: 2) summary illustrates the extremely detailed cost-effectiveness analysis such procedures may offer:

Table 6.1 EuroQOL EQ-5D health states

Scores for the EuroQOL EQ-5D are a measure of individual functioning in five dimensions.

___

Mobility
1. No problems walking about.
2. Some problems walking about.
3. Confined to bed.

Pain/discomfort
1. No pain or discomfort.
2. Moderate pain or discomfort.
3. Extreme pain or discomfort.

Self-care
1. No problems with self-care.
2. Some problems washing or dressing.
3. Unable to wash or dress self.

Anxiety/depression
1. Not anxious or depressed.
2. Moderately anxious or depressed.
3. Extremely anxious or depressed.

Usual activities (work, study, housework, leisure activities)
1. No problems in performing usual activities.
2. Some problems in performing usual activities.
3. Unable to perform usual activities.

As each dimension has three levels – no problem, some problems and major problems – the EuroQOL returns a total of 243 possible health states, which with the addition of 'unconscious' and 'dead' produce a total of 245 possible health states.

___

Paclitaxel generates 0.5111 QALYs and docetaxel 0.6016 QALYs – a difference of 0.0905 QALYs, equivalent to an additional 33 days of perfect health (0.0905 × 365). The additional costs of docetaxel amount to £220 per patient, which means that it costs £2,431 (£220/0.0905) to generate an additional QALY by using docetaxel.

Table 6.3 illustrates the wide range of procedures for which this sort of analyses have been conducted. The table also shows the huge variation in terms of cost per QALY. Such analyses may allow for relative weightings of intervention importance to be derived; thus we can see that neurosurgical intervention for malignant intracranial tumours is, at 1990 British prices, 97 times more expensive per QALY gained than pacemaker implantation.

What such figures conceal, however, is the details of both the procedures and the recipients of the intervention. That is, 'intracranial tumours' covers a

Table 6.2 EQ-5D health state valuations

Health state	Description	Valuation
11111	No problems	1.000
11221	No problems walking about; no problems with self-care; some problems with performing usual activities; some pain or discomfort; not anxious or depressed	0.760
22222	Some problems walking about; some problems washing or dressing self; some problems with performing usual activities; moderate pain or discomfort; moderately anxious or depressed	0.516
12321	No problems walking about; some problems washing or dressing self; unable to perform usual activities; some pain or discomfort; not anxious or depressed	0.329
21123	Some problems walking about; no problems with self-care; no problems with performing usual activities; moderate pain or discomfort; extremely anxious or depressed	0.222
23322	Some problems walking about, unable to wash or dress self, unable to perform usual activities, moderate pain or discomfort, moderately anxious or depressed	0.079
33332	Confined to bed; unable to wash or dress self; unable to perform usual activities; extreme pain or discomfort; moderately anxious or depressed	–0.429

Source: Phillips and Thompson (1998).

very wide range of conditions of differing severity. Secondly, it may be argued (see Cubbon, 1991) that life-saving brain surgery is more 'valuable' for a 35-year-old executive than it is for a 65-year-old pensioner.

Utility Measures

Utility measures can be employed to evaluate any health state – current health, previous health or, as in the Salkeld *et al.* (2000) study, *hypothetical* future states. Utility measures also allow for the evaluation of other outcomes, for example length of life. Using such measures allows respondents to evaluate the relative utility (or desirability) of various health states rather than simply reporting on their present symptoms or current functional status. Thus answers are influenced by the preferences and

Table 6.3 Relative costs of a variety of medical health care and health promotion activities and interventions

Intervention	£/QALY at 1990 prices
Cholesterol testing and diet therapy (all adults aged 40–69)	220
Neurosurgical intervention for head injury	240
GP advice to stop smoking	270
Neurosurgical intervention for subarachnoid haemorrhage	490
Antihypertensive treatment to prevent stroke (ages 45–64)	940
Pacemaker implantation	1,100
Hip replacement	1,180
Valve replacement for aortic stenosis	1,410
Cholesterol testing and treatment (all adults aged 40–69)	1,480
Kidney transplantation	4,710
Breast cancer screening	5,780
Heart transplantation	7,840
Home haemodialysis	17,260
Hospital haemodialysis	21,970
Neurosurgical intervention for malignant intracranial tumours	107,780

Source: Adapted from Phillips and Thompson (1998).

goals of individual respondents as well as their preparedness to take risks. Responses require respondents to make an explicit trade-off on their relative preferences for particular health states (again usually rated from 1.0 = perfect health to 0.0 = death).

Assessment of health utilities most commonly uses one or more of three techniques: direct rating scales, time trade-off (TTO) and standard gamble (SG). Using a direct rating scale respondents are presented with a description of a health state and asked to rate it on a 0 to 1 (or 0 = bad as death to 100 = good as perfect health) scale. For example Salkeld *et al.* (2000: 345) used ratings of four health states described as:

Full health – Anne
Anne is a similar age to you. She lives in her own home and cares for herself. Anne is active in her local community and is out and about with friends quite a bit. She swims regularly and enjoys visiting her children each weekend. Anne walks without any aids and can manage her 12 steps at home without any problems. She enjoys shopping and cooking for herself. Anne does not need any help with the housework and derives pleasure and relaxation from gardening.

Fear of falling – Mary
Mary is a similar age to you. She lives alone in her own home and cares for herself. Mary is involved in community fundraising and enjoys playing bridge. Mary recently had a fall. She did not break any bones but was

badly cut and bruised. She is scared of falling. Mary continues to walk without aids. She still looks after herself and does her own housework. Mary has been a bit depressed since her fall. She has returned to her bridge group but is anxious when she is outside the home because she is scared of falling again.

Good hip fracture – Jean
Jean is a similar age to you. She lives in her own home and cares for herself. Before her fall Jean was out and about quite a bit with her church group. She swam on a regular basis and occasionally looked after her grandchildren. Jean broke her hip when she fell. She is finding it difficult to do everything at home now that she walks with a stick. She needs help in shopping as she no longer drives or feels confident to shop alone. She can prepare only simple meals and is missing being able to bake for her friends. Jean can no longer manage the housework by herself. She misses her church activities but finds it too painful and tiring to be out for long periods. Jean experiences feelings of frustration and anger. Jean gets tearful thinking about all the things she can't do.

Bad hip fracture – Elizabeth
Elizabeth is a similar age to you. Until her recent fall, she lived in her own home and managed to care for herself. She was active in her local community. Elizabeth broke her hip when she fell. She is now unable to live alone as she requires a great deal of help to do most things. Elizabeth now lives in a nursing home near to her family but away from her friends. She is limited in where she can walk because of the frame and is unable to walk for long distances. She is unable to shower or dress without help from the nurse. She is unable to pursue her gardening or community work. Her leg aches sometimes at night. She has become anxious and is easily upset.

Having ranked and *directly rated* their 'preference' for these hypothetical scenarios a further time trade-off study was undertaken.

Time trade-off method

Time trade-off (TTO) studies use such hypothetical scenarios and offer respondents a forced choice between two states where outcomes are known with certainty (Dolan *et al.*, 1996). An example typical of a TTO study would offer respondents the following choices and establish the point at which they are, by increments, indifferent between them.

Imagine that you have chronic fatigue syndrome (CFS) and that you feel constantly tired, lethargic and have pain in your joints almost every day. You have some problems with shopping for yourself, lifting things and concentrating on work for more than an hour or so at a time. You have tried the most commonly prescribed medications, but they have not helped. Other than your CFS, you are in good health. You are 50 years old and can expect to live another 30 years.

An experimental drug is available that would totally eliminate your chronic fatigue syndrome and restore full health. However, this medication would decrease your life expectancy. If the medication decreased your life expectancy by five years you would have the following options. A. Live with CFS for 30 years B. Live in full health for 25 years Which option would you choose?

Patients are asked for the trade-off they are prepared to make in terms of years of life in full health for the benefit of the intervention (in this case the imaginary experimental drug). In Salkeld et al. (2000) the choice was between living in a state of less than full health for five or ten years (depending on the participants' age) and then dying, or living for a lesser period of time as 'Anne' (in full health) and then dying, with 'tradeable' time increments of six months or a year. The time in full health was varied until participants were indifferent between alternatives. The trade-off being asked for here was 'shorter periods of life in full health for longer periods of life with lower quality of life' (Salkeld et al., 2000: 342). Given the choices above, a person may respond to the preference options as follows, with a tick (√) indicating their preferred choice:

1.   A. CFS for 30 years   √   B. full health for 25 years
2.   A. CFS for 30 years   √   B. full health for 22 years
3.   A. CFS for 30 years   √   B. full health for 21 years
4.   A. CFS for 30 years   B. full health for 20 years
5. √ A. CFS for 30 years   B. full health for 19 years
6. √ A. CFS for 30 years   B. full health for 18 years

The 'point of indifference' between options is at option 4. This set of preference choices returns the conclusion that 20 years in full health is just as good as 30 years with CFS, or a willingness to 'trade-off' ten years of life. Using the utility weight formula x/t (where x = years in full health and t = years with disease) then U – the utility weight – is $20/30 = 0.67$. This figure may be transformed into a QALY: thus living with CFS for 1 year yields 0.67 QALYs. The result can also be specified in terms of QALYs 'gained': living with CFS for 30 years yields $0.67 \times 30 = 20$ QALYs.

In Salkeld et al.'s study, extremely low mean utility weights assigned to the three non-full health options (fear of falling 'Mary' = 0.67; 'good' hip fracture 'Jean' = 0.31; 'bad' hip fracture 'Elizabeth' = 0.05) suggested that 'most women were prepared to trade off considerable length of life to avoid the reduction in quality of life that happens after a hip fracture' (Salkeld et al., 2000: 343). Although Salkeld et al. compared the utility weights assigned by those women in their sample who had and had not actually suffered a hip fracture – and found no significant difference in weights – clearly there are issues to be addressed in this method. Firstly in real life, there can be no knowing of the two alternatives on offer with the 'certainty' that Dolan *et al.* (1996a, 1996b) indicate the TTO method requires. Secondly, the way that options get weighted clearly depends on the way they are described. As Table 6.1 shows, apparently fine-grained differences in EuroQOL health state descriptions produce quite divergent utility values. Other issues also arise – for example not only the questionable realism of many TTO 'choices' – but also the reliability and validity of measures such as the EuroQOL with very elderly people. Coast *et al.* (1997) assessed the validity and reliability of the EuroQOL in elderly people, focusing particularly on people's ability to self-complete the scale. They state:

> Ability to self-complete the EuroQOL was found to be strongly related to both increased age and reduced cognitive function ... This research points to the need for rigorous studies (such as randomized controlled trials) to assess the impact of the format of administration of the EuroQOL on the scores obtained. (Coast *et al.*, 1997: 1)

The third utility measure employs the standard gamble (SG) method. This method asks respondents to take a gamble, or to weigh the odds, in two alternative states of health to arrive at a utility judgment. To return to our earlier example, such a method might ask a person the following question.

> Imagine that you have chronic fatigue syndrome and that you feel constantly tired, lethargic and have pain in your joints almost every day. You have some problems with shopping for yourself, lifting things and concentrating on work for more than an hour or so at a time. You have tried the most commonly prescribed medications but they have not helped. An experimental drug is available that would totally eliminate your chronic fatigue syndrome and restore full health. Unfortunately it carries a small but serious risk of toxic side effects.

> Which would you prefer? 90 per cent chance of perfect health and 10 per cent chance of immediate death or 100 per cent chance of life with CFS.

Like the TTO method, the relative odds can be varied until the respondent is unable to express a clear preference for one state. Thus we could vary the odds such that the choice demanded was between an 85 per cent chance of perfect health and a 15 per cent chance of sudden death, or a 100 per cent chance of life with CFS; between a 95 per cent chance of perfect health and a 5 per cent chance of sudden death or a 100 per cent chance of life with CFS and so on. When a respondent is indifferent between the two options (say at the 90 per cent chance of perfect health and 10 per cent chance of immediate death or 100 per cent chance of life with CFS stage) the utility weight is calculable from the following formula:

$$U(CFS) = 0.90 \times U(\text{Perfect Health}) + 0.10 \times U(\text{Death})$$
$$U(CFS) = 0.90 \times (1.0) + 0.10 \times (0) \text{ thus } U(CFS) = 0.90$$

An alternative approach to using the standard gamble method may pose a question in terms of anticipated life expectancy. For example:

> you have been diagnosed with prostate cancer. This reduces your life expectancy to ten years compared to a healthy person your age. A surgical treatment is available. If this treatment is successful, it would increase your life expectancy to be the same as a healthy person your age – 30 years. However, this surgery involves a risk of death. What risk of death would you accept?

If a respondent was willing to accept a 25 per cent risk of death, this can be respecified as saying that a life expectancy of ten years and a 25 per cent chance of death within two weeks in exchange for a 75 per cent chance of life expectancy of 10 years become equivalently attractive options. As the standard utility of expectable life is $U(30 \text{ yrs}) = 1.0$ and that of death is $U(0 \text{ yrs}) = 0.0$, then the utility weight is simply derived from the relative odds accepted. That is $U(10 \text{ yrs}) = 0.75 \times U(30 \text{ yrs}) + 0.05 \times U(0 \text{ yrs}) = 1.00 \times U(10 \text{ yrs})$. Accordingly: $((0.75 \times 1.0) + (0.05 \times 0.0) = U(10 \text{ yrs}) = 0.75))$.

Such studies allow for the relative costing of medical procedures in terms of cost per QALY and, in principle, for the differential weighting of forms of health care provision into 'league tables'. Another key use for utility weight analyses is the investigation of the weights assigned not by patients, but by *their doctors*. While their study addressed doctors' HIV utilities, as Owens *et al.* (1997: 77) point out:

> understanding of quality of life (QOL) with human immunodeficiency virus (HIV) is important because the merits of prevention and treatment alternatives may depend substantially on how these interventions affect QOL. Physicians' views about QOL are important, because they influence the therapeutic options that physicians consider or offer, the recommendations that physicians make, and because they are important for the analysis of certain policy questions.

Owens *et al.*'s study assessed physicians' utilities of health states for HIV with hepatitis B as a comparison. The TTO method returned median utilities of 0.833 for asymptomatic HIV, 0.417 for symptomatic HIV and 0.167 for AIDS. Each two-way comparison was statistically significant at the 0.01 level. Median utilities for asymptomatic hepatitis B, mildly symptomatic hepatitis B, and severely symptomatic hepatitis B were 0.917, 0.667 and 0.167. Again each comparison was statistically significant. With one year in full health equal to one QALY, then living for one year with asymptomatic HIV equals 0.833 QALYs. One year with symptomatic HIV equals 0.417 QALYs (just under 60 per cent less 'valuable' than a year in full health) and one year with full AIDS (or severely symptomatic hepatitis B) is worth 0.167 QALY, or, in other words, this is a year of life that has only slightly more 'utility' than death.

Owens *et al.* (1997) show that, although *doctors* varied substantially in their ratings of health states, they assessed the utility of life with HIV, including asymptomatic infection, as so severely reduced as, in the case of AIDS itself, to be barely distinguishable from being dead. This finding is in tension with Tsevat *et al.* (1999) who found that when *patients* with HIV were asked to 'trade off' life years for a return to 'full health', they were reluctant to do so: not only did patients often report an *improved* QOL *after* infection, but they clearly differ from the physicians surveyed by Owens *et al.* (1997) in the 'utility' they assign to life with HIV.

That utility perceptions may shape treatment decisions is shown by Patil *et al.*'s (2001) study of the preference values of physicians with regard to hepatitis C (HCV) and the use of antiviral therapy treatment. Patil *et al.* (2001) note that while most people with hepatitis C are asymptomatic, infection can lead to cirrhosis, cancer and death. As such, doctors making treatment decisions, and their patients, have to balance (trade off) the potential costs of HCV treatment – medication side effects and the cost of therapy – against potential future benefits. The most frequently used medications cause a number of unpleasant side effects and the cost of treatment is high. On the other hand a good response to medication is associated with undetectable viral load, improved liver function, and gains in health-related QOL.

Patil *et al.* (2001) also note that 'physicians' perspectives on HCV and its treatment may influence the advice that they give about treatment appropriateness. Patil *et al.* (2001) used an alternative methodology for measuring utilities, a visual analogue scale anchored on 0 per cent = death and 100 per cent = life without hepatitis C. Participants rated vignette descriptions of health states (see Table 6.4), derived from 'findings of our previous study of symptoms in patients with HCV and on a consensus of a group of hepatologists' (Patil *et al.*, 2001). With visual analogue scales (as in the EuroQOL 5D) participants simply draw a line on the scale to indicate their preference value. Participants also nominated the threshold sustained viral response rate to medication that they believed would be necessary for them to make a recommendation to their patients that they commence treatment.

Patil *et al.* (2001) report that 'physicians felt that hepatitis C causes a dramatic reduction in health status'. Utility values decreased rapidly as the severity of symptomatology increased (with the correlation statistically significant at the 0.001 level). Median preference value for Health State 1 ('No Symptoms, No Cirrhosis') was 88 per cent (or 0.88 QALY), or asymptomatic HCV infection was rated as a 12 per cent reduction in life

Table 6.4 Descriptions of Hepatitis C health states and treatment side effects from the Patil et al. (2001) study

Health state 1	Hepatitis C with no symptoms, no cirrhosis	No physical symptoms May transmit to sexual partner May develop cirrhosis
Health state 2	Hepatitis C with mild symptoms, no cirrhosis	Sometimes do not feel rested Tire more easily than usual May transmit to sexual partner May develop cirrhosis
Health state 3	Hepatitis C with moderate symptoms, no cirrhosis	Frequently do not feel rested Tire easily Limited in physical activities May transmit to sexual partner May develop cirrhosis
Health state 4	Hepatitis C with mild symptoms, cirrhosis	Sometimes do not feel rested Tire more easily than usual May transmit to sexual partner Have cirrhosis May get liver cancer May get liver failure
Health state 5	Hepatitis C with severe symptoms, cirrhosis	Sleep is disturbed Usually feel tired Limited in physical activities including work Little interest in sex Have cirrhosis May get liver cancer May need liver transplant
Treatment side effects	Side effects of treatment for hepatitis C	Needle sticks three times a week Pills twice daily Flu-like symptoms Fever, chills, nausea, headache, poor appetite Tend to improve after the first two weeks Tiredness, difficulty sleeping irritability, difficulty concentrating Chance of other life threatening medical problems that go away after treatment is completed such as low blood count, hair loss and depression

quality as compared to life without. The median preference value for the most severe health state (Health State 5 'Severe Symptoms, Cirrhosis' was only 18 per cent (utility = 0.18 QALY) representing a decrement in QOL of 82 per cent compared to life without HCV.

The median preference value for life with the side effects therapy was 47 per cent (utility = 0.47) indicating that treatment side effects themselves were assigned a preference value suggesting that QOL was less than half as good on antiviral treatment as compared to life without HCV. In terms of level of therapeutic response necessary to recommend treatment, a median of a 60 per cent sustained response rate was obtained (in contrast to the 30 per cent response rate offered by current antiviral therapy). Patil *et al.* (2001) report no significant correlations between preference values for hepatitis C health states, ratings of side effects of therapy and treatment thresholds.

As they recognize, Patil *et al.*'s (2001) findings offer an interesting parallel to those of Owen *et al.* (1997). The parallels suggest that the two different methodologies (time trade-off and visual analogue scale) obtain sufficiently similar results to offer support to each other, a finding echoed by Hakim and Pathak's (1999) study of the comparability of rating scales, standard gamble and discrete choice conjoint modelling methods. The use of a visual analogue scale does, however, have considerable advantages in terms of its simplicity of administration (Nord, 1991), although Selai and Trimble (1997) have noted that a number of patient groups may have considerable difficulties with the technique.

As did Owen *et al.* (1997), Patil *et al.* (2001) report a very wide range for physicians' preference ratings of treatment side effects, suggesting that while doctors' beliefs about the impact of side effects vary substantially they are, overall, negative. The absence of a correlation between ratings of treatment side effects and thresholds for recommending treatment suggests either inadequate knowledge of the disease among primary care doctors or the operation of preconceived notions about the disease and its treatment. This finding is, again, in keeping with the literature which suggests that both doctors' health state preferences and the disability weights they assign to particular conditions, may differ substantially from their patients (Costantini *et al.*, 2000; Rothwell *et al.*, 1997), and are considerably less positive (AbouZahr and Vaughan, 2000).

Noting that Treadwell *et al.* (2000) showed that HCV patients preferred to expedite their periods of poor health and higher utilities for therapy, even with side effects, than for life with delayed treatment, Patil *et al.* (2001) suggest that, in their study, 'in contrast, the physicians…had a relatively high threshold for recommending treatment, which would lead them to postpone therapy in the majority of cases'. Patil *et al.* (2001) suggest that one of the ways in which utility analysis may be of benefit is in facilitating doctor–patient decision-making on the basis of mutually understood utility preferences.

DALYs and Their Difficulties

Brown (2001: 769) suggests, based on the WHO's 'World Health Report 2001' that:

> psychiatric and neurological disorders account for nearly a third of the world's disability, measured in years lived with a disability. The burden is currently greatest in the industrialised countries, mainly because their populations are older, but as life expectancy in developing nations rises, these countries too are expected to see mental health problems become more prevalent. By 2020, depressive disorders are expected to be the second biggest cause of disease burden worldwide. (WHO, 2001)

This view is based on the DALY, or disability adjusted life year, a statistic representing 'years lived with a disability' or, alternatively, the 'burden of disease'. As was noted in Chapter 1, such estimates are contrary to Cummins's (2001b) view that absolute levels of international subjective well-being have been unchanged over the last twenty or so years. Data in the *World Health Report 2001*, which also notes that 'in Australia ... depression is ranked as the fourth most common cause of the total disease burden, and is the most common cause of disability' (WHO, 2001: 88), are consistent with work by Lewis and Wilkinson (1993) which suggests that profound, persistent unhappiness and anxiety was reported by 22 per cent of respondents in 1977 and 31 per cent in 1986, or James's (1997) analysis of dramatically increased suicide rates in Western countries over the last 50 years.

Arnesen and Nord (1999: 1423) note that the aim of the DALY is ambitious: they cite the International Burden of Disease Network (1998, cited in Arnesen and Nord, 1999: 1423) as suggesting that, while 'the burden of disease has yet to entirely replace traditional approaches to the assessment of health needs as an influence on political decision making', this development is clearly anticipated by the project. The concept of the DALY is complementary to the QALY and is designed to assist with the identification of health problems and their relative magnitude, the recognition of disease patterns, the prioritization of health problems and to inform allocation of health care resources (AbouZahr and Vaughan, 2000; Murray, 1994; Murray and Acharya, 1997). In the World Health Report (e.g. WHO, 2000, 2001), the primary summary measure of population health used is otherwise known as Disability-Adjusted Life Expectancy, or DALE. DALEs are described by Sadana *et al.* (n.d.: 3) as:

> measures [of] the equivalent number of years of life expected to be lived in full health, or healthy life expectancy ... As a summary measure of population health, DALE combines information on the impact of premature death and of disability and other non-fatal health outcomes.

DALYs have also been described as a 'health gap measure that quantifies loss of health for a population against a normative standard, and are not intended to be a measure of total well-being' (Salomon *et al.*, 2001: 268). Murray and Lopez (1997, cited in AbouZahr and Vaughan, 2000: 656) suggest that the development of the DALY was driven by the fact that:

> given the current state of health measurement, most analyses must ultimately fall back on measures of mortality, morbidity and disability. Analyses of outcomes, determinants, resources and even intervention effectiveness in reproductive health require clear and unambiguous specificity to facilitate meaningful measurement.

DALYs are thus intended to offer 'clear and unambiguous specificity to facilitate meaningful measurement'. As QALYs represent numerically the years of healthy life lived, so DALYs are a measure of the number of years of healthy life lost. DALYs, like QALYs, multiply the number of years lived by a quantification of the quality of those years and, whereas we have seen that QALYs employ what are termed 'utility' weights of health states (for example, recall that the utility weight of a 'bad' hip fracture was = 0.05 in the Salkeld *et al.*, 2000 study), DALYs use 'disability weights' to summarize the 'burden of disease'. Disability weights are assigned according to the classification of diseases, injuries and their sequelæ in the International Classification of Diseases (ICD-9) ((WHO, 1975) into 107 causes of death and 483 disabling sequelæ of illness or injury. Determination of disability weights is achieved by a process which begins with premature mortality deaths being assigned to a disease category and grouped by age, sex and demographic region based on death records where these are available. Standard protocols for DALY calculation specify that each state of ill health is assigned a disability weight by 'expert judgment' on the familiar scale from death to perfect health on a metric from 1.0 to 0.0 where death records are unavailable (Murray and Lopez, 1996). Years of healthy life lost are estimated on the basis of the difference between actual ages of death and the ideal standard life expectancy (in the 1993 exercise, 82.5 years for women and 80 years for men).

In the case of specific disabilities, incidence by age, sex and demographic region are derived from official records where available, or from the opinions of experts where not. Years lived with a disability are obtained by multiplying the expected duration of the disability (to remission or death) by a disability weight which supposedly reflects the average severity of the disability 'burden' when compared to full health or death. Having defined seven disability classes the Global Burden of Disease (GBD) project then assigned a weighting, based on expert consensus, to each of the 483 disabling conditions using person trade-off methods (on which more follows). When these assessments were being made expert panels were 'asked to evaluate the average individual with the condition described taking into account the average social response or milieu' (AbouZahr and Vaughan, 2000: 656). Quite what 'the average individual' who is HIV positive could possibly be is difficult to imagine (are they male or female? young or old? gay, straight or bisexual? perhaps they are the arithmetic mean of these categories – an androgynous, middle-aged person with serious sexual identity issues?), and the notion that there might be such a thing as an 'average social response or milieu' for, say, HIV, which manages to take the mean response of societies across sub-Saharan Africa, the Asia/Pacific and the former socialist economies of the Eastern Bloc, actually is, in practice, unimaginable.

Such reliance on a priori categorization is (almost) guaranteed to produce such difficulties. In this context, it is of note that in their study of the QOL of people with HIV/AIDS in Dublin (using the SEIQoL-DW[2], Hickey *et al.* (1996) found that the higher order categorization 'people with HIV/AIDS' (precisely the variety of umbrella disease categorization employed in the ICD-9, and hence the global burden of disease project in the assignment of disability weights) was entirely inadequate to capture the variability in the commonalities that *sub-groups* of the diagnostic group 'people with HIV/AIDS' showed in their estimations of the domain weights of various QOL domains. For example, gay people with HIV/AIDS and injecting drug users with HIV/AIDS nominated different issues as having a major impact on their QOL and, similarly, those with asymptomatic HIV identified comparable issues both to those in the study with 'full-blown' AIDS and HIV negative controls. Similar problems of misleading patient groupings, and the questionable reliance on average population scores, are identified by Fayers and Bjordal (2001) in their critique of Sprangers *et al.* (2000) on the QOL of people with chronic medical conditions. Fayers and Bjordal (2001: 978) note that:

> the investigators group the disorders with abandon; they combine thyroid-gland impairments with diabetes, to form a 'disease cluster' of endocrinological disorders, and multiple sclerosis, a debilitating illness with no prospect of recovery, together with migraine … for some diseases, population surveys will commonly be characterised by many cases of low severity, which may make average HRQL values seem close to those of the normal population, even though for a common disease the small proportion of severely ill patients could represent a large number of individuals who urgently need attention.

Despite these difficulties DALYs are, like QALYs, straightforward to compute. DALYs are calculated by multiplying the disability weighting for the specific condition by the number of years lived in that health state and added to the number of years lost due to the disease. The initial calculation of unweighted DALYs lost due to a particular disease in a specific population group is then found by employing the formula:

Years lost due to premature death = Expected standard lifetime – Age at death + Time lived with a disability = Duration of disability × Severity weighting

With future burdens discounted at 3 per cent per annum and differential weightings that value the quality of years lived in childhood and old age less, we can see, in Arnesen and Nord's (1999: 1423) example, that:

If the utility of deafness is 0.67, the disability weight of deafness is 1 – 0.67 = 0.33.

Disregarding age weighting and discounting, and assuming life expectancy of 80 years, a deaf man living 50 years represents 0.67 × 50 = 33.5 QALYs gained and 0.33 × 50 + 30 × 1 = 46.5 DALYs lost.

By employing DALYs it is possible to identify – as the WHO has for depression – global patterns in the prevalence and 'burden' of various diseases. Table 6.5 illustrates the comparative rankings that may then be afforded by the methodology, in this case the differential burden of disease in the area of reproductive health 'carried' in various parts of the world by men and women.

Among the many objections to DALYs identified by Arnesen and Nord (1999) the foremost is perhaps the most difficult: they state that: 'While the idea of expressing burden of disease in a single index is tempting, any attempt to summarise information about quality of life and length of life in one number is bound to run into conceptual and methodological problems' – the same objection made by Edgerton (1996) and Taylor (1994) to expressing the concept of QOL itself in numerical terms. Arnesen and Nord (1999) identify a range of conceptual problems in the DALY. They suggest that the DALY procedures of discounting future health gains and losses and of age weighting not only discourage preventive medicine, but also discriminate against children, old people and future generations – with the estimates of life expectancy selected tending to discriminate against women. The expert panels' approach to the assignment of disability weights ensures that the weights assigned reflect the prior values, beliefs and expectancies of a skewed sample, who may or may not view, say, deafness in the same way that deaf people do or assign the same 'utility' to it. As Rothwell et al. (1997: 1582) put it, not only do doctors demonstrate that they do not understand which aspects of health actually matter to their patients but also that 'doctors are not good at estimating the overall quality of life of their patients'.

As such, age weighting and discounting measures central to the DALY procedure reflect not the *utility of life to individuals*, but rather the *societal usefulness of people's years of life*. Arnesen and Nord (1999) argue that 'the DALY approach implicitly attaches lower value to life extending

Table 6.5 Total DALYs lost due to reproductive ill-health in women and men of reproductive age as a percentage of total DALYs lost in the 15–44 year age group, 1990

	Total DALYs lost (%)												
	STDs excluding HIV		HIV		Maternal conditions	Reproductive cancers		Total	
	Female	Male	Female	Male		Female	Male	Female	Male
Established marked economics	2.36	0.10	0.99	4.08	2.09	3.18	0.02	8.62	4.20
Former socialist economies	3.52	0.30	0.03	0.09	6.25	2.83	0.03	12.63	0.41
Sub-Saharan Africa	6.31	1.79	8.38	6.29	24.45	0.54	0.02	39.69	8.54
India	6.58	2.49	0.20	0.43	19.19	1.42	0.01	27.40	2.93
China	0.21	0.05	0.00	0.01	6.91	0.99	0.01	8.12	0.06
Asia/Pacific	7.00	2.05	0.14	0.24	14.55	1.66	0.01	23.36	2.30
Middle East	1.47	0.32	0.03	0.18	18.70	0.97	0.02	21.17	0.51
Latin America/Caribbean	3.97	0.60	1.06	3.63	9.64	2.14	0.02	16.80	4.25
World	4.23	1.09	1.78	2.02	14.47	1.42	0.01	21.90	3.12

Source: AbouZahr and Vaughan (2000).

programmes for disabled people than to corresponding programmes for people without disability'. They illustrate the discriminatory possibilities of the DALY by offering a comparative quantification of the differential value (quality?) attached to one year of life for people with and without disabilities. Arnesen and Nord (1999: 1424) note that:

> disability weightings in use [Murray, 1996] tell us that the value of one year for 1000 people without disabilities on average is set equivalent to the value of one year for 9524 people with quadriplegia, 4202 people with dementia, 2660 blind people, 1686 people with Down's syndrome without cardiac malformation, 1499 deaf people, 1236 infertile people, and 1025 underweight or overweight people (2 SD from mean weight : height ratio)

Both AbouZahr and Vaughan (2000) and Arnesen and Nord (1999) are concerned with the very specific problems caused by the methodology used by the expert panels to assess disability weights such as these. The procedure used (an amended version of the time trade-off method) was the person trade-off technique (Murray, 1996). In the DALY protocol, the expert panels answered two person trade-off questions, and consistency between the two answers was then forced. The first question (Person trade-off 1 below) demands an abstract judgment about the relative value of the lives of people with and without disabilities, while the second asks experts to rate the value of cures for different chronic conditions in relation to therapeutic activities that may extend life. Arnesen and Nord (1999: 1424) explain the issue here clearly: 'How many people cured of blindness does the respondent consider equal to prolonging the lives of 1000 people? If the response is 5000, the corresponding disability weight of blindness is $1000 : 5000 = 0.2$.'

Calculating a disability weight from the first person trade-off is a rather chilling exercise. The question asked is:

> *Person trade-off 1*
> You are a decision maker who has enough money to buy only one of two mutually exclusive health interventions. If you purchase intervention A, you will extend the life of 1000 healthy [non-disabled] individuals for exactly one year, at which point they will all die. If you do not purchase intervention A, they will all die today. The alternative use of your scarce resources is intervention B, with which you can extend the life of n individuals with a particular disabling condition [blindness, deafness, Down syndrome] for one year. If you do not buy intervention B, they will all die today; if you do buy intervention B, they will die at the end of exactly one year.

The expert's task is to provide the *n* in question: how many disabled people's lives are worth the same as 1,000 'healthy' people's? The question presupposes that the answer will *have* to be more than 1,000 and the transformation of this hypothetical number to a disability weight is straightforward. As Murray and Lopez (1996) note: 'If the participant judges that 1000 healthy people would have an equal claim on the resources as 8000 people with some severe disability, the weight assigned to that particular disability is equal to 1 minus 1000 divided by 8000, or 0.875' (cited in Arnesen and Nord, 1999: 1424). Perhaps a more serious methodological concern is forced consistency between the two weightings. In methodological terms, it is important that two judgments should reflect the same valuation of the same health state. However, while *methodologically* coherent, this procedure raises many of the same *conceptual* incoherencies as the necessity of forced choice responses to individual items on psychometric QOL measures discussed in Chapter 4. Again Arnesen and Nord (1999: 1424) describe the difficulties engendered by the entirely sensible (in methodological terms) requirement that the two person trade-off valuations are equivalent:

> to see how this works, consider the case of blindness. Assume that a panellist, on ethical grounds, responds that extending the life of 1000 sighted people and 1000 blind people is equivalent. The resulting disability weighting for blindness is zero. Assume that in the second question the panellist answers that relieving 5000 people of blindness is as valuable as prolonging the lives of 1000 people. This gives a disability weighting of 0.2. The valuation so far has yielded two different disability weightings for the same health state. The panellist is now asked to reconsider these responses and choose a new pair of answers to produce the same disability weighting. The panellist might end up by selecting PTO1 = 1100 and PTO2 = 11 000, which together yield a disability weighting of 0.09. This weighting, however, does not correspond to any actual preference of the respondent: it is basically an artefact, generated by the requirement for consistency between questions that address different issues.

Such issues raise serious doubts about the validity of the disability weights calculation protocol. Indeed, so serious are the concerns raised that the continued use of the metric has been subject to critical review (Murray *et al.*, 1999) by the WHO. It would seem that these procedures must be considered extremely carefully: it is to such a review that we now turn.

Difficulties with the QALY and DALY Approach: Dying and Disability

Cummins (1997b: 126) describes the QALY as a 'bizarre notion based on invalid psychometric assumptions' and, in particular, is scathing of the standard use of hypothetical scenarios. He suggests that:

the QALY methodology is complete nonsense in that it implies any relationship with subjective QOL. No one can validly respond to such hypothetical situations... So how does all of this fit with the idea that people can validly report on the vicarious experience of disability? Of course it does not fit at all. The only people who can report on this experience are people who have the particular form of disability under discussion.

Nord (1999) argues that the key weakness of the QALY is that researchers ask healthy people to imagine they are ill and then ask them to describe their position on the allocation of medical resources. As we have seen, Polsky *et al.* (2001) suggest we should be very sceptical about accepting the preferences of the general public about the relative utility of various health states as representative of the views of patients. Nord (1999, 1992a) argues instead that we should be asking those with illnesses or disabilities the difficult questions about health resource allocation. A closely allied criticism of the approach is that both the measures themselves, and the procedures whereby they are arrived at, are highly technical for non-specialists and are not transparent to ordinary people. Work by Mulkay *et al.* (1987), Morris and Durand (1989) and Nord (1991) suggests that expressing QOL in terms of numbers is highly problematic: to most people such numbers have little meaning as they have no experience with them in everyday life.

In consideration of the views of 'ordinary people', Koch (2001) reports an intriguing study addressing precisely the points raised above. The notion that people *can* predict their evaluations of future health states is, clearly, central to the entire QALY programme. We have seen that there are reasons to be cautious about the use of hypothetical scenarios especially when we consider the artificial nature of the scenarios that people are asked to judge (Nord, 1999) as well as the artefactual nature of the choices experts (and patients) may be asked to make (Arensen and Nord, 1999), not to mention the dramatically different evaluations that asking 'experts' about their 'patients'' lives, and 'patients' about their own lives produce (Cummins, 1997b; Goodinson and Singleton, 1989; Ferrans, 1990). Indeed, in their study of terminally ill patients using the EORTC QOL Questionnaire,[3] Sahlberg-Blom *et al.* (2001: 550, my emphasis) report that, 'despite having an *assessed* lower quality of life in many dimensions than people in general ... patients experienced happiness and satisfaction during their last month of life'.

Koch's (2001) study, in an imaginative twist, takes Cummins's and Nord's point and does precisely what they suggest. Koch surveyed persons with acquired disabilities on a range of QOL issues and found, for example, that *after* disablement 'whatever the quantity of time spent with family, friends, and on spiritual matters the quality of the experience in each area was richer and more meaningful' (Koch, 2001: 459). As he notes, such a finding echoes Young and McNicoll's (1998) whose study of the perceived QOL of people with ALS (motor neuron disease) found that participants reported both a richer spiritual life and stronger interpersonal ties than before diagnosis.

Koch concludes that:

> the experience of disability forces changes in perception and values depending on a range of accommodations. These are based on the presence or absence of social and familial support as well as the specific nature of the physical restriction. If support exists – in the home, work place, and the greater community – people may decide to continue with a restricted life for far longer than might have earlier been anticipated. If however support is absent, and life becomes restricted ... life quality diminished as a result ... Prospective health planning instruments axiomatically assume individuals can predict accurately the choices they would make in the event of a physically limiting condition ... that among study respondents was extremely rare ... That most respondents report a strong life quality, despite their moderate to severe physical limitations, apparently speaks not to a 'disability paradox' ... but to a process of social and familial adaptation whose benefits were clearly unanticipated by respondents prior to injury or diagnosis.

Such findings are both immensely encouraging and simultaneously rather depressing: they raise very serious questions about assigning 'disability weights' to disease states, and must call into question the idea that it is possible to make, sensibly, statements like 'the utility of tetraplegia is 0.13'. Again we see that, when the 'patients' whose QOL researchers and practitioners attempt to fix numerically are *themselves* asked about it, QOL is better understood as a *process* phenomenon: not as a once-and-for-all metric.

The 'medical model' underpinning QALYs and DALYs uses 'the pathogenesis and natural history of disease as the conceptual framework for assessing morbidity and mortality and for interpreting the effects of various interventions' (Hyder *et al.*, 1998, cited by Koch, 2001: 455). The use of medicalized, or pathologized, conceptions of QOL (the absence of symptoms; the ability to score better than 'dead' or 'unconscious' on the EuroQOL; ideas like the QALY and the DALY) has been criticized on both empirical and theoretical grounds (for example, Cummins, 1997b; Koch, 1994; Kuczewski, 1999; Nord, 1992a, 1999; Young *et al.*, 1994). Koch notes that it is a perspective 'held in particular contempt by writers advancing a "disabilities perspective" who argue, with Chamie (1995), that physical differences are not illnesses and should not be treated as such' (Koch, 2001: 455). In closing this chapter, then, it would seem that many would agree with Aksoy's (2000: 22) evaluation of QOL measurement in medical settings when he argues that 'it is not possible to measure the QOL of an individual either accurately or reliably. It is, therefore, our duty to respect individuals' lives and try to improve their condition as much as possible'.

In Summary

QALYs and DALYs attempt to standardise the QOL provided by different interventions, to arrive at cost : benefit ratios for medical practices, and to express the 'burden of disease' in a 'common currency'. These approaches are taken very seriously by influential global organizations – such as the World Bank and the WHO. However, when doctors, patients and the general public rate different (ill) health states, using techniques such as TTO studies, they routinely return – sometimes grossly – divergent views about the utility or quality of life. Many people with conditions that doctors regard as so near to death as not to be worth arguing about regularly report that the quality of their life *after* diagnosis or disablement is higher than previously. Despite the serious conceptual, methodological and practical difficulties entailed, the future of this technology seems to be assured: the pressing question is, then, how to tame it.

Notes

1. The WHOQOL 100 Scale consists of six domains measuring QOL in the areas of physical, psychological, independence, social relationships, environment and spiritual well-being. As the title suggests the scale contains 100 items divided unevenly between the domains. Psychometric properties are reported by the WHOQOL Group (1998).
2. The SEIQOL (McGee *et al.*, 1991; O'Boyle *et al.*, 1993) rates subjective QOL in medical contexts using a complex scale and multiplies scores derived from 'best possible – worst possible' visual analogue scales by personally estimated weights on five descriptors of QOL selected by respondents.
3. The EORTC QLQ-30 (Aaronsson *et al.*, 1993) consists of 30 questions covering physical functioning (5), role functioning (2), cognitive functioning (2), emotional functioning (4), social functioning (2), general quality of life (2), fatigue (3), nausea and vomiting (2), pain (2), and six single items (short of breath, trouble sleeping, lack of appetite, constipation, diarrhoea and financial problems).

Study Questions

- How might one know, with enough certainty to meaningfully evaluate its 'utility', what it is like to be rendered paraplegic?
- How well do concepts like Disability Adjusted Life Years reflect the views of people with disabilities about their lives?

- How do decisions about the 'quality of life' of patients actually get made in particular health care settings?
- What criteria should we employ to judge what is an 'acceptable' or 'unacceptable' quality of life?

Suggestions for Further Reading

Baldwin, S., Godfrey, C. and Propper, C. (eds) (1990) *Quality of Life: Perspectives and Policies*. London: Routledge.

Koch, T. (2001) Future states: the axioms underlying prospective, future-oriented, health planning instruments, *Social Science and Medicine*, 52: 453–65.

Nord, E. (1999) *Cost-value Analysis in Health Care*. Cambridge: Cambridge University Press.

Nord, E. (1992a) An alternative to QALYs: the saved young life equivalent, *British Medical Journal*, 305: 875–8.

CHAPTER 7

QOL research with special populations

It has been suggested that QOL offers the 'ultimate criterion for the assessment of the effectiveness of social care delivery' (Perry and Felce, 1995: 1). This chapter examines applied QOL research with 'special' populations as this research illustrates with particular clarity many of the methodological issues involved in the use of structured questionnaires. The questionable theoretical coherence of using individually measured QOL as an outcome measure of the quality of care or service practices, the relationship between etic and emic constructions of what constitutes 'quality of life', and the theoretical place of particular life circumstances/ social arrangements in the conceptualization of QOL are examined.

Applied QOL Research

Heal and Sigelman (1990: 174–5) suggest that:

there are compelling philosophical reasons for providing mentally retarded consumers with opportunities to tell us how they perceive their lives and how they would like their lives to change ... developing any reliable and valid quality-of-life measure requires considerable effort ... [an] effort that promises to result in a fuller understanding of the lives of developmentally disabled citizens.

However, Emerson and Hatton (1994) suggest that, for this group and for people with mental health problems, the literature has, instead, focused on objective indices such as community participation, engagement in activity or skill levels. Reliance has been placed upon 'measurable "objective" indices which, by consensus are thought to be associated with a better quality of life ... such factors as physical health, access to health care, quality of housing ... employment status and disposable income' (Emerson and Hatton, 1994: 11). The relation of these variables to subjective assessments of life satisfaction or QOL is generally accepted as being weak. Where QOL has been employed as a variable in its own right, one of the major methodological difficulties in applied work has been the tendency for researchers to design their own scales, often with an unstated theoretical base, rather than conducting validation work on pre-existing scales. Cummins and co-workers suggested that, of over eighty such scales they had identified by 1994, none reached minimally acceptable standards of psychometric validation (Cummins *et al.*, 1994). Perhaps in conse-quence, in their review of the British applied research, Emerson and Hatton (1994: 12–13) noted that:

> given the generally acknowledged importance of listening to the views of the consumers of our services and the weak relationship between 'objective' indicators of quality of life and expressed life satisfaction, it is somewhat surprising that such a low proportion of studies have sought to elicit the views of service users.

It is not only British work that has failed to solicit the views of service consumers. In his review of American ethnographic research, Edgerton (1990: 153) suggested that while many studies have offered a rich picture of people's vocational, residential and recreational patterns, they have failed to give an adequate picture of:

> the actual quality of those lives, the life events that have had the greatest impact on these lives, or the feelings of the people themselves about their lives ... in short we know all too little about ... their satisfaction with those lives.

Edgerton advocates research based in ethnographic naturalism. Such an approach is often described as 'emic', or grounded in the perspective of the respondent, as opposed to 'etic' work which privileges the perspective of the analyst. Emic approaches offer the opportunity, often through prolonged contact with participants, 'to make inferences about individuals' satisfaction with the quality of their lives that we believe are both reliable and valid' (Edgerton, 1990: 155). As Edgerton suggests, this approach – drawn as it is from the traditions of ethnomethodology rather than 'positivistic behavioral science' (Edgerton, 1990: 154) – removes some of the dilemmas inherent in positivist research on QOL, for example of psychometric validity and reliability, discussed in Chapter 4, and is also attentive to the ethics of 'emancipatory research' discussed in Chapter 3.

Studies in this tradition have suggested that people with intellectual disabilities have a number of concerns about support services which have a bearing on *their* judgments of the quality of their lives. Cattermole *et al.* (1988), for example, found that people were deeply dissatisfied with the independence they were allowed in the home environment. Bowd (1989) observed that criteria employed by adults with mental retardation to evaluate their quality of life differed from those of professionals. Sands *et al.* (1991) found that, while levels of satisfaction with services were high over all, services tended to enculturate a 'sense of dependency and compliance' (Sands *et al.*, 1991: 313) and interviewees reported con-siderable dissatisfaction with the range of opportunities and choices offered. Rapley *et al.* (1998) reported that many Australian adults with intellectual disabilities are keenly aware of stigmatization and prejudice from 'normal' community members.

However, this work, while offering richly textured accounts of quality of life from the perspective of the individual participant, is difficult to use as a method for evaluating service quality. Such work is extremely time-consuming, is essentially open-ended and, by virtue of its attempted fidelity to the views of particular individuals, does not offer the sort of data that is readily amenable to aggregation and quantification. In consequence, there have been two major efforts to devise formal, psychometric QOL measures as evaluation tools in services for people with an intellectual disability. Cummins's work on the ComQOL has been discussed in Chapter 4. Here the focus is on the other widely used and researched measure, the Schalock and Keith (1996) *Quality of Life Questionnaire* (see Cummins, 1997c, for an overview and evaluation of scales used in applied intellectual disability research).

Population-Specific Measures – the Work of Schalock and Keith

Schalock and Keith have developed a conceptual model of QOL which is attentive to the issues discussed in Chapters 2 and 3. The Schalock and Keith model of QOL recognizes the multifactorial nature of the construct, its individually specific, yet culturally homogenous, domains of reference; and acknowledges that the experience of intellectual disability is essential to QOL judgments and, further, recognizes the interactive – indeed socially constructed – nature of the concept. From this explicit theoretical position they have developed a measurement instrument as an operationalization of their conceptual model in the form of the *Quality of Life Questionnaire* (QOL.Q; Schalock and Keith, 1996).

Schalock and Keith disagree with Cummins about whether QOL should be operationalized using a generic or population-specific conceptualiza-tion. Schalock and Keith's operationalization of 'quality of life' is such that four assumptions are reflected explicitly. They assume that (1) QOL is a unitary construct in the sense that there are no differences between the needs of people with mental retardation and those without for, for example 'affiliation, a sense of worthiness, decision making and choices'; that (2) QOL is the product of the interactions of self with others; that (3) QOL is an outcome of the meeting of basic needs and the discharge of basic responsibilities in community settings; and that (4) the QOL experienced by any individual is a subjective phenomenon determined by their perception of their situation rather than how the individual is seen by others (Schalock et al., 1990: ii–iii).

Schalock et al. (1990) and Schalock and Keith (1996) report the development and psychometric validation of the QOL.Q, a 40-item measure which, with an American standardization population, reliably discriminated between respondents across a range of living and work environments, for example between residents of independent apartments and group homes (Schalock and Keith, 1996). The standardization manual suggests that factor analysis shows that items load reliably onto four factors – Satisfaction, Competence/Productivity, Empowerment/Independence and Social Belonging/Community Integration, a structure replicated by Rapley and Lobley (1995) in Britain. These factors were designed to reflect the core domains of life quality identified by the work of Andrews and Withey (1976), Campbell *et al.* (1976), Flanagan (1978) and others discussed above. Items tap each of the five domains of life quality identified in the integrative model of QOL offered by Felce and Perry (1996a) which was discussed in Chapter 2, and address explicitly at least four of the seven components identified by Cummins's (1997a) comprehensive definition of QOL and the dimensions identified in his 1998 review.

The theoretical approach Schalock and Keith adopt recognizes that subjective evaluations of life quality are individually calibrated. However, for the purposes of measurement, the QOL.Q assumes that the importance of the core domains of QOL is sufficiently comparable across individuals to allow the specification of a range of items which are treated as being of equivalent importance. While this approach can be criticized for blurring the individual-specific comparative weightings of QOL domains (an essential component of Cummins's ComQOL), it does allow for higher-order comparisons between studies or units of service.

Unlike the ComQOL-ID which separates the measurement of satisfaction with objective circumstances from the estimation of their importance, Schalock and Keith (1990, 1996) treat satisfaction as a component part of QOL judgments. However, acknowledging that basic human needs hold across cognitive levels, Schalock and Keith reflect Cummins's insistence that QOL is a universal construct, despite their divergent assumption that, while the construct may have a higher-order generality, the detail of the items which reflect QOL domains is influenced by individuals' immediate circumstances. Accordingly, Schalock and Keith (1996) argue that, if we are to describe the utility of services well, it is essential to address those issues in the lives of people with intellectual disabilities which are pertinent purely to this group.

Population-Specific QOL Measures as Service Evaluation Tools

The following section of the chapter describes in detail three small-scale service evaluation studies conducted in services for people with intellectual disabilities in Britain and Australia. These studies were designed to do three things. Firstly, they were to *triangulate* the life experience of service users afforded by the service in question: to gather data on a range of experiences which the services claimed to be supporting or providing in order to arrive at a synthesis of converging data about people's lives. Secondly, they were to evaluate the *utility* of using a well-validated and psychometrically-sound quality of life questionnaire (the QOL.Q) as an outcome measure in service evaluation practice. (Does it add useful information? Is it feasible as a measure given the characteristics of the population? Does the measure return acceptable levels of data? Is the data set compromised by unacceptable levels of missing data? Does the QOL data tell us something we didn't know on the basis of established measures? Is QOL an 'ultimate criterion'?) Thirdly, the studies were designed to answer questions about the measure at a *conceptual/theoretical level*. (Does the measure show appropriate statistical relationships to other measures – that is does it show convergent validity? Does the measure demonstrate sensitivity to change in quality of life over time? Is the measure contaminated by confounding variables?)

The studies described are small in scale. However, their inclusion here is designed to demonstrate that it is both sensible and feasible to conduct such limited analyses. Such studies, by the use of appropriate statistical procedures (for example a stringent alpha criterion, the employment of non-parametric statistics, and the use of less frequently employed indices such as measures of effect size), can provide results in which reasonable confidence can be placed in terms of their *indicative* use. That is to say, if studies such as those discussed below return data which provide unsatisfactory answers to the questions identified above, then we can be reasonably certain that either the quality of life measure in question is of little use or that larger-scale studies are unwarranted.

Britain – the Rapley and Beyer (1996, 1998) Studies

Rapley and Beyer (1996) report the use of the QOL.Q[1] in the evaluation of a small community residential service. The study suggested that, in common with much of the literature, the experience of adults with intellectual disabilities in community-based services could be characterized as being one of 'isolation and disengagement' (Rapley and Beyer, 1996: 31). Contacts with other people in community settings were sparse and primarily functional, with staff contact with service users in the domestic setting generally occurring at a low level, particularly in the area of assistance giving. Measured QOL entered into theoretically appropriate, and statistically significant, relationships with objective measures of community integration; for example, 'the extent to which people had and met friends was correlated with higher QOL.Q scores' (Rapley and Beyer, 1996: 38). Rapley and Beyer (1996) concluded that, in view of the consistent relationships between measured QOL and established service quality criteria, the addition of QOL measurement to 'traditional' evaluative indices such as adaptive behaviour, engagement and community participation was a potentially useful development.

Emerson and Hatton (1994, 1996) have pointed out that the results of many longitudinal studies of service quality have been confounded by the effect of differing ability levels of service users on outcome variables such as social integration or engagement, or by the employment of different informants, in different settings, in the measurement of outcomes. To be useful service evaluation instruments, therefore, QOL measures need to be sensitive to changes in service users' experience over time that is not attributable to gross changes in residential setting and consequent differential staffing expectations or values. Furthermore, such instruments should be resistant to confounding by service users' adaptive behaviour levels. In order to examine the utility of the QOL.Q – and hence quality of life assessment more generally – as a service evaluation tool, the follow-up study reported by Rapley and Beyer (1998) took account of both of these potentially confounding variables, firstly by replicating the study reported by Rapley and Beyer (1996) in the same service after a two-year interval and, secondly, by statistically controlling for the effects of differing participant abilities on the outcome variables selected for study.

In order that the study could, meaningfully, be compared to the existing service evaluation literature, data were collected on service users' experience in the major outcome domains identified by Emerson and Hatton (1994, 1996) as the most frequently used in the international literature. As such, well validated measures of adaptive behaviour, involvement in domestic routines and contact with support staff, and participation in community life were used. Measures selected were thus representative of those used in the relevant literature and, also, represented life domains which could – on the basis of the theoretical model of quality of life informing the QOL measure used – be expected to enter into statistical relationships with quality of life scores.

The *adaptive behaviour* levels of service users were described using Part One of the AAMD Adaptive Behaviour Scale (ABS) (Nihira *et al.*, 1975).[2] *Involvement in routines and contact with staff* was measured by direct observation using the computerised Momentary Time Sampling[3] data collection system (Beasley *et al.*, 1993) loaded onto a hand-held Psion Organiser. Behaviour of staff and participants was observed and the behaviour exhibited by target participants was coded under four categories: Activity, Social Activity, Staff Contact and Problem Behaviour. Coding categories include behaviours which may readily be observed in the domestic setting. Owing to known problems of observer error and drift, on some occasions two observers attended each observation session to allow inter-observer coding reliability to be assessed. *Participation in community life* was assessed using the Social Networks Questionnaire[4], a slightly modified form of the Lifestyles Questionnaire employed in the evaluation of the All-Wales Strategy (Evans *et al.*, 1994).

As with the previous study, ABS data were analysed as raw scores. Data from direct observations were converted into percentage of observed points at which the target behaviour was observed employing the MTSTAB program (Stein and Mansell, 1992). As the study was part of a larger comparison of institutional and community-based services, inter-observer reliabilities were estimated across all settings. A 5.72 per cent reliability sample (23 hours reliability observations out of 402 hours total observations) was taken. Mean occurrence reliabilities across observers and settings by observation category were: Activity = 93.16 per cent; Social Activity = 96.11 per cent; Contact = 94.48 per cent; Problem Behaviour = 91.90 per cent. Total participant engagement was computed as a variant of the definition offered by Stein and Mansell (1992). Engagement was computed as the sum of the percentage time each participant's behaviour was coded as Leisure/Recreation, Personal/Selfcare, Chores/Electrical, Chores/Other, Clear Social Act and Unclear Social Act across sessions. In addition to client behaviours, Positive, Negative, Neutral and Assistance-giving staff contact were summed to provide an overall mean score of all participant activity and associated staff contact.

Data from the Social Networks Questionnaire were coded using a minimally revised version of the framework described by Evans *et al.* (1987). The summary variable of 'Community Participation' was computed as the sum of scores on all SNQ categories, offering a global index of the extent of participants' social networks and the level of integration opportunities afforded by community-based activity. Quality of Life was computed as total QOL.Q score.

Statistical procedures

At the 5 per cent level the non-parametric Wilcoxon signed-ranks test indicated that participants' ABS Total scores showed significant changes over the two years separating the studies ($z = -2.04$, $p = 0.02$). As a conservative procedure, and on the basis of the theoretical concerns outlined by Emerson and Hatton (1994, 1996), it was assumed that this change in scores represented a possible confound of the other outcome measures. Accordingly a repeated measures ANCOVA was computed to examine changes in scores on the three summary variables of Engagement, QOL and Social Integration. Individuals' total ABS score, as measured in the first and second studies, was used as a varying covariate to control for the influence of adaptive behaviour levels of participants. Because of the small sample size and concerns about violations of assumptions for parametric tests, non-parametric statistics were employed to examine changes in sub-items of the summary variables over time.

Results

Table 7.1 reports summary data for the main effects of the repeated measures analysis of variance. While only changes for the QOL main effect and sub-items of the QOL.Q and SNQ reached statistical significance, a number of theoretically appropriate and indicative changes in observed scores reached significance at the 0.05 level. For the RMANCOVA, the effect size (partial eta squared, η^2) was used as an index of the magnitude of the main effect. Green *et al.* (1997: 230) define η^2 for the factor interpreted as 'the proportion of the variance of the dependent variable related to the factor, holding constant (partialling out) the covariate. Traditionally an η^2 of .01, .06 and .14 represent small, medium and large effect sizes respectively.' In this analysis partial eta squared therefore represents an index of the size of the change in observed outcome measures (dependent variables) related to the passage of time (Time 1 and Time 2 representing the two levels of the time factor), with adaptive behaviour levels partialled out. Observed levels are adjusted for one-tailed tests of significance.

As Table 7.1 shows, when adaptive behaviour levels are controlled for, the QOL measure shows a significant difference in mean scores between T1 and T2. The Social Integration measure shows a marginally significant difference in mean scores between T1 and T2, but no significant difference in mean Engagement scores was observed. Partial eta squared values suggest that the effect size of both of the significant results is strong.

Table 7.1 Change in QOL.Q scores over time – repeated measures analysis of covariance

Variable	Sum of squares	d.f	Mean square	F	Prob.	η^2
Quality of Life						
QOL	659.14	1	659.14	17.55	0.01	0.66
Error	338.08	9	37.56			
Regression	220.18	1	220.18	5.86		
Social Integration						
Social Integration	28.31	1	28.31	5.13	0.03	0.50
Error	27.60	5	16.07			
Regression	12.40	1	12.40	2.25		
Engagement						
Engagement	19.43	1	19.43	0.00	0.47	0.00
Error	49688.97	9	5521.00			
Regression	39.07	1	39.07	0.01		

Source: Rapley and Beyer (1998).

As noted above, because of the very small sample sizes, Rapley and Beyer (1998) used non-parametric statistics for their univariate analyses. One-tailed Wilcoxon matched pairs signed-ranks tests were computed to examine the changes over time in component items of the summary variables. A conservative α level of 0.01 was set for these comparisons: z values and one-tailed p for comparisons are reported. Obtained scores for T2 exceed those for T1 for all statistically significant comparisons reported.

These results show that a number of small-scale changes appear to have occurred in the network in the two years separating the two evaluation studies. Although Adaptive Behaviour Scale scores increased, the possibility that this change is due to measurement error (Felce and Perry, 1996b) is strong. Although overall mean levels of Engagement did not differ significantly over time, the level of variation in scores decreased, suggesting that engagement was more evenly spread across service users in the network at the second round of data collection. The pattern of service users' engagement in a range of domestic activities also appeared to have changed: for example, at the second round of data collection levels of 'No activity' had decreased. A noticeable increase in community-based activity appeared to have occurred – for example average SNQ Total Scores rose from 24.71 to 28.77. These increases in purposeful domestic activity and community-based activity were accompanied by statistically significant changes in mean QOL on all but the Social Belonging subscale.

Rapley and Beyer (1998) drew *limited and tentative* conclusions from these studies. They noted that, while an AB comparison design can only provide an indicative result, the finding of increased service user ability levels was in contrast to many other UK studies which have reported a plateau effect after an initial, post-resettlement, increment (e.g. Lowe *et al.*, 1993; Emerson and Hatton, 1996). Noting that Felce and Perry (1996) suggested that small changes in ABS scores require corroborative observational data in order to be interpretable, they argued that the small increases in observed domestic activity possibly offered such corroboration.

Secondly, they concluded that – when the confounds were controlled – multivariate analyses suggested that measures of the social integration and the QOL showed small increases over two years. Possibly reflecting these small changes in domestic activity and community-based activity, mean QOL scores improved, suggesting that the instrument is sensitive to such change.

Thirdly they suggested that QOL measurement appeared to reflect the gains identified by the other measures, and thus may add to evaluative practice but that, alone, QOL was an insufficient index of service users' experience. In order to achieve a rich description of service quality, objective indices are required to describe the detail of the participation in ordinary communities afforded to people with intellectual disabilities by community-based services.

Australia – the Rapley and Hopgood (1997) Study

Thirty-four adults with intellectual disabilities in five supervised community based residences participated in this study. Two residences were located in suburbs of a large regional city; the remaining three were located in small country towns. The study was designed both to consolidate the findings of the Rapley and Beyer (1996, 1998) work and to test further ideas about factors contributing to the QOL of people with intellectual disabilities. As such the study sought to evaluate the contribution that place of residence (urban versus rural) might make to QOL, and to assess the relationship between participants' sense of belonging to their community and their QOL.

As in the Rapley and Beyer studies, ability levels of service users were measured using the AAMD Adaptive Behaviour Scale (Nihira *et al.*, 1975). Engagement in domestic activity was measured using of the Index of Participation in Domestic Life (Raynes *et al.*, 1989a)[5] and participation in community life was measured using the Index of Community Involvement (Form II) (Raynes *et al.*, 1989b).[6] Participants' sense of community was assessed by employing the Neighbourhood Sense of Community Index (NSCI) (Pretty *et al.*, 1994).[7]

Analysis

The study examined the relationship between measures of key outcomes identified in the literature and tested the ability of the measures to discriminate between residential settings and between urban and rural locations. All measures yielded individual data, and scores for individuals were averaged across settings and measures. Examination of the data revealed no missing data or outliers. Patterns of relationships between measures were examined with correlational analyses using the Pearson product-moment correlation coefficient. In order to explore variation between settings analyses of variance were employed.

Analysis of covariance, with ABS scores as covariate to control for confounding by ability levels (Emerson and Hatton, 1994), was not necessary as the correlation between ABS scores and the IPDL only achieved significance at the 0.05 level. A positive, but weak, relationship was observed between the ABS (Part 1) and QOL.Q total ($r = 0.3$) with a small percentage predictive variance in QOL scores by ability levels ($r^2 = 0.09$). ABS scores and other summary measures were not correlated.

Prior to ANOVA, Levene's test (Levene, 1960) for homogeneity of variance was conducted to check for violation of parametric testing assumptions. A conservative criterion of $\alpha = 0.05$ was set. In the case of violation of assumptions non-parametric Kruskall-Wallis or Wilcoxon tests were employed. Univariate ANOVAs were conducted to examine differences between residential settings and rural and urban locations. Post hoc comparisons (Bonferroni tests) were conducted. A stringent criterion alpha of 0.01 was set due to the large number of analyses planned.

Relationships between the measures: exploratory analysis

QOL.Q sub-scales showed moderate to high inter-correlations. As expected from the literature, engagement (IPDL) was related to both higher ability levels and to lower levels of problem behaviour, but only marginally. Main summary measures (apart from the NSCI) entered into theoretically appropriate relationships with QOL scores. A high correlation was obtained between the IPDL and the QOL.Q.

If staff activity were the central mediating factor in service users' activities shown in many studies, the ICI and the IPDL should be positively correlated. However, no correlation was observed. This result suggests that the influence of staff activity, a confound in other studies, does not appear to be unduly influencing results here, and that the measures are tapping clearly differentiable aspects of individual activity in community and domestic settings. Empowerment and Satisfaction correlate significantly with the IPDL and the ABS. A high correlation was found between the IPDL and Competence, with which the ICI displayed a weak relationship. NSCI scores were inversely related to Competence scores. These relationships indicate that opportunities for meaningful activity in both domestic and community environments are associated with higher QOL, but that (as the Competence sub-scale primarily measures job satisfaction) these opportunities are more readily available to service users who are involved in some form of employment and higher ability levels. A strong sense of community is, however, less likely to be reported by these participants.

Table 7.2 Relationships between summary measures and QOL.Q sub-scales

	IPDL	ICI	NSCI	ABS Part 1	QOL.Q
IPDL	–	–	–	–	–
ICI	0.11	–	–	–	–
NSCI	–0.19	0.22	–	–	–
ABS. Part 1	0.38*	–0.15	0.01	–	–
ABS. Part 2	–0.33*	0.06	0.27	0.35*	–0.27
QOL.Q	0.67**	0.35**	–0.17	0.30**	–
Competence	0.66**	0.35*	–0.35*	0.09	0.80**
Empowerment	0.48**	0.06	0.00	0.34*	0.67**
Satisfaction	0.55**	0.16	–0.02	0.40**	0.68**
Social Belonging	–0.19	0.27	0.17	–0.12	0.37**

*   = $p < 0.05$
** = $p < 0.01$
All other values non-significant at $p < 0.05$
Source: Rapley and Hopgood (1997).

Table 7.3 One-way of analyses of variance by place of residence

Variable	d.f.	F	Probability
QOL.Q Total	4,33	3.986	0.010
Competence	4,33	13.779	0.001
Levene's test	4,29	11.599	0.001
Kruskall-Wallis χ^2	4	13.874	0.007
ICI	4,33	12.612	0.001
IPDL	4,33	6.443	0.001
Levene's test	4,29	5.573	0.002
Kruskall-Wallis χ^2	4	16.462	0.002
NSCI	4,33	10.529	0.001

Source: Rapley and Hopgood (1997).

Univariate analyses

Univariate analyses were conducted to examine differences in outcomes by participants' place (specific group home) and location (urban vs. rural) of residence. Where the assumption of homogeneity of variance was violated, a non-parametric Kruskall-Wallis test was employed for the residence comparisons and the Wilcoxon rank sum test for the dichotomous urban vs. rural comparison. The results of the analysis of the summary measures are reported in Table 7.3.

Results of ANOVAs and subsequent post hoc analyses suggest that there are significant differences by residence on all summary measures – though marginally for total QOL (p = 0.010) – and on the Competence sub-scale.

For QOL total score, urban residences scored significantly higher (mean = 86.36, s.d. = 6.68) than rural residences (mean = 73.75, s.d. = 6.33). Individuals in urban locations also scored significantly higher on the ICI (mean = 10.09, s.d. = 1.97) than their rural counterparts (mean = 7.91, s.d. = 1.31). Wilcoxon rank sum tests confirmed that levels of community activity were significantly different, at the 5 per cent level, across urban and rural locations (ICI; z = –2.0323, p < 0.0421). Similar results were also observed on the IPDL, with the urban residences (mean = 21.00, s.d. = 3.33) scoring significantly higher than rural residences (mean = 15.83, s.d. = 4.87). Results of ANOVA for the NSCI did not support the hypothesis that individuals living in small towns in rural areas would exhibit a greater sense of community.

Rapley and Hopgood (1997) argued that the expected heterogeneity of service outcomes was observed. The hypothesis that QOL would display theoretically congruent relationships with objective indicators of service quality was broadly supported. Appropriate relationships were found between independent objective indices and QOL. For example, both the IPDL and the ICI were related to higher QOL – that is, higher levels of domestic activity and community involvement were associated with higher overall quality of life scores.

Rapley and Hopgood (1997) noted that the addition of the QOL.Q to the objective indicators provided some valuable insights. Thus, activity measures suggested that service users were engaging in domestic activities, and in a limited range of community based activities. However, when QOL.Q Empowerment scores were analysed, there was little evidence to suggest that service users' choices about important life decisions, such as where to live and whom to live with, or apparently trivial ones – such as possessing a key to their own home – were being supported.

In summary

Measures such as the QOL.Q and ComQOL-ID offer indices of quality of life that are derived from a theoretical base and are attentive – as much as is possible with formal psychometric measures – to individuals' concerns. Whereas a strength of the QOL.Q is that it measures specific aspects of the lives of people with intellectual disabilities that differentiate their experience from the rest of the 'normal' population, the ComQOL-ID has the strength of direct comparability to the 'normal' population via the parallel form. Both appear to relate sensibly to established measures of service quality. However, it is going too far to suggest that QOL offers the 'ultimate criterion for the assessment of the effectiveness of social care delivery' (Perry and Felce, 1995) for while QOL measurement may relate to other indices, it does not replicate or reproduce them. If we wish to know about the extent of people's participation in community, direct measures of such variables are still required. What QOL measurement may offer is a sense not only of matters that are not captured by existing objective indices, but also of how people feel about, say, their levels of social interaction.

It is also the case, of course, that formal operationally-defined measures are necessarily 'etic': that is they are based in the views of researchers about what QOL is and which aspects of life matter. Even a measure such as ComQOL, which allows individual weighting of the importance of domains, does not allow respondents to provide their own domains, but requires them to use pre-given scales. As such, it is necessary to supplement formal psychometric scales with an 'emic' methodology based in the perspective of participants, if both an aggregate, quantitative account *and* a richly textured description of service quality is to be achieved. Chapter 4 has shown what such studies may look like.

QOL Research with Psychiatric Populations

While, as yet, not as well developed as the intellectual disability literature, much of the research reported to date with people with mental health problems recapitulates the issues, debates and confusions found there. As in the intellectual disability literature, QOL has usually been assessed through questionnaires or structured interviews focusing on the person's satisfaction with various life domains. The psychiatric literature also conflates distinct theoretical concepts such as 'satisfaction within a range of community residential alternatives' and 'quality of life' (Anderson and Lewis, 2000: 580), or 'quality of life' and 'social functioning'. In the study reported by Dickerson *et al.* (2000), for example, the QOLI (Lehman, 1988)[8] is described not as a measure of quality of life, but rather as a 'measure of social functioning'. This is also true of the relationship between 'symptoms' and QOL across this literature: for instance, Kaiser (2000: 92) notes that 'it is not surprising that a relationship is found between cognitive functioning and quality of life when the quality of life measures seem to be confounded to a considerable extent by psychiatric symptomatology'.

Such confounding is apparent in the way this literature – presupposing the validity of psychiatric classifications – accomplishes diagnosis employing criteria of impaired social functioning which demonstrate considerable overlap with the criteria then used, supposedly independently, to infer QOL. The scope for circularity is considerable. In their study of the 'determinants of quality of life at first presentation with schizophrenia' Browne *et al.* (2000: 173) note that 'at presentation, subjects already had a diminished QOL'. Presumably, if this is a first presentation for 'schizophrenia' – which is diagnosed on the basis of impaired social activity, interpersonal relationships and so on – both diagnosis and QOL must be being identified on the basis of the same set of presented 'indicators'. Either the study is 'double-dipping' or these researchers, by virtue of the issuing of a diagnosis of schizophrenia, *knew before it was assessed* that 'subjects already had a diminished QOL'.

In consequence the psychiatric literature shows, similar, though less heated, debates about whether population-specific QOL measures and research approaches such as interviews should take cognizance of the particular life circumstances of people described as 'mentally ill'. As in the intellectual disability literature, debate occurs about the relationship between objective and subjective indicators of QOL (Barry and Crosby, 1996; Prince and Gerber, 2001; Ruggieri *et al.*, 2001; Skantze *et al.*, 1992).

As in general medicine, we see not so much population-, but 'disorder'-specific measures beginning to proliferate. As there, these measures typically conflate 'disease' and 'QOL' by including symptom scales within measures described as assessing quality of life. For example, Wilkinson *et al.* (2000) report the development of the 30-item 'Self-report Quality of Life measure for people with Schizophrenia' (SQLS) which consists of three sub-scales – 'psychosocial', 'motivation and energy' and 'symptoms and side-effects'. Similarly, Heinrichs *et al.* (1984) describe 'The Quality of Life Scale: An instrument for rating the schizophrenia syndrome'. The effect of psychotropic medication on QOL is another favoured site for psychiatric research, but again much of this work is confounded by the equation of measures of, for example, the side effects of Risperidone with QOL per se (Franz *et al.*, 1997; Priebe *et al.*, 1999; Sharma, 1999). In summarizing this work, Kaiser (2000: 92) has made what by now should be a familiar comment: he notes 'whether or not subjective quality of life is related to cognitive deficits in schizophrenia ... remains unclear and so far is only a hypothesis, although it is widespread as an advertising slogan for atypical antipsychotic medication'. Much of the work in this literature probably meets the criteria for advertising better than it does those for science.

Once more, the dissenting voices (those calling for an emic appreciation of the life circumstances of people with long-term mental health problems) appear to be in the minority. Furthermore, the psychiatric literature throws questions about the *purpose* of QOL research into particularly sharp relief. As we will see below, this literature has established conclusively that people with mental health problems score lower on QOL measures than do their 'healthy' peers; that people living in mental hospitals, by and large, report a lower QOL than people living in supported housing in the community; and that people with longstanding problems tend to have a lower QOL than those whose problems are relatively more recent. I am reminded that, as a psychology undergraduate, one of my lecturers was fond of telling us that the discipline was the 'science of the bloody obvious'.

Psychiatric Studies

Hermann *et al.* (2000) report a comparative study of patients with epilepsy and 'healthy' controls with three key aims: firstly to examine differences in self-reported psychiatric symptoms between patients with and without epilepsy; secondly, to assess the relationship between chronicity and co-morbid interictal psychiatric symptoms; and thirdly, to evaluate the impact of psychiatric symptoms on HRQOL. Using the Symptom Checklist-90-Revised[9] to assess psychiatric 'symptoms', participants with epilepsy also completed the Quality of Life in Epilepsy-89[10] to measure their HRQOL. Hermann *et al.* (2000) report that, compared to controls, epilepsy patients exhibited significantly higher (worse) scores on all but one of the 12 SCL-90-R scales. Increasing chronicity was associated with significantly higher scores across all SCL-90-R scales (indicating a worse state of affairs) and increased emotional-behavioural distress was associated with lower QOL scores across all 17 QOLIE-89 scales. Correlations between two SCL-90-R summary measures of emotional-behavioural distress (Global Severity Index, Positive Symptom Distress Index) and one specific scale

(Depression) with HRQOL were –0.54, –0.57, and –0.50 respectively, all significant at the p < 0.01 level. The authors conclude that interictal psychiatric symptoms are elevated among epilepsy patients compared with controls, and appear to be modestly associated with increasing chronicity of epilepsy. They suggest that 'this comorbid emotional-behavioural distress is specifically associated with a significantly poorer health-related quality of life, and suggests that quality-of-life research should devote greater attention to the potential impact of comorbid psychiatric distress' (Hermann et al., 2000: 184).

Anderson and Lewis (2000) examined the association between resident characteristics, clinical factors, mental health service utilization and QOL for people living in an Intermediate care facility (ICF) and compared outcomes with QOL reported by people with 'psychiatric disorders' living in other residential settings in the literature. Information was collected from patients' notes, discussions with staff and semi-structured interviews; 100 people diagnosed with 'schizophrenia' completed the Quality of Life Interview – Brief Version (QOLI; Lehman, 1988), the Severity of Psychiatric Illness scale (SPI)[11] (Lyons et al., 1997a; Lyons et al., 1997b) the Barthel Activities of Daily Living Index (BAI)[12] (Blass, 1985) and the SF-12 (Ware et al., 1998), a short form of the SF-36 discussed in Chapter 6.

Multivariate regression analyses suggested that higher levels of QOL were associated with reports that psychological problems did not interfere with work and activities, and with being rated as posing a lower level of danger to others. In other words, these variables were statistically significant predictors of a higher QOL score. A comparison of the QOL scores reported by ICF residents in Anderson and Lewis's (2000) study with other studies of the QOL of people with mental health problems (for example, Lehman et al.'s (1991) study of state hospitals) suggested that ICF residents reported significantly higher QOL scores than state hospital patients – but lower scores than community samples. Anderson and Lewis (2000: 580) suggest that their study:

> replicate[s] others in suggesting that persons living in state hospitals report a poorer quality of life than persons living in community residential alternatives (Lehman et al., 1991). That residents of the ICF reported a lower quality of life as compared to other community facilities may be better understood within the role of the residential settings ... As Slaughter et al. (1991) suggest, variability in quality of life outcomes across treatment settings may be due to the interaction of other service components and housing services ... Future research needs to examine whether different types of service utilization, for example mental health service use, has an impact on life satisfaction in other residential settings and whether the intensity of service use or the receipt over time is associated with improved quality of life.

Here again we see the difficulty of specifying the necessary and sufficient conditions for 'service components' to have a direct bearing on the QOL experienced by their users. 'Improved quality of life' is conflated with 'intensity of [mental health] service use'. Interestingly Hansson *et al.* (2001) suggested that the level of experienced 'self-directedness' best predicts the QOL of psychiatric patients, which may explain the routinely found gradient in QOL reported by people in psychiatric services: with lowest levels for people detained in secure settings to highest in community-based services.

The confusion of measures of psychiatric 'symptoms' and 'quality of life' is illustrated by Skevington and Wright (2001) of the WHO Centre for the Study of Quality of Life at the University of Bath. In a study of the QOL of people receiving antidepressant medication in primary care, funded by Glaxo-Wellcome, they suggest that the 'study arises from the need for good quality of life (QOL) assessment and a new comprehensive generic QOL profile for cross-cultural use' (Skevington and Wright, 2001: 261). How the study of depressed primary care patients in Bath fosters the development of 'cross-cultural' QOL is unclear. Using the WHOQOL-100[13] and the Beck Depression Inventory, they report an AB design study of 106 patients with 'moderate depression' treated by their GPs. Participants completed both measures at the start of treatment and again six weeks later. Oddly, claiming to have measured depression and QOL at *six weeks*, Skevington and Wright then report that:

> depression decreased significantly over 2 months and 74% reported feeling better. WHOQOL-100 scores increased in 24 of the 25 facets, demonstrating that QOL improves significantly in the 8 weeks following the start of antidepressant treatment. It also shows the instrument's validity and sensitivity to changes in clinical condition. The UK WHOQOL-100 is confirmed as excellent to good. Antidepressants significantly and comprehensively improve QOL. (Skevington and Wright, 2001: 261)

These are very strong claims indeed.

However, there is a raft of difficulties with the study. Apart from the fact that 26 per cent of participants *did not* report feeling better, and 10.5 per cent reported feeling worse or 'very much worse', the patient group is anything but homogenous. We are told that 'patients needed to be at the beginning of a first episode of depression and suited to taking a course of antidepressants. Alternatively, they could be at the start of a new episode of depression and a new course of pharmacological treatment' (p. 261). So, we have two completely different types of patients: those who have *never* been depressed and *never* taken antidepressants, and those who have *repeatedly* experienced these circumstances. We are told that 69 per cent of participants had been depressed for under a year, but the mean duration of depression was 2 years 3 months (with a huge standard deviation of 4 years

4 months). An unspecified number had had 'up to 20 years recurrent illness' (p. 262). Even at a purely common-sense level, it would seem that there may be a difference in how new patients and those with '20 years of recurrent illness' might experience their misery and the quality of their lives. Furthermore, the sample was strongly skewed in a number of potentially important ways: 76 per cent were women, 35 per cent were unemployed and, although three-quarters were prescribed SSRIs (selective serotonin reuptake inhibitors), the other 25 per cent of participants took antidepressant medications which are completely pharmacologically distinct.

The statistics presented to substantiate the claims that the WHOQOL is 'excellent', and that 'antidepressants significantly and comprehensively improve QOL' simply cannot be trusted. Inadequate data is presented on drop-out rates, meaning that the reader has to work out that the attrition rate for the study was nearly *one-quarter* by inspecting the degrees of freedom of the t test results presented for the test-retest analysis of changes in BDI scores. However, the scores on the BDI prove inconvenient: after an average of 55 days of treatment, the 80 or so patients still in the study recorded a statistically significant 'improvement' from 'moderate to severe depression' to 'moderate depression'. As such a finding clearly cannot provide strong support for the authors' (preconceived?) views, the BDI scores are abandoned in favour of two unstated 'transition questions' which are said to be 'equivalent', despite the fact that their correlation with BDI changes scores is of the order of only 0.4 (p. 262). On the basis of this statistical manipulation – a facet analysis which shows *no relationship* between depression and QOL on nine of the WHOQOL facets, a maximum correlation between depression scores and one facet of QOL as measured by the WHOQOL of 0.58 (Positive feelings) and the very strong possibility that the large number of tests conducted has led to Type 1 errors – the authors feel able to claim, unequivocally, that antidepressants 'comprehensively improve QOL'.

In the light of the extremely strong and unequivocal claims that are made, both for the WHOQOL (see Hagerty *et al.*, 2001) and for antidepressant medication, Skevington and Wright (2001: 261) make the remarkable claim that:

> for psychometric testing it is unnecessary to control for antidepressant type, size of dose, length of treatment, level of compliance or incidence of comorbidity ... it is sufficient to establish that scores of QOL are higher when people are well and lower when their health is worse.

Based on the study design reported, we cannot even know this with any certainty. If it doesn't matter what pills people take, if it doesn't matter what their problem is, if it doesn't even matter whether people actually take their pills or not, and if *we don't even bother to check*, then how can we claim that antidepressants have *anything to do with* QOL at all? If this is the rationale adopted, then this study does not *begin* to live up to the role it sets out for QOL research in psychiatry – namely that 'it is vital to the success of evidence-based medicine that the accuracy, reliability and validity of outcome measures are established' (p. 261). As it stands we cannot know what really happened to patients' depression or quality of life in this study, still less at *eight* weeks: what we can infer is that 25 per cent of patients had dropped out of the study by then. In passing, as Kaiser (2000) reminds us, eight weeks is the rule of thumb promoted by psychiatry and drug company advertising for the time that it takes 'antidepressants' to 'work'.

Somewhat more critically, Kemmler *et al.* (1997) report a study casting doubt on the rationale of the domains or 'facets' of life approach. Using a German version of the Lancashire QOL Profile,[14] the QOL of 48 'chronic schizophrenic outpatients with a long-term disease history' is reported. Correlations between general life satisfaction, satisfaction with specific life domains, psychological well-being and psychopathology were analysed using correlational and multiple linear regression analyses. Only social relations and health contributed significantly to the patients' general life satisfaction: the other domains (work, leisure, family relations and housing) failed to reach significance. Psychological well-being sub-scales (self-esteem, affective state) and 'psychopathology' were much more strongly related to general life satisfaction than the other life domains examined. What this study would seem to be telling us, then, is that people who meet current diagnostic criteria for schizophrenia are not terribly happy. Again, given that poor interpersonal relations is a key criterion indicator for such a diagnosis to be made, there would seem to be a high degree of redundancy in studies such as this.

Similarly, Taylor *et al.* (1998) analyse the differential impact of two types of community-based care ('intensive' and 'standard') on the QOL of 138 'people with psychosis' in London. Using the Lancashire Quality of Life Profile[14], Taylor and colleagues found that global QOL and the average of the domain-specific scores were stable over time. Weak improvements in the Living situation domain were noted in the 'intensive' sector. This improvement is accounted for by a large drop in in-patient admissions and increased social activity in the intensive sector. Over the entire study people reported poor objective QOL. Rather strangely, given that they document a 'large drop in in-patient admissions' and 'increased social activity', Taylor *et al.* (1998: 416) conclude that 'we failed to find an effect of intensive community care on QOL in people with psychosis. This may indicate an insensitivity to change in QOL measures, or that the intervention failed to produce the kind of changes in mental health and functioning which would be reflected in improved QOL.'

In contrast Simpson *et al.* (1989) report a comparative study of 'chronically mentally ill' patients in acute wards in a district general hospital, a hostel ward and group homes. They found that although 'severity of psychopathology corresponded to their placement' when analysis controlled for 'psychopathology', differences in quality of life were found between the three service settings – with residents in group homes and the hostel (as Anderson and Lewis, 2000 found) having a greater degree of similarity in QOL than those in the district general hospital. Precisely this profile was replicated in Shepherd *et al.*'s (1996) comparison of long-stay mental hospitals and community-based dispersed housing in outer London. Coid (1993: 611) has also noted that those who are involuntarily detained in mental hospitals have a 'poor quality of life'.

In Summary

Now clearly it is unfair to criticize those who have a direct interest in the provision of mental health services for assuming that these services must, of necessity, improve people's quality of life. It is probably unkind to note that it is unsurprising to discover that people diagnosed as 'severely mentally ill' are not very happy, that people incarcerated in mental hospitals report lower QOL than those in the community, or that 'psychopathology', impoverished social relations and low QOL are correlated. Equally it may be thought unnecessarily suspicious to be sceptical about reports produced by researchers funded by drug companies and affiliated to the World Health Organization, writing in psychiatric journals which depend on pharmaceutical advertising to stay in business, which find that the QOL measure developed by the WHO is 'excellent to good' and that 'antidepressants significantly and comprehensively improve QOL'. But the serious point here is that such assumptions and practices (and almost the entire psychiatric literature is predicated upon them), and the research studies which flow from them, show the wholesale adoption of an unthinking 'etic' procedural approach that 'tacitly treats common sense as both [its] resource and ... topic' (Silverman, 1998: 192). As Edwards (1997) has demonstrated, such an approach cannot but return incoherent results.

Notes

1. The QOL.Q is intended to be completed as a structured interview with service users with an intellectual disability. The QOL.Q presents respondents with a set of questions (such as 'how much fun and enjoyment do you get out of life?') which are answered by choosing between three alternatives (in this case 'not much/some/lots'). Answers are scored as 1, 2 or 3 and aggregated, higher scores indicating higher QOL. QOL.Q factors are: Satisfaction; Competence/ Productivity; Empowerment/Independence; and Social Belonging/Community Integration. Each factor has ten items, thus factor scores range from 10–30 and the total score is the sum of the factor scores. Psychometrics are reported by Rapley and Lobley (1995).

2. The ABS is a scale for the assessment of the activities-of-daily-living skills of people with intellectual disabilities. The ABS provides a criterion-referenced measure of individuals' effectiveness in coping with the natural and social demands of their environment. Part 1 is designed to evaluate an individual's skills and habits in ten behaviour domains considered important to the development of personal independence in daily living. Psychometrics are reported by Nihira *et al.* (1975) and Perry and Felce (1995).

3. MTS Activity codes provide for recording of engagement in activities such as 'Personal/Self-Care' (tasks such as grooming, washing and tooth-brushing) or 'Chores – electrical' (for example making toast). Staff Contact categories are coded as Positive, Negative, Neutral or Assistance completed using a 30-second momentary time sampling methodology. See Felce (1986) and Murphy (1987) for a detailed discussion of the use of direct observation as a research method.

4. The Social Networks Questionnaire measures three aspects of community life: the number of friends people had and the frequency of their meeting; the type and frequency of participation in social, sporting, recreational and any other activities outside of the home; and the degree to which these activities were specially organized for people with disabilities.

5. The IPDL measures the extent to which opportunities promoting individual independence and opportunities to participate in household maintenance are provided by intellectual disability services (Raynes *et al.*, 1989b). Each of 13 items is scored on a three-point rating scale; IPDL total score is the sum of item scores. The higher the total score the greater the indication of available opportunities for participation in domestic tasks. Raynes *et al.* (1989b) and Perry and Felce (1995) report psychometrics.

6. The ICI measures the extent of involvement in activities and use of facilities based in the local community (Raynes *et al.*, 1989a) and consists of 15 items. Raynes *et al.* (1989a) report psychometrics.

7. The NSCI consists of 12 items reflecting components of community membership, influence, integration and fulfilment of needs, and shared emotional connection. Pretty *et al.* (1994) report psychometric data.

8. The QOLI (Lehman, 1988, 1996) measures life circumstances and activities with indices of objective experiences and subjective feelings about these experiences. The short version contains 60 items. Objective items include Living Situation; Daily Activities and Functioning; Family; Social Relations; Work and School; Finances; Legal and Safety; and Health. Items are rated on dichotomous or ordinal scales with higher ratings indicating better functioning or more frequent behaviour except for the global ratings of health and general functioning. Sub-scale scores are the sums of items within each area that are rated on the same scale. The QOLI does not yield a total score. Psychometric properties are reported by Lehman *et al.*, (1986); Lehman *et al.*, (1982).

9. The SCL-90-R is a 90-item self-report inventory designed to reflect 'psychological symptom patterns' rated on a five-point scale of distress ranging from 'not at all distressed' to 'extremely distressed'. The SCL has nine symptom dimensions and three global distress scales. Symptom dimensions are: Psychoticism; Obsessive-compulsive; Paranoid ideation; Phobic anxiety; Hostility; Anxiety; Depression; Interpersonal sensitivity; and Somatization. The global distress scales are the Global Severity Index (the number of

symptoms reported with their intensity); Positive Symptom Distress Index (average level of distress reported for symptoms endorsed); and Positive Symptom Total (number of symptoms endorsed, regardless of the level of distress). For psychometrics see Derogatis (n.d.), Derogatis and Cleary (1977) and Derogatis et al. (1974).

10. The QOLIE-89 has 17 summary scales: Seizure worry; Medication effects; Health discouragement; Work/driving/social function; Language; Attention/concentration; Memory; Overall QOL; Emotional well-being; Role limitations – emotional; Social isolation; Social support; Energy/fatigue; Physical; Role limitations – physical; and Pain. Psychometrics are described by Devinsky et al. (1995).

11. The SPI assesses clinical status on 21 dimensions. Dimensions include Risk behaviours; Complications to illness and Complications to treatment. Details are reported by Lyons et al. (1997a) and Lyons et al. (1997b).

12. The BAI (Blass, 1985) covers ten self-care activities: Bathing; Dressing; Grooming; Toileting; Transferring from bed to chair; Mobility; Stairs; Continence (bowel and bladder), and Feeding. Total score is the sum of the ten activities with a lower score indicating greater dependence. For psychometrics see Mahoney and Barthel (1965).

13. The WHOQOL series of measures are critically reviewed by Hagerty et al., (2001). See Appendix 2 for the brief form, the WHOQOL-BREF.

14. The Lancashire QOL Profile (Oliver et al., 1996) has nine domains with objective questions and a satisfaction question scored 1–7. Domains are Work; Leisure; Religion; Finance; Living situation; Legal and safety; Family relations; Social relations; and Health. The LQOL incorporates a double question on global life satisfaction, Cantril's Ladder as a visual-analogue scale for global well-being, positive and negative affect scales and a self-esteem scale. Psychometric details are reported in Missenden et al., (1995-6) and Kaiser et al., (1998).

Study Questions

• What are the pros and cons of adopting emic and etic perspectives on quality of life?

• Is the quality of life of people with intellectual disabilities or mental health problems best understood from 'their' (emic) perspective or from 'ours' (etic)?

• Is an enhanced quality of life an appropriate outcome to specify for recipients of human services?

• Can specific quality of life 'outcomes' be tied to human service interventions sufficiently closely to warrant the use of QOL measures as indices of 'success'?

• Which aspects of the life experience of people with intellectual disabilities or mental health problems are most important to the quality of their lives?

Suggestions for Further Reading

Brown, R. I. (ed.) (1997) *Quality of Life for People with Disabilities: Models, Research and Practice*, 2nd edn. Cheltenham: Stanley Thornes.

Lyons, J. S., Howard, K. I., O'Mahoney, M. T. and Lish, J. (1997) *The Measurement and Management of Clinical Outcomes in Mental Health*. New York: Wiley.

Rapley, M. (2001) Policing happiness, in C. Newnes, G. Holmes and C. Dunn (eds), *This Is Madness Too*. Ross-on Wye: PCCS Books.

Schalock, R. L. (ed.) (1997) *Quality of Life Volume II: Application to Persons with Disabilities*. Washington: American Association on Mental Retardation.

CHAPTER 8

Researching QOL as a Psychological Object

The idea that individual-level QOL is best understood as a psychological state has grown in popularity over recent years, but, as we have seen in Chapter 5, the historical development of this piece of contemporary cultural common sense is *itself* a topic that repays attention. Here, to complement that analysis, a critical review of the concept of QOL as a psychological object is offered. The purpose of this chapter is to *demonstrate* how a critical reading of the psychological quality of life literature may be conducted, taking as its analytic site Cummins's homeostatic theory of subjective well-being. This analysis is itself a part of an ongoing dialogue in the literature between Bob and myself (see Rapley and Ridgway, 1998; Cummins, 2001a) – and is a further contribution to that critical engagement. Indeed, without Bob's unfailingly generous assistance, this book would be much the poorer. Of course, this does not mean that we cannot disagree or question each other's point of view: indeed, it is an important measure of any contribution to the literature that it is taken seriously enough to be challenged.

As Rose has shown, we have come to think ourselves as, fundamentally, psychological beings. *Cogito ergo sum* has little competition as the slogan of the present. The very persuasiveness and apparent 'intuitive' sense of this way of thinking ourselves demands that we rethink this way of thinking (Foucault, 1970, 1978).

QOL as a Psychological Object

A body of work suggests that QOL is a psychological state representing a summary of estimations of the satisfactoriness of life in a limited number of areas or 'domains'. Campbell (1981) suggested psychological well-being could be conceptualized in terms of twelve domains of QOL: marriage, family life, friendships, general standard of living, work, neighbourhood, city/town of residence, housing, health, self, education, and national concerns. These factors compare favourably with those identified in Lehman's (1988) study of the QOL of the 'chronically mentally ill' (health, safety, religious concerns, living circumstances, family relationships, social relationships more generally, recreational activity, work and financial concerns). Keith (1990: 94) summarizes the literature thus:

it would be fair to say that Americans ... are concerned in rating the quality of their own lives with relationships, work, general material standard of living, opportunities for learning, the neighbourhoods/communities/homes in which they live, health and safety, recreational/social activities, and perception of self.

Cummins (1996b) has suggested that seven domains (Material well-being, Emotional well-being, Productivity, Intimacy, Safety, Community and Health) capture the 'totality' of the QOL construct. However, Cummins has recently advanced a theory of subjective well-being which radically recasts the concept. This theory – of the 'homeostatic control' of subjective well-being – is critically scrutinized in this chapter.

Subjective Well-being as Brain State

Cummins and his co-workers offer perhaps the comprehensive theory to date of QOL as a hard-wired, biologically determined brain state. That this work is widely seen as important may be gauged partly by the inclusion of key elements of Cummins's position into major recent theoretical statements by organizations such as ISQOLS (Hagerty *et al.*, 2001) and IASSID (2001), and also by the claims he and colleagues make themselves. In their conclusions to a chapter describing 'subjective well-being homeostasis' Cummins *et al.* (in press) make powerful claims for the 'revolutionary' importance of their view. They state that:

> the idea that it is normal and adaptive to view one's life positively is revolutionary ... such an idea fundamentally challenges the ideas of many influential psychologists and psychiatrists from the last century as to what constitutes desirable psychological functioning. Most essentially, the idea that the accurate perception of reality equates to optimal psychological functioning is clearly wrong.

In keeping with the use of worked examples to illustrate major issues in this book, a detailed account is offered here of Cummins's work, as a perspicuous instance of the individualistic psychological ('modern') stream of QOL research. The 'homeostatic' theory of subjective well-being is critically examined, as are some of the major difficulties with, and implications of, this way of understanding of what are, after all, people's verbal reports of how their life is.

A Critique of the Homeostatic Model

Cummins (2001b) has claimed 'remarkable stability in population life satisfaction'. His 1995 study held that life satisfaction could be defined as

75.0 ± 2.5 per cent of QOL scale maximum scores (%SM) and, using two standard deviations as a normative band, population means fall in the range 70–80%SM. Cummins (1998b) reported a similar analysis for 45 Western and non-Western nations. This study found a 'population standard' (Cummins, 2001) of 75 ± 2.5%SM for Western nations, while others reported lower levels of life satisfaction. Grand mean life satisfaction was 70 ± 5.0%SM. Cummins (2001) argues that both the Western and world ranges have an upper margin at 80%SM, while the world range falls beneath the Western normative margin of 70%SM to 60%SM.

Cummins (2001b) bases his argument that life satisfaction is homeo-statically maintained largely on these data. He claims that:

> There are several reasons to posit such an idea. The first is based on the weight of empirical data that have been described. Despite very different circumstances of living, the World's populations have an average level of life satisfaction that varies by only about 20 percent. This is a strong indication that life satisfaction is not free to vary over its entire range. Second, it has long been speculated that animals like to feel good about themselves ... and it is intuitive that humans benefit from having a positive outlook on life ... So given these characteristics and the apparent benefits to the maintenance of life satisfaction ... human selection has favoured this attribute ... humans must also have evolved device(s) that allow the maintenance of life satisfaction.

Appeals to 'animals liking to feel good about themselves', evolutionary theory and the 'weight of empirical data' make a potent mix. However, the notion of an absolute range over which human life satisfaction may vary is *not* a given fact of nature – as its juxtaposition to evolution and the animal kingdom might imply. Such a joining is 'ontological gerrymandering' (Potter, 1996). We cannot ask animals if they 'feel good', and what contribution 'feeling good' might make to the individual reproductive success of specific animals – the fundamental criterion for the selection of characteristics in evolutionary theory – is nowhere addressed. Of course, if speculation about the evolutionary success of happy animals is not accepted, then there is no reason to countenance the idea that 'humans must also have evolved device(s) that allow the maintenance of life satisfaction within some range that is optimal for the survival of the population' (Cummins, 2001).

The idea of a fixed range over which 'a positive outlook' may fluctuate is a function of a pair of a priori decisions – firstly to regard 'feeling good about yourself' or 'life satisfaction' as a *thing* (to reify subjective experience), and secondly, to use the measurement technology of the physical sciences to quantify what has become an 'object'. It might also be thought that, if 'a positive outlook' can vary by 20 per cent depending on local conditions, a *contextual* understanding would be fruitful. This is not the case, however: Cummins *et al.* (in press) offer an extraordinarily detailed account – based on these speculations – which reduces 'having a positive outlook on life', later respecified as 'Subjective Well-Being output', to the automatic 'output' of the ghostly activities of the machine (Ryle, 1949).

Affective and Cognitive Components of Subjective Well-being

Cummins *et al.* (in press) argue that, since the seminal studies of Campbell *et al.* (1976), the view that personal (subjective) well-being is made up of affective and cognitive elements has been accepted. They refer to this phenomenon as *subjective well-being* (SWB).

In their analyses of six national samples Crooker and Near (1998) concluded that, in studies of subjective well-being, distinctions between cognitive and affective measures are *illusory*. However, Cummins *et al.* (in press) continue the dichotomization and use the term *happiness* to describe the affective component. For the putative cognitive element of SWB, it is suggested that personal evaluations of this dimension are generated via the computation of multiple internal comparisons. Net satisfaction is described as a positive linear function of the perceived differences between what one has versus (1) what one wants, (2) what others have, (3) the best one has had in the past, (4) what one expected to have in the past, (5) what one expects to have in the future, (6) what one deserves, and (7) what one needs. This yields a measurable state to provide a quantum of what Cummins *et al.* (in press) suggest should be called *life satisfaction*. The net satisfaction quantum thus derives from the meeting of what are termed 'multiple needs' (Cummins *et al.*, in press) on the basis of the assumption that the desire for satisfaction motivates people to act. Cummins *et al.* (in press) suggest that 'this applies to satisfaction with income, health, education, and other life facets, as well as with satisfaction with life as a whole' (Mallard *et al.*, 1997: 260). Other writers such as Veenhoven (1997: 29) are less sanguine, suggesting that, over and above 'sufficient food, housing and health care', what people 'need' is not the sort of thing which can be established *empirically*.

Having suggested that 'life satisfaction' is a 'linear function' of multiple comparisons, quite what arithmetic operations are then performed by the brain to produce a numerical value for SWB is not specified. We are not told if, across the hundreds of measures of SWB identified, SWB is (to be) treated as a simple additive product of separate affective and cognitive quanta, or whether their relationship is multiplicative, logarithmic or synergistic, nor the relative weights of each putative component. Similarly, it is not clear from the account how separate estimations of numerous different domains relate to numerical estimates of 'satisfaction' produced in response to single questions.

However, Cummins *et al.* (in press) go on to argue that, given its claimed ability to measure both cognitive and affective aspects of SWB, the ComQOL allows a measure of 'the aggregate of satisfaction across life domains [which] yields *Subjective Quality of Life* (SQOL)'. This is a little confusing given the earlier description of affective and cognitive evaluations of life as 'subjective well-being'. The ComQOL (Cummins, 1997a, 1997b) does, however, implicitly, answer the theoretical question about the arithmetic operations in the brain which produce well-being estimates: it is a simple procedure of adding up benefits on each domain, with domains weighted by importance, and then calculating an average. Whether the endorsement of this computational process is for psychological, physiological or neurological reasons, or just administrative convenience, is unclear. As Veenhoven (1997) has suggested, however, the mere fact of a correlation between sub-evaluations of domain benefit and overall ratings of happiness does not, and cannot, suggest that one causes the other.

A Normative Standard for Subjective Well-being

Cummins *et al.* (in press) state that: 'SQOL ... can be described in terms of an empirical normative standard ... Western population mean scores for SQOL predictably lie within the range 70 to 80 %SM' and claim that the measuring of such values reflects biologically based human universals (Cummins, 2001; Cummins *et al.*, in press). On the basis of meta analyses of general population surveys recalibrated to express scores as %SM, Cummins *et al.* (in press) claim that, when recoded in this manner, life satisfaction and SQOL scores consistently yield a mean of 75 and a standard deviation of 2.5. That is life satisfaction and subjective QOL scores across population samples usually fall into the 70–80%SM range as shown by Figure 8.1.

In other words, on average people around the world are 'normally' somewhere between three-quarters and 80 per cent satisfied with their life or, alternatively, the quality of their life is between 75 and 80 per cent (of what, one wonders?). Cummins (1995) suggests no study yet has returned an average value significantly above 80%SM. Further, even though the highest levels of life satisfaction are obtained from very wealthy people their values also average to around 80%SM (Cummins, 2000a). The findings of Groot and VandenBrink (2000) – who showed additional income made no difference to life satisfaction for people with minimum value of 80%SM – are cited to suggest a ceiling effect: that it is not physically possible to become happier than 80 per cent. Further evidence for biologically determined well-being is held to derive from the stability of these figures over time. On the basis of these data, and of a range of other studies, Cummins *et al.* (in press) argue that:

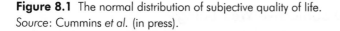

Percentage of scale maximum (%SM)

Figure 8.1 The normal distribution of subjective quality of life.
Source: Cummins *et al.* (in press).

These data, together with the predictable ranges of SQOL values, constitute converging evidence that SWB is not simply free to vary at the whim
of personal circumstances, but is managed. This idea, that SWB is under
active internal control, is termed SWB homeostasis.

The general idea of the proposed homeostatic system is that SWB is
managed, for each individual, within a 'set-point-range' (Cummins,
2000b). That is, each person has an in-built 'set-point' for their normal
level of SWB, as proposed by Headey and Wearing (1992), and their
perceived SWB is normally held within a narrow range around this setting.

A Role for Circumstances?

While these data are (intendedly) described by proponents of a biological
view as convincing evidence that 'SWB is not simply free to vary at the
whim of personal circumstances', the correlation coefficients relied upon
are quite *low* if a strong biological mechanism is determining people's
verbal behaviour. The shared variance between the satisfaction reports of
the highest coefficient cited – a value of 0.65 reported by Bowling (1996) – is
a mere 42 per cent, or well under half. If this is hard evidence for biological
control, what is influencing the other 58 per cent of the variance in
happiness reports? While Cummins (2001b) claims that the life satisfaction
of Western populations was stable between 1980 and 1990, Veenhoven cites
Witt *et al.* (1979) to suggest that elderly Americans became happier between
1950 and 1970 and also points out that the Heady and Wearing (1992) study
on which Cummins *et al.* (in press) draw to stake their 'satisfaction is

determined by biology' claim, actually demonstrated that 'life events explained some 25 per cent of the differences in life satisfaction' (Veenhoven, 1997: 15) and that 63 per cent of national differences in happiness 'can be explained by variation in societal qualities' (Veenhoven, 1997: 19). Contra Cummins *et al.* (in press) Veenhoven claims that: 'happiness does not remain the same over time: particularly not over the length of a lifetime … Happiness changes quite often; both absolutely and relatively towards others … Happiness is not insensitive to change in living-conditions … Happiness is not entirely an internal matter' (Veenhoven, 1997: 20). To accept Cummins *et al.*'s (in press) argument one has to believe that something dramatic happened to humanity as a whole between 1970 (when the data suggest that for at least some Americans happiness was changeable) and the decade 1980–1990 (when Western populations' levels of happiness suddenly became, after Cummins (2001b), fixed).

Life Events and Subjective Well-being

Cummins *et al.* (in press) allow a limited role for life events as temporary disruptions to biologically based well-being. If people experience an event which 'depresses their SWB below threshold', homeostatic control 'should improve their levels of SWB over time'. They cite data suggesting that people who have received bad medical news (Bloom *et al.* 1991) or have suffered spinal injuries (Bach and Tilton, 1994) report, later, that life satisfaction has returned to previous levels. They further suggest that the stability of SWB over time is restricted to two sorts of people, firstly those who score in the 'normal' range and experience no life events or, as they state, 'under maintenance conditions, where no threat to homeostasis can be recognized, there should be no systematic relationship between the objective circumstances of people's lives and their SWB'. This, of course, makes the measurement of SWB for almost any policy-relevant or service evaluation purpose, at any level, pointless. The second group are those who experience what is termed 'homeostatic defeat' due to some chronic condition, like extreme poverty, to which they cannot adapt (a position which blames individuals' biology rather than their circumstances for their misery).

As is shown in Figure 8.2, the influence of life events is modelled as dependent upon the 'strength of extrinsic conditions'. If these are strong, or 'if the strength of the agents exceeds the homeostatic threshold … the extrinsic agents begin to wrest control of SWB away from the homeostatic system, causing SWB to rise or fall. As this occurs, the agencies and SQOL start to co-vary' (Cummins *et al.*, in press). Of course this position presupposes that 'the strength of the agents' is universally determinable (as of course is their composition) and independent of the values, appraisals and social mores of people whose brain systems are so violently taken control of.

Figure 8.2 The relationship between subjective and objective quality of life.
Source: Cummins *et al.* (in press).

Personality and Subjective Well-being

Cummins *et al.* (in press) do allow for other putatively stable 'internal' brain systems to have a role in determining SWB, and here the 'affective' component of the two-factor model of SWB seems to come to the fore. These are the 'personality' factors of 'neuroticism' – which is described as 'the source of constitutional negative affectivity' – and 'extraversion' which is held to be 'the source of constitutional positive affectivity ... the natural opposing force to neuroticism'.

Despite a huge literature critical of the incoherence of the concept of 'personality', and the fact that the 'personality' literature is almost as internally fragmented and contradictory as the QOL literature itself, in a near perfect recapitulation of Kant's *Critique of Judgment* (see McHoul and Rapley, 2001),[1] Cummins *et al.* (in press) state that: 'It seems reasonable to suggest that it is the balance between these two personality dimensions that provides the set-point-range for SWB.' These 'dimensions' are then supported by a further set of proposed 'homeostatic variables' and mediated by what are called 'cognitive buffers'. On the basis of a review of some of this literature, Cummins *et al.* (in press) argue that:

> when the correlations are averaged across the five factors, the highest
> loading category is Self-esteem (.31) followed by SQOL and Ill-being,

both on .27. The lowest are Just World Beliefs (.14) and Motivation (.13).
… factors of neuroticism and extraversion, and to a lesser extent conscientiousness, have a robust relationship with subjective well-being conceptualised either as SWB or SQOL. In addition, these three factors also have a reliable influence on the two putative 'buffer' variables of self-esteem and control.

The conceptual coherence of this account is questionable, as indeed is the certainty of the claims given the psychometric marginality of many, if not most, tests of personality and its putative 'components'. Indeed, just such a caveat is later entered: Cummins *et al.* (in press) note that 'there are, however, many different ways to measure self-esteem, and these different instruments may yield very different results … self-esteem scales are not equivalent'. But to return to these claims: surely the initial claim that Cummins *et al.* made was that SWB and SQOL are different 'things', and that confusing one for the other is what the proposed model claimed to avoid? Isn't, according to the proposed model, 'motivation' to satisfaction the fundamental drive for the whole of human action and the SWB system itself? If so, then why is 'motivation' one of the lowest loading variables? What relationship do 'just world beliefs' have to anything under consideration here: surely there is an immensity of cultural variability in what constitutes a 'just world'? What clear theoretical bearing does 'conscientiousness' (not a component – until now – of the model) have on satisfaction, whether conceptualized as SQOL, SWB or happiness? Is 'control' really a 'personality' variable or better understood as the *actual* presence or absence of leverage over real-world events?

However, in keeping with the biological determinism of the model, personality – rather than real-world events – is identified as the serious contender for a role in the generation of the well-being reported by people. Cummins *et al.* (in press) note that:

> It seems that the strength of the relationship between personality and SWB will be situationally variable and, apart from being dependent on the nature of the measures employed, it will be determined by the degree of challenge that objective circumstances bring to the homeostatic system.
> … while it is clear personality and SWB are linked, no simple general estimate of the strength of this linkage can be made. However, it is possible that if samples were separated on the basis of their relative degree of homeostatic threat, more consistent estimates would emerge.

It seems rather optimistic to imagine that one could ever establish a universally agreed ranking of 'homeostatic threats', and hence this appeal employs wishful thinking to buttress an unsupported position. It may appear that the above view relegates personality (the nature of which 'thing', it is conceded, will vary according to the manner in which it is measured) to the second rank after 'situational variability', 'objective circumstances' and the 'homeostatic system'.

However, Cummins *et al.* then make a series of startling claims. Following Switzky (1999: 70) they assert that 'personality [is] at the center of operations', that personality is the 'fulcrum around which all other psychological, educational, and self-regulatory processes rotate to energize behavior and performance' and that personality is the key determinant of evaluations of the strength of met and unmet needs. Furthermore, apparently, when people are asked to consider whether the support they have from family, friends and others is adequate (presumably their 'level of satisfaction with social support') the startling claim is now advanced that, rather than such a judgment being a rational (albeit probably automatic and unconscious) calculation of 'have–want' discrepancies, or the relativities of benefits received weighed against actual requirements, this is not a matter of (rational) judgment or computation at all. Instead it is claimed that the 'evidence for a genetic link appears to be strongest in relation to perceived social support ... This link has special significance in terms of the model since it may represent the simplest connection between personality and motivation'.

Whether we believe that our levels of social support are adequate then is not to do with anything as messy as lived experience and recalcitrant relatives. Our perceptions of the social support we receive are merely a matter of our DNA. Notably this claim is buttressed, not by a review of the literature on genetic determinants of beliefs about social support (such a literature is sparse, and overlooks the fact – as does all so-called biological psychology – that genes code for proteins and not for beliefs, attitudes or values), but by an extended discussion of studies of 'extraversion with particular attention to the facet of 'sociability', as the enjoyment of social activities, preference for being with others and 'reward sensitivity'.'

From the other side of the 'personality' coin, it is claimed once more that real-world circumstances have little bearing on how persons describe them. Cummins *et al.* (in press) cite a study by Fyrand *et al.* (1997) that reported a 'strong correlation' (for once we are not given a value) between depression and the lack of social support (described as 'an unmet need') in people with arthritis. However, after statistically removing the effects of neuroticism on the relationship, the correlation 'virtually disappeared'. This, it is stated, means that 'neuroticism may, therefore, have caused the perceived lack of social support'. This is the production of persons as 'cultural dopes' (Garfinkel, 1967): depressed people don't know their own lives or circumstances, they cannot reliably report on whether they have adequate social support or not, their 'neuroticism' makes them incapable of telling it like it is. If we cannot trust people's reports on such a matter, surely people's reports of their 'satisfaction', 'happiness' or SWB on measures such as Cummins's own ComQOL should be regarded as equally unreliable.

'Buffers' of Subjective Well-being

Cummins *et al.* (in press) briefly move away from biology to account for the role of 'buffers' in SWB. Noting 'overwhelming evidence that the way people think about and explain what happens in their lives is intimately tied to their level of SWB', they claim that three 'cognitive protective factors' (self-esteem, perceived control and optimism) are crucial to well-being. In a tautologous argument it is suggested that feeling good about yourself (high self-esteem) produces a feeling of subjective well-being (or feeling good) and, contrariwise, feeling bad about yourself produces feeling of subjective ill-being, viz.: 'low self-esteem would be predicted to correlate with low values of the cognitive buffers…reflecting a weak buffering system that is susceptible to homeostatic defeat by negative life events'. Similarly it is contended that 'perceived control is central to life quality', that perceived control is another buffer that 'reinforces' SWB. The buffer's modus operandum is opaque: 'Under normal conditions, where the person believes their environment is under their control, they will evidence internal control. This, in turn, reinforces SWB.' Essentially what this says is that if people believe they are in control they will behave as if they believe they are in control, and probably tell us they believe they are in control. This tells us little: the link to SWB is, in effect, accomplished by authorial fiat. Cummins *et al.* (in press) then clarify:

> however, the extrinsic environment cannot always be perceived as under one's personal control, such as when negative life events must be endured. This is when the perception of external control can act as a buffer. That is, if negative life events were simply accepted as evidence of a complete loss of control this would be indicative of helplessness and very damaging to SWB. If, on the other hand, such events can be understood as simply bad luck (i.e. that the event is unlikely to recur) or the will of God (i.e. that there is a higher, but not understood purpose underlying the event), then the negative feelings associated with the event can be reduced, and the impact on SWB diminished. This is the proposed role of external control, not to directly enhance SWB but to buffer the potential negative impact of negative life events. The capacity of the buffer is, however, limited in this regard, and this capacity will be exceeded by either a strong or protracted negative event. As a consequence, high levels of external control will most commonly be linked to a measurable reduction in SWB, even though the model predicts such a reduction to be less than would be the case in the absence of the external control buffer.

It is somewhat perplexing then that such an account (which it must be remembered is embedded in an unambiguously biological account of a hard-wired brain system controlling SWB – that is, it is proposed that it is as much a condition of being human that SWB is 'not free to vary' as it is that humans have two legs and two arms, not three or four) immediately falls back on matters of cultural belief (and, it must be said, Western common sense) to account for the operation of what is claimed to be a neurological (brain) system. 'Negative life events', the 'will of God' and 'bad luck' too are, presumably, hard-wired into humans, as is the universality of lowered SWB as the inevitable human response to what is held to be 'helplessness'. That Buddhism, for example, enjoins its adherents actively to seek and to celebrate helplessness cannot be accommodated by this account. That one's own death (and presumably Cummins *et al.* (in press) would imagine this as a 'strong' 'negative life event') might be understood by some as a positive and control over its ending as enhancing the value and quality of what remains of it – as shown by van Hooff's (1990) study of self-killing in antiquity, Irish hunger strikers in the 1980s and many young Palestinians more recently – again cannot be accommodated.

Further difficulties arise with the third 'buffer', optimism, 'defined as a perception that the future will be to the perceiver's advantage or for their pleasure' and that 'studies have shown that people view themselves on an upward path of 'life getting better'.' In support of their claim that 'optimism' too acts to 'buffer' SWB, Glatzer's (1991) survey work is cited as evidence of 'optimism as a positive cognitive bias'.

> People were asked to rate their life satisfaction as they remembered it to be 5 years ago, in the present, and as they anticipated it would be 5 years hence. The mean scores, in %SM units, were as follows: past (73, 71, 74), present (78, 77, 77), future (80, 75, 76). These data do not confirm the future bias, perhaps due to the prevailing uncertainty in the country at that time. However, the present greater than the past bias is clearly evident and is consistent with the idea that the optimism buffer helps to maintain SWB through a downward comparison with the past.

Not only does this conclusion seem odd in face of the evidence, but it also demonstrates both the slipperiness of the concepts deployed and the flexibility of Cummins *et al.*'s arguments. Glatzer (1991) appears to have studied remembered, current and projected 'life satisfaction' not 'optimism'. The results cited directly contradict the central notion that people in the 'normal' range of homeostatically controlled SWB (remember this is supposed to be between 70%SM and 80%SM, into which bracket all estimates cited fall) would not be affected by extrinsic circumstances. The data also directly contradict Cummins's (2001b) claim that there is no evidence that levels of life satisfaction in Western nations changed in the period 1980–1990. How, then, did 'prevailing uncertainty in the country at that time' operate to change the reports offered of German life satisfaction? Prevailing uncertainty is a description of circumstances that clearly rules out what is claimed as the *necessary condition* for homeostatic control being 'wrested' out of the control of the brain – the severity of 'extrinsic threat'. Why then did the scores change?

However, suggesting that optimism shows a high relationship with internal control and 'the personality traits and self-esteem', Cummins *et al.* (in press) argue that 'the buffering aspect of optimism lies within the global expectation that things are going to get better with time and in the tendency to perceive things in a more positive light than may be objectively true'. It seems that these constructs are extremely hard to disentangle. Clarification follows:

> self-esteem, control and optimism buffers appear to display the necessary characteristics to justify their role [in the homeostatic model]. Each one has strong links to SWB consistent with SWB being a product of both the buffers and personality ... In addition, the buffers are highly correlated, consistent with the proposal that they constitute a single buffering system for the purpose of SWB output. While it has also been argued that these buffers, through the influence of personality, can be linked to motivation, the most central source of motivation is likely to be the cognitive appraisal of needs.

This account, then, presents putative 'buffers' as simultaneously separable and as a singular system, as 'highly correlated' (and hence conceptually overlapping) but as, in some sense, sufficiently discriminable to be distinct 'things'. They both 'produce' 'SWB output' in collaboration with 'personality' and yet are – at the same time – junior partners to personality when it comes to being 'influenced' about matters of 'motivation'. Such supposed aspects of persons are, as we have seen, understood as fixed, biologically given matters.

Motivation, Needs and Subjective Well-being

When it comes to motivation, earlier the well-spring for human action, a priori traits, buffers and personality types take second place to ratiocination. 'The most central source of motivation' we read 'is likely to be the cognitive appraisal of needs'. That basic needs, such as for food and drink, are not 'cognitive' but rather physical states, and that the logical grammar of statements such as 'I am thirsty' is such that they do not describe a 'cognitive state' but rather a physiological one (cf. Wittgenstein, 1953; Coulter, 1999) is unrecognized. Further to argue that 'unmet needs provide the basis for motivation ... the idea that they are directly linked to SWB levels is problematic' is itself problematic. How being unable to satisfy a basic need, for food say, could *not* be related to SWB as ordinary persons would understand the term is difficult to comprehend. And indeed precisely this point is later conceded. Cummins *et al.* write that 'What may, however, affect the levels of SWB is the presence of a strong, chronic, unmet need that acts to compromise the buffers, and thereby to reduce

SWB. For example, a person who is chronically very hungry or insecure is likely to have a level of SWB that lies below the normal range.'

The grounds offered for the counter-intuitive suggestion that SWB is all but impervious to anything but 'chronic unmet needs' is based on an acceptance of Maslow's (1954) theory of a hierarchy of needs. They argue that 'as most basic needs are met, higher level needs arise which, in Maslow's hierarchy, culminate in needs of self-actualization'. Cummins *et al.* (in press) then claim that, given the 'remarkable level of stability' SWB shows, 'to account for such stability it must be assumed either that some needs cannot be met or that met needs are seamlessly replaced by unmet needs, so as to maintain an average SWB level of 75%SM. Both of these ideas seem implausible.'

Not only are Cummins *et al.* (in press) conflating levels of analysis (*population* mean SWB levels and *individuals'* potential 100% SWB minus a supposed need to 'self-actualize'), but also their argument depends upon the prior assumption that Maslow's theory is itself a plausible account of human universals. Again one is reminded that Buddhism and variants of Islam encourage their adherents not to self-actualize but to self-negate, that as Rose (1992: 110) points out, the notion that the 'need' to 'self-actualize' was 'a part of human nature' was only invented in the West in the 1950s, and that, from a Wittgensteinian perspective, the logical grammar of the term 'need' refers not to putative internal states, but rather to conditions of deficit in the external world: for example the statement 'I need a pencil to sign my name' *cannot* index an intra-psychic state.[2]

Problems with the Assumption of Met Needs

Further, the argument depends on uncritically accepting that the idea that 'some needs cannot be met is implausible' is itself plausible. The argument here depends on the further acceptance of the claims that as:

> the majority of people in Western society do not experience chronic unmet needs at the lower levels of Maslow's hierarchy, and have their relationship needs reasonably well met, the assumption of 'unmet' needs, required to fulfil the average 25%SM deficit from complete life satisfaction, must be maintained via unmet 'self-actualization' needs. There is no evidence of which we are aware to support such an idea.

Of course, if one looks at 'hard' evidence relating to divorce rates, levels of domestic violence, homelessness, poverty, inequality of income distribution and lack of access to affordable healthcare across most of the Western world – all of which directly coincide with the 'lower levels of Maslow's hierarchy', and all of which show a steady worsening over the last twenty years (World Bank, 2000) – one might not so readily accept the contention that 'the majority of people in Western society do not experience chronic unmet needs ... and have their relationship needs reasonably well met'.

For example, the National Centre for Social and Economic Modelling in Australia has suggested that 'there is strong evidence that income inequality has increased between the late 1980s and mid-1990s and there is some evidence to suggest that it has continued increasing since then; this increase has been driven by a decline in the income share of the bottom 10 per cent of Australians ... and an increase in the income share of the top 10 per cent' (Harding and Greenwell, 2001: 22). World Health Organization projections for depression suggest that the global 'burden of disease' caused by depression will increase by at least 50 per cent by 2020 and will be the second most important cause of disability worldwide (WHO, 2001). The UK government has estimated that nearly 20 per cent of British adults have a 'neurotic disorder' (most commonly anxiety and depression) and that these rates have been static since the early 1990s (Ferriman, 2001). These figures suggest a generally widespread low-level misery.

Of course, if it is accepted for a moment that for a considerable number of people in the West there are very real difficulties with meeting basic subsistence and relational needs – as reports such as Harding and Greenwell's (2001) suggest – the argument about putative 25%SM self-actualization deficits runs into difficulties. A considerable body of work demonstrates that high levels of objective threat to the most basic of needs, life itself, are negatively correlated with mean ratings of happiness at the population level. Veenhoven (1997), for example, reports, across 48 countries, that levels of malnutrition, accessibility of safe drinking water, murder rates and lethal accident rates are negatively correlated with happiness. It is, of course, also the case that in Western society, where we are told 'most people do not experience chronic unmet needs...and have their relationship needs reasonably well met', respected psychiatrists such as Wolpert (1999) have described a huge increase in levels of depression since 1980 – an era when, pace Cummins, apparently world levels of SWB have not changed.

There are a number of further problems with this account. The first of these is that – as we all know – our personal estimates of how good life is are, in practice, likely to fluctuate over time. Contra Cummins et al. (in press) who object that if unmet needs had a major bearing on SWB, 'SWB would show marked fluctuations as unmet needs arise, and are then met. But this does not occur', data they have already drawn upon to make their argument shows precisely that SWB *does* fluctuate in response to events – such as serious injury or life-threatening illness – which challenge people's abilities to meet their basic needs (Bach and Tilton, 1994; Bloom et al., 1991).

Secondly, it only makes sense to speak of automata or alien beings as exhibiting an 'average 25%SM deficit from complete life satisfaction' as if this were a steady state of being-in-the-world. It is hard to imagine what 100%SM life satisfaction could actually mean, and, if Cummins is right that humans cannot biologically exceed 80%SM, then, ipso facto, 80%SM is as happy as one could be: in effect, this quantum actually represents 100 per cent satisfaction. However, if we talk about real-life human beings (presumably who the model is trying to account for), everyday members' understandings tell us that life is a dynamic process, not a steady state.

Thirdly, SWB may well be 'remarkably stable' when large population averages, derived from cross-sectional ('snapshot') studies, taken from different eras and sourced from completely different people, are what we are trying to explain. But such population averages are *abstractions*: they do not relate to any individual judgments of satisfaction with life and, again, it is surely this that we are trying to explain. Indeed, while Cummins *et al.* (in press) here and elsewhere maintain that SWB is stable, in Cummins (2001) it is suggested that: 'Rodgers (1982) ... reviewed national USA survey data from 1957 to 1978. He reported a slight but significant decrease up to the early 1970s followed by a gradual recovery. This latter increase was also reported by Andrews (1991) in respect of data derived from a life-as-a-whole survey conducted in 1972 and again in 1988' (Cummins, 2001b).

Similarly, in their discussion of the effects that needs being met have on the 'buffers' (which, following an exercise model, it is held 'strengthens' them) Cummins *et al.* (in press) discuss a study reported by Wolinski *et al.* (1985). Wolinski and co-workers found that, over a one-year study, people with high or low levels of SWB at the start of the study scored lower and higher, respectively, five or 12 months later. With socio-economic status (SES) overriding the regression to the mean effect, Cummins *et al.* (in press) acknowledge that a *direct relationship* between socio-economic status and SWB improvement over the course of the study exists. Wolinski *et al.* (1985) conclude that their results 'suggest a vicious cycle wherein lower SES elderly people will increasingly face declining SWB, while their higher SES counterparts will somehow be able to avoid and/or compensate for the circumstances and problems that would otherwise result in reducing their subjective well-being' (p. 102). This is described as: 'consistent with that emerging from the aforementioned review ... the perception of whether or not important needs are being met is strongly influenced by personality' (Cummins, *et al.*, in press). That high SES may be linked to access to resources and the ability to operate materially on the world is not canvassed: rather, again, we see that such matters (despite the contrary evidence Wolinski *et al.* provide) are overridden by 'personality'.

In summarizing their account Cummins *et al.* (in press) thus maintain, as shown in Figure 8.3, that:

> SWB is under the direct control of personality and the indirect control of the buffers, which together act to maintain SWB within its normal range ... chronic met needs will normally have little influence on SWB levels ... in such circumstances, the buffers will typically not be activated ... Consequently, the level of SWB will remain determined by the

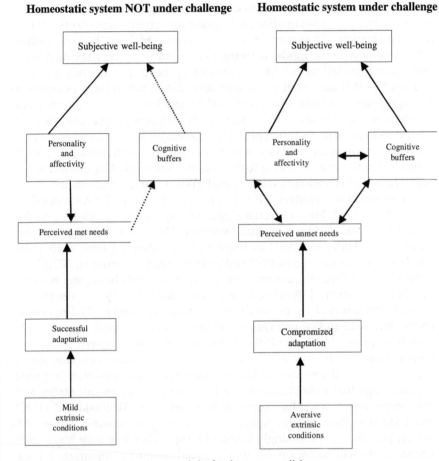

Figure 8.3 A homeostatic model of subjective well-being.
Source: Cummins *et al.* (in press).

dispositional set-point-range ... To summarize, it is proposed that, in the absence of strong unmet needs, the SWB homeostatic system will deliver a level of SWB that is within its set-point-range. The presence of strong unmet needs can defeat this system and, therefore, cause SWB to fall below its normal range ... The differential strength of the buffers combines to absorb the impact of threats causing needs to no longer be met, and as a consequence, act to maintain SWB within homeostatically determined levels.

Adaptation to Life and Subjective Well-being

One other matter needs to be addressed: adaptation. Having stated that 'personality provides a steady affective background that determines the set-point-range for the whole homeostatic system' and that 'a set of cognitive buffers, together with personality, create subjective well-being', Cummins *et al.* (in press) introduce the concept of adaptation as 'the most basic process in the homeostatic model', and describe adaptation as 'a psychological process that allows people, over some period of time, to experience a reduced reaction to some changed life circumstance that comes to represent their extrinsic experience'.

The fundamental postulate of Adaptation Level Theory (Helson, 1964) is that an individual's judgment of their current 'stimulation' level (whether that be positive or negative) is relative to the level to which they are accustomed. So, if current stimulation is higher than accustomed, change is experienced. Cummins *et al.* (in press) suggest that adaptation may be defined as the process by which the future experience of this new level of stimulation comes to seem unremarkable: that is an upward shift in adaptation level occurs 'because the novel stimulation has been added to the "accustomed" level of stimulation'. Secondly, habituation takes place: the idea being that people get used to (or become accustomed to) a given level of 'stimulation', and habituation is the term used to describe 'the idea that events are judged by the extent to which they deviate from adaptation level'.

While adaptation and habituation are usually concepts employed in behavioural psychological research looking at the way rats, for example, show decreased responsivity to painful stimuli over time, or the manner in which humans no longer consciously hear background noise after a certain period of exposure (and hence the use of the rather incongruous sounding term 'stimulation'), a number of studies have transplanted these concepts from the laboratory to examine the ideas of adaptation and habituation in relation to happiness and SWB. As Cummins *et al.* (in press) note, perhaps the most frequently cited study is that of Brickman *et al.* (1978) who compared the reported happiness of lottery winners, people with spinal injuries and a 'no-event' control group. When the happiness of the three groups was compared up to a year and a half later only minor differences in SWB could be found. Cummins *et al.* (in press) explain:

> the lottery winners' initial euphoria and changed life-style caused a massive upward shift in adaptation level … new pleasures lost their capacity to excite, and the ordinary events of their previous lives, that had been sources of pleasure, were now unable to do so because they fell below the new adaptation level. In contrast, the reduced level of positive stimulation experienced by people who had acquired paraplegia, caused their adaptation level to fall … these people increasingly experienced pleasure from minor positive events that would have previously gone unnoticed … due to the changed adaptation levels of these groups, their levels of happiness had returned close to the levels they had experienced prior to their life event.

Such an account, while sounding entirely plausible, does so only as long as it is assumed that 'happiness' is, actually, a static *thing* amenable to precision measurement. The account offered here, by *forcing* happiness into such a mould, neglects that whatever the measure of happiness suggests in terms of a producible quantum, it is not the same 'thing' or set of 'things' that was measured across time. As Cummins *et al.* (in press) note, the spinally injured participants 'increasingly experienced pleasure from minor positive events that would have previously gone unnoticed' whereas, for the lottery winners, the 'new pleasures lost their capacity to excite, and the ordinary events of their previous lives, that had been sources of pleasure, were now unable to do so'. So again, contra their argument, what we see is that what 'happiness' *consists in* changes in keeping with the circumstances of people's individual lives. If entirely different criteria are being used by the participants, at the different moments of measurement, to arrive at a happiness quantum – as Cummins *et al.*'s (in press) exposition so clearly suggests – then we are comparing apples with oranges.

Such confusion continues in the summary of adaptation research. It is suggested that 'data confirming the validity of Adaptation Level Theory in relation to SWB are unimpressive', but despite this Cummins *et al.* conclude that, as the theory is said to 'have a strong level of acceptance' and as 'no telling argument or data have been provided that reasonably question the validity of the main tenets ... it seems logical to incorporate the theory... into our Homeostatic model'. It must be noted at this point that Creationism has a 'strong level of acceptance' in many American educational circles, as did Lysenkoism in Soviet genetics and as did the ideas of phlogiston and the earth being a flat disc supported by tortoises in earlier times.

Subjective Well-being, Joy and Depression

The final aspect of the theory of SWB homeostasis concerns 'homeostatic maintenance and failure'. This aspect of the theory is described as 'speculative at this stage', but is necessitated by the fact that 'the maintenance of SWB within its set-point-range requires some kind of feedback loop'. Drawing on Carver (2000), it is suggested that human action is goal-directed and managed by two types of feedback loop: 'goal seekers' and 'anti-goal' avoiders. Checking the match between current conditions and goals, the loops adjust action as necessary. This theoretical speculation affords the insight that, in consequence 'people tend to do what they intend to do ... and avoid doing the things they regard as unpleasant'. The same is held to be true for how people feel, but with the added complication that the speed with which goals are being met is also at issue. Carver (2000: 339) suggests that 'if the sensed velocity is less than the reference point, the result is negative affect; if it exceeds the reference point, the result is positive affect' (Cummins *et al.* (in press) apply this logic to subjective well-being. They conjecture that:

> SWB lying either above or below the set-point-range constitutes a deviation from the velocity goal. Such deviations will then lead to internal adjustments that will, eventually, restore SWB to a level within its set-point-range ... Levels of SWB lying above the set-point-range should lead to 'coasting' ... to withdrawal of some effort, basking, or turning to some other behavioural domain. Levels of SWB lying below the set-point-range should lead to the more intense goal-seeking motivation or behaviour.

Lest the idea gain hold that 'coasting, basking' or lazing is under the control of human agency rather than under the direction of automated brain mechanisms whirring away inside their passive human vehicles, Cummins *et al.* (in press) quickly dispel such a thought. In considering 'joy' they note that this experience should be considered neither epihanous, transcendental nor exceptional. It is, rather, a mundane and temporary aberration, a consequence of 'acute homeostatic failure'. It is suggested that 'higher than normal SWB can be induced in the short-term by meeting a need (e.g., having a satisfying meal) or experiencing a highly positive life event (e.g., being promoted at work). Such situations represent homeostatic failure at the level of the cognitive buffers.' Such a notion also represents failure at the level of an account of *human* experience. Similarly with despair: 'depression', it is suggested:

> is conceptualised as the loss of SWB homeostasis ... Provided that some negative influence lacks the power to defeat homeostasis, the symptoms of depression should be virtually absent ... under conditions of homeostatic defeat, the symptoms of depression (i.e. scores on depression indices) are coincident with low values within the buffer systems and related personality trait constellations ... In summary, both joy and depression can be regarded as consequences of homeostatic failure. However, whereas joy is inevitably an acute state, defeated by homeostatic processes, depression can be chronic, representing the failure of homeostasis in the face of powerful and persistent negative experience.

Such an account of the (un)happiness or (dis)satisfaction of persons is flawed on a number of levels. To begin with 'having a satisfying meal' or 'being promoted at work' are not the kinds of events sensibly describable as engendering 'joy' in the usually accepted usage of the term. Secondly, why 'powerful and persistent negative experience' should be capable of producing chronic homeostatic control failure and 'powerful and persistent positive experience' should not, similarly, be capable of producing 'chronic' 'joy' – especially if all it takes is a decent meal – is unspecified.

Furthermore, 'scores on depression indices', which are here held to be 'coincident with low values within the [cognitive] buffer systems', are more often than not derived by asking people primarily about their *actions and bodily experiences*, not about their feelings or 'cognitions'. As such quite how sleeping more or less than usual, or losing or gaining weight, are supposed to be 'coincident with' low levels of optimism, self-esteem and perceived control is opaque. Secondly, just what 'depression' is thought to be happens to be extremely variable across cultures (Wolpert, 1999) and hence both 'symptoms of depression and scores on depression indices' will only have locally specific relationships (if any at all) to putative values of speculative 'cognitive buffers' rather than the universal connection which Cummins *et al.* (in press) wish to claim.

Finally, if SWB is, as Cummins *et al.* (in press) claim, controlled primarily by personality and 'cognitive buffering', it is entirely unclear how, and by what process, 'powerful and persistent negative experience' should overpower the mechanism whereby 'levels of SWB lying below the set-point-range should lead to the more intense goal-seeking motivation or behaviour'. Such an account adds nothing to common-sense understandings of everyday contentment, satisfaction with life or subjective well-being, still less to everyday conceptions of either ecstasy or misery: it merely repackages these in a depersonalized cognitive psychological terminology of 'feedback loops', 'velocity goals' and 'homeostatic failure'. As was noted above, to speak in such a manner of persons is to reduce being human to being a faulty radiator, robot or guided missile.

In Summary

The idea that biology determines lived experience is pervasive in contemporary psychology. Although a powerful and apparently per-suasive account of how things stand with persons, it is an extraordinarily problematic position, for all sorts of reasons. This chapter has sought to show how the assumptions underpinning one theory of QOL can be identified and unpacked. As such, this chapter has tried to demonstrate *how* it is possible to take a critical stance towards impressive sounding statistics and the elaborate psychological theories – which make up so much of our current common sense of ourselves. As Foucault (1978) observed, it is precisely *because* psychological ideas determine so much of how we understand ourselves that these notions, which after all are *only hypotheses*, demand detailed critical attention.

Notes

1. In brief Kant's *Critique of Judgement* (1978) attempts to reconcile the paradoxical view of human beings as rational animals, whereby pure reason and everyday earthly practical reason, become via the capacity for judgment a set of checks and balances on each other.
2. My thanks to Alec McHoul for this observation.

Study Questions

- What are the political, practical and ethical implications of understanding subjective well-being as a biological brain state?
- Is my QOL homeostatically controlled?
- How can we *know* how animals (or other persons) feel about themselves or the quality of their lives?
- How much reliance can we place on people's verbal reports of their happiness?

Suggestions for Further Reading

Butler, P. V. (1998) Psychology as history, and the biological renaissance: a brief review of the science and politics of psychological determinism, *Australian Psychologist*, 33, 1: 40–6.

Edwards, D. (1997) *Discourse and Cognition*. London: Sage.

Potter, J. (1996) *Representing Reality: Discourse, Rhetoric and Social Construction*. London: Sage.

Rose, S., Lewontin, R. C. and Kamin, L. J. (1984) *Not in Our Genes: Biology, Ideology and Human Nature*. London: Pelican.

CHAPTER 9

Should We 'Hang up Quality of Life as a Hopeless Term'?

Patients who are dying may find some quality in life, even when their quality of life as assessed by current measures is abysmal. (Farsides and Dunlop, 2001: 1481)

Malcolm: Nothing in his life / Became him like the leaving of it: he died / As one that had been studied in his death / To throw away the dearest thing he ow'd as t'were a careless trifle. (*Macbeth*, Act 1, Scene 4, 7–11)

In her foreword to the second American Association on Mental Retardation volume on quality of life (Schalock, 1997) Luckasson (1997: ix) noted that she had moved, over ten years, from being a sceptic about the value of quality of life research, to being at least persuadable that 'quality of life/ happiness, as a guide to good, may be absolutely appropriate'. Potter (2000) observed that, after one hundred years of psychological research, nearly all of the important questions were yet to be asked, let alone answered. In this final Chapter I outline a position congruent with both of these observations. In QOL research I believe, as with Potter's view of psychology, that we have yet to get any where near beginning to comprehend what asking serious questions about the quality of (a) life may mean – as the quotes heading this chapter suggest. Of course, Farsides and Dunlop's (2001) observation may be taken as an indication that what we need are measures or scales that more accurately measure the quality of life of the dying. Such a reading would, I believe, be to miss the point, and, below, I sketch a way forward which respects the view that, as Malcolm noted of the Thane of Cawdor's departure, the quality of a life (or death) is, in the end, a qualitative, or aesthetic, judgment.

So, with Luckasson, I have come to believe that the concept of QOL – or, as Taylor (1990) would have it, a definitively lower case 'quality of life' – may offer not so much a formalized, psychometric, conceptual framework for understanding quality of life as a (biological) human universal. Rather quality of life may offer us a 'sensitizing concept' for thinking through the purpose and methods of delivery of human services, or ways to enhance the 'liveability' of our particular communities in a democratic, inclusive and 'emancipatory' way. This final chapter then draws together the preceding discussion and summarizes the key philosophical, conceptual and methodological issues covered. Some avenues for further research are identified.

Rethinking Quality of Life

In his biography of Ludwig Wittgenstein, Monk (1991) describes the period, during the Second World War, when Wittgenstein collaborated with Grant and Reeve at Guy's Hospital in London. Grant and Reeve were studying the effects of injuries sustained by soldiers in battle and civilians in air raids. The project had begun as an attempt to specify more closely the nature of a condition, first identified in the Great War, described as 'wound shock'. Monk (1991: 445) writes that:

> Grant and Reeve's initial problem was that, in spite of a detailed study of the scientific literature, there seemed to be no satisfactory way of defining clinically the condition of 'wound shock'. Some authors identified the condition on the basis of haemoconcentration (the development of an abnormally high concentration of red blood cells in the blood thought to be due to the leakage of plasma from the blood into the tissue), while others recognized it as a syndrome of low blood pressure, skin pallor and rapid pulse.

The parallels with the social scientific research on quality of life reviewed in this book are striking. Despite claims of consensus, and what many see as inappropriate foreclosure in terms of theoretical models, it seems to be the case, that – as with 'wound shock' in the 1940s – 'in spite of a detailed study of the scientific literature, there seem[s] to be no satisfactory way of defining ... the condition'. Instead there exists a bewildering variety of different 'conditions', on the basis of which the construct is inferred. By the time of the final report of the 'wound shock' project, the project team had come to the conclusion, which gives every appearance of having been written by Wittgenstein himself, that:

> in practice we found that the diagnosis of shock seemed to depend on the personal views of the individual making it rather than on generally accepted criteria. Unless we were acquainted with these views we did not know what to expect when called to the bedside. The label alone did not indicate what signs and symptoms the patient displayed, how ill he was or what treatment he required. The *only common ground* for diagnosis that we could detect was that the patient seemed *ill*. We were led, therefore, to discard the word 'shock' in its varying definitions. We have not since found it to be of any value in the study of injury; it has rather been a hindrance to unbiased observation and a cause of misunderstanding. (Monk, 1999: 452, my emphasis)

'Wound shock' and 'quality of life' then share the quality that, while specific instances of the use of the terms seem to depend on the views of the individual using it, nevertheless, these usages show what Wittgenstein

(1953) calls, in the *Philosophical Investigations*, a 'family resemblance': in all cases 'the patient seemed *ill*'. The mistake with 'wound shock' was to look *beyond* the family resemblance, to imagine that an underlying relationship between the multiplicity of manifestations of illness was implied by the existence of a term which appeared to unite them into a singular entity. To pursue the family resemblance argument for a moment, it is clear that the terms 'mother', 'father', 'brother' and 'sister' can all be collected up into the superordinate category 'family' – or, by analogy with 'wound shock', can be seen as different manifestations of the condition 'family', and could be imagined as different forms of 'illness'. But while family members may indeed bear a family resemblance, to say that 'beneath' external appearances, all of these instances of 'family' are 'the same' is to make as little sense as holding that all forms of 'illness' are 'the same'.

If the logical grammar of the term 'quality of life' is examined it too can be seen to operate in this manner. Instances of the usage share a family resemblance with each other: but they do not point to a singular underlying 'thing' or entity. Pace Watson, we cannot make a term mean what we want it to mean. Thus while the field of quality of life research may show immense vigour and huge productivity, at the same time argument continues to rage about what QOL 'really is'. Paradoxically, the need for the field to produce 'consensus documents' points to the *absence* of any serious consensus on the central object of study. It is difficult to imagine any of the mature sciences, such as physics, needing to convene an expert working group to produce a consensus document on a basic concept. One doesn't, therefore, see publications entitled 'The Atom: A consensus document'.

Proponents of QOL research, however, argue that such documents are required because of the youth of the field. Cummins *et al.* (in press), for example, end their account of the homeostatic model of subjective well-being with the claim: 'Other data may cause a re-evaluation of the structure that has been described. We look forward to such developments and offer this homeostatic model only as a first step in out understanding of how it is that SWB is so effectively maintained.' Similarly, in their Preface to the *soi-disant* 'consensus document', *Quality of Life: Its Conceptualization, Measurement and Application* prepared for the International Association for the Study of Intellectual Disability, Schalock and Parmenter (2000: 5) write that 'concepts and models presented in this Consensus Document will potentially vary from country to country ... The cross-cultural understanding of the concept of quality of life is still in its infancy'. In their conclusion to the same document Felce *et al.* (2000: 31) *begin* by stating that: 'It is important to point out that the concept of quality of life is still emerging in the field.'

In the *Philosophical Investigations*, Wittgenstein (1953: 232) remarks of psychology that:

the confusion and barrenness of psychology is not to be explained by calling it a 'young science'; its state is not comparable with that of physics, for instance, in its beginnings. (Rather with that of certain branches of mathematics. Set Theory.) For in psychology there are experimental methods and *conceptual confusion*. (As in the other case conceptual confusion and methods of proof.) The existence of the experimental method makes us think we have the means of solving the problems which trouble us; though problem and method pass one another by.

The field of quality of life, it would seem, has the distinction of demonstrating the problems of both set theory and of psychology. As we have seen, it has 'experimental methods' and 'methods of proof' aplenty but, unlike physics in its beginnings, it is assailed by conceptual confusion. Despite the immense outpouring of QOL studies since the 1960s we are no closer to knowing how to answer questions such as 'what is quality of life'. As suggested above, this may be in part because, to paraphrase Wittgenstein, the existence of methods of study makes us think we have the means of solving the problems which trouble us, despite problem and method passing one another by. It is arguable that, in quality of life research across the social sciences, problem and method pass one another by, not so much because 'the science is undeveloped but because the methods it employs are inappropriate to its task' (Monk, 1991: 549).

Given that method is always already theory in disguise, the problem of method may be more to do with the way we theorize *persons*. Theories of the person are almost always implicit (if addressed at all) in currently dominant psychologistic theorizing across the social sciences (in whatever discipline), and the endeavour to measure the 'amount' of quality of life that persons 'have' trades on an entirely unstated theory of the person. The currently dominant theory of the person in the West holds that, after Descartes and Kant, to be human is to have a body and a psyche, a psyche, which may – indeed must – be disaggregated into parts for the purposes of (meaningful) counting. Thus we see that current efforts to measure the quality of life of individuals presuppose that there are such psychical *things* as 'life satisfaction', 'subjective well-being' and the rest, pre-existing inside people's heads, and that they too are subjectable to further disaggregation (into 'domains' or 'facets') that permit direct measurement.

That is – like memories, attitudes and beliefs – such objects exist, and along with the other inventoried 'contents' of the psyche, they *drive human acts*. The provision by a research participant of an answer to a social scientist's question about their quality of life, under such an account, is not then the *act* of a *person* but the act of a being that may, more accurately, be likened to a gas meter. The 'levels' of subjective well-being, satisfaction with relationships and the rest reported by persons are merely *readings* of objectified, 'inner', psychical dials. This surely is a misunderstanding not only of what it means to be a *person*, but also of what it means to *act*.

In *Being and Time* Martin Heidegger (1996: 44–5) writes that:

Acts are nonpsychical. Essentially the person exists only in carrying out intentional acts, and is thus essentially *not* an object. Every psychical objectification, and thus every comprehension of acts as something psychical, is identical with depersonalization. In any case, the person is given as the agent of intentional acts which are connected with the unity of a meaning. Thus psychical being has nothing to do with being a person. Acts are carried out, the person carries them out.

In order then to understand what human acts – such as individuals' descriptions, demonstrations or avowals of the quality of their life – may mean, it is necessary either to rethink our theories of personhood or to accept that currently given psychologistic theories of quality of life cannot, under this account, be theories of the quality of life of *persons*. Paradoxically, then, given their avowed purpose of furnishing an explanation of the quality of life which people experience, while current theories may (or may not) offer compelling accounts of depersonalized (and entirely hypothetical) homeostatically controlled cognitive componentry, they cannot tell us anything about the meaning of the quality of life, as a state of being-in-the-world, of *persons*. Such a state of affairs, it would seem, requires both that we suspend our habitual, a priori, beliefs about the nature of ourselves, and also that we retheorize not only the object of our enquiry (persons, and the quality of their lives), but also the procedures whereby we investigate ourselves.

Quality of Life as a Member's Term

There is, furthermore, another difficult problem to address which follows from the above. That is, debates about definitional matters, objective and subjective indices of QOL, whether subjective well-being is best understood as a function of self or circumstance and the rest, distract attention from a more fundamental issue – namely what is at stake in the everyday-life, normal, practical grounding of the concept of 'quality of life'. If we ask what it means, in ordinary practice, to 'assess someone's quality of life' we must immediately pause. We sense that there is something wrong with the question; that is we do not, in the very ordinary life which is meant both to warrant, and to be explained by, QOL research, 'assess' *anyone's* quality of life at all. To ask the question that way, and indeed to ask the closely related question 'what is quality of life' (on which more later), is to recast what are always already dynamic and interactional phenomena in terms which suggest formality, regularity and standardization (Garfinkel, 1967). QOL *qua* QOL, or 'quality of life' deployed as an *official* or *technical* term, operates in the same manner as all other social-scientific terms. That is it cannot but *homogenize* that which it intends (and claims) to pick apart.

However, 'assessing' the quality of life (whether in people's 'own words' (cf. Edgerton, 1990; Bryant *et al.*, 2001) or, in Edgerton's words, via 'simple scalar instruments' (cf. World Health Organization, 1997; Cummins, 2001c) suggests a range of practices which share a language-game similarity (Wittgenstein, 1953) with folk enquiries, but which have very different motivations, sources of evidence and consequences. That is, there will be circumstances in everyday life under which we care about some particular person's well-being sufficiently to listen out for worries they express and perhaps to check a range of things (whether they are eating and sleeping properly, have enough money to get their groceries and so on), all with the possible upshot (say) of encouraging them to see the doctor, apply for a particular job or take a holiday. Equally, we might read in the newspaper or hear on the radio that this or that group of people seems to be having a bad time of things, that thousands of workers in a particular industry have lost their jobs, that residents of a particular locality have had their homes destroyed by a natural disaster or whatever and talk to friends about it – all with the consequence of (say) warranting a certain argumentative position in casual political talk, organizing a petition or encouraging people to donate towards a relief operation. Note how these mundane examples of everyday occasions when someone's well-being, or some group of people's quality of life, is of concern have to be described in their local and particular details (even at this level of generalization) and how they wholly resist, within the commonsensically understood meaning and usage of the term, being cast as a generalized 'assessment' of 'quality of life'.

On either an ethnomethodological, or an 'ordinary language philosophy', reading it seems clear that each of these 'assessments' (or, to pre-empt a later point, 'appreciations') is occasioned by local demands and has its own motivations, sources of evidence and consequences. In other words, there seems to be in operation a template very like that which Sacks calls those sets of question forms which Members use, one of which is 'Why do you want to do X?' (Sacks, 1992: 33). The general template is familiar, but it has its particular effect from what goes through it locally – and here the template is understandable as 'Are you happy with/about X?' The difference between these ordinary forms of asking about people's 'quality of life' in various domains (are you happy with/about X?) and the form of the question in social scientific QOL research represents a paradox in Sack's (1992) sense. That is, it is precisely contrary to the prevailing social scientific QOL research enterprise that, in everyday life, assessment should be so particular, so local and so unsystematic. The very abstraction and formalism – not only of the term 'assessment of quality of life' – but also of the procedures and practices that most research in the social sciences is committed to – demand standardization, replicability and generality; but *none of these* are routine features of ordinary concerns about some particular person's, or group of persons', particular sort of well-being, for (someone's) particular reasons.

It is possible then that a question like 'what is quality of life' is not the sort of a question that can, sensibly, be asked within a social *scientific* framework as the framework of social *science* is conventionally understood. It is possible that the routine procedures of normal science (Kuhn, 1973) in the social scientific disciplines have misled us about what sort of question it is that we are actually asking when we enquire of people how 'satisfied' they are with their lives. As we have seen, debate rages in the literature about whether such judgments are 'affective' or 'cognitive' (see Cummins *et al.*, in press) or some blend of the two, about the correct methods of calibrating responses and the (conflicting) relationship of these responses to 'variables' of every imaginable stripe. But perhaps to ask someone about the quality of their life is not to request a 'cognitive', rational judgment derived from a calculus of wants and needs, met and unmet. Perhaps it is not, either, to seek a raw, emotional, 'affective' appraisal. Perhaps in seeking a telling about the quality of a life we are not asking such sorts of questions at all: rather perhaps we are asking for a qualitative *appreciation* of how things stand. As such, then, maybe asking about the quality of life amounts to a request for an *aesthetic judgment*.

In his discussion of Wittgenstein's (1978) *Lectures and Conversations on Aesthetics, Psychology and Religious Belief*, Monk (1991) offers an account of Wittgenstein's intellectual project there in 'rescuing' questions of appreciation from the idea that there could be a science of aesthetics, and from the broader project of the West – the 'idol worship', in Wittgenstein's words, of 'Science and the Scientist' (Wittgenstein, 1978: 27). Monk suggests that:

> rather than trying to answer the traditional questions of aesthetics ('What is beauty?' etc.), Wittgenstein gives a succession of examples to show that [artistic] appreciation does not consist (as one might think from reading some philosophical discussions of aesthetics) in standing before a painting and saying: 'That is beautiful'. Appreciation takes a bewildering variety of forms, which differ from culture to culture, and quite often will not consist in *saying* anything. Appreciation will be *shown*, by actions as often as by words, by certain gestures of disgust or satisfaction, by the way we read a work of poetry or play a piece of music, by how often we read or listen to the same piece, and how we do so. These different forms of appreciation do not have any one thing in common that one can isolate in answer to the question 'What is artistic appreciation?' They are, rather linked by a complicated series of 'family resemblances'.

Thus inasmuch as 'appreciation does not consist ... in standing before a painting and saying: "That is beautiful"', perhaps appreciating the quality of one's life does not consist in standing in front of a social scientist and saying '75 ± 2.5 per cent'. Equally, as we saw in Chapter 3, it is perfectly possible to see that people with intellectual disabilities understand Wittgenstein's point that 'appreciation takes a bewildering variety of forms, which differ from culture to culture, and quite often will not consist in *saying* anything. Appreciation will be *shown*, by actions as often as by words, by certain gestures of disgust or satisfaction.' That is, showing appreciation may not be a one-off event, but rather an extended process – as we also saw in the discussion of Koch's (2001) work in Chapter 6. Recall that, in Chapter 3, Bob displayed a comprehensive appreciation of the high quality of his life *not* by *saying* anything about the quality of his life *as such*, and most certainly not in a manner which could contribute to the 'scientific' measurement of his appreciation, satisfaction or whatever. Rather, Bob *displayed* the quality of his life by *showing*, over the course of an extended period – for example in his singing of 'Santa Claus is coming to town' – his warm and positive appreciation of his life circumstances.

Monk goes on to point out that, crucially, in attempting to find answers to the question of aesthetic understanding, we are not looking for a reductive, *causal* explanation. Inasmuch as there is no science of aesthetics, equally the methods, procedures and results of another science, such as physics, or what he terms 'some pseudo-science, such as psychology' (Monk, 1991: 405), cannot sensibly be addressed to these questions. The question of reductionism imported into the analysis of aesthetic questions by the adoption of (pseudo)scientific methods is also eloquently addressed in the *Lectures and Conversations*. There Wittgenstein notes that, although making the statement: 'If we boil Redpath at 200 degrees C. all that is left when the water vapour is gone is some ashes, etc. This is all Redpath really is', has a certain charm, 'it is misleading to say the least' (Wittgenstein, 1978: 24). In talking of appreciation or an aesthetic judgment, then, Wittgenstein observes that: 'it is not only difficult to describe what appreciation consists in, but impossible. To describe what it consists in we would have to describe the whole environment' (Wittgenstein, 1978: 11). And that project is, despite the willingness of the Australian Bureau of Statistics (as we saw in Chapter 2) to contemplate 'mapping the whole of life', in practice a very different, and non-statistical, undertaking.

In an analogous analysis, Leudar and Thomas (2000) discuss the ways in which the 'pseudo-sciences' have approached the puzzling phenomenon of 'auditory hallucinations', or 'hearing voices'. They conclude their magisterial historical survey of the experience – from the reports of Achilles in the *Iliad* to the present day – with a sobering reflection on the problems caused by the practice in the 'pseudo-sciences' of asking questions about lived human experience in the form: *'what is x?'*

The timeless and universal question 'what is hearing voices? period' is therefore not a happy one – it impoverishes the phenomenon studied. It impoverishes it because it treats as incidental and unimportant its context-contingent aspects. In psychology, which aims at biological and evolutionary explanations of mind, the timeless question implies there is a basic, raw experience of hearing voices ... This position is clearly not supported by the materials ... As there are no mechanical behaviours (except in abstractions) which become intentional conduct when combined with psychological phenomena, so there are no raw experiences which become meaningful under descriptions but can be lived without them ... So the general conclusion is really that local concepts are constitutive of local experiences and there cannot be a psychology or psychiatry which can do without them. (Leudar and Thomas, 2000: 209)

That is, if we read 'quality of life' for 'hearing voices' in Leudar and Thomas's account, it is difficult to escape coming to identical conclusions. To paraphrase: there is no raw experience of quality of life which becomes meaningful under descriptions but can be lived without them ... local concepts (of quality of life) are constitutive of local experiences (of quality of life) and there cannot be a psychology or psychiatry which can do without them.

Ways Forward

One aspect of a very different project that understanding quality of life might become is outlined by Rose (1992) when he calls for the development of a 'critical ontology of ourselves' (Rose, 1992: 160). Chapter 5 has offered a 'worked example' of what a contribution to such a project might look like. Rose suggests that the investigations of the forms of self that are presupposed within modern social, economic and political relations evokes a 'central question addressed by Max Weber ... a sustained reflection on *Mentschentum*, the history of what humans are in their nature and how human lives are conducted' (Rose, 1992: 160). Such a project is consonant with Foucault's (1986) suggestion that the central task of philosophy after Kant was to describe both the nature of our present and the nature of ourselves in that present. It is, says Rose (1992: 161):

to recognize the importance of historical investigations into the events through which we have come to recognize ourselves and act upon ourselves as certain kinds of subject. It is to interrogate what we have become, as subjects, in our individuality, and the nature of the present in which we are. Such an investigation would not attempt a psychological diagnosis of the modern soul. Rather it would seek to document the categories and explanatory schemes according to which we think ourselves, the criteria and norms we use to judge ourselves and one another in order to make particular kinds of being. We would, that is to say, endeavour to describe the historical *a priori* of our existence as subjects.

And, perhaps, we should take as a starting point the notions of subjectivity, autonomy and freedom themselves.

It is precisely because notions such as subjectivity, autonomy and freedom are so massively pervasive in the ways in which we think ourselves that it is essential that they be subject to scrutiny. The notion of quality of life too is becoming, if it has not already, so much a part of the mundane present, so closely bound up with 'the criteria and norms we use to judge ourselves and one another', that it is essential that this notion, too, be subject to critical scrutiny and analysis. Here too the purpose is emphatically not to 'attempt a psychological diagnosis of the modern soul' (there is more than enough literature essaying precisely that) but rather to understand the manner in which accounts of the 'modern soul' *as* an object amenable to psychological diagnosis and statistical modelling have come to be, how such accounts are constructed in order to persuade, and the relations between such accounting, the norms and criteria developed therein (such as ideas that, because happiness is homeostatically controlled, humans can and must be at best 75–80 per cent satisfied with their lives) and the forms of governmentality and the technologies of the self which flow from, and are naturalized by, such accounts.

In terms of the use of the QOL construct, in a 'scientific' manner, for example to gauge the success or otherwise of policy initiatives, human service structures or individualized care, the upshot of the current dominance of views which see QOL as an individualized aspect of the modern day psyche is paradoxical. If, pace Cummins *et al.* (in press) and Edgerton (1990), we are to believe that individuals' claims to contentment are, in some sense, not theirs to make – but rather are driven by temperamental, or biological, constraints and processes over which they, as persons, have no control – then, as Wolfensberger (1994) and Erikson (1993) have suggested, the practical utility of using measures of QOL as an index of policy success or service quality approximates to nil.

Of course this does not mean that seeking comments on aspects of personal experience which may be directly tied to the quality of health or social care interventions are of no value. In spite of the deprecation heaped on health-related quality of life because of its failure to employ a generic definition and measure of QOL (by Cummins, 1997b, for example), it is precisely the close relationship between, for example, matters such as the closeness of the car park to the outpatient oncology department and the experience of undergoing chemotherapy as more or less bearable which makes many measures in the HRQOL field of direct use in the evaluation of patient satisfaction. That 'patient satisfaction' and 'quality of life' are, in this literature, most often employed interchangeably, and that 'quality of life' here is used in its vernacular, or everyday, usage is only a problem if one wishes to claim a special technical status for what is always already a Member's term. This is not to suggest that other developments in HRQOL are unproblematic: as discussed in Chapter 6, the notions of QALYs and DALYs are not only deeply conceptually and methodologically difficult, they are also – for many – ethically unacceptable. I return to this point again below.

In assessing such matters, however, we have much to gain (as, for example, Thompson and Gifford's (2001) study discussed in Chapter 2 showed us) from the greater use of qualitative methods in the evaluation of quality of life. Edgerton (1990) has drawn the conclusion, from his close ethnographic study of the lives of people with intellectual disabilities, that we should be prepared to 'uncouple' objective standards of quality from subjective appraisals of the quality of life. The difficulties entailed by insisting on firm a priori categorizations of lived experience essential to quantitative work are well illustrated by public health researcher Eberhard Wenzel (2001) in the Internet diary he published up until his death from cancer in late 2001.

Wenzel writes of his first moments as a confirmed cancer patient (http://www.ldb.org/cancer/c1.htm). 'Objectively' he has – at the moment of his formal diagnosis – moved from the category of 'non-patient' into another: he has now become 'A Cancer Patient', and hence, by understood standards of HRQOL research, one might expect that this categorical membership would bestow a quality of life correspondingly reduced to whatever the 'disability weight' of oesophageal cancer is. However, in answer to the question 'how does it feel to be a C patient?', Wenzel notes that: 'Well, I don't know, because I don't feel like a C patient ... people call me and ask "how do you feel?", probably expecting me to respond with "uh, not so good ...". But that's not true for the time being. It may change though, who knows?' That is, we must be careful with the uncritical use of categories, and specifically the categorical (and dogmatic) use of diagnostic group labels and the values assigned to them. Wenzel shows very clearly that simply being objectively describable as a 'cancer patient' need not necessarily imply that one, 'subjectively', is a cancer patient. Thus, while Edgerton's work is specifically related to people with intellectual disabilities, there are no good reasons for assuming that his conclusions do not apply more widely. He notes (Edgerton, 1996: 88) that:

> improving the quality of a person's life may increase his or her sense of wellbeing, or it may not. That remains an empirical question and a difficult one to answer ... We should continue every effort to ensure that persons ... have access to better housing, health care, recreational activities, dignified employment, and everything else that an enlightened society can provide for its citizens. But we must never forget that all a society should do is provide options ... Nor should it imagine that all who accept its array of life-quality options will experience a greater sense of well-being than they did before, or that all who reject these options in favour of an alternative life-style will be less satisfied.

In a similar vein, in a letter to the editor, published by the *British Medical Journal*, the chair of the UK's Depression Alliance, Dr Chris Manning, wrote to express his disbelief at official government statistics which suggested that levels of everyday misery ('neurosis') had not increased in Britain over the course of the 1990s. In his letter Manning captures one of the major difficulties both with the use of aggregated statistics of population well-being per se, and with the use of what may be described as measures of individual, personal (un)happiness as indicators of the effectiveness of government policy. He suggests that:

> there may be areas of the country where neurosis is increasing and others where it is decreasing. An average would cancel this out. A man sitting with one foot in a bowl of ice and one of boiling water has his feet in water of averagely aggregated warmth – but that will not do justice to *his* description of [his] level of comfort. (Manning, 2001)

As such, there is much to commend – in my view at least – the 'Scandinavian' approach to matters of life quality. If it is (as Perry *et al.* (2000) and Cummins (2001c) would suggest on the basis of 'hard' empirical data) impossible to establish clear-cut and explicit links between human service structures, processes and activities and the expressed happiness or life satisfaction of service recipients, then it seems to make very little sense indeed to employ that happiness, or otherwise, as a measure of how well the service is serving its 'customers'. Of course, if, as I have suggested above, estimations of the quality of one's life are anyway primarily aesthetic, there is no reason to presuppose that 'hard data' would provide any connection in the first place. What such findings do suggest, however, is that whether or not service structures themselves have any bearing on the individual life satisfaction of service users, it is possible to devise sets of publicly verifiable desirable standards for the delivery of services that maximize the quality, or aesthetic, of their use. This is, in my view, a fruitful area for future research.

That is, following Taylor (1990), there is no reason at all that service planners, providers and evaluators, as well as governmental policy-makers, should not use 'quality of life' as a sensitizing notion. However, in the case of using QOL as a formally operationalized and measurable construct, it seems clear that the problems involved probably outweigh the putative benefits. That is to say, there is no reason why we should not set about designing human services by asking ourselves about how this or that service process or this or that service structure might affect the quality of the lived experience of persons served in such a way or such a place. As we saw earlier, in one HRQOL study the key factor determining the 'quality' of patients' cancer treatment experience was found to be the closeness and convenience of the public car park to the outpatients' department. That 'parking proximity' is not identified anywhere else in the literature (at least to my knowledge) as a domain of 'quality of life' is, in the final analysis, irrelevant. That convenience of access made a large contribution to the quality of the treatment experience of a specific group of people is, while a fairly unremarkable and possibly entirely unsurprising finding, a helpful contribution to our knowledge about ways of designing services such that future groups of patients experience a qualitatively different (and better) service. Research possibilities here are extensive, and entirely in keeping with the increasing 'consumerist' focus of health and social care services. In this regard, studies evaluating the outcomes and effectiveness of projects such as the UK Department of Health's 'Expert Patient' initiative are clearly needed. Questions might include: What maximizes doctors' take up of 'expert patients' advice? What factors act as barriers? What effect on medical practice do 'expert patients' have?

Similarly, while methodologically and ethically problematic as a metric for large-scale funding decisions, the Patil *et al.* (2000) study (Chapter 6) showed that the *joint* estimation of hepatitis C disease state and treatment utilities by patients and their doctors may have much to contribute as a method for establishing an explicit base upon which mutually cooperative helping relationships can be forged. An exploration of the comparative utilities of doctors and their patients in a wider range of illnesses, the analysis of the use of cooperative ratings as a possible technique to maximize doctor–patient communication, and the value of the employment of utility evaluation techniques in medical education are clearly exciting areas for further field research.

Furthermore, a range of approaches to the use of social indicators is available, at both the local level (such as the projects described by Salvaris in Chapter 2) and also at a national and supra-national level (such as the EUSI described in Chapter 2), which permit the collection of data which can be *coherently quantified* and *sensibly aggregated* to tell a story about the living conditions of the nation-state (levels of unemployment, income disparities, percentage of women in the labour force, proportion of population with access to fresh drinking water, adherence to international conventions, crime rates and so on). We saw in Chapter 2 some of the key areas for development in the social indicators field: detailed research projects looking at the use of community-derived quality of life indicators are clearly needed.

There is insufficient space here to argue the case in detail, but the adoption of conceptually coherent sets of such indicators at the national and international levels, I would argue, rules out the use of notions like DALYs, particularly in estimates of the 'global burden' of human misery or 'psychiatric disorder'. In the light of the documented disparities between doctors and patients in the 'utility' they assign to various states of health, the methodological and ethical difficulties of their measurement and calculation, and the questionable intellectual coherence of guesses at utilities for hypothetical states as a method of estimating anything (other than, as noted above, immediate and local preferences), the QALY and the DALY should, in my view, be regarded as a misleading and possibly dangerous development. If, as they do, open democratic societies' need mechanisms for the 'rationing' or allocation of healthcare funding, then in my view the preferred site for the making of such decisions is the public forum, and the preferred method is ethical debate. That is, as Luckasson (1997) noted, as a *guide to good*, in the making of what are always already *moral* choices, quality of life might be absolutely appropriate as a ethical or aesthetic concept. Such an approach may have the virtue of reinstating into the debate, explicitly, the fact that when we discuss the quality of people's lives we are engaged in the weighing of moral questions, not simply the dry dissection of putative biological mechanisms or hypothetical statistical abstractions.

That is, efforts to press Member's terms like 'quality of life' into the mould of 'hard science' are probably misguided. The forced quantification of qualitative experience permits the rhetorical invocation of ghostly 'market mechanisms' driven by cost-utility analysis, and the grinding out of impressive-looking, but publicly incomprehensible, utility values to the nth decimal place. Even the WHO has noted that this process serves to distract attention from more important matters (Sayers and Fliedner, 1997). As, in psychology, does the search for equally ghostly 'cognitive mechanisms' which, whirring away all by themselves, 'maintain SWB output'.

As Erikson (1993) put it, the place for citizens to comment on the success or otherwise of governments in raising their personal well-being, or quality of life, is at elections. And, as Ludwig Wittgenstein also clearly put it, on those matters of which we cannot speak, we must remain silent.

Study Questions

- Is the quality of one's life best considered as a psychological (cognitive and/or affective) brain state or as an aesthetic judgment?
- Is enhancing the quality of life, happiness or life satisfaction of individuals the proper role of the state or its institutions?
- How might the scientific study of 'quality of life' proceed?
- Should we 'hang up quality of life as a hopeless term' as Wolfensberger (1994) has suggested?

Suggestions for Further Reading

Heidegger, Martin (1996) *Being and Time*, trans. by J. Stambaugh. Albany, NY: State University of New York Press.

McHoul, A. and Rapley, M. (2001) Culture, psychology and 'being human', *Culture and Psychology*, 7, 4: 433–51.
Wittgenstein, Ludwig (1953) *Philosophical Investigations*, (eds) G. E. M. Anscombe and R. Rhees. Cambridge: Blackwell.

Transcription Conventions

The transcription conventions used here were derived from those developed by Gail Jefferson (see Atkinson and Heritage, 1984).

(.) (..) (...)	Pauses of, approximately, a fifth of a second, half a second and one second.
(2 secs)	A roughly timed period of no speech.
.hh	A dot before an 'h' denotes speaker in-breath. The more h's, the longer the in-breath.
hh	An 'h' denotes an out-breath. The more h's, the longer the out-breath.
hehh hahh	Laughter syllables with some attempt to capture 'colour'.
Go(h)d	(h) This denotes 'laughter' within words.
((slurps))	A description enclosed in double brackets indicates a non-speech sound.
cu-	A dash denotes a sharp cut-off of a prior word or sound.
lo::ng	Colons show that the speaker has stretched the preceding letter or sound.
(guess)	Material within brackets represents the transcriber's guess at an unclear part of the tape.
?	A question mark denotes a rising intonation. It does not necessarily indicate a question.
=	The 'equals' sign denotes utterances that run on.
↑↓	Arrows indicate rising or falling intonational shift. They are placed before the onset of such a shift. Double arrows indicate very marked shifts.

<u>un</u>der	Underlining indicates emphasis.
CAPITALS	Capital letters indicate a section of speech that is noticeably louder than that surrounding it.
° soft°	Degree signs indicate speech noticeably quieter than the surrounding talk.
>fast< <slow>	'Greater than' and 'less than' signs indicate that the talk they encompass was produced noticeably more quickly than the surrounding talk; the reverse for 'slow' talk.
he ⌈llo ⌊hello	Square brackets between adjacent lines of concurrent speech show overlapping talk.
[^t]	Dental 'click'.

Introduction

WHOQOL-BREF

INTRODUCTION

**ADMINISTRATION, SCORING AND
GENERIC VERSION OF THE ASSESSMENT**

Field Trial Version December 1996

PROGRAMME ON MENTAL HEALTH

WORLD HEALTH ORGANIZATION

GENEVA

This manual was drafted by Alison Harper on behalf of the WHOQOL group. The WHOQOL group comprises a coordinating group, collaborating investigators in each of the field centres and a panel of consultants. Dr J. Orley directs the project. He has been assisted in this by Professor M. Power, Dr W. Kuyken, Professor N. Sartorius, Dr M. Bullinger and Dr A. Harper. The field centres involved in initial piloting of the WHOQOL were: Professor H. Herrman, Dr H. Schofield and Ms B. Murphy, University of Melbourne, Australia; Professor Z. Metelko, Professor S. Szabo and Mrs M. Pibernik-Okanovic, Institute of Diabetes, Endocrinology and Metabolic Diseases and Department of Psychology, Faculty of Philosophy, University of Zagreb, Croatia; Dr N. Quemada and Dr A. Caria, INSERM, Paris, France; Dr S. Rajkumar and Mrs Shuba Kumar, Madras Medical College, India; Dr S. Saxena and Dr K. Chandiramani, All India Institute of Medical Sciences, New Delhi, India; Dr M. Amir and Dr D. Bar-On, Ben-Gurion University of the Negev, Beer-Sheeva, Israel; Dr Miyako Tazaki, Department of Science, Science University of Tokyo, Japan and Dr Ariko Noji, Department of Community Health Nursing, St Luke's College of Nursing, Japan; Dr G. van Heck and Mrs J. De Vries, Tilburg University, The Netherlands; Professor J. Arroyo Sucre and Professor L. PicardAmi, University of Panama, Panama; Professor M. Kabanov, Dr A. Lomachenkov and Dr G. Burkovsky, Bekhterev Psychoneurological Research Institute, St. Petersburg, Russia; Dr R. Lucas Carrasco, University of Barcelona, Spain; Dr Yooth Bodharamik and Mr Kitikorn Meesapya, Institute of Mental Health, Bangkok, Thailand; Dr S. Skevington, University of Bath, United Kingdom; Professor D. Patrick, Ms M. Martinand, Ms D. Wild, University of Washington, Seattle, USA and; Professor W. Acuda and Dr J. Mutambirwa, University of Zimbabwe, Harare, Zimbabwe.

New centres using the field version of the WHOQOL-100 are: Dr S. Bonicato, FUNDONAR, Fundacion Oncologica Argentina, Argentina; Dr A.E. Molzahn, University of Victoria, Canada; Dr G. Yongping, St Vincent's Hospital, Victoria, Australia; Dr G. Page, University of Quebec at Rimouski, Canada; Professor J. Fang, Sun Yat-Sen University of Medical Sciences, People's Republic of China; Dr M. Fleck, University of the State of Rio Grande do Sul, Brazil; Professor M.C. Angermeyer, Dr R. Kilian, Universitatsklinikum Klinik and Poliklinik für Psychiatrie, Leipzig, Germany; Mr Kwok Fai Leung, Hospital Authority, Hong Kong; Dr B.R. Hanestad, University of Bergen, Norway; Dr M.H. Mubbashar, Rawalpindi General Hospital, Pakistan; Dr J. Harangozo, Semelweis University of Medicine, Budapest & Dr L. Kullman, National Institute of Mental Rehabilitation, Budapest, Hungary; Professor I. Wiklund, Health Economics & Quality of Life, Astra Hassle AB, Sweden; Dr C. Fidaner, Dr Behget Uz Paediatric Hospital, Balqova/Izmir, Turkey; Dr G. de Girolamo, Servizio Salute Mentale USL 27, Italy; Professor P. Bech, Frederiksborg

General Hospital, Denmark; Dr R.S. Pippalla, Howard University, College of Pharmacy and Pharmaceutical Sciences, Washington, DC, USA and Dr H. Che Ismail, School of Medical Sciences, Kelantan, Malaysia.

Further information can be obtained from:
Dr John Orley
Programme on Mental Health
World Health Organization
CH-1211 Geneva 27, Switzerland

WHOQOL-BREF Introduction, Administration, Scoring and Generic Version of the Assessment

Introduction

The WHOQOL-100 quality of life assessment was developed by the WHOQOL Group with fifteen international field centres, simultaneously, in an attempt to develop a quality of life assessment that would be applicable cross-culturally. The development of the WHOQOL-100, has been detailed elsewhere (i.e. Orley & Kuyken, 1994; Szabo, 1996; WHOQOL Group 1994a, 1994b, 1995). This document gives a conceptual background to the WHOQOL definition of quality of life and describes the development of the WHOQOL-BREF, an abbreviated version of the WHOQOL-100. It also includes a generic English language version of the WHOQOL-BREF, instructions for administering and scoring, and proposed uses for this short form of the WHOQOL.

Rationale for the development of the WHOQOL-100

WHO's initiative to develop a quality of life assessment arose for a number of reasons. In recent years there has been a broadening in focus in the measurement of health, beyond traditional health indicators such as mortality and morbidity (e.g. World Bank, 1993; WHO, 1991), to include measures of the impact of disease and impairment on daily activities and behaviour (e.g. Sickness Impact Profile; Bergner, Bobbitt, Carter et al, 1981), perceived health measures (e.g. Nottingham Health Profile; Hunt, McKenna and McEwan, 1989) and disability/functional status measures (e.g. the MOS SF-36, Ware et al, 1993). These measures, whilst beginning to provide a measure of the impact of disease, do not assess quality of life *per se*, which has been aptly described as "the missing measurement in health" (Fallowfield, 1990). Second, most measures of health status have been developed in North America and the UK, and the translation of these measures for use in other settings is time-consuming, and unsatisfactory for a number of reasons (Sartorius and Kuyken, 1994; Kuyken, Orley, Hudelson and Sartorius, 1994). Third, the increasingly mechanistic model of medicine, concerned only with the eradication of disease and symptoms, reinforces the need for the introduction of a humanistic element into health care. By calling for quality of life assessments in health care, attention is focused on this aspect of health, and resulting interventions will pay increased attention to this aspect of patients' well-being. WHO's initiative to develop a quality of life assessment arises from a need for a genuinely international measure of quality of life and a commitment to the continued promotion of an holistic approach to health and health care.

Steps in the development of the WHOQOL-100

The WHOQOL-100 development process consisted of several stages. These are explained in brief within this document. For a detailed description, the reader is referred to the WHOQOL Group (1994a, 1994b, in preparation). In the first stage, concept clarification involved establishing an agreed upon definition of quality of life and an approach to international quality of life assessment.

Quality of life is defined as individuals' perceptions of their position in life in the context of the culture and value systems in which they live and in relation to their goals, expectations, standards and concerns.

This definition reflects the view that quality of life refers to a subjective evaluation which is embedded in a cultural, social and environmental context. Because this definition of quality of life focuses upon respondents' "perceived" quality of life, it is not expected to provide a means of measuring in any detailed fashion symptoms, diseases or conditions, but rather the effects of disease and health interventions on quality of life. As such, quality of life cannot be equated simply with the terms "health status", "life style", "life satisfaction", "mental state" or "well-being". The recognition of the multi-dimensional nature of quality of life is reflected in the WHOQOL-100 structure.

In the second stage of development, exploration of the quality of life construct within 15 culturally diverse field centres was carried out to establish a list of areas/facets that participating centres considered relevant tb the assessment of quality of life. This involved a series in meetings of focus groups which included health professionals, patients and well subjects. A maximum of six specific items for exploring each proposed facet were generated by each centre's focus group. To enable the collaboration to be genuinely international the 15 field centres were selected world-wide to provide differences in level of industrialisation, available health services, and other markers relevant to the measurement of quality of life (e.g. role of the family, perception of time, perception of self, dominant religion). In the third stage of development, questions from each centre were assembled into a global pool. After clustering semantically equivalent questions, 236 items covering 29 facets were included in a final assessment. Pilot work involved administration of this standardised assessment to at least 300 respondents within each centre. Following field testing in these 15 centres, 100 items were selected for inclusion in the WHOQOL-100 Field Trial Version. These included four items for each of 24 facets of quality of life, and four items relating to the 'overall quality of life and general health' facet (see Table 1). The method by which these 100 items were selected is fully documented elsewhere (The WHOQOL Group, in preparation). The WHOQOL-100 Field Trial Version is currently being tested in new centres world-wide (these centres are outlined on page 6 of this document). The initial conceptual framework for the WHOQOL-100 proposed that the 24 facets relating to quality of life should be grouped into 6 domains. Recent analysis of available data, using structural equation modelling, has shown a four domain solution to be more appropriate. For a more detailed explanation of this, the reader is referred to The WHOQOL Group (in preparation). The WHOQOL-BREF is therefore based on a four domain structure (see Table 1).

Table 1: WHOQOL-BREF domains

Domain	Facets incorporated within domains
1. Physical health	Activities of daily living Dependence on medicinal substances and medical aids Energy and fatigue Mobility Pain and discomfort Sleep and rest Work Capacity
2. Psychological	Bodily image and appearance Negative feelings Positive feelings Self-esteem Spirituality / Religion / Personal beliefs Thinking, learning, memory and concentration
3. Social	Personal relationships Social support Sexual activity
4. Environment	Financial resources Freedom, physical safety and security Health and social care: accessibility and quality Home environment Opportunities for acquiring new information and skills Participation in and opportunities for recreation / leisure activities Physical environment (pollution / noise / traffic / climate) Transport

Development of the WHOQOL-BREF

The WHOQOL-100 allows detailed assessment of each individual facet relating to quality of life. In certain instances however, the WHOQOL-100 may be too lengthy for practical use. The WHOQOLBREF Field Trial Version has therefore been developed to provide a short form quality of life assessment that looks at Domain level profiles, using data from the pilot WHOQOL assessment and all available data from the Field Trial Version of the WHOQOL-100. Twenty field centres situated within eighteen countries have included data for these purposes (see Table 2). The WHOQOL-BREF contains a total of 26 questions. To provide a broad and comprehensive assessment, one item from each of the 24 facets contained in the WHOQOL-100 has been included. In addition, two items from the Overall quality of Life and General Health facet have been included.

Table 2: Centres included in development of the WHOQOL-BREF

Centres in the pilot version of the WHOQOL	Centres in the field trial of the WHOQOL-100
Bangkok, Thailand	Bangkok, Thailand
Beer Sheva, Israel	Beer Sheva, Israel
Madras, India	Madras, India
Melbourne, Australia	Melbourne, Australia
New Delhi, India	New Delhi, India
Panama City, Panama	Panama City, Panama
Seattle, USA	Seattle, USA
Tilburg, The Netherlands	Tilburg, The Netherlands
Zagreb, Croatia	Zagreb, Croatia
Tokyo, Japan	Tokyo, Japan
Harare, Zimbabwe	Harare, Zimbabwe
Barcelona, Spain	Barcelona, Spain
Bath, UK	Bath, UK
St Petersburg, Russia	Hong Kong
Paris, France	Leipzig, Germany
	Mannheim, Germany
	La Plata, Argentina
	Port Alegre, Brazil

The WHOQOL-BREF is available in 19 different languages. The appropriate language version, and permission for using it, can be obtained from The WHOQOL Group, Programme on Mental Health, World Health Organisation, CH-1211 Geneva 27, Switzerland. Under no circumstances should the WHOQOL-BREF be used without consultation with The WHOQOL Group. A methodology has been developed for new centres wishing to develop a further language version of the WHOQOL-100 or the

WHOQOL-BREF. This can be obtained from The WHOQOL Group, Programme on Mental Health, World Health Organisation, CH-1211, Geneva 27, Switzerland.

Questions should appear in the order in which they appear in the example WHOQOL-BREF provided within this document, with instructions and headers unchanged. Questions are grouped by response format. The equivalent numbering of questions between the WHOQOL-BREF and the WHOQOL-100 is given in the example version of the WHOQOL-BREF to enable easy comparison between responses to items on the two versions. The WHOQOL-100 field test permitted centres to include national items or facets that were thought to be important in assessing quality of life. Where centres wish to include additional national items or modules to the WHOQOL-BREF, these should be included on a separate sheet of paper and not scattered amongst the existing 26 items. There are three reasons for this:

1. To control for item order effects which could occur and change item meaning.
2. The WHOQOL-BREF represents an agreed upon core set of inter-national items.
3. The WHOQOL-BREF is likely to be used where quality of life is amongst one of several parameters being assessed. Therefore additional national information can be obtained by including additional modules and measures.

Administration of the WHOQOL-BREF

For any new centre not previously involved in either the development or field testing of the WHOQOL-100, the procedure being followed to field test the WHOQOL-BREF should be identical to that used to field test the WHOQOL-100. The instrument should be piloted on at least 300 people. This figure is based on the required numbers of respondents needed for analysis of pilot data. The sample of respondents to whom the assessment should be administered ought to be adults, with 'adult' being culturally defined. While stratified samples are not essential, a sampling quota should apply with regard to:

- Age   (50% = <45 years, 50% = 45+ years)
- Sex   (50% = male, 50% = female)
- Health status (250 persons with disease or impairment; 50 well persons)

With respect to persons with disease or impairment, this group should contain a cross-section of people with varied levels of quality of life. One way of attempting this would be to include some people with quite severe and disabling chronic diseases, some people in contact with health facilities for more transient conditions, possibly some attending a family practitioner, and others who are in contact with the health service for reasons that are not likely to impinge upon their quality of life to any great extent. By sampling patients from a cross-section of primary care settings, hospitals and community care settings this could most likely be achieved.

The WHOQOL-BREF should be self-administered if respondents have sufficient ability: otherwise, interviewer-assisted or interview-admini-stered forms should be used. Standardised instructions, given on the second page of the WHOQOL-BREF example assessment, should be read out to respondents in instances where the assessment is interviewer-administered.

For centres who have already participated in the development and field testing of the WHOQOL100, the above option of testing the WHOQOL-BREF is preferred, but not imperative where specific studies of patient groups are planned.

Frame of reference and time frame

A time frame of two weeks is indicated in the assessment. It is recognised that different time frames may be necessary for particular uses of the instrument in subsequent stages of work. For example, in the assessment of quality of life in chronic conditions, such as arthritis, a longer time frame such as four weeks may be preferable. Furthermore, the perception of time is different within different cultural settings and therefore changing the time scale may be appropriate.

Proposed uses of the WHOQOL-100 and the WHOQOL-BREF

It is anticipated that the WHOQOL assessments will be used in broad-ranging ways. They will be of considerable use in clinical trials, in establishing baseline scores in a range of areas, and looking at changes in quality of life over the course of interventions. It is expected that the WHOQOL assessments will also be of value where disease prognosis is likely to involve only partial recovery or remission, and in which treatment may be more palliative than curative.

For epidemiological research, the WHOQOL assessments will allow detailed quality of life data to be gathered on a particular population, facilitating the understanding of diseases, and the development of treatment methods. The international epidemiological studies that would be enabled by instruments such as the WHOQOL-100 and the WHOQOL-BREF will make it possible to carry out multi-centre quality of life research, and to compare results obtained in different centres. Such research has important benefits, permitting questions to be addressed which would not be possible in single site studies (Sartorius and Helmchen, 1981). For example, a comparative study in two or more countries on the relationship between health care delivery and quality of life requires an assessment yielding cross-culturally comparable scores. Sometimes accumulation of cases in quality of life studies, particularly when studying rare disorders; is helped by gathering data in several settings. Multi-centre collaborative studies can also provide simultaneous multiple replications of a finding, adding considerably to the confidence with which findings can be accepted.

In clinical practice the WHOQOL assessments will assist clinicians in making judgements about the areas in which a patient is most affected by disease, and in making treatment decisions. In some developing countries, where resources for health care may be limited, treatments aimed at improving quality of life through palliation, for example, can be both effective and inexpensive (Olweny, 1992). Together with other measures, the WHOQOL-BREF will enable health professionals to assess changes in quality of life over the course of treatment.

It is anticipated that in the future the WHOQOL-100 and the WHOQOL-BREF will prove useful in health policy research and will make up an important aspect of the routine auditing of health and social services. Because the instrument was developed cross-culturally, health care providers, administrators and legislators in countries where no validated quality of life measures currently exist can be confident that data yielded by work involving the WHOQOL assessments will be genuinely sensitive to their setting.

Scoring the WHOQOL-BREF

The WHOQOL-BREF (Field Trial Version) produces a quality of life profile. It is possible to derive four domain scores. There are also two items that are examined separately: question 1 asks about an individual's overall perception of quality of life and question 2 asks about an individual's overall perception of their health. The four domain scores denote an individual's perception of quality of life in each particular domain. Domain scores are scaled in a positive direction (i.e. higher scores denote higher quality of life). The mean score of items within each domain is used to calculate the domain score. Mean scores are then multiplied by 4 in order to make domain scores comparable with the scores used in the WHOQOL-100. Explicit instructions for checking and cleaning data, and for computing domain scores, are given in Table 3. A method for the manual calculation of individual scores is given on page 1 of the WHOQOL-BREF assessment form. The method for converting raw scores to transformed scores when using this method is given in Table 4, on page

11 of these instructions. The first transformation method converts scores to range between 4–20, comparable with the WHOQOL-100. The second transformation method converts domain scores to a 0–100 scale.

Where more than 20% of data is missing from a assessment, the assessment should be discarded (see Step 4 in Table 3). Where an item is missing, the mean of other items in the domain is substituted. Where more than two items are missing from the domain, the domain score should not be calculated (with the exception of domain 3, where the domain should only be calculated if ≤ 1 item is missing).

Any national items should be scored separately from the core 26 item of the BREF. During the analysis the performance of any national items will be examined for possible use in alter national studies. At this stage of field testing national and core items must not be mixed in administration or scoring of the BREF.

able 3: Steps for checking and cleaning data and computing domain scores

teps	SPSS syntax for carrying out data checking, cleaning and computing total scores
Check all 26 items from assessment have a range of 1–5	RECODE QI Q2 Q3 Q4 Q5 Q6 Q7 Q8 Q9 Q10 Q11 Q12 Q13 Q14 Q15 Q16 Q17 Q18 Q19 Q20 Q21 Q22 Q23 Q24 Q25 Q26 (1=1) (2=2) (3=3) (4=4) (5=5) (ELSE=SYSMIS). (This recodes all data outwith the range 1–5 to system missing).
Reverse 3 negatively phrased items	RECODE Q3 Q4 Q26 (1=5) (2=4) (3=3) (4=2) (5=1). (This transforms negatively framed questions to positively framed questions)
Compute domain scores	COMPUTE DOM1=MEAN.6(Q3,Q4,Q10,QI5,Q16,QI7,Q18)*4. COMPUTE DOM2=MEAN.5(Q5,Q6,Q7,QI 1,Q19,Q26)*4. COMPUTE DOM3=MEAN.2(Q20,Q21,Q22)*4. COMPUTE DOM4=MEAN.6(Q8,Q9,Q12,Q13,Q14,Q23,Q24, Q25)*4. (These equations calculate the domain scores. All scores are multiplied by 4 so as to be directly comparable with scores derived from the WHOQOL-100. The '.6' in 'mean.6' specifies that 6 items must be endorsed for the domain score to be calculated).
Delete cases with > 20% missing data	COUNT TOTAL=Q1 TO Q26 (1 THRU 5). (This command creates a new column 'total'. 'Total' contains a count of the WHOQOL-100 items with the values I–5 that have been endorsed by each subject. The 'Q1 TO Q26' means that consecutive columns from 'Q1', the first item, to 'Q26', the last item, are included in the count. It therefore assumes that data is entered in the order given in the assessment). FILTER OFF. USE ALL. SELECT IF (TOTAL > = 21). EXECUTE. (This second command selects only those cases where 'total', the total number of items completed, is greater or equal to 80%. It deletes the remaining cases from the data set).
5. Check domain scores	DESCRIPTIVES VARIABLES=DOMI DOM2 DOM3 DOM4 /STATISTICS=MEAN STDDEV MIN MAX. (Running descriptives should display values of all domain scores within the range 4–20).
5. Save data set	Save data set with a new file name so that the original remains intact.

Table 4: Method for converting row scores to transformed scores

DOMAIN 1			DOMAIN 2			DOMAIN 3			DOMAIN 4		
Raw Score	Transformed scores		Raw Score	Transformed scores		Raw Score	Transformed scores		Raw Score	Transformed scores	
	4–20	0–100		4–20	0–100		4–20	0–100		4–20	0–100
7	4	0	6	4	0	3	4	0	8	4	0
8	5	6	7	5	6	4	5	6	9	5	6
9	5	6	8	5	6	5	7	19	10	5	6
10	6	13	9	6	13	6	8	25	11	6	13
11	6	13	10	7	19	7	9	31	12	6	13
12	7	19	11	7	19	8	11	44	13	7	19
13	7	19	12	8	25	9	12	50	14	7	19
14	8	25	13	9	31	10	13	56	15	8	25
15	9	31	14	9	31	11	15	69	16	8	25
16	9	31	15	10	38	12	16	75	17	9	31
17	10	38	16	11	44	13	17	81	18	9	31
18	10	38	17	11	44	14	19	94	19	10	38
19	11	44	18	12	50	15	20	100	20	10	38
20	11	44	19	13	56				21	11	44
21	12	50	20	13	56				22	11	44
22	13	56	21	14	63				23	12	50
23	13	56	22	15	69				24	12	50
24	14	63	23	15	69				25	13	56
25	14	63	24	16	75				26	13	56
26	15	69	25	17	81				27	14	63
27	15	69	26	17	81				28	14	63
28	16	75	27	18	88				29	15	69
29	17	81	28	19	94				30	15	69
30	17	81	29	19	94				31	16	75
31	18	88	30	20	100				32	16	75
32	18	88							33	17	81
33	19	94							34	17	81
34	19	94							35	18	88
35	20	100							36	18	88
									37	19	94
									38	19	94
									39	20	100
									40	20	100

References

Bergner, M., Bobbitt, R.A., Carter, W.B. *et al.* (1981) The Sickness Impact Profile: Development and final revision of a health status measure. *Medical Care*, **19**, 787–805.

Fallowfield, L. (1990) *The Quality of Life: The Missing Measurement in Health Care*. Souvenir Press.

Hunt, S.M., McKenna, S.P. and McEwan, J. (1989) *The Nottingham Health Profile. Users Manual*. Revised edition.

Kuyken, W., Orley, J., Hudelson, P. and Sartorius, N. (1994) Quality of life assessment across cultures. *International Journal of Mental Health*, **23** (2), 5–27.

Olweny, C. L. M. (1992) Quality of life in developing countries. *Journal of Palliative Care*, *8*, 25–30.

Sartorius, N. and Helmchen, H. (1981) Aims and implementation of multi-centre studies. *Modern Problems of Pharmacopsychiatry*, **16**, 1–8.

Sartorius, N. and Kuyken, W. (1994) Translation of health status instruments. In J. Orley and W. Kuyken (Eds) *Quality of Life Assessment: International Perspectives*. Heidelberg: Springer Verlag.

Szabo, S. (1996) The World Health Organisation Quality of Life (WHOQOL) Assessment Instrument. In *Quality of Life and Pharmaeconomics in Clinical Trials* (2nd edition, Edited by Spilker B.) Lippincott-Raven Publishers, Philadelphia, New York.

The WHOQOL Group. The World Health Organization Quality of Life assessment (WHOQOL): position paper from the World Health Organization. *Soc. Sci. Med.*, **41**, 1403, 1995.

Ware, J. E., Snow, K., K., Kosinski, M. and Gandek, B. (1993) SF-36 *Health Survey: Manual and Interpretation Guide*. New England Medical Center, MA, USA.

World Bank. (1993) *World Development Report: Investing in Health*. New York: Oxford University Press.

World Health Organization. (1991) *World Health Statistics Annual*. Geneva: WHO.

The WHOQOL Group. (1994a) Development of the WHOQOL: Rationale and current status. *International Journal of Mental Health*, **23** (3), 24–56.

The WHOQOL Group. (1994b) The development of the World Health Organization quality of life assessment instrument (the WHOQOL) In J. Orley and W. Kuyken (Eds) *Quality of Life Assessment: International Perspectives*. Heidelberg: Springer Verlag.

The WHOQOL Group. (In preparation) The World Health Organisation Quality of Life Assessment (WHOQOL): Development and General Psychometric Properties.

WHOQOL-BREF

PROGRAMME ON MENTAL HEALTH
WORLD HEALTH ORGANIZATION
GENEVA

For office use only

Equations for computing domain scores	Raw score	Transformed scores*
Domain 1 (6-Q3)+(6-Q4)+ Q10 + Q15 + Q16 + Q17 + Q18 ☐ + ☐ + ☐ + ☐ + ☐ + ☐ + ☐ =	4–20	0–100
Domain 2 Q5 + Q6 + Q7 + Q11 + Q19 +(6-Q26) ☐ + ☐ + ☐ + ☐ + ☐ + ☐ =		
Domain 3 Q20 + Q21 + Q22 ☐ + ☐ + ☐ =		
Domain 4 Q8 + Q9 + Q12 + Q13 + Q14 + Q23 + Q24 + Q25 ☐ + ☐ + ☐ + ☐ + ☐ + ☐ + ☐ + ☐ =		

* Please see Table 4 on page 10 of the manual, for converting raw scores to transformed scores.

ABOUT YOU

I.D. number

efore you begin we would like to ask you to answer a few general questions about yourself: by rcling the correct answer or by filling in the space provided.

What is your **gender**?   Male   Female

What is your **date of birth**?   _____ / _____ / _____
                                                                   Day   Month   Year

What is the highest **education** you received?   None at all
                                                                   Primary school
                                                                   Secondary school
                                                                   Tertiary

What is your **marital status**?   Single   Separated
                                                                   Married   Divorced
                                                                   Living as married   Widowed

re you currently **ill**?   Yes   No

something is wrong with your health what do you think it is?_____illness/ problem

Instructions

This assessment asks how you feel about your quality of life, health, or other areas of your life. **Please answer all the questions**. If you are unsure about which response to give to a question, **please choose the one** that appears most appropriate. This can often be your first response.

Please keep in mind your standards, hopes, pleasures and concerns. We ask that you think about your life **in the last two weeks**. For example, thinking about the last two weeks, a question might ask:

	Not at all	Not much	Moderately	A great deal	Completely
Do you get the kind of support from others that you need?	1	2	3	4	5

You should circle the number that best fits how much support you got from others over the last two weeks. So you would circle the number 4 if you got a great deal of support from others as follows.

	Not at all	Not much	Moderately	A great deal	Completely
Do you get the kind of support from others that you need?	1	2	3	4	5

You would circle number 1 if you did not get any of the support that you needed from others in the last two weeks.

Please read each question, assess your feelings, and circle the number on the scale for each question that gives the best answer for you.

		Very poor	Poor	Neither poor nor good	Good	Very good
1 (G1)	How would you rate your quality of life?	1	2	3	4	5

		Very dissatisfied	Dissatisfied	Neither satisfied nor dissatisfied	Satisfied	Very satisfied
2 (G4)	How satisfied are you with your health?	1	2	3	4	5

The following questions ask about **how much** you have experienced certain things in the last two weeks.

		Not at all	A little	A moderate amount	Very much	An extreme amount
3 (F1.4)	To what extent do you feel that physical pain prevents you from doing what you need to do?	1	2	3	4	5
4 (F11.3)	How much do you need any medical treatment to function in your daily life?	1	2	3	4	5
5 (F4.1)	How much do you enjoy life?	1	2	3	4	5
6 (F24.2)	To what extent do you feel your life to be meaningful?	1	2	3	4	5

		Not at all	A little	A moderate amount	Very much	Extremely
7 (F5.3)	How well are you able to concentrate?	1	2	3	4	5
8 (F16.1)	How safe do you feel in your daily life?	1	2	3	4	5
9 (F22.1)	How healthy is your physical environment?	1	2	3	4	5

The following questions ask about **how completely** you experience or were able to do certain things in the last two weeks.

		Not at all	A little	Moderately	Mostly	Completely
10 (F2.1)	Do you have enough energy for everyday life?	1	2	3	4	5
11 (F7.1)	Are you able to accept your bodily appearance?	1	2	3	4	5
12 (F18.1)	Have you enough money to meet your needs?	1	2	3	4	5
13 (F20.1)	How available to you is the information that you need in your day-to-day life?	I	2	3	4	5
14 (F21.1)	To what extent do you have the opportunity for leisure activities?	1	2	3	4	5

		Very poor	Poor	Neither poor nor good	Good	Very good
15 (F9.1)	How well are you able to get around?	1	2	3	4	5

The following questions ask you to say how **good or satisfied** you have felt about various aspects of your life over the last two weeks.

		Very dissatisfied	Dissatisfied	Neither satisfied nor dissatisfied	Satisfied	Very satisfied
16 (F3.3)	How satisfied are you with your sleep?	1	2	3	4	5
17 (F10.3)	How satisfied are you with your ability to perform your daily living activities?	1	2	3	4	5
18 (F12.4)	How satisfied are you with your capacity for work?	1	2	3	4	5
19 (F6.3)	How satisfied are you with yourself?	1	2	3	4	5
20 (F13.3)	How satisfied are you with your personal relationships?	1	2	3	4	5
21 (F15.3)	How satisfied are you with your sex life?	1	2	3	4	5
22 (F14.4)	How satisfied are you with the support you get from your friends?	1	2	3	4	5

23 (F17.3)	How satisfied are you with the conditions of your living place?	1	2	3	4	5
24(F19.3)	How satisfied are you with your access to health services?	1	2	3	4	5
25(F23.3)	How satisfied are you with your transport?	1	2	3	4	5

The following question refers to **how often** you have felt or experienced certain things in the last two weeks.

		Never	Seldom	Quite often	Very often	Always
26 (F8.1)	How often do you have negative feelings such as blue mood, despair, anxiety, depression?	1	2	3	4	5

Did someone help you to fill out this form?...

How long did it take to fill this form out? ....

Do you have any comments about the assessment?

....

....

THANK YOU FOR YOUR HELP

An SPSS syntax file that automatically checks, recodes data and computes domain scores may be obtained from Professor Mick Power, Department of Psychiatry, Royal Edinburgh Hospital, Morningside Park, Edinburgh, EH10 5HF (email: mj@srv2.med.ed.ac.uk; fax: + 131 447 6860)

Resources

The following resources offer some useful places to start in thinking about QOL research.

Websites

Australian Centre for Quality of Life (ACQOL)
   <http://acqol.deakin.edu.au/>
International Society for Quality of Life Studies
   <http://www.cob.vt.edu/market/isqols/>
Internet Resources – Quality of Life Assessment in Medicine
   <http://www.QLMed.org/url.htm>
Quality of Life Assessment in Medicine
   <http://www.QLMed.org/LIST/index.html>
Social Indicators: an annotated bibliography on trends, sources and
   developments, 1960–1998
   <http://www.ag.iastate.edu/centers/rdev/indicators/anbib.html>
Social Indicators Europe
   <http://www.gesis.org/en/social_monitoring/social_indicators/EU_
   Reporting/eusi.htm>
UK National Statistics
   <http://www.statistics.gov.uk/>
World Bank Group – World Development Indicators
   <http://www.worldbank.org/data/wdi/>
World Database of Happiness
   <http://www.eur.nl/fsw/soc/database.happiness>
World Health Organization
   <http://who.int/>

Journals

Social Indicators Research
   <http://www.wkap.nl/journalhome.htm/0303-8300>
Quality of Life Research
   <http://www.wkap.nl/journalhome.htm/0962-9343>

Societies and Research Units

International Society for Quality of Life Studies
    <http://www.cob.vt.edu/market/isqols/>
University of Toronto Quality of Life Research Unit
    <http: //www.utoronto.ca/dol/unit.htm>
Redefining Progress
    <http://www.rprogress.org/index.html>

Quantitative Methods

Cummins, R. A. (2001) *Directory of Instruments to Measure Quality of Life and Cognate Areas*, 6th edn. Melbourne: School of Psychology, Deakin University,<http://acqol.deakin.edu.au/instruments/instrument.php>.

Nussbaum, M. and Sen, A. (eds) (1993) *The Quality of Life*. Oxford: Clarendon Press.

Sarantkos, S. (1993) *Social Research*. Melbourne: Macmillan Academic.

Staquet, M., Hays, R. and Fayers, P. (eds) (1998) *Quality of Life Assessment in Clinical Trials: Methods and Practice*. Oxford: Oxford University Press.

Lyons, J. S., Howard, K. I., O'Mahoney, M. T. and Lish, J. (1997) *The Measurement and Management of Clinical Outcomes in Mental Health*. New York: Wiley.

Qualitative Methods

Bernard, B. (1994). *Research Methods in Anthropology. Qualitative and Quantitative approaches*. London: Altamira Press.

Lepper, G. (2000) *Categories in Text and Talk: A Practical Introduction to Categorization Analysis*. London: Sage.

McHoul, A. and Rapley, M. (eds) (2002) *How to Analyse Talk in Institutional Settings: A Casebook of Methods*. London and New York: Continuum International.

Patton, M. Q. (1990) *Qualitative Evaluation and Research Methods*. Newbury Park, CA: Sage.

Puchta, C. and Potter, J. (1999) Asking elaborate questions: focus groups and the management of spontaneity, *Journal of Sociolinguistics*, 3: 314–35.

Richardson, J. T. E. (ed.) (1996) *Handbook of Qualitative Research Methods for Psychology and the Social Sciences*. Leicester: BPS Books.

Silverman, D. (1997) *Qualitative Methods: Theory, Method and Practice*. London: Sage.

tenHave, P. (1999) *Doing Conversation Analysis: A Practical Guide*. London: Sage.

Yates, S., Taylor, S. and Wetherell, M. (2001) *Discourse as Data: A Guide for Analysis*. London: Sage.

REFERENCES

Aaronsson, N. K., Ahmedzai, S., Bergman, B., Bullinger, M., Cull, A., Duez, N. J. *et al.* (1993) The European Organization for Research and Treatment of Cancer QLQ-C30: a quality of life instrument for use in international clinical trials in oncology, *Journal of the National Cancer Institute*, 85: 365–76.

AbouZahr, C. and Vaughan, J. P. (2000) Assessing the burden of sexual and reproductive ill-health: questions regarding the use of disability-adjusted life years, *Bulletin of the World Health Organization*, 78, 5: 655–66.

Adams, D. (1979) *The Hitch Hikers' Guide to the Galaxy*. London: Pan Books.

Addington-Hall, J. and Kalra, L. (2001) Who should measure quality of life? *British Medical Journal*, 322: 1417–20.

Ager, A. and Hatton, C. (1999) Discerning the appropriate role and status of 'quality of life' assessment for persons with an intellectual disability: a reply to Cummins, *Journal of Applied Research in Intellectual Disabilities*, 12: 335–9.

Ahuvia, A. C. and Friedman, D. C. (1998) Income, consumption, and subjective well-being: toward a composite macromarketing model, *Journal of Macromarketing*, 18: 153–68.

Aksoy, S. (2000) Can the 'quality of life' be used as a criterion in health care services? *Bulletin of Medical Ethics*, October: 19–22.

Albrecht, G. L. and Devlieger, P. J. (1998) The Disability Paradox: high quality of life against all odds, *Social Science and Medicine*, 48: 977–88.

Alderson, P. (2001) Down's syndrome: cost, quality and value of life, *Social Science and Medicine*, 53, 5: 627–38.

Anderson, R. L. and Lewis, D. A. (2000) Quality of life of persons with severe mental illness living in an intermediate care facility, *Journal of Clinical Psychology*, 56, 4: 575–81.

Andrews, F. M. (ed.), (1986) *Research on the Quality of Life*. Ann Arbor: MI: Institute for Social Research.

Andrews, F. M. (1989) The evolution of a movement, *Journal of Public Policy*, 9: 401–5.

Andrews, F. M. (1991) Stability and change in levels and structure of subjective well-being: USA 1972 and 1988, *Social Indicators Research*, 25: 1–30.

Andrews, F. M and Withey, S. B. (1976) *Social Indicators of Well-Being: Americans' Perceptions of Life Quality*. New York: Plenum.

Anson, J. and Anson, O. (2001) Death rests a while: holy day and Sabbath effects on Jewish mortality in Israel, *Social Science and Medicine*, 52: 83–97.

Antaki, C. (1994) *Explaining and Arguing: The Social Organisation of Accounts*. London: Sage.

Antaki, C. (1999) Assessing quality of life of persons with a learning disability: how setting lower standards may inflate well-being scores, *Qualitative Health Research*, 9: 283–300.

Antaki, C. and Houtkoop-Steenstra, H. (1998) Creating happy people by asking yes–no questions, *Research on Language and Social Interaction*, 30: 285–314.

Antaki, C. and Rapley, M. (1996a) 'Quality of Life' talk: the liberal paradox of psychological testing, *Discourse and Society*, 7, 3: 293–316.

Antaki, C. and Rapley, M. (1996b) Questions and answers to psychological assessment schedules: hidden troubles in 'quality of life' interviews, *Journal of Intellectual Disability Research*, 40, 5: 421–37.

Antaki, C., Condor, S. and Levine, M. (1996) Identities in talk: speakers' own orientations, *British Journal of Social Psychology*, 35: 473–92.

Antaki, C., Houtkoop-Steenstra, H. and Rapley, M. (2000) 'Brilliant. Next question ...': high-grade assessment sequences in the completion of interactional units, *Research on Language and Social Interaction*, 33: 235–62.

Arendt, H. (1958) *The Human Condition*. Chicago: University of Chicago Press.

Arnesen, T. and Nord, E. (1999) The value of DALY life: problems with ethics and validity of disability adjusted life years, *British Medical Journal*, 319: 1423–5.

Atkinson, D. (1988) Research interviews with people with mental handicaps, *Mental Handicap Research*, 1, 1: 75–90.

Atkinson, J. M. and Heritage, J. (eds.), (1984) *Structures of Social Action: Studies in Conversation Analysis*. Cambridge: Cambridge University Press.

Australian Bureau of Statistics (2001) *Measuring Wellbeing: Frameworks for Australian Social Statistics*. Canberra: Australian Government Printing Service.

Australia Institute and City of Newcastle (2000) *Indicators of a Sustainable Community: Improving Quality of Life in Newcastle*. Newcastle: Newcastle City Council.

Bach, J. R. and Tilton, M. C. (1994) Life satisfaction and well-being measures in ventilator assisted individuals with traumatic tetraplegia, *Archives of Physical Medicine and Rehabilitation*, 75: 626–32.

Baldwin, S., Godfrey, C. and Propper, C. (eds), (1990a) *Quality of Life: Perspectives and Policies*. London: Routledge.

Baldwin, S., Godfrey, C. and Propper, C. (1990b) Introduction, in S. Baldwin, C. Godfrey, and C. Propper (eds.) *Quality of Life: Perspectives and Policies*. London: Routledge.

Barnes, M., Mercer, G. and Shakespeare, T. (1999) *Exploring Disability: A Sociological Introduction*. Oxford: Polity Press.

Barry, M. M. and Crosby, C. (1996) Quality of life as an evaluative measure in assessing the impact of community care on people with long-term psychiatric disorders, *British Journal of Psychiatry*, 168: 210–16.

Bauer, R. A. (ed.) (1966) *Social Indicators*. Cambridge, MA, and London: MIT Press.

Beasley, F., Hewson, S., Mansell, J., Hughes, D. and Stein, J. (1993) *MTS: Handbook for Observers*. Canterbury: Centre for the Applied Psychology of Social Care, University of Kent at Canterbury.

Berger-Schmitt, R. and Jankowitsch, B. (1999) *Systems of Social Indicators and Social Reporting*, EuReporting Working Paper No. 1. Mannheim: Centre for Survey Research and Methodology.

Berger-Schmitt, R. and Noll, H. -H. (2000) *Conceptual Framework and Structure of a European System of Social Indicators*, EuReporting Working Paper No. 9. Mannheim: Centre for Survey Research and Methodology. Available from: <http://www.gesis.org/en/social_monitoring/social_indicators/EU_Reporting/concept. htm>.

Bergner, M., and Rothman, M. L. (1987) Health status measures: an overview and guide for selection, *Annual Review of Public Health*, 8: 191–210.

Bergner, M., Bobbitt, R. A., Carter, W. B. and Gilson, B. S. (1981) The Sickness Impact Profile: Development and final revision of a health status measure, *Medical Care*, 19, 8: 787–805.

Bernard, B. (1994) *Research Methods in Anthropology: Qualitative and Quantitative Approaches.* London: Altamira Press.

Billig, M. (1991) *Ideology and Opinions: Studies in Rhetorical Psychology*, London: Sage.

Blass, J. P. (1985) Mental status tests in geriatrics, *Journal of the American Geriatric Society*, 33: 461–2.

Bloom, J. R., Fobair, P., Spiegel, D., Cox, R. S., Varghese, A. and Hoppe, R. (1991) Social supports and the social well-being of cancer survivors, *Advances in Medical Sociology*, 2: 95–114.

Blunden, R. (1988) Quality of life in persons with disabilities: issues in the development of services. In R. I. Brown (ed), *Quality of Life for Handicapped People*. London: Croom Helm. pp. 37–55.

Boden, D. and Zimmerman, D. H. (eds), (1991) *Talk and Social Structure*. Cambridge: Polity Press.

Bonicatto, S. C., Dew, M. A., Zaratiegui, R., Lorenzo, L. and Pecina, P. (2001) Adult outpatients with depression: worse quality of life than in other chronic medical diseases in Argentina, *Social Science and Medicine*, 52: 911–19.

Bowd, A. D. (1989) Client satisfaction and normalization of residential services for persons with developmental handicaps, *Canadian Journal of Community Mental Health*, 8, 1: 63–73.

Bowling, A. (1995) What things are important in people's lives? A survey of the public's judgments to inform scales of health related quality of life, *Social Science and Medicine*, 41: 1447–62.

Bowling, A. (1996) Associations with changes in life satisfaction among three samples of elderly people living at home, *International Journal of Geriatric Psychiatry*, 11: 1077–87.

Boyle, M. (1990) *Schizophrenia: A Scientific Delusion?* London: Routledge.

Boyle, M. (2002) *Schizophrenia: A Scientific Delusion?* 2nd edn. London: Routledge.

Brickman, P., Coates, D. and Janoff-Bulman, R. (1978) Lottery winners and accident victims: is happiness relative? *Journal of Personality and Social Psychology*, 36: 917–27.

Brock, D. (1993) Quality of life measures in health care and medical ethics. In M. Nussbaum and A. Sen (eds), *The Quality of Life*. Oxford: Clarendon Press.

Brown P. (2001) Effective treatments for mental illness not being used, WHO says, *British Medical Journal*, 323: 769.

Brown, R. I. (ed) (1997) *Quality of Life for People with Disabilities: Models, Research and Practice*, 2nd edn. Cheltenham: Stanley Thornes.

Brown, R. I. (2000) Quality of life: Challenges and confrontation, In: K. D. Keith and R. L. Schalock (eds), *Cross-cultural Perspectives on Quality of Life*. Washington: AAMR. pp. 347–62

Browne, S., Clarke, M., Gervin, M., Waddington, J. L., Larkin, C. and O'Callaghan, E. (2000) Determinants of quality of life at first presentation with schizophrenia, *British Journal of Psychiatry*, 176: 173–6.

Bryant, L. L, Corbett, K. K. and Kutner, J. S. (2001) In their own words: a model of healthy aging, *Social Science and Medicine*, 53: 927–41.

Butterworth, J., Steere, D. E and Whitney-Thomas, J. (1997) Using person-centred planning to address personal quality of life, In: Robert L. Schalock (ed), *Quality of Life: Volume II: Application to Persons with Disabilities*. Washington, DC: AAMR, pp. 5–23.

Button, G., Coulter, J., Sharrock, W. and Lee, J. (1997) *Computers, Minds and Conduct*. Cambridge: Polity Press.

Cagney, K. A., Wu, A. W., Fink, N. E., Jenckes, M. W., Meyer, K. B., Bass, E. B. *et al.* (2000) Formal literature review of quality-of-life instruments used in end-stage renal disease, *American Journal of Kidney Diseases*, 36, 2: 327–36.

Campbell, A. (1976) Subjective measures of well-being, *American Psychologist*, 31: 117–24.

Campbell, A. and Converse, P. E. (1972) *The Human Meaning of Social Change*. New York: Russell Sage Foundation.

Campbell, A., Converse, P. E. and Rodgers, W. L. (1976) *The Quality of American Life: Perceptions, Evaluations, and Satisfactions*. New York: Russell Sage Foundation.

Carley, M. (1981) *Social Measurement and Social Indicators: Issues of Policy and Theory*. London: George Allen and Unwin.

Carr, A. J. and Higginson, I. J. (2001) Are quality of life measures patient centred? *British Medical Journal*, 322: 1357–60.

Carr, A. J., Gibson, B. and Robinson, P. G. (2001) Is quality of life determined by expectations or experience? *British Medical Journal*, 322: 1240–3.

Carroll, L. (1982) *Alice's Adventures in Wonderland and Through the Looking-glass and What Alice Found There*, ed. and intro. Roger Lancelyn Green, illust. John Tenniel, Oxford and New York: Oxford University Press.

Carver, C. S. (2000) On the continuous calibration if happiness, *American Journal on Mental Retardation*, 105: 336–42.

Cattell, V. (2001) Poor people, poor places, and poor health: the mediating role of social networks and social capital, *Social Science and Medicine*, 52: 1501–16.

Cattermole, M., Jahoda, A. and Marková, I. (1988) Leaving home: The experience of people with a mental handicap, *Journal of Mental Deficiency Research*, 32, 1: 47–57.

Centers for Disease Control and Prevention (2000) *Measuring Healthy Days*. Atlanta, GA. CDC.

Chamie, M. (1995) What does morbidity have to do with disability? *Disability and Rehabilitation*, 17: 323–37.

Chassany, O., Bergmann, J. F. and Caulin, C. (1999) Authors are creating a database of quality of life questionnaires (letter), *British Medical Journal*, 318: 1142.

Chorover, S. (1979) *From Genesis to Genocide: The Meaning of Human Nature and the Power of Behaviour Control*. Cambridge, MA: MIT Press.

Clements, J., Rapley, M. and Cummins, R. A. (1999) On, to, for or with? Vulnerable people and the practices of the research community, *Behavioural and Cognitive Psychotherapy*, 27, 2: 103–16.

Coast, J., Peters, T. J., Richards, S. H. and Gunnell, D. J. (1997) Use of the EuroQOL among elderly acute care patients, *Quality of Life Research*, 7, 1: 1–10.

Coates, A. S., Kaye, S. B., Sowerbutts, T., Frewin, C., Fox, R. N. and Tattersall, M.

H. N. (1983) On the receiving end: patient perceptions of side-effects of cancer chemotherapy, *European Journal of Clinical Oncology*, 13: 203–8.

Cobb, C., Goodman, G. S. and Kliejunas, J. C. M. (2000) *Blazing Sun Overhead and Clouds on the Horizon: The Genuine Progress Report for 1999*. Oakland, CA: Redefining Progress.

Coid, J. W. (1993) Quality of life for patients detained in hospital, *British Journal of Psychiatry*, 162: 611–20.

Collins, J. (1992) *When the Eagles Fly: A Report on Resettlement of People with Learning Difficulties from Long-stay Institutions*. London: Values Into Action.

Collins, J. (1993) *The Resettlement Game: Policy and Procrastination in the Closure of Mental Handicap Hospitals*. London: Values Into Action.

Costantini, M., Mencaglia, E., Giulio, P. D., Cortesi, E., Roila, F., Ballatori, E. *et al.* (2000) Cancer patients as 'experts' in defining quality of life domains: A multi-centre survey by the Italian Group for the Evaluation of Outcomes in Oncology (IGEO), *Quality of Life Research*, 9, 2: 151–9.

Coulter, J. (1979) *The Social Construction of Mind: Studies in Ethnomethodology and Linguistic Philosophy*. London: Macmillan.

Coulter, J. (1999) Discourse and mind, *Human Studies*, 22: 163–81.

Crooker, K. J. and Near, J. P. (1998) Happiness and satisfaction: measures of affect and cognition? *Social Indicators Research*, 44, 2: 195–224.

Cubbon, J. (1991) The principle of QALY maximisation as the basis for allocating health care resources, *Journal of Medical Ethics*, 17: 181–4.

Cummins, R. A. (1995) On the trail of the gold standard for life satisfaction, *Social Indicators Research*, 35: 179–200.

Cummins, R. A. (1996) The domains of life satisfaction: an attempt to order chaos, *Social Indicators Research*, 38: 303–28.

Cummins, R. A. (1997a) *The Comprehensive Quality of Life Scale – Intellectual Disability, Fifth Edition (ComQol-ID5): Manual*. Toorak: Deakin University School of Psychology.

Cummins, R. A. (1997b) Assessing quality of life, in: R. I. Brown (ed), *Quality of Life for People with Disabilities: Models, Research and Practice*, 2nd edn. Cheltenham: Stanley Thornes, pp. 116–50.

Cummins, R. A. (1997c) Self-rated quality of life scales for people with an intellectual disability: a review, *Journal of Applied Research in Intellectual Disability*, 10: 199–216.

Cummins, R. A. (1998a) *Use of proxy responding in QOL measures*. Paper presented at the Annual Conference of the Australian Society for the Study of Intellectual Disability, Adelaide, SA, August.

Cummins, R. A. (1998b) The second approximation to an international standard for life satisfaction, *Social Indicators Research*, 43: 307–34.

Cummins, R. A. (2000a) Objective and subjective quality of life: an interactive model, *Social Indicators Research*, 52: 55–72.

Cummins, R. A. (2000b) A homeostatic model for subjective quality of life, *Proceedings, Second Conference on Quality of Life in Cities*. Singapore: National University of Singapore, pp. 51–9.

Cummins, R. A. (2001a) Self-rated quality of life scales for people with an intellectual disability: A reply to Ager and Hatton, *Journal of Applied Research in Intellectual Disabilities*, 14: 1–11.

Cummins, R. A. (2001b) Life satisfaction: measurement issues and a homeostatic model, in B. Zumbo (ed), *Social Indicators and Quality of Life Research Methods: Methodological Developments and Issues, Yearbook, 1999*. Amsterdam: Kluwer Academic.

Cummins, R. A. (2001c) Living with support in the community: predictors of satisfaction with life, *Mental Retardation and Developmental Disabilities Research Reviews*, 7: 99–104.

Cummins, R. A., Gullone, E. and Lau, A. L. D. (in press) A model of subjective well-being homeostasis: the role of personality, in E. Gullone and R. A. Cummins (eds), *The Universality of Subjective Well-Being Indicators*. Dordrecht: Kluwer Academic.

Cummins, R. A., McCabe, M. P., Romeo, Y., Reid, S., and Waters, L. (1997) An initial evaluation of the Comprehensive Quality of Life Scale – Intellectual Disability, *International Journal of Disability, Development and Education*, 44: 7–19.

Cummins, R. A., Andelman, R., Board, R. Carman, L., Ferriss, A., Friedman, P. et al. (1998), *Quality of Life Definition and Terminology: A Discussion Document from the International Society for Quality-of-Life Studies*. The International Society for Quality-of-Life Studies (ISQOLS).

Davis, J. A. (1984) New money, an old man/lady and 'two's company': Subjective welfare in the NORC General Social Survey, *Social Indicators Research*, 15: 319–51.

De Neve, K. M. (1999) Happy as an extraverted clam? The role of personality for subjective well-being, *Psychological Science*, 8: 141–4.

De Vries, J., Seebregts, A. and Drent, M. (2000) Assessing health status and quality of life in idiopathic pulmonary fibrosis: which measure should be used? *Respiratory Medicine*, 94, 3: 273–8.

Debats, D. L. (1996) Meaning in life: clinical relevance and predictive power, *British Journal of Clinical Psychology*, 35: 503–16.

Department of Health (1989) *Caring for People: Community Care in the Next Decade and Beyond*, Cmnd. 849. London: HMSO.

Department of Health (1991) *Stephen Dorrell's MENCAP Speech/Statement on Services for People with Learning Disabilities – Tuesday 25 June 1991*. London: HMSO.

Department of Health (1992) *Social Care for Adults with Learning Disabilities (Mental Handicap)* LAC (92) 15. London: HMSO.

Department of Health (1993) *Services for People with Learning Disabilities and Challenging Behaviour or Mental Health Needs* (Chairman: Professor J. Mansell). London: HMSO.

Department of Health (2001) *The Expert Patient – A New Approach to Chronic Disease Management for the 21st Century*. London: HMSO.

Department of Health and Social Security (1969) *Report of the Committee of Inquiry into Allegations of Ill-treatment of Patients and Other Irregularities at the Ely Hospital*. Cardiff: HMSO.

Department of Health and Social Security (1971) *Better Services for the Mentally Handicapped*, Cmnd, 4683 London: HMSO.

Department of Health and Social Security (1979) *Report of the Committee of Enquiry into Mental Handicap Nursing and Care*, Vols. I and II, Cmnd. 7468-I, 7468-II. (Chairman: Mrs. P. Jay). London: HMSO.

Department of Health and Social Security (1980) *Mental Handicap: Progress, Problems and Priorities – A Review of Mental Handicap Services in England Since the*

1971 White Paper 'Better Services for the Mentally Handicapped'. London: HMSO.

Department of Health and Social Security (1981a) Care in the Community: A Consultative Document on Moving Resources for Care in England, HC(81)9/LAC(81)5. London: HMSO.

Department of Health and Social Security (1981b) Care in Action: A Handbook of Policies and Priorities for the Health and Personal Social Services in England, Cmnd. 8173. London: HMSO.

Department of Health and Social Security (1983) Care in the Community and Joint Finance, HC(83)21/LAC(83)15. London: HMSO.

Derogatis, L. R. (n. d.) Manual for the Symptom Checklist 90-Revised. Minneapolis: NCI.

Derogatis, L. and Cleary, P. (1977) Confirmation of the dimensional structure of the SCL-90: a study in construct validation, Journal of Clinical Psychology, 33: 981–9.

Derogatis L., Lipman, R. S., Rickels, K., et al. (1974) The Hopkins Symptom Checklist (HSCL): a self-report symptom inventory, Behavioral Science, 19: 1–13.

Deutscher, I. (1973) What We Say/What We Do: Sentiments and Acts. Glenview, IL: Scott Foresman.

Devinsky, O., Vickrey, B. G., Cramer, J., Perrine, K., Hermann, B. P., Meador, K. et al. (1995) Development of the Quality of Life in Epilepsy Inventory, Epilepsia, 39: 399–406.

Dickerson, F. B., Parente, F. and Ringel, N. (2000) The relationship among three measures of social functioning in outpatients with schizophrenia, Journal of Clinical Psychology, 56: 1509–19.

Dolan, P., Gudex, C., Kind, P. and Williams, A. (1996) The time trade-off method – results from a general population survey, Health Economics, 5: 141–54.

Drenowski, J. (1974) On Measuring and Planning the Quality of Life. The Hague: Mouton de Gruyter.

Drew, P. and Heritage, J. (eds) (1992) Talk At Work: Interaction in Institutional Settings. Cambridge: Cambridge University Press.

Dubos, R. (1959) Mirage of Health. New York: Harper Row.

Duckett, P. S. and Fryer, D. (1998) Developing empowering research practices with people who have learning disabilities, Journal of Community and Applied Social Psychology, 8: 57–65.

Easterlin, R. (1973) Does money buy happiness? The Public Interest, 30: 3–10.

Eckermann, L. (2000) Gendering indicators of health and well-being: is quality of life gender neutral? Social Indicators Research, 52, 1: 29–54.

Eckersley, R. (1998) Redefining progress: shaping the future to human needs, Family Matters, 51: 6–12.

Edgerton, R. B. (1990) Quality of Life from a longitudinal research perspective, In: R. L. Schalock (ed), Quality of Life: Perspectives and Issues. Washington: AAMR pp. 149–60.

Edgerton, R. B. (1996) A longitudinal-ethnographic research perspective on quality of life, In: R. L. Schalock (ed), Quality of Life: Volume I: Conceptualization and Measurement. Washington: AAMR, pp. 83–90.

Edgerton, R. and Gaston, J. (1993) I've Seen it All! Cambridge: Brookline Books.

Edwards, D. (1997) Discourse and Cognition. London: Sage.

Edwards, D. and Potter, J. (1992) Discursive Psychology. London: Sage.

Edwards, D. and Potter, J. (2002) Discursive psychology, In: A. McHoul and M. Rapley (eds), *How to Analyse Talk in Institutional Settings: A Casebook of Methods*. London and New York: Continuum International.

Edwards, D., Ashmore, M. and Potter, J. (1995) Death and furniture: the rhetoric, politics and theology of bottom-line arguments against relativism, *History of the Human Sciences*, 8, 2: 25–49.

Ehrs, P. O., Åberg, H. and Larsson, K. (2001) Quality of life in primary care asthma, *Respiratory Medicine*, 95, 1: 22–30.

Emerson, E. and Hatton, C. (1994) *Moving Out: Relocation from Hospital to Community*. London: HMSO.

Emerson, E. and Hatton, C. (1996) Deinstitutionalisation in the UK and Ireland: outcomes for service users, *Journal of Intellectual and Developmental Disabilities*, 231, 1: 17–37.

Ergene, E., Behr, P. K. and Shih, J. J. (2001) Quality-of-life assessment in patients treated with vagus nerve stimulation, *Epilepsy and Behavior*, 2, 3: 284–7.

Erikson, R. and Uusitalo, H. (1987) *The Scandinavian Approach to Welfare Research*, Reprint Series No. 181. Stockholm: Swedish Institute for Social Research.

Erikson, R. (1993) Descriptions of inequality: the Swedish approach to welfare research, in: M. Nussbaum and A. Sen (eds), *The Quality of Life*. Oxford: Clarendon Press, pp. 67–87.

Estes, R. J. (1984) *The Social Progress of Nations*. New York: Praeger.

Estes, R. J. (1997) Social development trends in Europe, 1970–1994: development prospects for the new Europe, *Social Indicators Research*, 42, 1: 1–19.

EuroQOL Group (1990) EuroQOL – a new facility for the measurement of health-related quality of life, *Health Policy*, 16: 199–208.

Evans, G., Beyer, S. and Todd, S. (1987) *Evaluating the Impact of the All-Wales Strategy on the Lives of People with a Mental Handicap: A Report of a Survey Methodology*, Research Report No. 21. Cardiff: Mental Handicap in Wales – Applied Research Unit.

Evans, G., Todd, S., Beyer, S., Felce, D. and Perry, J. (1994) Assessing the impact of the All-Wales Mental Handicap Strategy: a survey of four districts, *Journal of Intellectual Disability Research*, 38, 109–33.

Fairclough, N. (1993) Critical discourse analysis and the marketisation of public discourse: the universities, *Discourse and Society*, 4: 133–59.

Fairclough, N. (2002) Critical discourse analysis, in A. McHoul and M. Rapley (eds), *How to Analyse Talk in Institutional Settings: A Casebook of Methods*. London and New York: Continuum International, pp. 25–38.

Farlinger, S. (1996) Quality of life for women, *Social Indicators Research*, 39, 1: 109–19.

Farsides, B. and Dunlop, R. J. (2001) Is there such a thing as a life not worth living? *British Medical Journal*, 322: 1481–3.

Fayers, P. and Bjordal, K. (2001) Should quality-of-life needs influence resource allocation? *The Lancet*, 357, 9261: 978.

Felce, D. (1986) Evaluation by direct observation, In: J. Beswick, T. Zadik and D. Felce (eds), *Evaluating Quality of Care*. Kidderminster: BIMH Publications.

Felce, D. and Perry, J. (1993) *Quality of Life: A Contribution to its Definition and Measurement*. Mental Handicap in Wales – Applied Research Unit, University of Wales College of Medicine.

Felce, D. and Perry, J. (1995) Quality of Life: its definition and measurement, *Research in Developmental Disabilities*, 16, 1: 51–74.

Felce, D. and Perry, J. (1996a) Assessment of quality of life, In: R. L. Schalock (ed), *Quality of Life: Volume I: Conceptualization and Measurement*. Washington: AAMR, pp. 63–72.

Felce, D. and Perry, J. (1996b) Adaptive behaviour gains in ordinary housing for people with intellectual disabilities, *Journal of Applied Research in Intellectual Disabilities*, 9, 2: 101–14.

Felce, D., Matikka, L. and Schalock, R. L. (2000) Conclusion: In the Special Interest Research Group on Quality of Life of the International Association for the Scientific Study of Intellectual Disabilities (ed), *Quality of Life: Its Conceptualization, Measurement, and Application. A Consensus Document*. Washington: IASSID.

Ferrans, C. E. (1990) Quality of life: conceptual issues, *Seminars in Oncology*, 6: 248–54.

Ferriman, A. (2001) Levels of neurosis remained static in the 1990s, *British Medical Journal*, 323: 130.

Ferriss, A. L. (1988) The uses of social indicators, *Social Forces*, 66: 601–17.

Feyerabend, P. (1974) *Against Method*. London: Verso.

Finkelstein, V. (1993) Disability: a social challenge or an administrative responsibility? In: J. Swain, V. Finkelstein, S. French and M. Oliver (eds), *Disabling Barriers – Enabling Environments*. London: Sage.

Flanagan, J. C. (1978) A research approach to improving our quality of life, *American Psychologist*, 33: 138–47.

Forbes, A. and Wainwright, S. P. (2001) On the methodological, theoretical and philosophical context of health inequalities research: a critique, *Social Science and Medicine*, 53: 801–16.

Fordham Institute: (1999) *Index of Social Health*. Tarrytown, NY: Fordham Graduate Center.

Foucault, M. (1970) *The Order of Things: An Archaeology of the Human Sciences*. London: Tavistock.

Foucault, M. (1973) *The Birth of the Clinic: An Archaeology of Medical Perception*. New York: Pantheon.

Foucault, M. (1977) *Discipline and Punish: The Birth of the Prison*. London: Allen Lane.

Foucault, M. (1978) *The History of Sexuality Volume 1: An Introduction*. New York: Pantheon.

Foucault, M. (1985) *The Use of Pleasure*. New York: Pantheon.

Foucault, M. (1986) *The Care of the Self: The History of Sexuality Volume 3*. New York: Pantheon.

Franz, M., Lis, S., Pluddemann, K. and Gallhofer, B. (1997) Conventional versus atypical neuroleptics: subjective quality of life in schizophrenic patients, *British Journal of Psychiatry*, 170: 422–5.

Frey, R. S. and Al-Roumi, A. (1999) Political democracy and the physical quality of life: the cross-national evidence, *Social Indicators Research*, 47,1: 73–97.

Fyrand, L., Wichstom, L., Moum, T., Glennas, A. and Kvien, T. K. (1997) The impact of personality and social support on mental health for female patients with rheumatoid arthritis, *Social Indicators Research*, 40: 285–98.

Garfinkel, H. (1967) *Studies in Ethnomethodology*, Englewood Cliffs, NJ: Prentice Hall.

Garro, L. C. (1992) Chronic illness and the construction of narratives, In: M. D. Good, B. J. Brodwin, B. J. Good and A. Kleinman (eds), *Pain as Human Experience: An Anthropological Perspective*. Berkeley, CA: University of California Press, pp. 100–37.

Garro, L. C. (1994a) Individual or societal responsibility? Explanations of diabetes in an Anishinaabe (Ojibway) community, *Social Science and Medicine*, 40, 1: 37–46.

Garro, L. C. (1994b) Narrative representations of chronicling experience: cultural models of illness, mind and body in stories concerning the temporomandibular joint, *Social Science and Medicine*, 38: 775–88.

Gergen, K. (1992) Organization theory in the postmodern era, In: M. Reed and M. Hughes (eds), *Rethinking Organization: Directions in Organization Theory and Analysis*. London: Sage, pp. 207–26.

Gilbert, P. (1986) *The Holocaust: The Jewish Tragedy*. London: William Collins.

Gill, T. M. and Feinstein, A. R. (1994) A critical appraisal of the quality of quality-of-life measurements, *Journal of the American Medical Association*, 272, 6: 619–26.

Glaser, B. G. and Strauss, A. L. (1967) *The Discovery of Grounded Theory: Strategies for Qualitative Research*. New York: Aldine.

Glatzer, W. (1991) Quality of life in advanced industrialized countries: the case of West Germany. In: F. Strack, M. Argyle and N. Schwarz (eds), *Subjective Well-being: An Interdisciplinary Perspective*. New York: Plenum Press, pp. 261–79.

Glover, J. (1977) *Causing Death and Saving Lives*. Harmondsworth: Penguin.

Good, B. J. (1994) *Medicine, Rationality and Experience: An Anthropological Perspective*. Cambridge: Cambridge University Press.

Goode, D. A. (ed) (1994a) *Quality of Life for Persons with Disabilities: International Perspectives and Issues*. Cambridge: Brookline Books.

Goode, D. A. (1994b) The national quality of life for persons with disabilities project: a quality of life agenda for the United States, In: D. A. Goode (ed), *Quality of Life for Persons with Disabilities: International Perspectives and Issues*. Cambridge: Brookline Books.

Goodinson, S. M. and Singleton, J. (1989) Quality of life: a critical review of current concepts, measures and their clinical implications, *International Journal of Nursing Studies*, 26: 327–41.

Goodley, D. (1996) Tales of hidden lives: a critical examination of life history research with people who have learning difficulties, *Disability and Society*, 11, 3: 333–48.

Goodley, D. (2000) *Self-advocacy in the Lives of People with Learning Difficulties: The Politics of Resilience*, Buckingham: Open University Press.

Goodley, D. and Rapley, M. (2001) How do you understand 'learning difficulties'? Towards a social theory of impairment, *Mental Retardation*, 39, 3: 229–32.

Goodwin, C. and Heritage, J. (1990) Conversation analysis, *Annual Review of Anthropology*, 19: 283–307.

Green, S. B., Salkind, N. J. and Akey, T. M. (1997) *Using SPSS for Windows: Analyzing and Understanding Data*. Upper Saddle River, NJ: Prentice Hall.

Greig, R. (1993) *The replacement of hospital services with community services based on individual need: Where are we now?* Paper presented at Hester Adrian Research Centre Conference: Resettlement: New Directions in Services for People with Learning Disabilities, University of Manchester, Manchester, UK. November.

Griffiths, R. (1988) *Community Care: Agenda for Action*. London: HMSO.

Groenewoud, J. H., van der Maas, P. J., van der Wal, G., Hengeveld, M. W., Tholen, A. J., Schudel, W. J. *et al.* (1996) Physician-assisted death in psychiatric practice in the Netherlands, *New England Journal of Medicine*, 336: 1795–801.

Groot, W. and VandenBrink, M. (2000) Life satisfaction and preference drift, *Social Indicators Research*, 50: 315–29.

Groulx, R., Doré, R. and Doré, L. (2000) My quality of life as I see it, In: K. D. Keith and R. L. Schalock (eds), *Cross-cultural Perspectives on Quality of Life*. Washington: AAMR, pp. 23–7.

Gudex, C. (1990) The QALY: how can it be used? In: S. Baldwin, C. Godfrey and C. Propper (eds), *Quality of Life: Perspectives and Policies*. London: Routledge, pp. 218–30.

Gullone, E. and Cummins, R. A. (eds) (2002) *The Universality of Subjective Well-Being Indicators*. Dordrecht: Kluwer.

Haase, J. and Rostad, M. (1994) Experiences of completing cancer treatments: child perspectives, *Oncology Nursing Forum*, 21: 1483–94.

Haase, J. E., Heiney, S. P., Ruccione, K. S. and Stutzer, C. (1999) Research triangulation to derive meaning-based quality-of-life theory: adolescent resilience model and instrument development, *International Journal of Cancer*, 12 (supplement): 125–31.

Habich, R. and Noll, H. -H. (1994) *Soziale Indikatoren und Sozialberichterstattung. Internationale Erfahrungen und gegenwrtiger Forschungsstand*. Bern: Bundesamt für Statistik.

Hagerty, M. R., Naik, P. and Tsai, C.-L. (2000) The effects of quality of life on national elections: a multi-country analysis, *Social Indicators Research*, 49, 3: 347–62.

Hagerty, M. R., Cummins, R. A., Ferriss, A. L., Land, K., Michalos, A. C., Peterson, M. *et al.* (2001) Quality of life indexes for national policy: review and agenda for research, *Social Indicators Research*, 55: 1–96.

Hakim, Z. and Pathak, D. S. (1999) Modelling the EuroQol data: a comparison of discrete choice conjoint and conditional preference modelling, *Health Economics*, 8: 103–16.

Hammerlid, E. and Taft, C. (2001) Health-related quality of life in long-term head and neck cancer survivors: a comparison with general population norms, *British Journal of Cancer*, 84, 2: 149–56.

Hansson, L., Eklund, M. and Bengtsson-Tops, A. (2001) The relationship of personality dimensions as measured by the temperament and character inventory and quality of life in individuals with schizophrenia or schizoaffective disorder living in the community, *Quality of Life Research*, 10, 2: 133–9.

Harding, A. and Greenwell, H. (2001) *Trends in Income and Expenditure: Inequality in the 1980s and 1990s*. Canberra: National Centre for Social and Economic Modelling/University of Canberra.

Harris, J. (1987) QALY-fying the value of life, *Journal of Medical Ethics*, 13: 117–23.

Harris, J. (1991) Unprincipled QALYs: a response to Cubbon, *Journal of Medical Ethics*, 17: 185–8.

Harris, J. (1995) Double jeopardy and the veil of ignorance: a reply, *Journal of Medical Ethics*, 21: 151–7.

Hatton, C. (1995) Linking quality of life to service provision: squaring the quality circle, *Clinical Psychology Forum*, 79: 25–8.

Hatton, C. (1998) Whose quality of life is it anyway? Some problems with the emerging quality of life consensus, *Mental Retardation*, 36: 104–15.

Hays R. D., Sherbourne, C. D. and Mazel, R. M. (1993) The RAND 36-Item Health Survey 1. 0, *Health Economics*, 2: 217–27.

Hays, R. D., Kallich, J. D., Mapes, D. L., Coons, S. J. and Carter, W. B. (1994) Development of the Kidney Disease Quality of Life (KDQOL) Instrument, *Quality of Life Research*, 3: 329–38.

Hays, R. D., Kallich, J. D., Mapes, D. L., Coons, S. J. and Carter, W. B. (1997) *Kidney Disease Quality of Life Short Form (KDQOL-SF),Version 1. 3: A Manual for Use and Scoring*. Santa Monica, CA: RAND.

Headey, B., and Wearing, A. (1989) Personality, life events, and subjective well-being: toward a dynamic equilibrium model, *Journal of Personality and Social Psychology*, 57: 731–9.

Headey, B. and Wearing, A. (1992) *Understanding Happiness: A Theory of Subjective Well-being*. Melbourne: Longman Cheshire.

Headey, B., Veenhoven, R. and Wearing, A. (1991) Top-down versus bottom-up theories of subjective well-being, *Social Indicators Research*, 24: 81–100.

Heal, L. W. and Sigelman, C. K. (1990) Methodological issues in measuring the Quality of Life of individuals with mental retardation. In: R. L. Schalock (ed), *Quality of Life: Perspectives and Issues*. Washington: AAMR, pp. 161–76.

Heidegger, M. (1996) *Being and Time*, trans. J. Stambaugh. Albany, NY: State University of New York Press.

Heinrichs, D. W., Hanlon, T. E. and Carpenter, W. T. Jr (1984) The Quality of Life Scale: an instrument for rating the schizophrenia syndrome, *Schizophrenia Bulletin*, 10: 388–98.

Helson, H. (1964) *Adaptation-level Theory*. New York: Harper and Row.

Hendriks, A. H. C., De Moor, J. M. H., Oud, J. H. L. and Savelberg, M. M. H. W. (2000) Perceived changes in well-being of parents with a child in a therapeutic toddler class, *Research in Developmental Disabilities*, 21: 455–68.

Hermann, B. P., Seidenberg, M., Bell, B., Woodard, A., Rutecki, P. and Sheth, R. (2000) Comorbid psychiatric symptoms in temporal lobe epilepsy: association with chronicity of epilepsy and impact on quality of life, *Epilepsy and Behavior*, 1: 184–90

Hester, S. and Francis, D. (2002) Is institutional talk a phenomenon? In: A. McHoul and M. Rapley (eds), *How to Analyse Talk in Institutional Settings: A Casebook of Methods*. London and New York: Continuum International, pp. 209–20.

Hickey, A. M., Bury, G., O'Boyle, C. A., Bradley, F., O'Kelly, F. D. and Shannon, W. (1996) A new short form individual quality of life measure (SEIQoL-DW): application in a cohort of individuals with HIV/AIDS, *British Medical Journal*, 313: 29–33.

Higginson, I. J. (1993) *Clinical Audit in Palliative Care*. Oxford: Radcliffe Medical Press.

Higginson, I. J. and Carr, A. J. (2001) Using quality of life measures in the clinical setting, *British Medical Journal*, 322: 1297–300.

Hogenraad, R. and Grosbois, T. (1997) A history of threat in Europe and Belgium (1920–1993) *Social Indicators Research*, 42, 2: 221–44.

Houtkoop-Steenstra, H. (2000) *Interaction and the Standardised Interview: The Living Questionnaire*. Cambridge: Cambridge University Press.

Hughes, C., Hwang, B., Kim, J. H., Eisenman, L. T. and Kilian, D. J. (1995) Quality of life in applied research: a review and analysis of empirical measures, *American Journal on Mental Retardation*, 99, 6: 623–41.

Hyder, A. A., Rotllant, G. and Morrow, R. H. (1998) Measuring the burden of disease: healthy life-years, *American Journal of Public Health*, 88, 2: 196–202.

Idler, E. L. and Benyamini, Y. (1997) Self-rated health and mortality: a review of twenty-seven community studies, *Journal of Health and Social Behavior*, 38: 21–37.

James, O. (1997) *Britain on the Couch*. London: Century/Random House.

Johnston, D. F. (1988) Toward a comprehensive 'quality of life' index, *Social Indicators Research*, 20: 473–96.

Jones-Lee, M., Hammerton, M. and Phillips, P. R. (1985) The value of safety: results of a national sample survey, *Economic Journal*, 95: 49–72.

Jordan, T. E. (1998) John O'Neill, Irish bootmaker: a biographical approach to quality of life, *Social Indicators Research*, 48, 3: 297–317.

Jordan, T. E. (2001) Quality of life, hegemony, and social change in rural Ireland: W. Bence Jones, 'A Landlord Who Tried to do His Duty', *Social Indicators Research*, 55, 2: 199–221.

Joseph, G. A. and Rao, P. S. S. S. (1999) Impact of leprosy on the quality of life, *Bulletin of the World Health Organization*, 77, 6: 515–7.

Juster, F. T. and Land, K. C. (eds) (1981) *Social Accounting Systems: Essays on the State of the Art*. New York: Academic Press.

Kaiser, W. (2000) Cognitive effects of antipsychotics in schizophrenia and relationship to quality of life, *British Journal of Psychiatry*, 176: 92–3.

Kaiser, W., Priebe, S., Barr, W., Hoffman, K., Isermann, M., der-Wanner, U-U. *et al.* (1998) Profiles of subjective quality of life in schizophrenic in-and out-patient samples, *Psychiatry Research*, 66: 153–66.

Kant, I. (1978 [1798]) *Anthropology from a Pragmatic Point of View*, trans. V. L. Dowdell, rev. and ed. H. H. Rudnick. Carbondale, IL: Southern Illinois University Press.

Keith, K. D. (1990) Quality of life: issues in community integration, In: R. L. Schalock (ed), *Quality of Life: Perspectives and Issues*. Washington: AAMR.

Keith, K. D. and Schalock, R. L. (eds) (2000) *Cross-cultural Perspectives on Quality of Life*. Washington: AAMR.

Kemmler, G., Holzner, B., Neudorfer, C., Meise, U. and Hinterhuber, H. (1997) General life satisfaction and domain-specific quality of life in chronic schizophrenic patients, *Quality of Life Research*, 6, 3: 265–73.

Kendall, G. and Wickham, G. (1999) *Using Foucault's Methods*. London: Sage.

Kind, P. (1990) Issues in the design and construction of a quality of life measure, In: S. Baldwin, C. Godfrey and C. Propper (eds), *Quality of Life: Perspectives and Policies*. London: Routledge.

Kind, P., Dolan, P., Gudex, C. and Williams, A. (1998) Variations in population health status: results from a United Kingdom national questionnaire survey, *British Medical Journal*, 316: 736–41.

King's Fund Centre (1980/1982) *An Ordinary Life: Comprehensive Locally Based Services for Mentally Handicapped People*. Project Paper No. 24, London: King's Fund.

Klarman, H. E., O'Francis, J. and Rosenthal, G. D. (1968) Cost-effectiveness analysis applied to the treatment of chronic renal disease, *Medical Care*, 6, 1: 48–54.

Klassen, A. F., Newton, J. N. and Mallon, E. (2000) Measuring quality of life in people referred for specialist care of acne: comparing generic and disease-specific measures, *Journal of the American Academy of Dermatology*, 43, 2: 229–33.

Knapp, M. (1988) Construction and expectation: themes from the care in the community initiative, in P. Cambridge and M. Knapp (eds), *Demonstrating Successful Care in the Community*. Canterbury: University of Kent/PSSRU.

Koch, T. (1994) *A Place in Time: Care Givers for Their Elderly*. New York: Praeger.

Koch, T. (2000) Future states: the axioms underlying prospective, future-oriented, health planning instruments, *Social Science and Medicine*, 52: 453–65.

Kuczewski, M. G. (1999) Narrative views of personal identity and substituted judgment in surrogate decision making, *Journal of Law, Medicine and Ethics*, 27, 1: 32–5.

Kuhn, T. S. (1970) *The Structure of Scientific Revolutions*, 2nd edn. Chicago: University of Chicago Press.

Kuhse, H. and Singer, P. (1985) *Should the Baby Live?* Oxford: Oxford University Press.

Land, K. C. (1975) Theories, models and indicators of social change, *International Social Science Journal*, 27: 7–37.

Land, K. C. (1983) Social Indicators, *Annual Review of Sociology*, 9: 1–26.

Land, K. (2000) *Social indicators*. Available from <http://www.cob.vt.edu/market/isqols/kenlandessay. htm> [accessed 08. 11. 01].

Landesman, S. (1986) Quality of life and personal life satisfaction: definition and measurement issues, *Mental Retardation*, 24: 141–3.

Landgraf, J. M., Abetz, L. and Ware, J. E. (1996) *The CHQ User's Manual*. Boston: Health Institute, New England Medical Center.

LaPointe, L. L. (2001) Quality of Life with brain damage, *Brain and Language*, 71: 135–7.

Lauritzen, S. O. and Sachs, L. (2001) Normality, risk and the future: implicit communication of threat in health surveillance, *Sociology of Health and Illness*, 23, 4: 497–516.

Lehman, A. F (1988) A quality of life interview for the chronically mentally ill, *Evaluation and Program Planning*, 11: 51–62.

Lehman, A. F (1996) Measures of quality of life among persons with severe and persistent mental disorders, *Social Psychiatry and Psychiatric Epidemiology*, 31: 78–88.

Lehman, A. F., Ward, N. C., and Linn, L. S. (1982) Chronic mental patients: the quality of life issue, *American Journal of Psychiatry*, 139, 10: 1271–6.

Lehman, A. F., Possidente, S. and Hawker, F. (1986) The quality of life of chronic patients in a state hospital and in community residences, *Hospital and Community Psychiatry*, 37,9: 901–7.

Leidy, N. K. and Haase, J. E. (1999) Functional status from the patient's perspective: the challenge of preserving personal integrity, *Research in Nursing and Health*, 22: 67–77.

Lennon, J. and McCartney, P. (1964) Can't Buy Me Love, From *A Hard Day's Night*, London: Parlophone/EMI. CDP7-46437-2. Recorded by The Beatles 29 January 1964.

Levene, H. (1960) Robust tests for equality of variance. In: I. Olkin (ed), *Contributions to Probability and Statistics*, Palo Alto, CA: Stanford University Press.

Leudar, I. and Thomas, P. (2000) *Voices of Reason, Voices of Insanity: Studies of Verbal Hallucinations*, London: Routledge.

Levinson, S. (1983) *Pragmatics*. Cambridge, Cambridge University Press.

Lewis, G. and Wilkinson, G. (1993) Another British disease? A recent increase in the prevalence of psychiatric morbidity, *Journal of Epidemiology and Community Health*, 47: 358–361.

Loomes, G. and McKenzie, L. (1990) The scope and limitations of QALY measures, In: S. Baldwin, C. Godfrey and C. Propper (eds), *Quality of Life: Perspectives and Policies*. London: Routledge.

Lovett, H. (1993) Foreword, In: P. Kinsella *Supported Living: A New Paradigm*. Manchester: National Development Team.

Lowe, K., dePaiva, S. and Felce, D. (1993) Effects of a community-based service on adaptive and maladaptive behaviours: a longitudinal study, *Journal of Intellectual Disability Research*, 37: 3–22.

Luckasson, R. (1997) Foreword, In: R. L. Schalock (ed.), *Quality of Life: Volume II: Application to Persons with Disabilities*. Washington: AAMR, pp. vii-x.

Lyons, J. S., Howard, K. I., O'Mahoney, M. T. and Lish, J. (1997a) *The Measurement and Management of Clinical Outcomes in Mental Health*. New York: Wiley.

Lyons, J. S., O'Mahoney, M. T., Miller, S. I., Neme, J., Kabat, J. and Miller, F. (1997b) Predicting readmission to the psychiatric hospital in a managed care environment: implications for quality indicators, *American Journal of Psychiatry*, 154: 337–40.

McCormick, R. (1978) The quality of life, the sanctity of life, *Hastings Center Report*, 8: 32.

McGee, H. M., O'Boyle, C. A., Hickey, A., O'Malley, K. and Joyce, C. R. B. (1991) Assessing the quality of life of the individual: the SEIQol with a healthy and a gastroenterology unit population, *Psychological Medicine*, 21: 749– 59.

McHorney, C. A, Ware, J. J. and Raczek, A. E. (1993) The MOS 36-Item Short-Form Health Survey (SF-36): II. Psychometric and clinical tests of validity in measuring physical and mental health constructs, *Medical Care*, 31: 247–63.

McHoul, A. and Rapley, M. (2002b) 'Should we make a start then?' A strange case of (delayed) client-initiated psychological assessment. *Research on Language and Social Interaction*, 35, 1, 73–91.

McHoul, A. and Rapley, M. (2001) Culture, psychology and 'being human', *Culture and Psychology*, 7, 4: 433–51.

McHoul, A. and Rapley, M. (eds) (2002a) *How to Analyse Talk in Institutional Settings: A Casebook of Methods*. London and New York: Continuum International.

Mackenzie, G. (2001) Neurosis may be increasing (e-letter), *British Medical Journal*, <http://www. bmj. com/cgi/eletters/323/7305/130/a#EL3> [accessed 16/10/01].

McLintock, A. (1992) The angel of progress, *Social Text*, 10, 2 and 3: 84–98.

McNamee, D. and Horton, R. (1996) Lies, damn lies, and reports of RCTs, *Lancet*, 348: 562.

MacRae, D., Jr (1985) *Policy Indicators: Links Between Social Science and Public Policy.* Chapel Hill, NC: University of North Carolina Press.

Maguire, P., Booth, K., Elliot, C. and Jones, B. (1996) Helping health care professionals involved in cancer care acquire key interviewing skills: the impact of workshops, *European Journal of Cancer,* 32 (suppl.): 1486–9.

Mahoney, F. I., and Barthel, D. W. (1965) Functional evaluation: the Barthel Index, *Maryland State Medical Journal,* 14, 2: 61–5.

Mallard, A. G. C., Lance, C. E. and Michalos, A. C. (1997) Culture as a moderator of overall life satisfaction-life facet of satisfaction relationships, *Social Indicators Research,* 40: 259–84.

Manning, C. (2001) I don't believe the figures (e-letter), *British Medical Journal,* <http://www. bmj. com/cgi/eletters/323/7305/130/a#EL3> [accessed 16/ 10/01].

Martin, C. R. and Thompson, D. R. (2001) Does dialysis adequacy impact on the quality of life of end-stage renal disease patients? *Clinical Effectiveness in Nursing,* 5, 2: 57–65.

Martin, A. R., Lookingbill, D. P., Botek, A., Light, J., Thiboutot, D. and Girma, C. J. (2001) Health-related quality of life among patients with facial acne – assessment of a new acne-specific questionnaire, *Clinical and Experimental Dermatology,* 26: 380–5.

Maslow, A. H. (1954) *Motivation and Personality.* New York: Harper.

Mattes, R. and Christie, J. (1997) Personal versus collective quality of life and South Africans' evaluations of democratic government, *Social Indicators Research,* 41, 1/3: 205–28.

Megone, C. B. (1990) The quality of life: starting from Aristotle, In: S. Baldwin, C. Godfrey, and C. Propper (eds), *Quality of Life: Perspectives and Policies.* London: Routledge, pp. 28–41.

Michalos A. C. (1985) Multiple discrepancies theory (MDT), *Social Indicators Research,* 16: 347–413.

Miller, P. (1986) Critical sociologies of madness, In: P. Miller and N. Rose (eds), *The Power of Psychiatry.* Cambridge: Polity Press.

Miller, T. and McHoul, A. (1998) *Popular Culture and Everyday Life.* London: Sage.

Missenden, K., Oliver, N., Carson, J., Holloway, F., Towey, A., Dunn, L. *et al.* (1995–6) Understanding quality of life: a comparison between staff and patients, *Social Work and Social Sciences Review,* 6, 2: 117–29.

Monk, R. (1991) *Ludwig Wittgenstein: The Duty of Genius.* London: Random House.

Morreim, H. (1992) The impossibility and the necessity of quality of life research, *Bioethics,* 6, 3: 218–32.

Morris, J. and Durand, A. (1989) *Category Rating Methods: Numerical And Verbal Scales.* York: Centre for Health Economics, University of York (mimeograph).

Mozes, B., Maor, Y. and Shmueli, A. (1999) Do we know what global ratings of health-related quality of life measure? *Quality of Life Research,* 8, 3: 269–73.

Muldoon, M. F., Barger, S. D., Flory, J. D. and Manuck, S. B. (1998) What are quality of life measurements measuring? *British Medical Journal,* 316: 542–5.

Mulkay, M., Ashmore, M. and Pinch, T. (1987) Measuring the quality of life, *Sociology,* 21: 541–64.

Murphy, G. (1987) Direct observation as an assessment tool in functional analysis and treatment, In: J. Hogg and N. V. Raynes (eds), *Assessment in Mental Handicap.* Beckenham: Croom-Helm.

Murray, C. J. L (1994) Quantifying the burden of disease: the technical basis for disability-adjusted life years, *Bulletin of the World Health Organization*, 72, 3: 429–45.

Murray, C. J. L (1996) Rethinking DALYs, In: C. J. L. Murray and A. D. Lopez (eds), *The Global Burden of Disease: A Comprehensive Assessment of Mortality and Disability from Diseases, Injuries, and Risk Factors in 1990 and projected to 2020 – Summary*. Cambridge, MA: Harvard School of Public Health, pp. 1–98.

Murray, C. J. L. and Acharya, A. K. (1997) Understanding DALYs, *Journal of Health Economics*, 16: 703–30.

Murray, C. J. L. and Lopez, A. D. (eds) (1996) *The Global Burden of Disease: A Comprehensive Assessment of Mortality and Disability from Diseases, Injuries, and Risk Factors in 1990 and projected to 2020 – Summary*. Cambridge, MA: Harvard School of Public Health.

Murray, C. J. L, Salomon, J. A. and Mathers. C. (1999) *A Critical Examination of Summary Measures of Population Health*, GPE Discussion Paper No. 2, Geneva: World Health Organization.

Navarro, V. and Shi, L. (2001) The political context of social inequalities and health, *Social Science and Medicine*, 52: 481–91.

Nihira, K., Foster, R., Shellhaas, M. and Leland, H. (1975) *AAMD Adaptive Behaviour Scale*. Washington: American Association on Mental Deficiency.

Noll, H.-H. (2000) Social indicators and social reporting: the international experience, <http://www. ccsd. ca/noll1. html> [accessed 17. 09. 01].

Noll, H.-H. and Zapf, W. (1994) Social indicators research: societal monitoring and social reporting, in I. Borg and P. Mohler (eds), *Trends and Perspectives in Empirical Social Research*, New York: Walter de Gruyter.

Nord, E. (1991) The validity of a visual analogue scale in determining social utility weights for health states, *International Journal of Health Planning and Management*, 6: 234–42.

Nord, E. (1992a) An alternative to QALYs: the saved young life equivalent, *British Medical Journal*, 305: 875–8.

Nord, E. (1992b) Methods for quality adjustment of life years, *Social Science and Medicine*, 34: 559–69.

Nord, E. (1999) *Cost-Value Analysis in Health Care*. Cambridge: Cambridge University Press.

O'Boyle, C. A., McGee, H., Hickey, A., Joyce, C. R. B., Browne, J. and O'Malley, J. (1993) *The Schedule for the Evaluation of Individual Quality of Life Administration Manual*. Dublin: Department of Psychology, Royal College of Surgeons in Ireland.

O'Connor, R. (1993) *Issues in the Measurement of Health-related Quality of Life*, Working Paper 30. Melbourne: National Center for Health Program Evaluation.

Oliver, J. P. J., Huxley, P. J., Priebe, S. and Kaiser, W. (1997) Measuring the quality of life of severely mentally ill people using the Lancashire Quality of Life Profile, *Social Psychiatry Epidemiology*, 32, 76–83.

Oliver, N., Carson, J., Missenden, K., Towey, A., Dunn, L., Collins, E., and Holloway, F. (1996) Assessing the quality of life of the long-term mentally-ill: a comparative study of two measures, *International Journal of Methods in Psychiatric Research*, 6: 161–6.

Oliver, M. (1996) *Understanding Disability: From Theory to Practice*. Chatham: McKays.

Organization for Economic Cooperation and Development (2001) *The Well-being of Nations: The Role of Human and Social Capital*. Paris: OECD.

Organization for Economic Cooperation and Development (1982) *The OECD List of Social Indicators*, OECD Social Indicator Development Programme. Paris: OECD.

Ostroot, N. and Snyder, W. (1996) The quality of life in historical perspective. France: 1695–1990, *Social Indicators Research*, 38, 2: 109–28.

Owens, D. K., Cardinalli, A. B. and Nease, R. F. (1997) Physicians' assessments of the utility of health states associated with Human Immunodeficiency Virus (HIV) and Hepatitis B Virus (HBV) Infection, *Quality of Life Research*, 6. 1: 77–86.

Parker, I. (ed) (1998) *Social Constructionism, Discourse and Realism*. London: Sage.

Patil, R., Cotler, S. J., Banaad-Omiotek, G., McNutt, R. A., Brown, M. D., Cotler, S. et al. (2001) Physicians' preference values for hepatitis C health states and antiviral therapy: a survey, *BioMed Central Gastroenterology*, 1: 6. <http://www.biomedcentral. com/1471-230X/1/6> [accessed 02. 08. 01].

Patton, M. Q. (1990) *Qualitative Evaluation and Research Methods*. Newbury Park, CA: Sage.

Peräkylä, A. (1997) Reliability and validity in research based on transcripts, In: David Silverman (ed.), *Qualitative Methods: Theory, Method and Practice*. London: Sage, pp. 201–20.

Perry, J. and Felce, D. (1995) Objective indicators of quality of life: how much do they agree with each other? *Journal of Community and Applied Social Psychology*, 5: 1–19.

Perry, J., Felce., D. and Lowe, K. (2000) *Subjective and Objective Quality of Life Assessment: Their Interrelationship and Determinants*. Cardiff: Welsh Centre for Learning Disabilities – Applied Research Unit/University of Wales College of Medicine.

Personal Social Services Research Unit (1987) Consumerism and care in the community, *Care in the Community Newsletter*, No. 7. Canterbury: University of Kent/PSSRU.

Petersen, A. and Lupton, D. (1996) *The New Public Health: Health and Self in the Age of Risk*. London: Sage.

Phillips, C. and Thompson, G. (1998) *What is a QALY?* London: Hayward.

Pilgrim, D. and Bentall, R. (1999) The medicalisation of misery: a critical realist analysis of the concept of depression, *Journal of Mental Health*, 8, 3: 261–74.

Plato (1903) *The Four Socratic Dialogues of Plato*, trans. B. Jowett, with a preface by E. Caird. Oxford: Clarendon Press.

Pollard, B. and Johnston, M. (2001) Problems with the Sickness Impact Profile: a theoretically based analysis and a proposal for a new method of implementation and scoring, *Social Science and Medicine*, 52: 921–34.

Polsky, D., Willke, R. J., Scott, K., Schulman, K. A. and Glick, H. A. (2001) A comparison of scoring weights for the EuroQol derived from patients and the general public, *Health Economics*, 10: 27–37.

Potter, J. (1996) *Representing Reality: Discourse, Rhetoric and Social Construction*, London: Sage.

Potter, J. (2001) Beyond cognitivism, *Research on Language and Social Interaction*, 32, 1/2: 119–27.

Potter, J. and Wetherell, M. (1987) *Discourse and Social Psychology: Beyond Attitudes and Behaviour*. London: Sage.

Pretty, G. M. H., Andrewes, C. C. and Collet, C. (1994) Exploring adolescents' sense of community and its relationship to loneliness, *Journal of Community Psychology*, 22: 346–58.

Priebe, S., Oliver, J. P. J. and Kaiser, W. (eds), (1999) *Quality of Life and Mental Health Care*. Petersfield: Wrightson Biomedical.

Prieto, L., Santed, R., Cobo, E. and Alonso, J. (1999) A new measure for assessing the health-related quality of life of patients with vertigo, dizziness or imbalance: the VDI questionnaire, *Quality of Life Research*, 8, 1/2: 131–9.

Prince, P. N. and Gerber, G. J. (2001) Measuring subjective quality of life in people with serious mental illness using the SEIQoL-DW, *Quality of Life Research*, 10, 2: 117–22.

Puchta, C. and Potter, J. (1999) Asking elaborate questions: focus groups and the management of spontaneity, *Journal of Sociolinguistics*, 3: 314–35.

Puchta, C. and Potter, J. (forthcoming) *Focus Group Practice: Moderating Interaction in Market Research Focus Groups*. London: Sage.

Putnam, R. (1995) Bowling alone: America's declining social capital, *Journal of Democracy*, 6, 1 (Jan.): 65–78.

Putnam, R. (2002) Bowling together, *The American Prospect*, 11 February: 20–22.

Ramsey, P. (1978) *Ethics at the Edges of Life*. New Haven, CT: Yale University Press.

Rapley, M. (2001) Policing happiness, In: C. Newnes, G. Holmes, and C. Dunn, (eds), *This is Madness Too*. Ross-on-Wye: PCCS Books.

Rapley, M. and Antaki, C. (1996) A conversation analysis of the 'acquiescence' of people with learning disabilities, *Journal of Community and Applied Social Psychology*, 6: 207–27.

Rapley, M. and Beyer, S. (1996) Daily activity, community activity and quality of life in an ordinary housing network, *Journal of Applied Research in Intellectual Disabilities*, 9, 1: 31–9.

Rapley, M. and Beyer, S. (1998) Daily activity, community activity and quality of life in an ordinary housing network: a two-year follow-up, *Journal of Applied Research in Intellectual Disabilities*, 11, 1: 34–43.

Rapley, M. and Hopgood, L. (1997) Quality of life in a community-based service in rural Australia, *Journal of Intellectual and Developmental Disability*, 22, 2: 124–41.

Rapley, M. and Lobley, J. (1995) Factor analysis of the Schalock and Keith (1993) Quality of Life Questionnaire: a replication, *Mental Handicap Research*, 8, 3: 194–202.

Rapley, M. and Ridgway, J. (1998) Quality of Life talk: the corporatisation of intellectual disability, *Disability and Society*, 13, 3: 451–71.

Rapley, M., Kiernan, P. and Antaki, C. (1998) Invisible to themselves or negotiating identity? The interactional management of 'being intellectually disabled', *Disability and Society*, 13, 5: 807–27.

Rapley, M., Ridgway, J. and Beyer, S. (1998) Staff : staff and staff : client reliability of the Schalock and Keith (1996) Quality of Life Questionnaire, *Journal of Intellectual Disability Research*, 42, 1: 37–43.

Ravenscroft, A. J. and Bell, M. D. D (2000) 'End-of-life' decision making within intensive care – objective, consistent, defensible? *Journal of Medical Ethics*, 26: 435–40.

Raynes, N. V., Sumpton, R. C. and Pettipher, C. (1989a) *The Index of Participation in Domestic Life*. Manchester: Manchester University Department of Social Policy and Social Work.

Raynes, N. V., Sumpton, R. C. and Pettipher, C. (1989b) *The Index of Community Involvement*. Manchester: Manchester University Department of Social Policy and Social Work.

Reicher, S. (2001) Studying psychology, studying racism, In: M. Augoustinos and K. Reynolds (eds), *Understanding Prejudice, Racism and Social Conflict*. London: Sage, pp. 273–98.

Reiter, S. and Bendov, D. (1996) The self concept and quality of life of two groups of learning disabled adults living at home and in group homes, *British Journal of Developmental Disabilities*, xlii, 2, 83: 97–111.

Richardson, J. T. E. (1996) *Handbook of Qualitative Research Methods for Psychology and the Social Sciences*. Leicester: BPS Books.

Rodgers, W. (1982) Trends in reported happiness within demographically defined subgroups, 1957–78. *Social Forces*, 60: 826–42.

Rogers-Clark, C. (1998) Women and health, In: C. Rogers-Clark and A. Smith (eds), *Women's Health: A Primary Health Care Approach*. Sydney: MacLennan & Petty.

Rose, N. (1986) Psychiatry: the discipline of mental health, In: P. Miller and N. Rose (eds), *The Power of Psychiatry*. Cambridge: Polity Press.

Rose, N. (1992) Governing the enterprising self, In: P. Heelas and P. Morris (eds), *The Values of Enterprise Culture: The Moral Debate*. London: Routledge.

Rose, N. (1999) *Governing the Soul: The Shaping of the Private Self*, 2nd edn. London: Free Association Books.

Rosen, M. (1986) Quality of life for persons with mental retardation: a question of entitlement, *Mental Retardation*, 24: 365–6.

Rothwell, P. M., McDowell, Z., Wong, C. K. and Dorman, P. J. (1997) Doctors and patients don't agree: cross-sectional study of patients' and doctors' perceptions and assessments of disability in multiple sclerosis, *British Medical Journal*, 314: 1580–3.

Ruggieri, M., Bisoffi, G. and Fontecedro, L. (2001) Subjective and objective dimensions of quality of life in psychiatric patients: a factor analytic approach, *British Journal of Psychiatry*, 178: 268–75.

Ryle, G. (1949) *The Concept of Mind*. Oxford: Clarendon Press.

Sacks, H. (1992) *Lectures on Conversation, vols 1 and 2*, ed. G. Jefferson, intro. E. A. Schegloff. Oxford: Blackwell.

Sadana, R., Mathers, C. D., Lopez, A. D., Murray, C. J. L. and Iburg, K. (n. d.) *Comparative Analyses of More than 50 Household Surveys on Health Status*, GPE Discussion Paper Series No. 15. Geneva: World Health Organization.

Sahlberg-Blom, E., Ternestedt, B.-M. and Johansson, J.-E. (2001) Is good 'quality of life' possible at the end of life? An explorative study of the experiences of a group of cancer patients in two different care cultures, *Journal of Clinical Nursing*, 10: 550–62.

Salkeld, G., Cameron, I. D., Cumming, R. G., Easter, S., Seymour, J., Kurrle, S. E. *et al.* (2000) Quality of life related to fear of falling and hip fracture in older women: a time trade-off study, *British Medical Journal*, 320: 241–6.

Salomon, J. A., Mathers, C. D. and Murray, C. J. L. (2001) Applying DALYs to the burden of infectious disease (letter) *Bulletin of the World Health Organization*, 79, 3: 268.

Salvaris, M. (2000) *Community and Social Indicators: How Citizens Can Measure Progress. An Overview of Social and Community Indicator Projects in Australia and Internationally*. Hawthorn: Institute for Social Research, Swinburne University of Technology.

Samli, A. C. (1987) *Marketing and the Quality-of-Life Interface*. Westport, CT: Quorum Books.

Sanders, C., Eggerm, M., Donovan, J., Tallon, D. and Frankel, S. (1998) Reporting on quality of life in randomised controlled trials: bibliographic study, *British Medical Journal*, 317: 1191–4.

Sands, D. J., Kozleski, E. B. and Goodwin, L. D. (1991) Whose needs are we meeting? Results of a consumer satisfaction survey of persons with developmental disabilities in Colorado, *Research in Developmental Disabilities*, 12: 297–314.

Sarantkos, S. (1993) *Social Research*. Melbourne: Macmillan Academic.

Sawyer, M., Antoniou, G., Toogood, I. and Rice, M. (1999) A comparison of parent and adolescent reports describing the health-related quality of life of adolescents treated for cancer, *International Journal of Cancer*, 12 (supplement): 39–45.

Sayers, B. M. and Fliedner, T. M. (1997) The critique of DALYs: a counter-reply, *Bulletin of the World Health Organization*, 75: 383–4.

Schalock, R. L (1994) The concept of quality of life and its current applications in the field of mental retardation/developmental disabilities, In: D. A. Goode (ed), *Quality of Life for Persons with Disabilities: International Perspectives and Issues*. Cambridge: Brookline Books, pp. 266–84.

Schalock, R. L. (ed) (1996) *Quality of Life: Volume I: Conceptualization and Measurement*. Washington: AAMR.

Schalock, R. L. (ed) (1997) *Quality of Life: Volume II: Application to Persons with Disabilities*. Washington: AAMR.

Schalock, R. L. and Keith, K. D. (1993) *Quality of Life Questionnaire*. Worthington, OH: IDS Publishing Corporation.

Schalock, R. L. and Parmenter, T. (2000) Preface, In: *Quality Of Life: Its Conceptualization, Measurement, and Application A Consensus Document*. Washington: IASSID.

Schalock, R. L., Bonham, G. S. and Marchand, C. B. (2000) Consumer-based quality of life assessment: a path model of perceived satisfaction, *Evaluation and Program Planning*, 23, 1: 77–87.

Schalock, R. L., Keith, K. D. and Hoffman, K. (1990) *Quality of Life Questionnaire: Standardization Manual*. Hastings, NE: Mid-Nebraska Mental Retardation Services.

Schrecker, T., Acosta, L., Somerville, M. A. and Bursztajn, H. J. (2001) The ethics of social risk reduction in the era of the biological brain, *Social Science and Medicine*, 52: 1677–87.

Selai, C. E. and Trimble, M. R. (1997) Patients' assessments of disability in multiple sclerosis, *British Medical Journal*, 315: 1305 (letter).

Sharma, T. (1999) Cognitive effects of conventional and atypical antipsychotics in schizophrenia, *British Journal of Psychiatry*, 174 (suppl. 38): 44–51.

Shaw, C., McColl, E. and Bond, S. (2000) Functional abilities and continence: the use of proxy respondents in research involving older people, *Quality of Life Research*, 9, 10: 1117–26.

Shea, W. R. (1976) Introduction: the quest for a high quality of life, In: W. R. Shea and J. King-Farlow (eds), *Values and the Quality of Life*. New York: Science History Publications, pp. 1–5.

Sheldon, T. (2000) Dutch GP cleared after helping to end man's 'hopeless existence', *British Medical Journal*, 321: 1174.

Shepherd, G., Muijen, M., Dean, R. and Cooney, M. (1996) Residential care in hospital and in the community – quality of care and quality of life, *British Journal of Psychiatry*, 168: 448–56.

Sigelman, C. K., Budd, E. C., Spanhel, C. L. and Schoenrock, C. J. (1981) When in doubt, say 'yes': acquiescence in interviews with mentally retarded persons, *Mental Retardation*, 19: 53–8.

Silverman, D. (1997) Towards an aesthetics of research, In: D. Silverman (ed.), *Qualitative Methods: Theory, Method and Practice*. London: Sage, pp. 239–53

Silverman, D. (1998) *Harvey Sacks: Social Science and Conversation Analysis*. Cambridge: Polity Press.

Simpson, C. J., Hyde, C. E. and Faragher, E. B. (1989) The chronically mentally ill in community facilities: a study of quality of life, *British Journal of Psychiatry*, 154: 77–82.

Singer, P., McKie, J., Kuhse, H. and Richardson, J. (1995) Double jeopardy and the use of QALYs in health care allocation, *Journal of Medical Ethics*, 21: 144–50.

Sirgy, M. J. and Samli, A. C. (eds) (1996) *New Dimensions in Marketing/Quality-of-Life Research*, Westport, CT: Quorum Books.

Skantze, K., Malm, U., Dencker, S. J., May, P. R. and Corrigan, P. (1992) Comparison of quality of life with standard of living in schizophrenic outpatients, *British Journal of Psychiatry*, 161: 797–801.

Skevington, S. M. and Wright, A. (2001) Changes in the quality of life of patients receiving antidepressant medication in primary care: validation of the WHOQOL-100, *British Journal of Psychiatry*, 178: 261–7.

Slaughter, J. G., Lehman, A. F., and Myers, C. P. (1991) Quality of life of severely mentally ill adults in residential care facilities, *Adult Residential Care Journal*, 5, 2: 97–111.

Slevin, M. L., Plant, H., Lynch, D., Drinkwater, J. and Gregory, W. M. (1988) Who should measure quality of life, the doctor or the patient? *British Journal of Cancer*, 57: 109–12.

Smith, J. A, (1995) Semi-structured interviewing and qualitative analysis, In: J. A. Smith, R. Harré and L. Van Langenhove (eds), *Rethinking Methods in Psychology*. London: Sage.

Spencer, B., Leplège, A. and Ecosse, E. (1999) Recurrent genital herpes and quality of life in France, *Quality of Life Research*, 8, 4: 365–71.

Spitzer, W. O. (1987) State of science 1986: quality of life and functional status as target variables for research, *Journal of Chronic Diseases*, 40: 465–71.

Sprangers, M. A. G., de Regt, E. B., Andries, F., van Agt, H. M. E., Bijl, R. V., de Boer, J. B., *et al.* (2000) Which chronic conditions are associated with better or poorer quality of life? *Journal of Clinical Epidemiology*, 53, 9: 895–907.

Staquet, M., Hays, R. and Fayers, P. (eds) (1998) *Quality of Life Assessment in Clinical Trials: Methods and Practice*. Oxford: Oxford University Press.

Stein, R. and Jessop, D. (1990) Functional Status II(R) A measure of child health status, *Medical Care*, 28: 1041–55.

Stein, R. and Jessop, D. (1991) *Manual for the Functional Status II(R) Measure*. New York: Albert Einstein College of Medicine of Yeshiva University.

Stein, J. and Mansell, J. (1992) *MTSTAB: A Program for Analysing the Output of MTS on the PC*. Canterbury, Centre for the Applied Psychology of Social Care, University of Kent at Canterbury.

Stein, R. E. K. and Riessman, C. K. (1980) The development of an impact-on-family scale: preliminary findings, *Medical Care*, 18: 465–72.

Stones, M. J., Hadjistavropoulos, T., Tuuko, J. and Kozma, A. (1995) Happiness has traitlike and statelike properties, *Social Indicators Research*, 36: 129–44.

Swales, J. M. and Rogers, P. S. (1995) Discourse and the projection of corporate culture: the mission statement, *Discourse and Society*, 6: 223–42.

Switzky, H. N. (1999) Intrinsic motivation and motivational self-system processes in persons with mental retardation: a theory of motivational orientation, In: E. Zigler and D. Bennet-Gates (eds), *Personality Development in Individuals with Mental Retardation*. Cambridge: Cambridge University Press, pp. 70–106.

Tabachnick, B. G. and Fiddell, L. S. (1989) *Using Multivariate Statistics*, 2nd edn. New York: Harper and Row.

Taylor, S. J. (1994) In support of research on Quality of Life, but against QOL, In: D. Goode (ed) *Quality of Life for Persons with Disabilities: International Perspectives and Issues*. Cambridge: Brookline Books, pp. 260–65.

Taylor, S. J. and Bogdan, R. (1990) Quality of Life and the individual's perspective, In: R. L. Schalock (ed), *Quality of Life: Perspectives and Issues*. Washington: AAMR. pp. 27–40.

Taylor, R. E., Leese, M., Clarkson, P., Holloway, F. and Thornicroft G. (1998) Quality of life outcomes for intensive versus standard community mental health services, PRiSM Psychosis Study, *British Journal of Psychiatry*, 173: 416–22.

tenHave, P. (2002) Applied conversation analysis, In: A. McHoul, and M. Rapley (eds), *How to Analyse Talk in Institutional Settings: A Casebook of Methods*. London and New York: Continuum International, pp. 3–11.

Testa, M. A. and Nackley, J. F. (1994) Methods for quality-of-life studies, *Annual Review of Public Health*, 15: 535–59.

Thompson, S. J. and Gifford, S. M. (2000) Trying to keep a balance: the meaning of health and diabetes in an urban Aboriginal community, *Social Science and Medicine*, 51: 1457–72.

Treadwell, J. R., Kearney D. and Davila, M. (2000) Health profile preferences of hepatitis C patients, *Digest of Disease Science*, 45: 345–50.

Tsevat, S. N., Sherman, D. P. A. and McElwee, J. A. (1999) The will to live among HIV-infected patients, *Annals of Internal Medicine*, 131, 3: 194–8.

United Nations (1975) *Towards a System of Social and Demographic Statistics*. New York: United Nations.

United Nations (1995) *Human Development Report 1995*. New York and Oxford: Oxford University Press.

United Nations Human Development Program (UNHDP) (1990) *Human Development Report*. New York and Oxford: Oxford University Press.

United States Department of Health, Education, and Welfare (1969) *Toward a Social Report*. Washington, DC: US Government Printing Office.

van der Maas, P. J., van der Wal, G., Haverkate, I., de Graaff, C. L. M., Kester, J. G. C., Onwuteaka-Philipsen, B. D. *et al.* (1996) Euthanasia, physician-assisted suicide, and other medical practices involving the end of life in the Netherlands, 1990–1995, *New England Journal of Medicine*, 335: 1699–705.

van Hooff, A. J. L. (1990) *From Autothanasia to Suicide: Self-killing in Classical Antiquity*. London: Routledge.

van Thiel, G. J. M. W., van Delden, J. J. M., de Haan, K. and Huibers, A. K. (1997) Retrospective study of doctors' 'end of life' decisions in caring for mentally handicapped people in institutions in the Netherlands, *British Medical Journal*, 315: 88–91.

Veenhoven, R. (1984) *Conditions of Happiness*. Reidel: Dordrecht.

Veenhoven, R. (1991) Is happiness relative? *Social Indicators Research*, 24: 299–313.

Veenhoven, R. (1994) Is happiness a trait? Tests of the theory that a better society does not make people any happier, *Social Indicators Research*, 33: 101–60.

Veenhoven, R. (1996) Happy Life-expectancy: a comprehensive measure of quality-of-life in nations, *Social Indicators Research*, 39: 1–58.

Veenhoven, R. (1997) Advances in the understanding of happiness, *Revue Québécoise de Psychologie*, 18: 267–93.

Veenhoven, R. (1998) Two state-trait discussions on happiness: a reply to Stones *et al.*, *Social Indicators Research*, 43: 211–25.

Verri, A., Cummins, R. A., Petito, F., Vallero, E., Monteath, S., Gerosa, E. *et al.* (1999) An Italian-Australian comparison of quality of life among people with intellectual disability living in the community, *Journal of Intellectual Disability Research*, 43, 6: 513–222.

Verrips, G. H. W., Vogels, A. G. C., den Ouden, A. L., Paneth, N. and Verloove-Vanhorick, S. P. (2000) Measuring health-related quality of life in adolescents: agreement between raters and between methods of administration, *Child: Care, Health and Development*, 26, 6: 457–69.

Virginia Tech Center for Survey Research (1998) *Quality of Life in Virginia: 1998*. Blacksburg, VA: Center for Survey Research, Virginia Polytechnic Institute and State University.

Vogels, A. G. C., Verrips, S. P., Verloove-Vanhorick, M., Fekkes, R. P., Kamphuis, H. M., Koopman, H. *et al.* (1998) Young children's health related quality of life: development of the TACQOL, *Quality of Life Research*, 7: 457–65.

Walker, S. R. (1992) Quality of life measurement: an overview, *Journal of the Royal Society of Health*, 112: 265.

Walker, S. R. and Rosser, R. M. (eds) (1988) *Quality of Life: Assessment and Application*. Lancaster: MTP Press.

Wallcraft, J. and Michaelson, J. (2001) Developing a survivor discourse to replace the 'psychopathology' of breakdown and crisis, In: C. Newnes, G. Holmes and C. Dunn (eds), *This Is Madness Too*. Ross-on-Wye: PCCS Books.

Ware, J. J. and Sherbourne, C. D. (1992) The MOS 36-item short-form health survey (SF–36) I. Conceptual framework and item selection, *Medical Care*, 30: 473–83.

Warr, J. E. Jr, Kosinski, M. and Keller, S. D. (1998) *SF-12: How to Score the SF-12 and Mental Health Summary Scales*. Lincoln, RI: Quality Metric Inc. and The Health Assessment Lab.

Watson, D. R. (2000) The anthropology of communication: foundations, futures and the analysis of 'constructions' of space, in T. Lask (ed), *Social Constructions of Space: The Territories of the Anthropology of Communication*. Liège: Presses Universitaires de Liège.

Wearing, A. (1992) *Understanding happiness: A Theory of Subjective Well-being*. Melbourne: Longman Cheshire.

Webb, N. L. and Drummond, P. D. (2001) The effect of swimming with dolphins on human well-being and anxiety, *Anthrozoös*, 14, 2: 81–6.

Welsh Office (1991) *The Review of the All-Wales Mental Handicap Strategy: Proposals for Development from April 1993*. Cardiff: HMSO.

Wenzel, E. (2001) *The Big 'C' Report*. <http://www. ldb. org/cancer/c1. htm> [accessed 18. 10. 01].

Westerhof, G. J., Dittmann-Kohli, F. and Thissen, T. (2001) Beyond life satisfaction: lay conceptions of well-being among middle-aged and elderly adults, *Social Indicators Research*, 56, 2: 179–203.

WHOQOL Group (1993) *WHOQOL Study Protocol*. Geneva: WHO.

WHOQOL Group (1996) *WHOQOL-BREF: Field Trial Version: Introduction, Administration, Scoring and General Version of the Assessment*. Geneva: WHO.

WHOQOL Group (1998) The World Health Organization Quality of Life Assessment (WHOQOL): development and general psychometric properties, *Social Science and Medicine*, 46, 12: 1569–85.

Wiklund, I., Lindvall, K. and Swedberg, K. (1986) Assessment of quality of life in clinical trials, *Acta Medica Scandinavia*, 220: 1–3.

Willig, C. (2001) *Introducing Qualitative Research in Psychology: Adventures in Theory and Method*. Buckingham: Open University Press.

Wilkinson, G., Hesdon, B., Wild, D., Cookson, R., Farina, C., Sharma, V. *et al.* (2000) Self-report quality of life measure for people with schizophrenia: the SQLS, *British Journal of Psychiatry*, 177: 42–6.

Witt, D. D., Lowe, G. D., Peek, C. W. and Curry, E. W. (1979) The changing relationship between age and happiness: emerging trend or methodological artefact? *Social Forces*, 58: 1302–7.

Wittgenstein, L. (1953) *Philosophical Investigations*, trans. G. E. M. Anscombe and R. Rhees. Oxford: Blackwell.

Wittgenstein, L. (1961) *Tractatus Logico-Philosophicus*, trans. D. F. Pears and B. F. McGuinness. London: Routledge.

Wittgenstein, L. (1978) *Lectures and Conversations on Aesthetics, Psychology and Religious Belief*, ed. C. Barrett. Oxford: Blackwell.

Wolfensberger, W. (1972) *The Principle of Normalization in Human Services*. Toronto: National Institute of Mental Retardation.

Wolfensberger, W. (1994) Lets hang up 'Quality of Life' as a hopeless term, In: D. Goode (ed) *Quality of Life for Persons with Disabilities: International Perspectives and Issues*. Cambridge: Brookline Books.

Wolinsky, F. D., Roe, R. M., Miller, D. K. and Prendergast, J. M. (1985) Correlates of change in subjective well-being among the elderly, *Journal of Community Health*, 10: 93–107.

Wolpert, L. (1999) *Malignant Sadness*. London: Faber and Faber.

Woodill, G., Renwick, R., Brown, I. and Raphael, D. (1994) Being, belonging, becoming: an approach to the quality of life of persons with developmental disabilities. In: D. A. Goode (ed), *Quality of Life for Persons with Disabilities: International Perspectives and Issues*. Cambridge: Brookline Books, pp. 57–67.

Woodrow, P. (2001) Measuring quality of life, *Journal of Medical Ethics*, 27: 205.

World Bank (1997) *World Development Indicators*. Washington, DC: World Bank.

World Bank (2000) *World Development Report 2000/2001: Attacking Poverty*. Oxford: Oxford University Press and the World Bank. <http://publications. worldbank. org/ecommerce/catalog/product?item_id=217116> [accessed 25. 09. 01].

World Health Organization (1997) *WHOQOL: Measuring Quality of Life*. Geneva: WHO.

World Health Organization (2001) *World Health Report 2001: New Understanding, New Hope*. Geneva: WHO.

Wu, A. W., Fink, N. E., Cagney, K. A., Bass, E. B., Rubin, H. R., Meyer, K. B. *et al.* (2001) Developing a health-related quality-of-life measure for end-stage renal disease: the CHOICE health experience questionnaire, *American Journal of Kidney Diseases*, 37, 1: 11–21.

Young, J. M. and McNicoll, P. (1998) Against all odds: positive life experiences of people with advanced amyotrophic lateral sclerosis, *Health and Social Work*, 23, 1: 253–260.

Young, J. M., Marshall, C. L. and Anderson, E. J. (1994) Amyotrophic lateral sclerosis patients' perspectives on use of mechanical ventilation, *Health and Social Work*, 19, 4: 253–60.

Zapf, W. (1977) Soziale Indikatoren – eine Zwischenbilanz, In: H. -J. Krupp and W. Zapf (eds), *Sozialpolitik und Sozialberichterstattung*. Frankfurt am Main and New York: Campus, pp. 231–246.

Zapf, W. (1984) Individuelle Wohlfahrt: Lebensbedingungen und wahrgenommene Lebensqualität in der Bundesrepublik, In: W. Glatzer and W. Zapf (eds), *Lebensqualität in der Bundesrepublic*. Frankfurt am Main and New York: Campus, pp. 13–26.

INDEX